Being Local Worldwide

Being Local Worldwide

ABB and the Challenge of Global Management

Edited by

Jacques Bélanger,

Christian Berggren,

Torsten Björkman,

and Christoph Köhler

ILR Press
an imprint of
Cornell University Press
Ithaca and London

First published 1999 by Cornell University Press

Printed in the United States of America

Library of Congress Cataloging-in-Publication Data

Being local worldwide : ABB and the challenge of global management / edited by Jacques
    Bélanger . . . [et al.].
        p.   cm.
    Includes index.
    ISBN 0-8014-3650-8 (cloth)
        1. ABB Asea Brown Boveri Ltd.—Management.   2. Electric transformer industry—
    Management Case studies.   3. International business enterprises—Management Case
    studies.   I. Bélanger, Jacques.
    HD9697.T694A233   1999
    338.8'8721314—dc21   99-33981
                                                                                    CIP

Cornell University Press strives to use environmentally responsible suppliers and materials to the fullest extent possible in the publishing of its books. Such materials include vegetable-based, low-VOC inks, and acid-free papers that are recycled, totally chlorine-free, or partly composed of nonwood fibers. Books that bear the logo of the FSC (Forest Stewardship Council) use paper taken from forests that have been inspected and certified as meeting the highest standards for environmental and social responsibility. For further information, visit our website at www.cornellpress.cornell.edu.

Cloth printing   10 9 8 7 6 5 4 3 2 1

Contents

Preface

"Being local worldwide" is a slogan closely associated with the electrotechnical multinational Asea Brown Boveri (ABB) and with its famous current chairman and former chief executive officer, Percy Barnevik. Of all the core policies of ABB, this one has attracted the most interest and controversy since the merger of Swedish ASEA and Swiss Brown Boveri in 1987. What that policy looks like empirically is the focus of this book.

The research design underlying the book is simple and straightforward. My colleagues and I have studied a number of local companies within the same multinational company, ABB, all having the common policy of promotion of "being local." At the same time we have opted for maximum variety and diversity in local conditions by selecting the cases "worldwide." We are interested in the degree of correspondence between what ABB says it does and what local ABB companies actually do. We have been fortunate in negotiating access to the most critical test of "the being local worldwide" policy, that is, the cluster of companies within ABB responsible for the design, manufacturing, and sales of power transformers. That part of ABB is by far the most duplicated business within the multinational and has since the early 1990s been running more than twenty plants around the globe, all making in essence the same thing: power transformers. From a researcher's point of view, the company is running a huge field experiment qualifying the true meaning of the "being local worldwide" policy. We have had the advantage of using this field experiment for our purposes. We have also wanted to put this business area (BA), one of forty within ABB and also one of the largest, in perspective. Consequently we have undertaken complementary case studies of two other BAs.

The implementation of our simple research design has proved to be a complex and demanding endeavor. Our policy was to entrust the case studies to researchers living in the same country the study was made. One implication of that policy is that we had to find interested researchers around the globe who could find local research funds to guarantee their independence. Once successfully formed and funded, the local team of researchers then had to start working on gaining access from local management and trade union representatives. The studies did not proceed at the same pace in all countries. Timing has been one of our trickier tasks. Our ambition of studying corporate policies at the headquarters, at the same time as local diversity, has added to our practical challenges.

Some twenty-five researchers have been involved in our case studies. This book has a dozen authors, and four of us are editors. The project has been ongoing worldwide for more than five years. One would expect some turbulence in such a large network, and we have had our share. Many researchers did not make it to the end because of new assignments, and others were able to continue often boosted by promotion to professorships. Of the departments and institutes involved I am most grateful to ISF (Institut für Sozialwissenschaftliche Forschung) in Munich, a copartner from a very early stage of the project. Our researchers from this renowned institute, Marhild von Behr, Hartmut Hirsch-Kreinsen, Christoph Köhler, and Rainer Schultz-Wild in particular, have made very important contributions to our methodology and comparative analyses. Our Australian colleague, Russell D. Lansbury, an authority on industrial relations, has proved to be a very keen observer of ABB policies and workplace realities not simply in Sydney but worldwide. A latecomer who made a great impact on this project is our driving coeditor Jacques Bélanger of Université Laval, Quebec, and my Swedish colleague, Christian Berggren, has contributed much by virtue of his relentless analytical skills. We have also all benefited from the help of our excellent assistant editor-in-chief, Cecilia Runnström, who has helped us with ruthless cutting, improving the quality of this book.

I originally initiated this project and network of researchers, and that is why I have the honor of acknowledging some of our best supporters and copartners over the years. Bert-Olof Svanholm, the former chief executive officer (CEO) of ABB Sweden, who died much too early, meant very much to this project. He understood our research interests and advised us to focus on the power transformers BA worldwide. Kenneth Synnersten, the first T-50 "general" in Sweden (T-50 was a time-based management program aimed at reducing total throughput times by 50 percent in three years), was also very helpful with the early negotiations. They took quite some time, and we had almost lost hope of ever getting access, when a research protocol was settled in March 1993. It was finalized in Mannheim, Germany, with Sune Karlsson, then Customer Focus program president and Bo-Göran Persson, BA president at that time. Within the BA no one has facilitated the project as much as Kjell Magnusson, the quality expert and Six Sigma enthusiast now in Zürich.

With this book an unusual research cooperation has come to an end.

Thousands of ABB employees around the globe have made our fieldwork possible, worthwhile, and rewarding. The informants are managers from every level of the lean ABB hierarchy. They are trade union representatives. They are rank-and-file employees. Most of them have a local orientation; the "globally oriented" are exceptional. Around the world are numerous ABB employees who have been very important to the success of this project. Each and every case study has had some "to be or not to be" moments, when key persons acted on our behalf and helped us get the right kind of access and quality of data. These helpers and supporters are too numerous to be presented here, but know that we thank you warmly.

Of all our many funding agencies I want to highlight The Swedish Council for Work Life Research ("RALF" in Swedish) because they took the greatest risk. They gave us funding on a sketch of an ABB study, on why the whole is more than the sum of its parts, the "being local worldwide" theme. RALF was first and has since made the greatest contributions, and without it this project would not have been possible.

Writing this in December 1998, I am back from a visit to ABB Powertech in Pretoria, South Africa, the world's most complete power transformer plant. Apart from the pleasure of trading Swedish fall for South African spring, it was a profound experience to visit this plant in the post-apartheid era and get some insights into the dramatic changes transforming South African society and working life. That visit was the latest in a long string of encounters with "local" conditions worldwide, trips that have taken me to Brazil, Australia, the United States, and so many places in Europe. Ironically the most rewarding study visit was made to a plant close by from a Swedish perspective, the ABB plant in Vaasa in northern Finland. I know that I speak on behalf of all the editors when I say that we found the organization and operation of this plant sensational; more on that in the coming chapters. The days in May 1996 that we on the editors' team spent with the architects of that organization, Kalevi Somppi, the local production manager, and Erik Nylund, the plant manager, were most inspiring.

With the South African visit I myself have come full circle in my study of ABB. It began with a meeting at ASEA, the Swedish predecessor of ABB, in May 1969. As a young sociologist I had done a study of Swedish public opinion, judging the performance of large companies and multinationals. ASEA management was interested in the results, because they were very concerned over the negative Swedish opinion toward their bidding on the Cabora Bassa project in Mozambique, widely seen in Sweden as indirect support of the Portuguese colonial system and oppressive regimes in Rhodesia and South Africa. In September 1969 ASEA withdrew from the bidding, owing to the risk of breaking the international boycott against the regime in Rhodesia. It was a tough decision in the sense that it gave the competitors a chance to build a HVDC (high-voltage direct-current) distribution system over long distances, until that moment a technology that ASEA had invented and considered its specialty. A German-Swiss consortium, including the Swiss archrival Brown Boveri, got the order instead. For ASEA this was a difficult lesson about the new interplay between domestic and global politics and how it influences ways of doing business.

The Cabora Bassa crisis awakened a renewed interest in opinion making within ASEA, and I was engaged in these studies during the 1970s. ASEA, throughout this century the "flagship" of the powerful Wallenberg group, was in the 1930s the first Swedish company to import the human relations philosophy from the United States. During the 1970s many rediscoveries were made about the importance of cohesion and team spirit. In accordance with corporate culture the employees called themselves "Vi Aseater" ("we Asians"). My own focus during these years shifted toward the organizational transformations taking place within ASEA. Great things were happening, basically due to another American import called "the rationalization of capital." With Curt Nicolin as CEO, cash flows and throughput times were enhanced. Organizationally these new ideas had important consequences, driving departmental integration, job rotation, multiskilling, and flexibility. This paradigmatic turnaround of an old institution such as ASEA became the theme for a dissertation that I wrote, in close cooperation with my wife, Karin Lundqvist. We were already familiar with the organization in 1981, at a time when the company had a new CEO, Percy Barnevik.

During Barnevik's aggressive leadership, the company attracted a lot of media attention and steeply rising stock market value (tenfold increase from 1980–1987, the year of the merger with Brown Boveri). But mass media tend to forget history and overestimate the present. ASEA's organizational developments of the 1980s had the same focus as those of the 1970s: speed and shortening of throughput times. The change was quantitative rather than qualitative. As the company increased its competitive strength, however, these new advantages were used for a striking merger and acquisition offensive. ASEA started growing at a swift pace (increasing turnover five times and doubling the number of employees from 1980 to 1987), and by and large integrated its competitors in the Nordic countries. The growth was a decisive factor in making the big merger with Brown Boveri possible. The two rivals started to look like equals. Brown Boveri was even larger (in 1987 it had 100,000 employees versus the 70,000 of ASEA), but ASEA's stock market value was twice that of the Swiss company for which the 1980s was a period of stagnation. The merger created ABB, which began operations in 1988, with Percy Barnevik, the leading merger architect, as CEO. After the merger followed many acquisitions in the late 1980s, most notably Combustion Engineering and parts of old Westinghouse, according to the dictum that a marked presence on the American market is part of the definition of being a "global player."

At the beginning of the 1990s ABB still had its stronghold in Europe (roughly 60 percent of its business), but year after year it becomes ever more global. This period is the basis for the studies in this book. It coincides with the latter half of the Barnevik reign over ABB, a period much acclaimed in management literature and often referred to when "modern" leadership and organization are discussed. Whether you find our conclusions different from and more interesting than the many ABB references circulating in management literature is up to you as reader to decide. We believe you will find ours a truer story, but be prepared to find that reality does not always surpass imagination. Not all of Barnevik's ideas survived the test of time. ABB is now downplaying the local, domestic dimension in its matrix structure and even further strengthening its emphasis on the global business dimension.

Reading this book will give you a deeper understanding of the tensions between global and local presences in a corporation. From a historical perspective it makes sense to enter our story at Ludvika. To a foreigner Ludvika might seem "in the middle of nowhere." But despite looking isolated and peripheral, this company town was for a long time a world-class center of technical expertise resting on excellence in HVDC transmission, including the manufacturing of power transformers. Ludvika was a cornerstone for the ascendancy of ASEA and later ABB. From a Swedish perspective Ludvika is part of the cultural heartland of our country, Dalecarlia. It is in a sense the Swedish "Middletown" at lake Väsman, where the Swedish trade union movement has chosen to locate its most important educational center, Brunnsvik, the starting point of so many political careers. The seemingly idyllic company policy of "being local worldwide" has turned out to have important and unforeseen consequences for this "Middletown." It hit another "Middletown," the legendary Muncie, even harder, where the once-huge power transformer plant was closed in 1998. Indeed this is the key theme that underlies the case studies as a whole—the complex tensions arising between the immense variety of local conditions on the one hand and the intriguing character of the ongoing process of globalization on the other.

Torsten Björkman

Stockholm, Sweden

Being Local Worldwide

Introduction
Between Globalization and Multidomestic Variation

Christian Berggren

Asea Brown Boveri—The Modern Way of Coping with Local and Global Logics at the Same Time?

The 1990s saw an enormous interest in new forms of international management: What type of companies and what management models will survive and thrive in the new global economy? What kind of impact will these international corporations have on local economies and workplace relations? Will anything be left of national traditions? In the business world, there has been a steady rise in corporate mergers, ranging from national deals to mergers across countries and oceans, as in the spectacular Daimler-Chrysler merger. Many of the merged entities face hard times, because of internal political struggles and cultural friction: a well-publicized case is the American, previously American-Swedish, drug company Pharmacia-Upjohn. There are some success stories, which have received a lot of attention. One of the most prominent of these is Asea Brown Boveri (ABB), created in 1987 by the merger of two national champions in the electrotechnical industry, Swiss Brown Boveri and Swedish ASEA. Under its forceful first chief executive officer Percy Barnevik, ABB became synonymous with a new and innovative way of managing large organizations and running international business. According to *Fortune*, ABB was "the most successful cross-border merger since Royal Dutch linked up with Britain's Shell in 1907" (Rapoport 1992, 24). In the annual survey by *Financial Times* and Price Waterhouse of Europe's most respected companies, ABB has come out on top and Percy Barnevik was twice ranked as the most respected European manager, in particular for his strategic vision.

There are several reasons for this spotlight on ABB. One is that this company, with a strong presence in a variety of countries ranging from the United States, Brazil, Germany, Switzerland, Sweden, and Poland to India and Australia, belongs to the still rather exclusive group of companies with genuine global aspirations. Two surveys reported by Hirst and Thompson (1996) demonstrate that most multinational companies are regional rather than global and strongly dependent on their domestic market. According to these surveys, the North American market accounts for two-thirds of the sales of U.S. manufacturing multinationals, the Japanese market for 75 percent of Japan's manufacturing multinationals, and the European market for 75 percent of the sales of French and German multinationals. In the service sector, the dominance of the home region is even more pronounced. The authors conclude: "International businesses are still largely confined to their home territory; in terms of their overall business activity, they remain heavily 'nationally embedded'" (98).

A second reason is that ABB's model of management, and Percy Barnevik in particular, has been portrayed as a cure for "big company disease." In the management press as well as in business strategy literature, ABB's policies of trimming staffs and focusing on speed and time have been seen as a recipe for how to overcome the tendency of giant companies to become as slow as dinosaurs (Kanter 1989; Peters 1992; Keller 1993). At ABB, corporate staffs have been ruthlessly downsized. The German headquarters of Brown Boveri, the original Swiss partner of ABB, once had a staff of 1600 people. After the merger it was reduced to 100. At the Finnish company, Strömberg, which was acquired by ASEA a few years before the merger with Brown Boveri, headquarters staff was trimmed from 800 to 60 employees. American Combustion Engineering Inc., acquired in 1990, had to reduce its staff from 600 to 90 — and the fleet of corporate jets was eliminated. The cutbacks in central bureaucracies have been only the first step. At the same time ABB headquarters in Zürich has espoused a worldwide rationalization program, centered on a customer focus strategy. A crucial part of this agenda is the insistence on responsiveness and speed, on short delivery times, and on rapid introduction of new products inspired by the concept of time-based management and the Boston Consulting Group (Stalk and Hout 1990).

Third, ABB's way of combining international strategy with local presence and autonomy has been praised as a most sophisticated way of responding to the complexities of the new competitive environment.

There are good reasons for studying international corporations. The production of these companies dominates international commercial transactions and is more important than trade. And the role of multinational enterprises is not restricted to economic factors: "Multinational corporations are at the forefront of organizational and managerial innovation, since they have both a greater need for advanced organizational strategy and managerial practices compared with indigenous firms, and greater abilities to develop them" (United Nations [UN] 1995, 173). Moreover, multinationals are successfully globalizing major consumer markets. Coca-Cola, Levi's jeans, Philip Morris cigarettes or Sony camcorders are not only sold over the world but also marketed in an almost identical manner from one country to the other (Levitt 1991). Ford's "world car concept" and similar initiatives are intended to achieve the same globalization of manufacturing.

The increasing capital mobility and international economic integration, the penetration of global competition into new areas, and the powerful role of multinational corporations have generated persuasive visions of the imminent rise of a global economy. According to an influential proponent of this argument, Kenichi Ohmae (1990, 1995), multinational companies are spearheading a new borderless economy, where national states and institutions will wither away.

The globalization thesis has met several counterarguments, however, which stress the continuing role of national and regional variation. Claiming the importance of "culture" is a common denominator for many of these opponents. In this tradition the concept of "cultural programming" has gained much acclaim (Hofstede 1980; Hampden-Turner and Trompenars 1993). A different critique of the global convergence thesis is implied in Michael Porter's analysis of national competitive advantage as clusters of advanced skills and specialized relationships built over long periods of time (Porter 1990). In this perspective, the international economy is a dynamic system with great potential to create advantages from national or regional peculiarities. The two perspectives, the vision of the frictionless international economy versus the insistence on local and cultural particularity, are often squarely juxtaposed. The strategic vision of ABB, which has attracted so much interest from academics and business journalists alike, is to combine the two perspectives: enjoying global scale but at the same time "being local everywhere."

The Purpose of this Book

The intent of this book is to advance the debate concerning the strategies of multinationals and implications of internationalization by stepping inside a "global" corporation and capturing its dynamics from both a local and an international perspective. We are convinced that general concepts of global convergence or national diversity need to be assessed by detailed, comparative case studies at the plant and local level. In the research for this book we attempted to cross the traditional boundaries between management science, sociology, and comparative industrial relations. Studies in management and business strategy are often strong in concepts but weak in empirical detail as well as in the real-world implementation of corporate policies at different organizational levels. Programs and declarations of chief executives are often taken at face value. The strengths of industrial sociology are the reverse of management science. There is an abundance of empirical data from the local level, but a lack of understanding of the managerial level. The complexity of different organizational models is reduced to simple dichotomies such as "traditional" versus "modern." In this book, our intention is to combine management science and comparative industrial sociology in a multilevel organizational study, but we have made no systematic efforts to compare workers' views through an ethnographic approach. ABB's fundamental claim has not been about changing the world of work, but of "reinventing the multinational." By transcending disciplinary boundaries we attempt to capture the inner workings of, and tensions within, this giant multinational organization.

Further, this book is informed by a conviction that culture and national institutions do matter. If they did not, international trade rather than international investment would be preferred by expanding companies in a world of rapidly improving logistics. In fact, the very structure of ABB, the central object of study in this book, is predicated on the assumption that adaptation to national markets and relationships are of major importance for international success. The relations between national culture and institutions on the one hand and corporate culture and structure on the other are not static and symmetric, however. Japanese multinationals have provided some of the most spectacular cases in which supposedly unique management systems have been successfully transplanted to very different social and cultural contexts. This testifies to the potential power of corporate systems and the plasticity of national traditions. The interchange between corporate and national institutions can also work in the other direction, however, and outcomes are seldom determined in advance. The dynamics between forces of convergence and forces of diversity, in organization of work and production, in managerial forms and levels of performance, in institutions of industrial relations and labor regulation, is a central area in our inquiry.

Finally, this book was written with the assumption that highly global multinationals such as ABB are of special importance. In quantitative terms they compose a minority of multinational companies, but if there is a long-term tendency toward a more global economy, these companies are the pioneers and early movers. In many cases they have been at the forefront of international restructuring. In the white goods industry, Electrolux was an early international mover, prompting previously domestically oriented U.S. firms to move into Europe. The emergence of ABB in 1987 inspired another cross-border merger in the electrotechnical industry within only one year: the creation of British-French GEC-Alsthom. ABB has also exerted pressure on American General Electric to increase its international presence. The importance of studying the most international companies is also a case for focusing on multinational enterprises originating from small countries. As a matter of fact, most companies that can claim to be global are from small countries. This is confirmed by the list of the top 100 presented by the World Investment Report (UN 1995). In terms of absolute size of foreign assets, the list is dominated by giant American and Japanese companies. But when an index of multinationality is calculated as the average of foreign assets to total assets, of foreign sales to total sales, and of foreign employment to total employment, the picture is completely different. On the list of the ten most internationalized companies referred to above, eight originate from small countries: three from Switzerland (Nestlé, Holderbank, CIBA-Geigy), one from Sweden (Electrolux), one from the Netherlands (Philips), one from Belgium (Solvay), one from Canada (Thomson), and one, finally is both Swiss and Swedish—ABB! The relative insignificance of the domestic market tends to force small-country multinationals to become more international than companies from large countries in terms of sales. There is also a cultural aspect. American and Japanese multinationals tend to be heavily dominated by their respective national culture, whereas small-country multinationals more easily adopt and promote an "international" culture. Large-country multinationals, especially the American ones, enjoy the support and promotion of a powerful state apparatus. Small-country multinationals have to fend for themselves.

A Hybrid in Tension

Historical origin and the size of domestic market are closely related to the structure and organization of international companies.[1] There is a long debate on how to distinguish between different structures and there is no generally accepted terminology. The taxonomy below is mainly inspired by Perlmutter's important study (1979). An early and still very important type is the *ethnocentric multinational*, characterized by a heavy economic and cultural base in its home country. Export sales, supported by sales subsidiaries and marketing agencies, are normally complemented or replaced by local manufacturing, but strategic functions remain centralized in the home country headquarters. No major responsibilities devolve to centers outside the traditional center, and the domestic market continues to be the most important. In the classic U.S. case of ethnocentric companies, the non-American businesses are subsumed into an "international department" (Malnight 1993). This type of multinational could be described as "national in disguise" and figures prominently on the list of the world's largest multinational companies, measured by value of foreign assets: Exxon, General Electric, Hitachi, and Mitsubishi are all major international players but in the sense given above also very ethnocentric companies. This is even truer for most American computer and software companies.

Among companies with a more genuine multinational orientation, two major types can be distinguished. One is the *geocentric*, or globalist, company. This is also a centralized organization but, in contrast to the ethnocentric type, policies are developed on a worldwide basis. Geocentric companies tend to adopt global policies with little interest in national variation

---

[1] In this book, *multinational* is used as a generic term for international companies, without any connotation of a specific organizational solution. Accordingly, multinational must be clearly distinguished from *multidomestic*, which implies a particular type of multinational, contrasted to the ethnocentric and geocentric species, described in this section.

and tradition. Evans and Lorange (1989) describe this kind of organization in the following way: "It adapts to different local environments by controlling selection. . . . [N]ational differences are statistical differences in means between the normal curve distribution of values and attitudes in any given population. . . . When a globally oriented company, for example, Hewlett-Packard, is recruiting a German manager for a career at their plant near Munich, they are not simply seeking any technically qualified German manager, they are looking for a German whose personality matches Hewlett-Packard's cultural values" (153).

In contrast to this centralized type of corporate organization, there is also a decentralized type, the *polycentric company*, which has delegated responsibilities to many centers. In the literature, the polycentric, federalist character of European multinationals has often been contrasted with the centralized and/or ethnocentric character of American MNEs. The Dutch Philips corporation has been a prominent representative of this European, small-country tradition (Bartlett and Ghoshal 1990).

ABB's claims of being a corporation that is "being local worldwide" is clearly associated with European polycentrism. However, ABB has also sought to avoid the principal problem of this tradition: the emergence of powerful national fiefdoms, pursuing their own product and market strategies and eroding the potential economies of scale and scope of international coordination. Using Perlmutter's terminology, ABB could be described as a hybrid, striving to integrate the different logics of global business and local embeddedness, to combine a geocentric and a polycentric or, in the ABB parlance, a *multidomestic* approach. This hybrid character is embodied in ABB's cherished but controversial matrix structure. Corporate headquarters are small, major "centers of excellence" are located in several countries, and adaptation to local variety is an article of faith. At the same time, the company pursues a strong global agenda including rationalization programs, management practices, and corporate expansion targets. The "hybrid structure" implies tensions and dynamics: the balance between the two principles, which is reflected in the matrix structure, is constantly evolving. These dynamics are explored in rich detail in the case studies in Chapters 4–9. For details on ABB's structure and organization, see Box 1.

An important mechanism to achieve uniformity within this empire is the accounting system Abacus, which collects monthly performance data from every profit center. The Abacus figures are closely monitored by corporate headquarters. Red figures are expected to prompt immediate action. Financial control is complemented by social and cultural mechanisms of coordination and integration. International management training ranks high on the agenda. In the two years 1990–91, for example, one thousand managers participated in a series of three-day corporate seminars, attended by members of the executive board. Another method for fostering the development of global managers is the assignment of specialists and managers to international tasks. In 1992 international assignments were awarded to more than

ABB Presentation

The Asea Brown Boveri Group was formed in 1987 by a merger between Swedish ASEA and Swiss Brown Boveri. Both had a history going back almost one hundred years, since their foundation at the onset of the second industrial revolution. They had always been minor players in the international electrotechnical oligopoly. With the formation of ABB they entered the center. In a series of acquisitions in Western and Eastern Europe and North America, ABB rapidly established an international presence. The number of employees rose from 169,000 in 1989 to 215,000 in 1990, but then stabilized. In spite of continued acquisitions, albeit on a smaller scale, total employment stabilized around 210,000 in the mid-1990s. ABB is a nonpublic company, owned fifty-fifty by the Swiss and Swedish partners. The chief executive officer is a Swede, the corporate headquarters are located in Zürich, Switzerland; the company language is English. The head office is inconspicuous, the corporate staff small, approximately 150 persons. In the electrotechnical industry, ABB together with the much smaller GEC-Alsthom is the most focused group—and by far the most internationalized. (see Table I.A.)

Table I.A. Degree of Internationalization in the Electrotechnical Industry, 1993

Company	Country	Total employment (thousands)	Foreign employment (thousands)	(percent)
ABB	Sweden/Switzerland	213	172	81
Siemens	Germany	404	153	38
GEC-Alsthom	France/Britain (1992)	80	23	29
General Electric	USA	222	59	27

To structure its broad product scope and geographically dispersed structure, the ABB group applies an elaborate matrix. One dimension is products and markets. The organizing principle is business areas, which are grouped into major business segments. In 1993 there were forty-five business areas and five segments—Power Generation, Power Transmission and Distribution, Industry and Building Systems, Traction and Financial Services. The senior executives running the segments are located in Zürich and are members of the executive board. The headquarters, sometimes called "coordination offices," of the business areas are located in several different countries. The five most important business areas in terms of sales are listed in table I.B.

Table I.B. Major business areas within ABB, 1993

	Revenues (billion $US)	Employees
Gas Turbine Power Plants	3.5	3,400
Automation and Drives	2.6	16,300
Electrical and Mechanical Installations	1.8	13,000
High Voltage Switchgear	1.7	7,500
Fossil Combustion Systems	1.2	7,300

The business area at the center of this study, Power Transformers, ranked no. 9 on this list with revenues amounting to $US 1 billion and 7500 employees. Of the 20 most important business areas in 1993, 5 were headquartered in Switzerland, 4 in Germany, 4 in Sweden, 3 in the United States, and the remaining 3 in Finland, Britain, and Belgium. In these terms ABB is still very much a European company. The structure of business segments and areas has been modified several times. In 1995, the seven business areas of ABB's traction segment were merged with the rail transportation business of Daimler Benz to form a new fifty-fifty owned joint venture, Adtranz. In the same year several other business areas, mainly in the industry segment, were consolidated. As a result, the business structure of ABB in 1996 contained only four segments and thirty-five business areas.

Geography constitutes the other dimension of the ABB matrix. Local operations are federated into national or sometimes regional structures. In countries with a strong ABB presence, such as Sweden, Germany and Switzerland, the national presidents enjoy a powerful role in the organization. The national-regional organizations are consolidated in three continental groups, namely, Europe, the Americas, and Asia–Pacific. The most important countries in the ABB group in terms of employment are listed in table I.C.

Table I.C. The Ten Most Important Countries of ABB (1995)

Country	Employment
Germany	33,000
Sweden	26,300
USA	21,900
Switzerland	12,700
India	10,200
Finland	8,900
Italy	8,800
UK	7,900
Norway	7,100
Czech Republic	6,500

In the group as a whole, the employment in Europe and the Americas has been shrinking, whereas there has been a strong increase in South and East Asia, expanding from 19,400 to 26,400 between 1994 and 1995.

one thousand people. A more controversial cultural coordination mechanism is the widespread network of Swedish managers. When ASEA and Brown Boveri merged, the two companies were roughly equal in size and technological capabilities. Brown Boveri was in a severe financial plight, however, while ASEA enjoyed robust earnings. The new corporate management was chiefly recruited from ASEA and immediately set out to shake up the unprofitable Brown Boveri subsidiaries. This resulted in a strong Swedish and Scandinavian presence not only in corporate and business area management, but also at the local level, where many national presidents are Swedes.

This has created an ABB paradox: the company is striving to be global and multidomestic, but at the same time it has been heavily reliant on expatriate Swedish managers.

ABB and Its Critics

Most of the many articles written about ABB have been extremely positive or outright adulatory. There has also been some criticism, however. ABB's matrix organization remains controversial. This form gained wide popularity among multinational firms in the 1970s but was later criticized for drawbacks such as ambiguity, increased costs of communication, slow decision making, and lack of clear responsibility (see, e.g., Evans and Lorange 1989). Another difficulty in ABB's matrix structure is the policy to reconcile local embeddedness and low cost, when the latter calls for cross-country consolidation and restructuring. At ABB, Barnevik defended the matrix principle as the only one possible in a complex world. The basic argument is quite similar to Evans and Lorange's discussion (1989) of the two logics behind human resource management: the product-driven logic of business dynamics and the geographically based sociocultural logic. According to Barnevik, the matrix "is a fact of life. If you deny the formal matrix, you wind up with an informal one—and that's much harder to reckon with" (Taylor 1991: 95–96).

Another criticism is that the image of lean staffs is deceptive: actual costs of management and coordinating staffs are much higher than represented by the inconspicuous headquarters, but because they are dispersed among various international and national centers they are much less visible than in traditional centralized organizations (Hoffmann and Linden 1994). Unions, particularly in Germany, have reacted strongly against ABB's American style of downsizing and lean staffing.

Further, there have been doubts about the long-term sustainability and economic effectiveness of ABB's professed internationalism, with its lack of anchorage in a strong national culture. ABB grew to international prominence by acquiring companies across Europe and North America. But is it really possible to buy into local markets in this tradition-bound industry? In what markets is the company a genuine insider? A related issue concerns possible national tensions and friction across the global company and how these could affect recruitment and promotion at leading positions: What will happen when the Barnevik generation leaves the scene? Will it be possible to recruit a new top management team without conflicts and struggle between the different nationalities in the company? In an ethnocentric company, the succession process is easier, because the dominance of one nationality is taken for granted and there is less need for maintaining a delicate balance.

Finally, there has been concern relating to ABB's financial performance. The first six years after the merger it was rather uninspiring, lower than the performance of ABB's major competitors. This testifies to the costs of consummating complex mergers and also to some strategic mistakes, such as the expensive effort in the early 1990s to enter the American power-generation market, which then turned out to be virtually dead. The confidence of major institutional investors in ABB and Barnevik remained solid, however. In the mid-1990s the company enjoyed major earning increases, but in 1997, once again ABB had to report significant restructuring costs.

In the final chapter we return to several of these concerns and analyze them against the backdrop of our international case studies.

Three Major Issues

Global Standards versus Local Innovation

A key issue in the book is to understand and assess the mechanics of globalization versus the dynamics of local variation within a hybrid-type multinational, which is simultaneously pursuing global scale and local presence, cross-border learning and national embeddedness. How do global efforts to standardize product and processes intersect with the resilience of national institutions and local initiatives? How are previously insulated local companies transformed when they are exposed to the rationalization programs of international management? Specifically, we are interested in the meaning of the ABB policy of "being local worldwide." Does it allow for genuine and unexpected local innovations, or is it more a case of modifications of centrally espoused programs? How does this policy evolve over time: is it a temporary phenomenon devised to facilitate the integration of acquired companies, to be followed by a regime of international consolidation and standardization? Or is "being local worldwide" a persistent program, although the geographical configuration may change in response to overall growth patterns in the world's infrastructure demand?

Another perspective on the globalization-localization logic within ABB concerns its internal mechanisms of coordination. Since the mid-1980s, the process school in international management research has emphasized subtle methods of coordination, at the expense of formalized procedures and central control: "lateral communication," "horizontal organizations," "heterarchy" instead of hierarchy, "networks" instead of vertical coordination (Bartlett 1986; Hedlund 1986; Prahalad and Doz 1991; White and Poynter 1990). These mechanisms have been linked to notions of the heterarchic company with many centers (Hedlund 1994). However, the focus on novelty and fluidity has often come at the expense of the classic interest in structure, organization, and control (Berggren 1996). In a review of the literature on multinational corporations, Martinez and Jarillo (1989) have provided a comprehensive list of coordination mechanisms, starting with structural and formal mechanisms and ending with informal and subtle means. In the case of the electrotechnical industry with its enormous scope of products and technologies, there is arguably much variation in coordination and control mechanisms across the product range. An important point made by Martinez and Jarillo is that "complex strategies (those resulting from interrelated, multi-plant, multi-market policies) need an enormous coordinating effort, and so are implemented through both types of mechanisms, structural and formal, plus informal and subtle. Thus mechanisms at the bottom of the list are added to, not substituted for, those high on the list" (494). An interesting question is whether ABB supports the agenda for subtle coordination proposed by the process school in international management, or whether this "hybrid-type of multinational" is much closer to the composite-type co-ordination observed by Martinez and Jarillo.

Dynamics of Learning: No One-way Street

A second important issue concerns organizational learning within a multinational that has been formed by mergers and acquisitions and has to cope with entrenched technological traditions. In ethnocentric multinationals, learning is a straightforward process of transferring manufacturing systems and management practices from domestic operations to peripheral units. It is a one-way movement of methods from headquarters to affiliates, in which learning is basically viewed as an imitation process. Referring to the so-called network or process school within international management studies, the World Investment Report (UN 1995) notes that "at least in principle, every part of the corporate system can become the source of new organizational and managerial practices," but it then reports that "evidence relates mostly to the transfer from parent firms to their foreign affiliates" (UN 1995, 174, 176). The approach to learning is steeped in the belief in a globally applicable "one best way."

ABB represents a more complex case, and by means of our in-depth study of one business area, Power Transformers, this book views learning processes from several different angles:

The catch-up process at the periphery, illustrating the argument by Glasmeier and Fuellhart (1996) that nonroutine learning is dependent on external linkages;

The reorientation at the traditional European core, linked to a belated awareness of the need to learn from others; and

The reversal of roles within the business area, in which former teachers have to become pupils, and previous marginal units emerge as new teachers.

Another aspect concerns the different approaches to learning and competitiveness that exist in the company. According to the hard-core, total quality management approach, which is favored by a significant part of the international management community, local variation in product and process is treated as a problem and an obstacle and should be progressively eliminated. For every process step there is one and only one best way, but it could be German, Finnish, Canadian, or Brazilian. Inferior country performance should not be confused with corporate performance. In principle, new best practices could emerge anywhere. The task of international management is to identify such practices, elevate them to the global standards, and then go on to find new best practices.

A different logic of learning views local variation and innovation, beyond a certain level of technological standardization, as competitive advantages. Horizontal exchange and knowledge diffusion within the business area are encouraged, but top-down programs are viewed with suspicion, because they could frustrate local ingenuity and responsiveness. This approach is less oriented toward global scale in hardware and software and more toward the creative use of local skills, opportunities, and networks. The tension between the two approaches, the geocentric and the polycentric, is an important theme in the following case studies.

Process Management and the Dilemmas of Lean Staffing

Finally, the book intends to contribute to the discourse in sociology and management concerning the implementation of a new production regime at the plant level. Generally there is a strong American influence within ABB. Modern management is inundated by three-letter acronyms—total quality management (TQM), time-based management (TBM), business process reengineering (BPR). ABB has tried them all, but in different local contexts. In Sweden, for example, the interest in American and Japanese methods is mixed with a strong sociotechnical heritage and professed belief in goal-directed groups. Everywhere within ABB, however, there is an insistence on change, speed, improvement, and global performance standards. What are the consequences for the various labor regimes within the company? The focus varies somewhat among the case chapters, but mainly they deal with institutional changes, workforce restructuring, the agenda of expanded or redirected management control, and the potential conflicts between different goals, for example, broad skills and lean staffing. At this level, too, processes of convergence as well as persistent local variation are of central interest.

Research Design and Methodology

The book is based on a sample of national case studies. There are good arguments for a case study approach. As Raymond Vernon has observed, "Some of the most provocative work of researchers from the business school community has come from those who have plumbed in depth the behavior of individual firms, or the interplay of a limited cluster of firms competing in a well-defined product market" (1994, 141).

The core of the research is a multicountry study of one business area, Power Transformers. This business area constitutes one of ABB's core technologies. From the early days of ASEA (ABB's Swedish predecessor), mastery of the technology of power transmission and distribution has played a major role in establishing its solid reputation in the electrotechnical industry and has been prominent in the development of ABB management. Over the years, several managers of the large Ludvika complex, a stronghold in the transformer business, have become members of the select executive board of ABB. Of course, ABB now has a more global reach, and no sector can be seen as representative of such a huge and complex corporation. Nevertheless, the power transformers business area has often been referred to, within ABB and in the international literature, as an example of the way this multinational responds to globalization (see, e.g., Taylor 1991). This business area manufactures basically the same product in twenty-two plants in seventeen countries (1996). Economies of scale are limited, especially in the assembly and testing processes. Close relations with local customers are of crucial importance. Hence this industry can rightly be seen as a critical case in the study of the meaning of "being local worldwide." If the idea of the multidomestic organization does not work in its most likely setting, it is unlikely to work well in other segments of the ABB corporation.

A frequent problem in international comparisons is to identify the causes for observed differences in institutional structures or organizational performance. Our research design eliminates a theoretically trivial cause for such variation between local companies: differences in products and technologies. There is a further advantage in choosing ABB and the power transformers business area. Many multinational companies operate plants producing the same or similar products in several locations. Tetrapak, for example, a Swedish specialist in packaging of perishable products, has a worldwide structure of fifty plants that produce packaging materials in close proximity to its customers, local breweries and dairies. All of these plants have been established by the Swedish parent as green-field sites. The ABB power transformers business area is different, because it is a result of the merger of several different companies: ASEA, Brown Boveri, and Westinghouse plus various local contenders. As a result, it is possible to study the influence of both national and corporate cultures within this business area.

Mirroring ABB, the intention of our project has been to develop a multidomestic research structure. For several years, local research teams have studied seven transformer operations in six countries on three continents: Australia, Canada (Ontario and Quebec), Germany, Spain, Sweden, and the United Kingdom. As a part of the broader study, research visits have also been extended to Guarulhos in Brazil, Vaasa in Finland, Lodz in Poland, and Sécheron in Switzerland in 1995–1996. To coordinate methods, compare observations, and foster a "global orientation," a systematic exchange of visits has taken place between the national teams, and all members of the editorial committee have visited several plants in addition to their "home site." The national case studies include institutional environment, market situation, plant history, production organization, industrial relations, and plant performance. The local studies, often referred to as plant studies, should not be construed as narrow "factory studies," because the local transformer operations include custom design, planning, and purchasing, as well as production and shipping. The process focus, which has become so important within the business area, spans the entire value chain from order receipt to delivery.

Fieldwork has mainly consisted of on-site interviews with general managers; personnel and production managers; engineers in design, planning, purchasing, and quality functions; as well as union officers. Detailed case reports have been presented and discussed with local management. The international business area management has generously supplied statistics from its 7-ups-program, which compares the performance of all plants on a monthly basis. An ongoing dialogue with BA management has helped to interpret local developments and international trends.

In addition to this major international case study, the research program has taken advantage of the scope of ABB to conduct auxiliary studies in two very different fields: turbines, in the Power Generation business segment, and automation, a part of the business area Automation and Drives in the Industry and Building Systems segment. These businesses differ from the power transformers business area in a number of ways. Whereas power transformers belong to the classic and now mature electrotechnical products, process automation is a young business, with a high research and development intensity, rapidly evolving technologies, and a fluid competitive situation. In power transformers, ABB's competitive advantage rests on product technology and local manufacture; in automation, advanced research and customized software applications using centrally produced hardware are of chief importance. Turbine production is organized by the business area, Power Plant Production, which applies an international division of labor very similar to the European production network for Airbus. In 1994 this business area comprised twenty-two plants in thirteen countries, a vast international structure but operating entirely different from the power transformers business area. The differences among these three business areas make it highly interesting to compare the outcomes of ABB's specific policies and the various forms of cross-border organizational learning.

Overview

Chapter 1 gives a broad overview of the historical development of the electrotechnical industry, its major players in Europe and the United States, and industry restructuring in the 1980s. Chapter 2 zooms in on the area at the center of our study, that is, the power transformers business area, presenting its structure, markets, and competitors as well as the policies and politics of the business area management. Then Chapter 3 provides the basics for those interested in transformer technology and transformer production. This chapter includes a detailed account of ABB's system of plant metrics, which is used for international comparisons. Chapters 4 to 9 are devoted to national case studies on Scotland, Spain, Australia, Canada, Sweden, and Germany. In fact, the Canadian study contains two cases, the Anglo-Canadian Guelph plant and the Varennes plant located in the Province of Quebec. The basic issues are the same in all the cases, but the personal style of writing differs, and so does the extent and depth of the analysis of the social context.

Chapter 10 brings the case studies together. It starts with a discussion of their different starting points and then proceeds to an analysis of the "business area drama." The next two chapters (11 and 12) broaden the perspective by bringing the results of research into two other business areas into the picture. Finally, in conclusion Chapter 13 takes the reader back to the original issue: the dynamics of global aspirations and local embeddedness, "being local worldwide," its challenges and dilemmas. This casts light on the broader interpretation of the ABB trajectory. In the final analysis, is ABB a trendsetter, a model of the future to come, or a highly inspiring but still exceptional case?

1   ABB and the Restructuring of the Electrotechnical Industry

Torsten Björkman

This chapter focuses on the electrotechnical industry, one of the first science-based industries. Not only has it reshaped our material culture but it has also exerted an influence on organizational thinking and practice far beyond the boundaries of the industry. The chapter also deals with how far the globalization process has come in the electrotechnical industry. Is Asea Brown Boveri a trendsetter in globalization of the industry? The ABB merger and other recent corporate restructuring are analyzed from both historical and strategic perspectives.

The Role of the Electrotechnical Industry

Electricity is of primary importance in a modern society. Computers are not possible without electricity. In telecommunications it is taken for granted. Television sets and radios, stoves and refrigerators, washing machines and irons, all presuppose electricity. Before the invention of the incandescent lamp (the lightbulb), humanity had to rely on the dim light from candles and later, kerosene lamps. Electricity ended those "Dark Ages."

Electricity consumption is an important indicator of the standard of living a society enjoys. It is generally ten times higher in developed compared with developing countries.[1] World consumption of electricity has roughly kept on doubling every decade. Industrialization without electricity would be very primitive. All kinds of industries from mines and steelworks to traction and financial services use electricity as a power source. The electrotechnical industry facilitates these developments by providing all the other industries with the necessary equipment.

[1] *United Nations energy statistics yearbook. 1995.*

16

The electrotechnical industry is the third largest manufacturing industry in the world measured by revenues, after autos and petroleum refining. It is the largest industry if measured by the number of its employees.[2] A handful of multinational corporations dominate the industry, for example, General Electric (GE), Siemens, ABB, General Electric Company–Alsthom (GEC-Alsthom), Mitsubishi Heavy Industries, Hitachi, and Samsung. In addition a vast number of small and medium-sized enterprises (SMEs) compete beside these giants (see discussion later in the chapter.)

Since we are all users of electricity, the organization and administration of that use is a major service industry of its own, traditionally dominated by public utilities. Historically many of the electrotechnical giants have lived in symbiosis with public or private electric utilities of similar sizes. That is one reason why so many of them use the word *general* in their names thereby emphasizing their public importance.[3] Most industrialized countries have had a combination of utilities and electrotechnical manufacturers analogous to military industrial complexes, which have armed forces and arms industries. That stable state is coming to an end. To a large extent the electric utilities have been or soon will be privatized. The United Kingdom was an international trendsetter that privatized its electricity nets in 1990. The new utilities the world over are often less faithful to their industrial suppliers than the old ones used to be. The competition is consequently increasing, which is to many a new experience.

The electrotechnical industry has been regarded as of vital importance to national defense throughout most of its history, fostering arguments for protectionism and technical trade barriers. National differences are many and varying, ranging from the provision of direct or alternating electric current with different voltages and amperages, to peculiar standards for points and switches. Differences in security regulations, surveillance, and stipulations concerning technical documentation abound. Lack of international standardization makes sense from a military point of view, but this state of affairs makes international trade more difficult and tends to make each domestic market a protected and closed one. Many international actors, most prominently the International Standardization Organization (ISO) in Geneva, have attempted to dismantle the whole system of national standards in favor of international ones. Although some progress is recorded, most of that work remains to be done.

A company that crosses borders and frontiers has much more difficulty because of the focus on domestic markets. Domestic competition has until re-

---

[2] The *Fortune* Global. 1995. *Fortune* (August 7).

[3] General Electric in the United States, General Electric Company (GEC) in the United Kingdom, Compagnie Générale d'Électricité (CGE) in France, Allgemeine Elektrizitäts Gesellschaft (AEG) in Germany, and Allmänna Svenska Elektriska Aktiebolaget (ASEA) in Sweden, all starting their names with "General," "Générale" in French, "Allgemein" in German, "Allmänna" in Swedish.

cently been at the forefront in most countries; GE against Westinghouse in the United States; Siemens versus Allgemeine Elektrizitäts Gesellschaft (AEG) in Germany; and Hitachi, Mitsubishi, and Toshiba battling in Japan. Internationally it has been a relatively closed industry, with many cartels putting competitors from smaller countries in a disadvantaged position. Both ASEA in Sweden and Brown Boveri in Switzerland experienced the handicap of doing business as an outsider. Competition has been restricted mostly to developing countries that have no electrotechnical companies of their own. Today international competition is gaining momentum, particularly within the three trading blocks of the European Union (EU), the North American Free Trade Agreement (NAFTA) and the Association of South East Asian Nations (ASEAN). Consequently corporations once shielded and protected have to improve quickly or perish.

The Structure of the Electrotechnical Industry

The electrotechnical industry is clearly molded by the giants but that does not exclude companies of smaller sizes, many of which are newcomers. Historically "mortality" among the SMEs in the industry has been high. To be swallowed by one of the giants is a fate shared by many. These acquisitions have been ongoing throughout the twentieth century, but they were particularly intense in the very early twentieth century and later, in the 1980s and 1990s. Still many independent SMEs remain, and new ones are founded occasionally. Nevertheless, SMEs do not alter the fundamental fact that the giants dominate the electrotechnical industry, which is one of the most important characteristics of this industry. Corporations such as GE, Siemens, and Mitsubishi have become institutions in their countries of origin. ABB shares the industry's ambitions of being valued as more than a company by its customers. ABB is different with its insistence on having many homes, on being multidomestic.

Some industries are relatively easy to define. The motor vehicle industry is a good example. A core product is manufactured in the millions, namely, the automobile with its parts and components. The other products that make up the industry are also well-known and distinct. To autos one usually adds motorcycles, vans, trucks, buses, road graders, earth movers, bulldozers, and other off-road vehicles. Since the auto industry is selling to the end users and since its products are eagerly sought after, the visibility of companies in the auto industry is very high.

Defining the electrotechnical industry is a tougher task. To a large extent it is an industry behind other industries providing them with power equipment and machinery. Some products such as household appliances are known to everyone but many of the core products of the industry are more or less anonymous, for example, generators, turbines, transformers, switch gear, and robots. The range of electrotechnical products is enormous, from the tiniest electronics to the mightiest power stations. ABB is presently the only company remaining with a complete range of power electrical products for generation, transmission, and distribution.

Some electrotechnical product clusters merit industries of their own. The computer industry is one example. Home electronics, with products like televisions, radios, and recorders, is another subgroup, as well as companies manufacturing household appliances such as refrigerators, vacuum and other cleaners, washing machines, and dishwashers. The traction industry, in which electrical applications are used in railbound traffic, has also come of age. The same holds true for the telecommunications industry. Alcatel, Ericsson, Motorola, Nokia and Northern Telecom are relatively specialized telecommunication companies, but a conglomerate like Siemens also belongs to this group. To lump all these industries and subclusters together and call them the electrotechnical industry, a common practice, might make the world more understandable but it does not facilitate comparative analysis.

The smaller companies in the electrotechnical industry are more focused, for obvious reasons. The smaller corporations do not have the resources to cover the whole range of possible technologies and products. Even among the giants, however, there are substantial differences. ABB would have to merge with Ericsson and Electrolux as well as with a computer manufacturer to get the same complex internal structure as Siemens, a company almost notorious for its many specializations, as are the Japanese giants. Siemens, together with GE, is also a world leader in medical engineering. GE also has quite a number of military products. That military profile is a legacy from World War II, when the company devoted much of its resources to the manufacturing of armaments.[4] Aircraft engines belong to that category. Turbines, a standard element in power stations, have a lot in common with aircraft engines both in design and manufacturing, so the competence was already there. The most important British company in the industry, GEC, also has a strong position in defense applications and for the same reasons as GE.

Thus far we have only talked about products and technologies with electricity as the common denominator, but electrotechnical companies have moved further into distant branches of manufacturing or into the service sector. The industry leader, GE, has amassed many service companies especially in the finance sector. The service part of that corporation's revenues has now surpassed 40 percent.[5] Westinghouse, a once very important electrotechnical company, has almost abandoned its origins and since December 1997

---

[4] See Robert Slater. 1992. Shining in the Palace of the Mikado. In *The new GE: How Jack Welch revived an American institution.* New York: Irwin.

[5] *Fortune* Magazine celebrated the 40th anniversary of its corporate rankings by merging its rankings of the 500 top industrial and 500 top service corporations into a new ranking of the top 500 corporations. The corporation used as an example of the integration is GE. "Far more than a manufacturer, GE writes mortgages, leases airplanes, and broadcasts TV signals for its own NBC and for others, such as Viacom." See *Fortune* (May 15). 1995.

was renamed CBS Group and is now predominantly a media company. In fact none of the electrotechnical corporations have an identical structure: all are unique combinations of products and businesses.

Needless to say, after more than a hundred years, the electrotechnical industry has changed greatly and today is in the midst of dynamic technical development. The rapid establishment and expansion of the industry occurred in the 1880s. From a few fundamental inventions in electrical power generation, transmission, and application, the industry has grown in numerous directions. We now take a closer look at technological developments in the industry from telegraphy and batteries to nuclear power and automation and lately, changes in organization from corporate bureaucracies to "boundaryless" organizations.

The Formation of a Science-Based Industry

The latter part of the nineteenth century was the golden era of electrification. From a technological perspective, turbines, generators, transformers—all the building blocks of an electrical infrastructure—were created in this period. In theory there is a close connection between the most important technological achievements in the field of electricity and the scientific foundations of those innovations. In the practical world there is usually a lag between discovery and application, one that takes decades or, as with power transformers, half a century.

The prehistory of the electrotechnical breakthroughs that came at the end of the nineteenth century is a long one. Electrical phenomena such as electrostatics were known already to the ancient Greeks. Thales (fl. 600 B.C.) knew that amber could attract a feather, if rubbed with some soft cloth. ("Electron" is, by the way, the Greek word for amber.) The founding of the science of electricity, however, (e.g., electrodynamics, electromagnetism) took place more than two thousand years later. In 1600 the Englishman William Gilbert coined the term *electricity* in his book on magnetism. The terminology used in electrical measurements and calculations pay tribute to some of the great scientists in the field. An electrical charge is called *coulomb* (C), named after the Frenchman Charles de Coulomb (1736–1806), who studied electrical attraction and repulsion. *Volt* (V), the unit of electrical potential difference (or colloquially, "live wire," "tension"), refers to its Italian discoverer, Alessandro Volta (1745–1827). Electrical current is measured in *ampère* (A) in honor of the Frenchman André-Marie Ampère (1775–1836), the founder of electrodynamics. The German Georg Ohm (1789–1854) demonstrated that there are no perfect conductors. The intensity of electrical current is reduced by resistance, since called *ohm* and symbolized by the Greek character omega (ω). Inductance is measured in *henry* (H), named after the American Joseph Henry (1797–1878), one of the great names in electrodynamics. The electrical unit for capacitance, giving the quantity of electrical charge a capacitor can store per unit of electrical potential difference, is called *farad* (F) after the Englishman Michael Faraday (1791–1867).[6] Faraday is often considered the most influential researcher in general electrical phenomena, working in the field of electrochemistry in particular.[7] To the work of the Scotsman James Clerk Maxwell (1831–1879) and the German Heinrich Hertz (1857–1894) we owe the theoretical understanding and experimental verification of electromagnetism. In commemoration of Hertz's achievements we measure frequency in *hertz*.

This short overview of the historical development of the field of electricity proves the point that electrical engineering is unthinkable without the preceding scientific discoveries. This scientific base did not underpin the first industrial revolution in the eighteenth century that took place in textiles, transportation, and mining. The ascent of the new electrotechnical industry and the simultaneous rise of the chemical industry at the end of the nineteenth century are often called a second industrial revolution. Their close dependence on scientific discoveries and an emerging profession of specialized engineers are two of its most salient features.[8] Inventions still played a central role but the process of innovation was becoming institutionalized. The industries of the second wave fostered the creation of the first huge industrial laboratories. The leading corporations of the electrotechnical industry played an important part in the scientific development of the field.[9]

GE is a telling example. The company was a result of the merger in 1892 between Thomas Alva Edison's Edison General Electric Company (started 1878) and Elihu Thomson's Thomson-Houston Electric Company. Edison General Electric's strength was its many inventions, its weakness the fact that Edison favored direct current instead of alternating current. Elihu Thomson staked alternating current, the key to his fortunes. The choice between direct and alternating current was strategic in the early period of the industry, similar to the choice between lighter or heavier than air aircraft in aviation. Alternating current came out as the winner.

Edison had created his famous laboratory in Menlo Park, New Jersey, with the ambition of "a minor invention every ten days, and a big one every six months or so."[10] Strange as it may seem, his plans came close to reality: Edison took out more than four thousand patents. The single most acclaimed

[6] Harris Benson. 1996. *University physics*. New York: John Wiley & Sons.

[7] From our perspective in this book, devoted to the study of ABB's power transformers business area, it is of special interest that Faraday in principle created the first transformer in 1831.

[8] The American Institute of Electrical Engineers was founded in 1884. In Germany and Scandinavia the engineering field of electrotechnology is often divided into heavy and light current. This is seldom the case in the Anglo-Saxon countries, which emphasize the unity of the field and its strong ties to general physics.

[9] See, for instance, Wolfgang König. 1996. *Science-based industry or industry-based science? Electrical engineering in Germany before World War I*. The Society for the History of Technology.

[10] Quoted from David Noble. 1977. *America by design*. Oxford: Oxford University Press: 8.

of all his patents was the incandescent lightbulb (1879)[11] but on his impressive list are also the phonograph and the kinetoscope (the movie camera), and improvements in dynamos and batteries. Later GE organized research and development in an even more systematic way than at Menlo Park. The new establishment in Schenectady, New York, with famous researchers and inventors like Charles Steinmetz (an immigrant from Germany, who was a brilliant mathematician and engineer with a new vision of how to run a laboratory) and Nikola Tesla (a Croatian born inventor and one of the great names in the science of electricity), perfected laboratory organization and concentrated on alternating current applications instead of Edison's focus on direct current. The laboratory approach to innovation was copied by some of the other high-tech corporations of the time, the telephone giants, AT&T and Western Electric in particular, forming the famous Bell Labs in 1925.[12]

The other multinationals in the emerging electrotechnical industry have trajectories similar to that of GE. As a rule they were started by or with the expertise of some prominent inventors. Westinghouse, once the very important other American electrotechnical giant, was founded by George Westinghouse, famous for some four hundred patents, most of them using alternating current. One of the early successes of Westinghouse was William Stanley's transformer based on alternating current.[13]

With companies like Siemens and AEG, Germany used to be the second most important country in this industry. Until the 1880s it was number one. Siemens and Halske, which is the old name, started as a family business in telegraphy in 1847[14] and grew to become the dominant German corporation. Werner von Siemens (1816–1892) is distinguished for many patents in telegraphy and power generation and also for theoretical breakthroughs. In 1866 he discovered the dynamo principle for generating electric power as well as inventing the dynamo (or generator). The Siemens corporation also became well-known for being first in mastering electrification of railways, trams and elevators. Later it also commercialized applications of X-rays, discovered in 1895 by Wilhelm Conrad Röntgen, the first recipient of the Nobel Prize in physics.

In the 1880s Siemens lost its monopolistic position in Germany, when a number of competitors were established, all of them in Berlin: AEG, Schuckert, Osram, Bergmann, and Telefunken.[15] AEG, founded in 1883 by Emil

---

[11] The first central generating plants to supply electrical lighting with power were set up in London and New York in 1882, the beginning of the end of the "Dark Ages."

[12] In the 1920s Bell Laboratories surpassed Schenectady and became the world's largest industrial laboratories of that time employing more than a thousand engineers.

[13] "Westinghouse Electrical Systems Division Flexible Manufacturing System." Robert Lund, Albert Bishop, Anne Newman, eds. 1993. *Designed to work: Production systems and people.* New Jersey: Prentice Hall.

[14] Siemens celebrated its 150th anniversary in 1997.

[15] Heidrun Homburg. 1991. *Rationalisierung und Industriearbeit. Arbeitsmarkt, Management, Arbeiterschaft im Siemens-Konzern Berlin 1900–1939.* Berlin: Haude und Spener, 348ff. Also see Jürgen Kocka. 1972. *Siemens und der aufhaltsame Aufstieg der AEG.* In *Tradition 17* Jahrgang.

Rathenau, made innovative investments in lighting.[16] The company compensated for its late start relative to Siemens by becoming more export oriented. At the beginning of the twentieth century it reached the status of the world's leading electrotechnical exporter. During the first half of the twentieth century Siemens as a rule had a third, and AEG a fourth, of German electrotechnical production.

In a number of countries the electrotechnical industry remained domestic. Countries such as the United Kingdom and France somewhat belatedly got strong electrotechnical companies, but they were geared toward the domestic market and the semidomestic markets in their colonies. In the United Kingdom GEC became the star. In France, Compagnie Générale d'Electricité (CGE) was set up in 1898 in close cooperation with Compagnie Française Thomson-Houston. The product range was limited in the beginning with a focus on lamps and batteries.[17] CGE got heavily involved in telecommunications during the First World War. Alsthom (founded as late as 1928) and Schneider (owned by one of the oldest French industrial dynasties) became the leading French firms in the field of electrical power technology. Many countries followed the French and British models, with their high degree of self-reliance on domestic electrotechnical companies often combined with protective tariffs against foreign competition. Countries fitting that description were Italy, Spain, Brazil, and Japan.

Broadly speaking, there are two types of electrotechnical companies: the domestic players and the global contenders. In two small countries, Switzerland and Sweden, the domestic players outgrew their domestic markets. The two countries have excellent hydropower potential in common as well as pioneering companies in the industry. The Swedish ASEA was founded in 1883 and the Swiss Brown Boveri in 1891. The two companies had many traits in common and both from the start were dominated by inventing engineers. Of the two founding fathers of the Swiss company, Walter Boveri was the entrepreneur and businessman; Charles Brown, the inventor. A native Englishman working in Switzerland, Brown's inventions made the distribution of electrical power over long distances possible. Brown Boveri engineers were among the pioneers in the electrification of railways, such as the ones on the Matterhorn and Jungfraujoch. One of the founders of ASEA, Jonas Wenström, built many of his inventions on three-phase current proving its applicability for transmission. ASEA also pioneered in the electrification of steelworks and some other trades. The business side of ASEA was very turbulent during its first two decades, the company falling prey to raiders and speculators. At the turn of the new century stability was found by the famous Wallenberg family gaining control and the appointment of a legend-

[16] His son and successor as CEO in 1915, Walther Rathenau, organized the German economy during World War I and later became foreign minister in the Weimar Republic, which speaks for his talents but also bears witness to the societal importance and prestige of the electrotechnical industry. He was murdered by anti-Semitic officers in 1922.

[17] The name was changed to "Alcatel Alsthom" as recently as 1991.

ary chief executive officer, Sigfrid Edström, who ruled the company for half a century.

Brown Boveri and ASEA made heroic efforts to keep pace technologically across the wide range of electrotechnical products and systems. Both companies became very proficient in power generation as well as power transmission. Another similarity is the way the two companies were strengthened by domestic competition. Brown Boveri had to compete with Maschinenfabrik Oerlikon and a number of other smaller Swiss producers, which in due time were acquired and merged with Brown Boveri. The history of ASEA is similar insofar as ASEA also took over most of its domestic competitors— in 1916 the famous Swedish turbine manufacturer, STAL (Svenska Turbinfabriks Ab Ljungström) in Finspång and the Swedish transmission manufacturer, Förenade Elektriska in Ludvika, still a center for transmission research and transformer manufacturing.[18]

Brown Boveri and ASEA, respectively, became export oriented early on. Their international growth patterns were different, however. Germany and North America were more or less closed to ASEA; consequently, expansion was in other directions, that is, Russia, southern Europe, and Latin America. Brown Boveri, on the other hand, had established a presence in Germany. In 1900 Brown Boveri started its operations in Mannheim, its daughter company soon becoming twice as big as its parent company in Baden, Switzerland. During this period Brown Boveri also acquired an important subsidiary in Italy, Tecnomasio Italiano in 1903 and its daughter company in Austria in 1910. By and large Brown Boveri was more international and cosmopolitan than ASEA. The Swiss company had more of a multidomestic structure. ASEA was accustomed to treating its international operations as daughter companies to its Swedish operation. In Norway ASEA and Brown Boveri met head-on through the daughter companies, ASEA Per Kure and Norsk Elektrisk Brown Boveri. No single company succeeded in towering over the others. After Norway gained its independence, leaving the union with Sweden in 1905, it had two "domestic" producers as well, the Norwegian National Industri and the Elektrisk Bureau.[19] Few countries had a more competitive electrotechnical market than the hydropower nation Norway.

The Period between the Wars

In the 1920s and even more so in the 1930s there was a tendency to up-scale electrical technology. The power plants became ever more powerful. New records were broken almost yearly. The volt-ampère figures for generators and transformers kept on growing.

[18] Jan Glete. 1983. *ASEA under hundra år, 1883–1983*. Västerås: ASEA AB.
[19] Nina Berg. 1993. *Medbestemmelse i et overnasjonalt konsern. En studie av ABB ASEA Brown Boveri*. Bergen: Universitetet i Bergen.

After World War I the U.S. economy had become by far the world's largest. The late 1920s were unprecedented boom years. GE took the lead in electrifying the American home and kitchen. Refrigerators, ovens, toasters, mixers, clocks, radios, air conditioners, vacuum cleaners, dishwashers, washing machines, and many other twentieth-century inventions were launched by GE and several smaller competitors. The market response was overall very favorable. These new products and the markets they created contributed to a steady rise in electricity consumption and continuing demand and investments in power stations as well as turbines, generators, transformers, cables, switch gear, capacitors, and the many peripheral products of electrification such as relays, sockets, meters, fuses, and the like. In the late 1920s two-fifths of the world's manufactured goods were made in the United States. The great depression of the 1930s more than halved the American output, but its repercussions in countries such as Japan and Germany were even more severe.

Electrification under the Soviet regime was of great magnitude. The famous Lenin quotation, "The power of Soviets + Electrification = Communism," was used as a slogan during the era of the first five-year plans with their vast electrification programs. The building of the Dnjeprostojan hydropower station and similar investments resulted in a twenty-fold jump in the Soviet electrical power supply during the years between the wars. The electrification program started with concessions and licensee agreements between the Soviet Union and major multinationals and ended with complete nationalization, autonomy, and self-sufficiency.[20]

In the United States the New Deal program of the 1930s included many large-scale investments in electrification, such as the exploitation of hydroelectric power in the Tennessee Valley. The period between the wars put an end to the old practice of belt-driven machines, which caused a quantum leap in the demand for electrical motors. The change to self-propelled machines made life easier for smaller companies and enhanced their competitiveness, gave more freedom in the layout of shops and workplaces, and opened the possibility of more autonomous work groups and workstations.

The electrotechnical industry tried to become "scientifically" managed during these years. Siemens introduced Taylor's principles in the early 1920s and Ford's mass-production ideas late in the same decade (Homburg 1991, 653). In the United States Westinghouse did more than copy the methods of the auto industry and in the 1930s took the lead in restructuring the jobs and tasks of batch production. The new production technology became known as MTM (Methods—Time Measurement), and could be implemented without the use of time-study men, since the measurements were made in the laboratory only once. MTM was exported to the world's auto industries beginning in the 1950s.

During the turbulent 1920s the German electrotechnical giants had diffi-

---

[20] A precedent that some corporate pessimists say will repeat itself in China.

culties in regaining their very impressive prewar strength. According to the peace of Versailles, Germany had to pay substantial war damages. That created a market for replacements in Germany, for example the one in the wake of delivery of thousands of locomotives to France after World War I. Siemens positioned itself in medical technology, among many other specialties. Both Siemens and AEG joined the armaments race in the 1930s. During the Second World War they administered their former competitors in occupied countries; the Dutch Philips, for instance, became a kind of subsidiary to Siemens.

In the 1930s ASEA became a leading company in transmission technology, much helped by its new high voltage laboratory in Ludvika. ASEA developed high voltage ovens for industrial applications. Brown Boveri was technologically advanced in turbines, superchargers, and turbocompressors. Internationally it acquired a strong position in some Eastern European countries such as Poland and Czechoslovakia. In Latin America, Argentina and Brazil market gains also contributed to the growth of Brown Boveri.[21]

The period between the wars is the era of the big cartels. The oligopolistic world leaders of this industry, for example, GE, Westinghouse, Siemens, and AEG, tried to divide the world into spheres of interest. On the whole, the largest companies managed a peaceful coexistence but some smaller territories were contested. AEG and Siemens tried to "colonize" Scandinavia in the 1920s, and GE tried it in the early 1930s, but on the whole both attempts failed. The Swedish ASEA not only survived domestically but gained strength internationally.

The Early Postwar Period

The Marshall Plan helped to support the boom years in the 1940s and 1950s. German development, in particular, the *Wirtschaftswunder*, was very different from the inflation and depression that followed the First World War. After World War II Siemens had lost 80 percent of its capacity, but was soon back to its prewar strength. The other defeated Axis power, Japan, was also regaining momentum. The groups of Japanese companies that dominated the economy of Japan between the wars, the *zaibatsu*, were dismantled by the American occupation forces under General MacArthur. It did not take long, however, before the old pieces were put together again, but with a new name, *keiretsu*. Companies like Mitsubishi and Hitachi reemerged on the scene. These companies soon grew to become some of the biggest in the world, but in the electrotechnical industry they remained primarily domestic and were technologically dependent on American and European license

---

[21] Werner Catrina. 1991. *BBC. Glanz—krise—fusion. 1891–1991: Von Brown Boveri zu ABB.* Zürich: Orell Füssli.

holders. The Japanese electrotechnical industry has so far not been as export oriented as the Japanese auto industry. The different corporations of the Mitsubishi group that have made a place in the electrotechnical industry, Mitsubishi Electric and Mitsubishi Heavy Industries, are each roughly of the same size as ABB revenuewise, but the profitability of some of these Japanese giants is meager indeed. In the case of Mitsubishi it has been close to zero for many years.[22] Apart from all their Western competitors, Japanese corporations in this industry are also challenged by companies from its former "colony," Korea.

The technology that enabled the atom bomb was soon applied in power generation.[23] The nuclear power industry emerged as an important part of the electrotechnical industry. Westinghouse became a market leader in the application of nuclear energy, a market that has not recovered since the accident in the nuclear power plant at Three Mile Island in 1979. Industry automation emerged as another new field. GE became one of the most important developers of the numerical control (NC) technology for operating machine tools; later it became known as computerized NC (CNC). Most of the major electrotechnical companies followed the lead of GE and founded or acquired units of automation expertise.

From a power generation and transmission perspective the industry surpassed its previous size and strength. Power stations reached new record capacities, such as the Brazilian hydropower station in Itaiphu and many similar gigantic projects in Third World countries (e.g., Assuan in Egypt and Cariba in Mozambique). Faster transmission became possible with ever higher voltages owing to breakthroughs made by ASEA and Brown Boveri. For a few years in the 1940s and early 1950s each of these two companies had very advantageous positions. Its German competitors, Siemens and AEG, were literally in ruins and the order books of Brown Boveri and ASEA were filled. In the early 1950s ASEA advanced to world leader status in electrical power transmission by developing the new technology of long-range, high-voltage, direct current transmission.

The Sixties and Seventies

Brown Boveri developed ever larger turbines and became a dominant player in the area of induction ovens, used in foundries for instance. This success led to the opening of green-field plants in Birr, Switzerland, the biggest in Europe of its kind in 1960. In 1967 Brown Boveri acquired one of its oldest Swiss competitors, Maschienenbau Oerlikon, and in 1969 another one, the Geneva company Sécheron (manufacturer of transformers). In 1970

[22] Lee Smith. 1995. Does the world's biggest company have a future? *Fortune* (August 7).
[23] A leading manager from Westinghouse was administering the Manhattan project that produced the first atom bombs.

Brown Boveri strengthened its position in Italy by acquiring Sace in Bergamo. In Italy, the Swiss company had gotten the reputation of giving its subsidiaries a great deal of local freedom.[24] The German Brown Boveri subsidiary in Mannheim, with more than 40,000 employees, also had much local freedom, but in contrast to the Italian operation it was much larger than its parent company in Baden. Headquarters in Baden had difficulty in exercising effective command and control over Mannheim.

Noteworthy during this period is the organizational reform that reshaped ASEA under its new chief executive officer (CEO), Curt Nicolin.[25] In hindsight it is interesting that ASEA implemented rationalization of capital, a forerunner of time-based management, already in the 1960s. Relative to the competition, ASEA became more performance oriented relying on facts and figures. A typical slogan of the time was "Management by Facts."

The Eighties: Dramatic Change in the Electrotechnical Industry

The 1980s were dramatic in the electrotechnical industry. Two century-old giants, Westinghouse and AEG, almost disappeared from the industry. Two big mergers contributed to reshaping it. The mergers resulted in ABB and GEC-Alsthom. The formation of ABB in 1987, from Swedish ASEA and Swiss Brown Boveri, created a new world leader in the core businesses of power generation and transmission. GE strengthened its number one position in terms of total revenues and profitability.

GE Versus Westinghouse

At the beginning of the postwar period GE and Westinghouse were relatively similar in size. Today GE's net earnings are considerably larger than Westinghouse's revenues. The stock market growth of GE during the last decade has been its biggest ever; Westinghouse has been shrinking for years. What can explain a shift of this magnitude?

GE, with $US 90 billion in 1997 sales (three times ABB's revenues) and $US 8 billion in net earnings (roughly six times ABB's net earnings), is in many respects the star of this industry. GE began doing radical things back in 1981, headed by its newly appointed CEO, Jack Welch. Most of the competition followed suit a decade later and some, for example, Siemens, have just begun. Welch applied simple rules but with great consistency. GE was not opting for completeness or integration but supremacy and consequently sold out large parts of its electrotechnical business. Jack Welch became fa-

---

[24] Catrina. 1991, page 168.
[25] As chairman of ASEA in the mid-1980s he was one of the architects behind the merger with Brown Boveri.

mous for policy formulations; for example, in 1982 he told his managers: "Let's compete only in businesses that we have a chance to tower over. The options for the rest are fix, close or sell," the essence of GE's so-called Number One and Number Two Strategy. A related policy formulation runs: "Change before you have to; if you don't have a competitive advantage, don't compete."

The GE restructuring program of the 1980s aimed at downsizing personnel in general, white-collar staff in particular, and shifting the company's product mix toward high-tech with high margins. GE targeted automation equipment as the most potential growth area. Power generation (meaning mostly generators and gas turbines), medical systems, and aerospace were also named high-tech priority areas. The other side of its high-tech strategy was selling off or dismantling low-tech businesses, for example, smaller consumer appliances (called "housewares" in the old GE), wire, cables, and switch gear. In the high-tech–high margins formula the emphasis was on margins. If you could get high margins without high-tech that was even better, for example, expanding into financial services, an early GE offensive that became very successful.

The reduction in employees within GE during the first half of the 1980s was 25 percent or 130,000, more than during the Great Depression in the beginning of the 1930s. The CEO earned the nickname "Neutron Jack," alluding to the bomb that kills people but leaves buildings standing. Welch even abandoned buildings. The old legendary center of GE in Schenectady, New York, where Edison once used to work, was stripped of its functions and employees were moved to low-cost southern states. Nonetheless GE's profitability increased substantially, and the stock exchange evaluation of the company improved dramatically. The personnel reductions seemed farsighted in retrospect. Jack Welch was reassessed. In recent years he has been named America's most respected manager.

Globally GE has had a rather cautious approach preferring joint ventures, for instance, with Britain's GEC and Japanese Fanuc. GE bought Thorn, the British company, in 1990 and is the owner of the National Broadcasting Company (NBC). Immediately after the fall of the Berlin Wall GE bought the Hungarian lighting firm Tungsram and started an Eastern European company-buying offensive, one that so far has not been overly successful.

The delayering within GE started at lower levels of management but by 1985 the divisional organization, and with that all the vice presidents, was eliminated giving the CEO direct access to the main business areas. A lot was done to change the corporate culture toward entrepreneurship and speedy decision making.[26] A kind of time-based management (TBM) program called

---

[26] Noel Tichy and Stratford Sherman. 1993. *Control your destiny or someone else will: How Jack Welch is making General Electric the world's most competitive company*. New York Doubleday, p. 199.

Work-Out was started in 1988 backed by a lot of training at the corporation's secretive management school at Croton-on-Hudson.[27] In 1990 the Quick Response program was introduced as the new ideal, the objective being to shorten the response time from order to delivery. Empowerment of the rank and file was another major theme, expressed in GE jargon as High Involvement Teams. Later than ABB but with a lot more managerial backing, GE launched a Six Sigma quality program in 1995. GE is a major exponent of what they themselves call "the boundaryless organization," a flexible organization with permeable vertical, horizontal, external, and geographical boundaries.[28]

Westinghouse in Pennsylvania has been shrinking for years, ever since its nuclear strategy ran into difficulties in the aftermath of the Three Mile Island incident. A common denominator of the many initiatives undertaken by its rapidly changing top managers has been diversification into services and sell-offs of its power segments. Westinghouse's big move into financial services in the 1980s, inspired by GE's successes with the same strategy, failed utterly and endangered the very existence of the whole company. How and when a company implements a strategy seems to be as important as the strategy itself, judging from the opposite outcomes for GE and Westinghouse applying the same strategy of diversification into the finance sector. GE's power transmission and distribution divisions were sold to Westinghouse in the late 1980s and acquired by ABB in 1989. From Westinghouse's old base in the electrical power industry nuclear energy and power generation still remain. Westinghouse tried diversification ultimately leading to retreat from the electrotechnical industry.

Swedish ASEA and Swiss Brown Boveri Form the Multidomestic ABB

The merger was a well kept secret until the news of it "detonated" in the summer of 1987. The merger made sense to most observers. Brown Boveri was very strong in the German-speaking countries of Europe plus Italy. ASEA had recently made the Nordic countries a domestic market (employees in Nordic countries other than Sweden increased from 2,500 in 1980 to 15,000 in 1986).[29] Brown Boveri was very proficient in power generation (12 percent of revenues compared with 3 percent in ASEA) and ASEA was superior in industrial, building, and environmental systems (22 percent versus 16 percent) as well as in traction (5 percent versus 3 percent). Power

---

[27] By its admirers named the Harvard Business School of American Industry.

[28] Ron Ashkenas, Dave Ulrich, Todd Jick, Steve Kerr. 1995. *The boundaryless organization*. San Francisco: Jossey-Bass.

[29] In particular through the acquisition of Finland's leading electrotechnical corporation, Strömbergs.

transmission, an old ASEA strength, was heralded as the business with the greatest rationalization potential. Brown Boveri was strong in research and development but not in profits; ASEA was advanced in organization and sales and very profitable. The new CEO of ABB, Percy Barnevik, had an excellent track record as CEO of ASEA and was met with respect from the very start. Brown Boveri brought 97,500 employees to the merger; ASEA 71,000. Together they formed the biggest corporation in electrotechnology proper. Mitsubishi, Hitachi, GE, and Siemens are larger than ABB owing to their other operations but not larger in electrical power technology.

The merger was followed by dramatic downsizing and slashing of headquarters and managerial layers. The reduction resulted in cutting away 90 percent according to the formula of 30 percent laid off, 30 percent transferred to operating units, and 30 percent moved into newly created companies offering services on a competitive basis.[30] The old Brown Boveri alone had 4,000 employed at headquarters in Baden. ABB started with less than 100 employed at the new headquarters in Zurich and roughly 500 altogether, if we add all national, business segment, and business area managers as well.

After the merger followed a number of swift acquisition offensives all launched in the late 1980s. The media were fond of comparing Barnevik to Napoleon[31] and calling these offensives "campaigns," the one in southern Europe, Italy and Spain in particular, followed by the campaign in North America including the acquisition of Combustion Engineering and the joint Westinghouse-GE transmission operation.

The Eastern European campaign, launched after the fall of the Berlin Wall, had its biggest gains in Poland but aimed for Russia as well. The Pacific Rim campaign focused on China at the start but now is targeting a number of other Asian countries as well, for example, Vietnam, Malaysia, Thailand, Indonesia, and India.

From the very start ABB chose a "multidomestic" approach, keeping local production but trying to improve competitiveness vigorously with the help of a number of strategies and methodologies, for example, Customer Focus, TBM, total quality management, Six Sigma, Seven-Ups (these strategies are discussed more thoroughly in the following chapters).

The GEC-Alsthom Merger

The ABB merger triggered defensive action from two of its French and British competitors. The state-owned CGE, nationalized in 1946, became

---

[30] Described many times; see for instance, *The New York Times*, 2 March 1992, "The Very Model of Efficiency," an interview with Gerhard Schulmeyer, at that time in charge of ABB's American operations.

[31] Catrina. 1991, p. 299.

privatized in 1987. That increased the possibilities for cooperation and joint ventures. CGE (since 1991 called Alcatel Alsthom) was and still is strong in telecommunications, energy, and transport. GEC with heavy reliance on defense products (the Marconi corporation is for instance part of the group), telecommunications, and medical equipment had also some presence in power systems. The GEC-Alsthom merger in 1989 is partial in the sense that only power systems and transportation (traction and marine equipment) are run by GEC-Alsthom as a special sector and daughter company within the two mother companies. The ABB merger, on the other hand, reduced ASEA and Brown Boveri to mere holding companies (ASEA ceased to exist altogether in 1996). Measured as percentage of turnover or number of employees GEC-Alsthom represents roughly a third of GEC and Alcatel, respectively. GEC-Alsthom is, with some 70,000 employees, a third as big as ABB. Transport and Power Generation are the two strongest divisions, their most famous product the high-speed train, the TGV (Trains à Grande Vitesse). In power generation, gas turbines are the prime product, for which they are in close cooperation with GE.

Siemens Versus AEG

AEG, the old German industry champion, was shrinking in the 1980s. In 1985 Daimler-Benz started a takeover that was completed in 1988. Ever since those years top management has tried to stem or compensate for the losses by selling off parts and subsidiaries of AEG, for instance, Transformatoren Union (in 1987) and Olympia Office (in 1992). These sales have not helped very much. The losses have some years been staggering.

Siemens (DM 94 billion, roughly $US 55 billion, in revenues for 1996) has fared much better than AEG. Siemens is well-known for its high standard of technological development. The company spends some 10 percent of its revenues on research and development.

In this mighty conglomerate a number of the many divisions are growing, for example, telecommunications (by far the largest) and medical engineering and industrial automation. Siemens has well-known trouble spots as well. The acquisition of Nixdorf did not make its computer division profitable. Likewise Siemens has lost money on its semiconductor operations although the world market has been booming.[32] The most common criticism against Siemens has been its lack of focus. It looks as if CEO Heinrich von Pierer has listened. He is selling off businesses that are judged to be noncore. The energy sector in general (roughly 15 percent of revenues) and power generation in particular have been given high priority.

---

[32] Plaut, Jones and Sanne. 1994. *Siemens*. London: Goldman Sachs; Miller. 1995. Siemens shapes up. *Business Week*, 1 May.

Another long-standing criticism deals with Siemens' alleged bureaucracy.[33] To cope with that Siemens is applying some of the same methodology as ABB and GE, that is, trying to change the corporate culture by introducing TBM (in Siemens called Time Optimized Processes, or TOP), reducing staff, de-layering, downsizing, and relocating to low-cost countries (e.g., the Czech Republic). It is too early to evaluate the effects, but there are signs indicating that Siemens will regain some of its former competitiveness.

Summary: Scale Versus Scope

The 1980s and even more so the 1990s have been critical for the manufacturers of electrical power generation and transmission equipment as well as for many other high-tech producers. To quote Jack Welch of GE: "If you thought the 1980s were tough, the 1990s will make the 1980s look like a cakewalk. It will be brutally competitive."[34] The truth of that predication has been brought home to such profitable companies as IBM, Philips, and many of the Japanese multinationals. Many of these stars of the 1980s have already lost 50 percent of both employees as well as revenues and are down to a fraction of their former stock market value.

For decades the oligopolistic giants of the industry were spoiled by benevolent public utilities and high "price quality" (characteristic jargon in this line of industry) on their products and services. The demand in North America and Europe has shown signs of stagnation. In some product ranges overcapacity has intensified competition. In many countries privatization among utilities has made prices fall. In particular, privatized utilities have postponed replacements, a tempting cost-cutting alternative because these products are often characterized by a longevity of twenty years and upward. Price erosion has been dramatic in some years during the 1990s, in the neighborhood of 20 percent and 30 percent yearly. The customer base of the industry has been shifting as well; more tend to buy less. Services and replacements gain in importance compared with investments in new equipment and capacity. Long-term growth is found in developing countries, for example, the Asia–Pacific region. The cumulative effects of these changes make the electrotechnical industry crowded and concentrated in the "wrong" parts of the world. What have the major corporations done in order to cope with these changed societal and market conditions?

Textbook solutions for the industry's woes would include cost-cutting and downsizing in high-cost countries, while making investments in and relocating to low-cost countries. Another classical alternative would be to speed up

[33] Homburg. 1991.
[34] Tichy and Sherman. 1993, p. 240.

technological development and the creation of new values with the aim of becoming the only or leading producer of a particular product or service. A typical move also might be abandoning this ageing industry in favor of a more dynamic environment.

Electrotechnical companies are moving targets for the business analyst. They change their scope of products and services as well as presence in different countries. Some companies are hard to follow, for example, Westinghouse, which experiments with many different strategies and changes them radically from one year to the next. In the long run it almost looks like trial and error. Still, through all the smoke of day-to-day variation, we can discern some fundamental structural strategic alternatives. Let us briefly look at some of the alternatives chosen by the well-known electrotechnical companies: GE, Westinghouse, Siemens, AEG, GEC-Alsthom, and last but certainly not least, ABB.

Diversification. This alternative leads to retreat away from the stagnant markets and the industry as a whole. Examples are Westinghouse and to some extent AEG.

Opting for scale. Companies retain core businesses within the electrotechnical industry in combination with diversification. GE and Siemens have taken this approach. GE's diversification has led to a new kind of conglomerate, in which a company combines all businesses in which they are able to become superior to the competition.

Opting for scope. Choosing scope as the major competitive advantage, a company plans mergers to hopefully optimal bigness in the core businesses. The ABB merger, which became effective in January 1988, has been praised for these qualities in the international business press.[35] GEC in the United Kingdom and Alcatel in France tried this strategy when they formed GEC-Alsthom in 1989.

The results of the restructurings during the 1980s are obvious in some respects. We have one clear winner, GE, and two obvious losers, Westinghouse and AEG. In the United States there is now one dominant player, GE. In Europe it is a more mixed picture, with ABB and Siemens as the two on top. In Asia no single company is leading the electrotechnical industry. Below or along with the international ranking, there are domestic champions in many countries, for example, GEC-Alsthom in France, Samsung in South Korea, and Mitsubishi in Japan. Added to these top players are international and domestic niche companies, mostly mid-sized, seldom commanding more than a thousand employees.

In the new competition that will rage at the turn of the millennium, the major alternative seems to be scale versus scope. GE has opted for economies of scale and become the trendsetter in aggressive cost-cutting and downsizing, starting that process in the early 1980s. Siemens has recently started

[35] References to important articles are already cited in the Introduction.

cost-cutting and prioritizing but has obviously a long way to go. From a distance it looks as if ABB also is mimicking GE in cost-cutting and racing for scale, but a closer look reveals that this is only partly true. The scope of electrotechnical products within ABB and the extent of its local presence add up to an important competitive advantage in bidding for really big orders, particularly in industrializing countries. Scope, the ability to deliver compatible electrical power systems from power station over long-distance transmission to distribution to consumers and end users, turnkey if asked for, has become one of ABB's key strengths and most valued competitive advantages. Scope has a real chance of winning over scale.

2 Lean Management in Practice
The Headquarters Perspective

Torsten Björkman

A Core Business Area within Asea Brown Boveri

The Power Transformers business area (BA) has a unique position within Asea Brown Boveri (ABB). It is regarded as a test case of the ABB policy of being local worldwide, since no other BA even comes close to this one's global presence (in 1996 the BA had 24 plants in 18 countries).[1] When the merger was announced by the new chief executive officer (CEO) Percy Barnevik,[2] he used transformers as an example: "We do it [the merger between ASEA and Brown Boveri] for synergy effects. Transformers as an example are made in different countries; *if they cannot make money out of this merger, who else can do it?*"

Power transformers form one of some thirty-five business areas within the ABB group.[3] It is one of the bigger BAs (number ten in economic ranking) with around $US 1 billion in turnover per year and approximately 7,500 employees. Like ABB, this business area has a short history. Its formative years were 1988 and 1989, when ABB became the world leader in the power transformer branch of the electrotechnical industry. As a result of the merger and several later acquisitions, the BA doubled in size and number of plants and came to own all major power transformer technologies in the world (seven altogether). ABB's power transformers BA is still the leader of this industry with a fifth of the world market. Siemens, the closest competitor, has less than 5 percent of the market.

---

[1] United States, Canada, Brazil, South Africa, Australia, Thailand, China, United Kingdom, Norway, Sweden, Finland, Poland, Germany, Switzerland, Spain, Italy, Turkey, and Vietnam.

[2] On August 11, 1987.

[3] Career patterns within ABB also tell the story of this BA's importance. Göran Lindahl, Percy Barnevik's successor as CEO of ABB since January 1997, was once plant manager of ASEA Power Transformers in Ludvika (1983–85), Sweden, with global responsibility for transformers. Sune Karlsson, now a member of the executive committee and in charge of the Power Transmission business segment worldwide succeeded Lindahl in Ludvika (1985–87) and became the first ABB president for the power transformers BA in 1988.

36

The ABB organization is structured as a matrix with responsibilities divided between national ABB companies (48 in 1996) and business areas (36 in 1996). As a consequence of this matrix a local plant manager has in principle two lines of authority above him (so far no women in that position), namely, the international BA managers and the national ABB managers. Jokingly, but only partly so, the BA managers are called the "bad guys," looking for results expressed in profits and physical performance, throughput times in particular. The BA managers are blamed for initiating downsizing and closedowns. The national ABB managers, on the other hand, are called the "good guys," taking responsibility for local customers and their own employees and honored for defending threatened workplaces.

A local plant manager has as a consequence two bosses, the BA president and the national ABB president.[4] The power transformers BA is the extreme example of ABB's matrix owing to the fact that 18 national presidents are directly affected by this BA's policy for the 24 plants currently in operation. To understand the intricacies of ABB matrix functioning, studying this BA is most rewarding.

The power transformers BA is facing falling prices and rising costs and has to learn how to cope with markets by and large stagnant. The worldwide trend of protected and monopolized public utilities that are deregulated and often privatized continues. Increased cost and price awareness among customers is a common effect. BA Management of course assumes responsibility for a happy ending despite these challenges. How do you improve performance worldwide? A synthesis of small-scale local manufacturing and at the same time economies of scale through a number of universal BA programs such as time-based management (TBM) and the Six Sigma program (see details later in chapter) is the general formula for survival and success. In this chapter the power transformers BA initiatives in strategy and structure are presented.

The Demand for Power Transformers

Power transformers play a vital role in electrical power transmission. The main product of this BA, the power transformer is a necessary link in the chain of power transmission from turbines (the primary mover) and generators to transformers and finally to equipment and machinery powered by electricity, for example, motors, robots, ovens and, of course, electric lighting. The transmission network forms a chain made up of these links. The network needs control equipment and switch gear, cables and transformers,

---

[4] In the core ABB countries such as the United States, Germany, Switzerland and Sweden, the business segment executive vice president is the immediate superior, not the national ABB company president.

before it is operational. To use an analogy with the mechanical gearbox, the "gearbox" of electrical transmission is the power transformer.

Power transformers are made in many sizes, but all of them are rather large, varying from a few cubic meters in volume to the size of a villa. Power transformers are primarily used to increase the voltage between the generation of electrical power and the long-distance transmission network. They are also regularly used in intermediate transmission and transformer substations along the network. The distance from power station to consumer is often a very long one; several thousand kilometers is not unusual. The increase of voltage at the beginning of the network creates a corresponding need for voltage decrease at the users' end of the network, a task that is handled by distribution transformers, technically a "cousin" to power transformers. Both voltage increase and voltage decrease are often divided into several steps and handled by transformers of different sizes, until electrical current reaches the end user, for instance, the single household.

The main reason for all this voltage transformation work is the fact that high voltage transmission is far more efficient, with less energy loss, than low voltage transmission. In comparing transformers with the mechanical gearbox, a popular metaphor, one has to keep in mind that in electricity the "gearbox" is split into two. We need one kind of "gearbox" for voltage increase, called "step-up transformation," an operation performed by the power transformer, and another "gearbox" for voltage decrease, called "step-down transformation," which is performed either by power or distribution transformers.

Power transformers are generally more complicated than the distribution transformers from an engineering point of view. The engineering design of a power transformer is a demanding task requiring a hundred times more hours spent on mathematical analyses and calculations than is the case with the design of a distribution transformer. From a manufacturing perspective the power transformer usually comes out of unit production as a uniquely customized product, whereas distribution transformers as a rule are manufactured in batches and in North America sometimes even in mass produced series.

The manufacturing of transformers is very dependent on first-quality materials and meticulous work practices. Each winding turn round the core of the transformer must be carried out exactly right. One tiny defect in spacing or isolation and the transformer might fail in the test laboratory. Normally several hundred turns are needed in a single transformer. The requirement of exact stacking of the hundreds of leaf-thin steel plates forming the core is equally rigorous. Difficulties tend to multiply with size. The test of mastery is the ability to design and build large transformers. Many companies are able to produce smaller ones.

Power transformers were invented more than a century ago. In the 1950s

Table 2.1. The World Markets for Power Transformers

Europe, Americas, Africa 45% of world market	Asia 55% of world market
Specified	
Western Europe, 15%	China, 19%
Eastern Europe, 7%	Japan, 10%
North America, 16%	India, 7%
Latin America, 3%	Rest of Asia–Pacific, 14%
Africa, 4%	Middle East, 5%

Estimated total world market in 1995 was 450,000 MVA, ABB's share was roughly 20%.

and 1960s transformers tended to become larger. High voltage transmission as well as direct current transformation were already achieved in the 1950s. Over a few years transmitted voltages increased more than ten times. Since those decades the technological development of the product has been rather slow, although the materials used have improved in quality and efficiency, environmental concerns are better met, and the control equipment is swifter and more precise. Design methodology has improved. Software packages have become more sophisticated using expert systems and knowledge-based systems for support. Modularization of the designs and reuse of tested design elements is another important tendency. By and large these developments have been moderately paced. A dramatic change in this situation is not generally foreseen, with the exception of software development.

Quality power transformers last very long, three to four decades, if you do not expose them for relocation and transportation but leave them in peace at their original installation. "They will last forever," is a common saying in the industry. There is considerable freedom of choice on when to renew them, which is very important to keep in mind if you want to forecast the demand for power transformers. Even a very large installed base of transformers does not necessarily create a market for renewals (repeat business) in the short run. See Table 2.1 for an area breakdown of the world market for power transformers.

Power transformers basically have two kinds of customers: first and foremost are public or private utilities supplying electric power, second in demand are industrial corporations with high consumption of electricity, for example, aluminum manufacturers and steelworks.

In many countries the power transformers market is oligopolistic; in a few, cutthroat competition is the norm. ABB's power transformer business area has to adapt and find appropriate responses in very varying competitive environments. The strength and status of the market are also very different from one country to the next. In some, ABB power transformers is number one and undisputed market leader; in other countries it is an outsider and very far from being considered as "domestic."

The international power transformer market is varied and filled with contrasts. Annual world electrical power production and consumption rose eleven-fold from 1950–1990 (11.5 trillion kWh in 1990). In North America and Western Europe the electrification wave culminated many years ago. Electricity consumption has stabilized or is stagnant owing to deindustrialization, more efficient equipment, and generally rising cost awareness. Overcapacity is maintaining a buyer's market. In the Asia–Pacific region, on the other hand, the electrification wave is rising and market conditions are dynamic. Latin America is also a new investor in electricity. The overcapacity of the European and American transformer industries affects the Asian markets to a lesser degree, making Asian demand very attractive and well worth fighting for among the Western power transformer makers.

The single most important market change is probably the trend toward privatization of public power utilities and the resulting change in purchasing behavior among the most important customers of power transformer producers. The traditional symbiosis between utilities and electrotechnical companies is generally coming to an end. Protectionistic and national patterns of alignments are weakening. The United Kingdom, during the government of Margaret Thatcher at the beginning of the 1980s, was an early proponent of deregulation and privatization. North America did the same thing a decade later. Many European countries, for example, Italy and Spain, have begun slowly dismantling some of their protectionistic utility systems with increased competition as a result.

The Competition

With a fifth of the world market ABB is by far the biggest contender in the electrotechnical industry. ABB is number one in the power transformer business. A closer analysis of ABB's market shares reveals that its share averages 40 percent for markets in which ABB has "domestic" manufacturing but is only about 10 percent on the "open" export markets, in which ABB has no local power transformer plants. That lesson has been learned the hard way. In the past, to get an order it was often mandatory to make part of the production locally. Many of the world's power transformer plants exist as a result of such demands. That is true as well for the cluster of power transformer plants, 24 in 1996, run by ABB and a core argument in favor of ABB's general policy of "being local worldwide."

The averages—a 40 percent market share with local production and a 10 percent share without it—conceal much variation among countries. Even with local production in common, ABB's power transformer plants have to cope with very different market shares. Their position is very strong in the Nordic countries (Sweden, Norway, and Finland) and in Switzerland, where ABB has domestic markets in the traditional sense. The power transformers BA also has a firm local presence in the power transformer markets of Spain, South Africa, and Turkey. ABB is meeting none or very little domestic competition in those countries and the market shares for their power transformers are above 40 percent. In the United States, Canada, Brazil and Italy, the BA has both a strong manufacturing presence and is number one in the market. In Germany, the United Kindgom, Australia, and Poland the power transformers BA has a substantial base but it is not in the number one position. In China, the BA has little more than a bridgehead but still operates a couple of plants. The BA is in operation in Thailand and Vietnam as well. Even in those countries in which ABB's power transformers BA has no plants, and supposedly a 10 percent market share, the implications of not being local vary. Russia, Japan, France, South Korea, India, Mexico, and some smaller European countries (e.g., Belgium, the Netherlands, Austria, and Portugal) have important power transformer companies of their own. Few industrialized countries are completely lacking in power transformer manufacturing, but the few who do lack such capability are somewhat more accessible customers.

Protectionistic trade policies are reducing ABB's power transformers' market shares down to zero in some countries. In the world market of power transformers there still are countries in which monopolies govern and many countries with less than perfect competition. A number of countries are for various reasons shielded from international competition, among them France, Japan, India, and China. A minor share of the Chinese market is open for international joint ventures, though, and given the vastness of that country, even a trifle of its growing market is of great interest. In the longer perspective competition is increasing and prices are coming down, but free trade is still the exception rather than the rule for power transformers as for so many other products in the world.

ABB's power transformers BA has a solid market share in a class of its own, but even so it has many strong competitors. Five to ten bidders for the same order is not uncommon. Contenders are mostly medium-sized companies and many of them are owned by large corporations, such as Siemens or the Japanese electrotechnical giants. There are also a number of "local" competitors, for example, Pauwels in Belgium, Elin in Austria, Tamini in Italy, and Smit in the Netherlands, all of which make power transformers only. The twenty largest competitors meet 60 percent (267,600 MVA) of the worldwide demand (Table 2.2).

There are some twenty more, still smaller, power transformer plants around the world, for example, Federal Pacific in Canada, Coemsa and Trafo in Brazil, Wilson Transformers in Australia, Starkstrom Gerätebau Regens-

Table 2.2. Ranking of Competitors in the Power Transformer Business

1. **ABB:** More than twenty power transformer plants and several more plants supplying materials and components, 85,500 MVA, 20% of the world market.
2. **Siemens:** Two plants in Germany (Nürnberg and Dresden) and four more in Portugal, Brazil, Colombia, and Pakistan.
3. **Zaporoche** in the Ukraine: The world's biggest transformer plant, operating far below capacity.
4. **Melco Ako Works/Matsushita** in Japan.
5. **Hitachi** in Japan.
6. **Schneider** in France.
7. **GEC-Alsthom,** plants in France and Australia.
8. **North American** in the United States (parent company is Rockwell International).
9. **Toshiba,** Hamakawasaki Works in Japan and one plant in the United States.
10. **Hyundai** in South Korea.
11. **Pauwels** in Belgium (including the daughter company, Federal Pioneer in Canada).
12. **Elin** in Austria.
13. **Peebles Transformers** in the United Kingdom.
14. **AEG,** with two plants in Germany.
15. **Tamini,** with four Italian plants.
16. **Magnetek** in Wisconsin, formerly owned by ABB, presently by General Signal.
17. **Fuji** in Japan.
18. **Prolec/GE** in Mexico.
19. **Takaoka** in Japan.
20. **Smit** in the Netherlands.

Ranking according to delivered power transformers in 1995 measured by their Megavolt-ampère (MVA) producing potential.

burg in Germany, Hawker Siddley in the United Kingdom, and Efasec in Portugal. The power transformer plant structures of China and India are partly kept in secrecy; some of their plants might be large enough to earn them positions on the top twenty list, but reliable evidence is lacking.

Merger Paradox—From Global Exporter to Local Producer

The structure of the ABB power transformers business area is impressive in its global reach. It is unique; there is nothing like it among the competitors. Still it is far from ideal compared with the policy of being local worldwide. Too much of the BA's capacity is located in northern Europe and North America, while the growing markets are to be found in Asia. The misfit between demand and the BA's manufacturing facilities presently makes exporting a necessity; without exporting the BA would shrink substantially. ABB's long-term policy is relocation of plants to the growing markets of Asia. The latest additions to the BA's cluster of plants are located in Vietnam and China.

"Being local worldwide" is a stated policy of ABB. The power transformers BA is the reference point for that policy. There are many arguments in this BA for remaining local. Managers conclude that "we live in the same

Table 2.3. Three Clusters of Power Transformer Plants within the Business Area

Former ASEA plants	Former Westinghouse plants	Former Brown Boveri plants
Ludvika, Sweden*: 10,000 MVA Bad Honnef, Germany: 5,000 MVA Pretoria, South Africa: 5,000 MVA Guarulhos, Brazil: 5,000 MVA Varennes, Canada: 4,000 MVA Istanbul, Turkey: 3,000 MVA (Oskarshamn, Sweden, closed in 1990; Oslo, Norway, closed in 1989)	**Muncie, United States***: 10,000 MVA St. Louis, United States: 5,000 MVA Guelph, Canada: 4,000 MVA Cordoba, Spain: 3,000 MVA Bilbao, Spain: 2,000 MVA Moorebank, Australia: 2,000 MVA	(**Mannheim, Germany,** closed in 1994)* Sécheron, Switzerland: 3,000 MVA (Osasco, Brazil, closed in 1992)

The MVA figures, roughly measuring the relative size of the plants, refer to 1995.
* The core plant in bold.

time zone, near our customers. We talk their language. We are part of their culture. We know them and their expectations for power transformers."

The present structure of the BA is very much the result of the merger and acquisition offensive of the late 1980s. ABB and its CEO Percy Barnevik were on the offensive. ABB's ownership of power transformer plants is often the result of package deals during different acquisition "campaigns": Nordic, Continental, southern European, North American, East European, and Asian. Basically three clusters of ABB power transformer plants were brought together. As can be seen from Table 2.3, the Westinghouse acquisition in 1989 was more important for this BA than the big merger between ASEA and Brown Boveri in 1987. The Westinghouse cluster is the result of General Electric (GE) more or less abandoning the power transformer business. That decision was in line with their policy, "If neither number one nor number two on the world market of a certain product, you either fix it or leave it." In the case of power transformers, GE and Westinghouse formed a joint transformer company in the mid-1980s run by Westinghouse, the very same group of plants bought by ABB in 1989.[5]

To these major clusters we can add a number of mid-sized and smaller acquisitions also dating from the late 1980s. Legnano, close to Milan, earlier owned by the Marelli company, was acquired by ABB in 1988. Pomezia, close

[5] According to the antitrust negotiations concerning the Westinghouse acquisitions, ABB had to sell off its pearl of American plants, the one at Waukesha in Wisconsin, now called Magnetek and owned by General Signal, a distressing loss for the ABB power transformers BA.

to Rome, was formerly part of the state-owned Ansaldo company. Vaasa in the northern part of Finland, formerly Strömberg, was acquired by ASEA in 1986, the year before the announcement of the big merger. Other acquisitions include Drammen (formerly National Industri cooperating with Westinghouse and Sarpsborg [closed 1994]; before that, National Industri was owned by Pfeiffer), with two plants situated near Oslo, and Dundee in Scotland, formerly Elektrisk Bureau and National Industri of Norway and before that the Scottish company, Bonar Long.

Within the BA management the dynamic years of restructuring are often referred to as "the opening of the books." Seven different power transformer technologies were gathered within the ABB company and an even greater variation on the ways to manufacture them. For many decades the former competitors had pondered the secret strengths and weaknesses of the other competitors and now all information was available under one corporate roof. The lasting impression of this opening of the books, among the small circle of experts who possessed the skills and had the opportunity to enjoy it, was one of disappointment. There were few secrets worth unveiling.

Performance left a great deal to be desired. For some plants a lot of catch-up work and housecleaning was required to lift them up to world class standard, at that time defined by some of the former ASEA plants such as Ludvika and Bad Honnef or the Sécheron plant in Geneva, belonging to the Brown Boveri camp since the late 1960s.

Compared with the merger and acquisition offensive of the late 1980s, the structural changes during the 1990s appeared modest. In 1990 the small Bangkok plant (1,000 MVA) got started, an ABB investment with equipment from the closed ASEA Oskarshamn plant in southern Sweden. In 1992 the equally small Halle plant in Germany (1,000 MVA) and the Polish Lodz plant (2,000 MVA), formerly the state-owned company Elta cooperating with the Austrian Elin company, became members of the ABB cluster. The Hefei plant, not very far from Shanghai, China, is a joint venture that for ABB got started in 1994; and in Hanoi, Vietnam, an ABB plant began operation in 1996.

A semiofficial policy of the power transformers BA is to have one plant per country. The actual closings have been rather few, especially benchmarked against what is more or less normal procedure after a takeover. In the old ASEA cluster, ASEA Per Kure in Oslo, the so-called Hasle plant, was closed in 1989 as well as an ASEA plant in Oskarshamn (not far from Kalmar, Sweden). Norway was also hit by a second closing, the Sarpsborg plant in 1994, a plant that once belonged to Elektrisk Byrå/National Industri. In the smaller Brown Boveri cluster Osasco in Brazil was shut down in 1992 and the manufacturing part of Mannheim closed in 1995. Muncie, Indiana, in the United States was closed in 1998.

Swedish, Norwegian, Brazilian, and German closings have adhered to the policy of one plant per country. Still there are four exceptions to this rule

Table 2.4. ABB Power Transformer Plants around the World in 1995

The Americas	Africa
United States: Muncie (1) and St. Louis (7) *Canada: Varennes (11) and Guelph (10)* Brazil: Guarulhos* (9)	South Africa: Pretoria (6)
	Australia
	Australia: Moorebank (Sydney) (19)
Europe	**Asia**
Sweden: Ludvika (2) Norway: Drammen (8) Finland: Vaasa* (14) *United Kingdom: Dundee (13)* Poland: Lodz* (21) *Germany: Bad Honnef (5)* and Halle (18) Switzerland: Sécheron (Geneva)* (15) Italy: Pomezia (3) and Legnano (4) *Spain: Cordoba (12) and Bilbao (17)*	Turkey: Istanbul (16) Thailand: Bangkok (20) Vietnam: Hanoi (22) China: Hefei and joint ventures

* Complementary study visits made to these plants.
Italics denote coverage in case study chapters.
Number in parentheses indicates rank order by size within the BA according to delivered MVA.

within the BA; namely, there are two plants in Canada, Italy, Spain and Germany, respectively. Does the second plant in each of these countries belong to the endangered species? Their existence is probably conditional not only on how profitable and generally speaking, what good performers they are but also on the cost of a plant closedown. ABB's power transformer plants worldwide are listed in Table 2.4.

If closings are exceptional, downsizing, on the other hand, has become a normal fate for ABB power transformer plants. A lot of cost-cutting has been executed at the plant level. Is there more yet to be done? Is there an optimal plant size for which to aim? These are controversial topics within the BA. Some plant managers advocate bigness and consequently, concentration. At BA headquarters they tend to disagree: the BA managers have had difficulties in detecting economies of scale in the larger plants. The larger plants seem to have few if any advantages. The optimal plant size is becoming smaller and smaller, according to BA management. The break-even point is lowered as well, making local presence feasible with even smaller plants. Some of the most profitable plants are quite small. None of the bigger ones is showing above average profits. Size is certainly not the only explanation for that relationship but still it is of importance. Some of the most successful plants both in economic and physical performance, for example, the plants in Vaasa, Geneva, and Guarulhos, Brazil, operate in the interval 2500–4500 MVA, the present ideal of optimal size.

If one measures the size of the plants according to their number of employees many are quite small. ABB plants in Turkey, Thailand, Australia, and Finland employ less than 200 employees. Most of the others are in the range of 200–400 employees; only the Ludvika plant has more than 500 employees. The "company-company" idea has become popular with the BA management; that is, military company size of around 200 employees as a norm for single companies in a cluster. The total power transformers BA does not have more than around 7,500 employees.

The most important export markets for the power transformers BA are in the Middle East and Asia–Pacific, China in particular. Eastern Europe, Africa, and Latin America are also of some importance as export markets. A strong BA policy is to prohibit the different BA plants to compete with one another for export orders; all orders are allocated. Before becoming part of ABB some of the BA plants used to compensate for downturns in their domestic market by increasing their exports. As part of ABB that policy might collide with the interests of other plants within the BA. The allocation of export opportunities has become a very important function of the BA management. The rule of thumb is that 70 percent of revenues derive from the domestic market and consequently 30 percent come from exports. For peak performers among the plants percentages might be reversed: 70 percent from exports and 30 percent from domestic revenues. There are also exceptions to these general rules. If a particular plant has a long-standing relationship with a certain customer, that customer normally gets the order; some types of transformers are made only at certain plants, and so on.

The paradoxical outcome of joining a global giant corporation has for many of the BA plants proved to be an increased focus on the domestic market and restrictions on exports—less not more internationalization. The more multinational the whole company has become, the less global and export oriented is the local plant.

At Headquarters of the Power Transformers Business Area

The power transformers business area management was formed in 1988 with Sune Karlsson (Swede) as the first president of the BA. He remained in that position until 1992, when he was succeeded by Bo-Göran Persson (Swede), formerly the country manager of ABB in Brazil. In 1997 François Gabella (Swiss), formerly in charge of the Sécheron and later Bad Honnef plants, became president. BA management in the narrow sense is the small BA headquarters with a handful of vice presidents and a secretary (Table 2.5). From 1988 to October 1996 it was situated in Mannheim but has since moved to Zurich, located in a few rooms in a building near the small ABB top management headquarters in the suburb of Oerlikon.

After the move to Zurich, headquarters became even leaner, reduced to six

Table 2.5. Business Area Headquarters: Eight Positions in the Mid-1990s

President	Six Sigma Management
Controller	Supply Management
Technology Management	Marketing Coordination
Process Management	Information Systems

positions. The Marketing Coordination and Information Systems functions were finalized. The vice presidents have decades of shared experience in the power transformer business. Four in the old team, the Swedes, had a common background from Ludvika. The new team, since 1996, is a slightly more international mix with three Swedes remaining.

The leanness of BA headquarters poses a challenge. Traditional ways of managing are taking too much time. Headquarters with fewer than ten persons would be demanding, even if the BA were concentrated in one place. Because the BA is spread all over the world mixing at least twenty national cultures—from northern, continental, eastern and southern Europe, from Canada and the United States, from Brazil and South Africa, from Australia, Thailand, China, and Vietnam—opportunities and difficulties are multiplying. National cultures are not necessarily monolithic, for example, operations in West or East Germany or in French- or English-speaking Canada, pose quite different problems. In addition the power transformers BA is the result of an integration of some ten different corporate cultures. Thus the magnitude of the management challenges becomes obvious. For two years the lean management of this BA was also in charge of a related BA of similar size, Distribution Transformers. In short, time-consuming activities need to be minimized and rationalised. Personal relations and business contacts belong to this category of management responsibilities in need of timesaving.

BA meetings have become one way of economizing on personal relations. For a while BA headquarters and the plant and company managers met regularly for strategy and BA meetings at least four times a year. These latter meetings are attended by some fifty participants including a few "outside" guests, mostly from other ABB companies. The duty of host rotates among the different plant managers. The meetings are held at various locations around the world, but always close to one of the BA's power transformer plants. The meetings are referred to by location, for example, "the Edinburgh meeting" (1989), "the Brazilian meeting" (1993), "the Warsaw meeting" (1994), and so on. At these meetings, which are no longer held with the same regularity, BA management is represented in the broader sense, including all the company and plant managers belonging to the BA and the deputies of those managers. The plants in question are not only the power transformer plants but also a few internal component suppliers such as ABB Components, Figeholm, Micafil, and Pucaro.

BA headquarters has allocated a tax on the local plants, the revenue from which enables the many headquarter management initiatives. The BA initiatives and programs that we analyze in the following sections, for example, Common Product, Customer Focus, and Six Sigma, have all been discussed and anchored in the enlarged BA management and are partly financed over the headquarters budget. The benchmarking and performance measurements called "Seven-Ups" are also evaluated during the regular BA meetings. These meetings play an important role in the organizational development of the BA, and they also provide feedback on the division of roles and responsibilities within the BA. Who is playing by the book, who is deviating?

Running the Business Area Using "Program Management"

The limited resources available to BA headquarters makes management initiatives at each of the plants relatively more important. Headquarters has to prioritize first or be lost. Since the merger the BA presidents authorized five major programs to improve plant and business area performance, discussed in the following sections.

The Common Product Program

Common Product is the first BA-wide program.[6] It is not hard to understand why it evolved. With the mergers and acquisitions of the late 1980s the power transformers BA had five major technologies to work with: the power transformer designs of ASEA, Brown Boveri, Elektrisk Bureau in Norway, Strömbergs in Finland, and IEC (Legnano) in Italy. At the turn of the decade the total had increased to seven different technologies with the acquisition of Ansaldo (Pomezia, Italy) and Westinghouse (with plants in the United States, Canada, Spain, and Australia). Numerous reasons account for the drive toward a common technology; without it the BA's products would differ and coordination among suppliers would be difficult. A lean supply program would be hard to maintain without a common technology built into the products.

The Common Product program is an example of multidomestic research and development. One explanation for the very federate organization of the Common Product program was the disappointment after "the opening of the books." No thrilling technological secrets were unveiled. No single design was superior to others. They all looked like variations on a theme, at least that is the story. Some postmerger technologies were admired for their technical elegance, others for their manufacturability, but their many similarities were the most striking feature.

Kickoff for the Common Product program took place at a BA strategy

---

[6] Its earlier name was the Common Technology program.

meeting in Edinburgh in 1989. Estimated costs for the whole project were at that time around $US 10 million. Fifteen sub-projects were started engaging some seventy-five engineers globally. One of the first tasks was to reach agreement on and define all important aspects of a transformer. At a later strategy meeting in Toronto (1990), a detailed implementation plan was adopted. The program has had a soft-sell approach in the BA. Common products were seen as a compromise, metaphorically an "Esperanto"-solution. No single transformer technology would be completely dominant. Many engineers believe that common products are very similar to the former ASEA technology, the interpretation the low-key approach was supposed to falsify. In hindsight an alternative would have been "colonization," that is, adopting the ASEA technology as the new norm.

The project has become much more complicated than was foreseen. Releases of new common products have been more numerous than planned, more like a new computer or software package and not a transformer being developed. (Software is, by the way, essential in the designing and manufacturing of a modern transformer and more effective software is made available almost constantly.) For program engineers it has been very frustrating to try to freeze the designs, for they are devoted to continuous improvements. It has been equally hard to try to freeze expectations from local plant experts. Plants were promised shop floor–ready designs, which often were considered not detailed enough by the locals.

In 1993 the program reached a crisis. A few catch-up plants, like those in Bangkok, Istanbul, and Halle, had considerable extra trouble in producing a number of common product transformers. Most plants made only one or two. The crisis was overcome and the program gained new momentum. In 1996 some 20 percent of transformers produced in the BA were made according to the new common product designs. This had a favorable effect on another of the BA programs, considered in the next section.

Lean Supply Program

The Lean Supply program was begun to effect new economies of scale in material and components, an advantage that will increase in proportion to the growing share of "common product" transformers in the BA output. Materials and components bought from suppliers constitute 50 percent of the cost of producing a power transformer. In countries with low labor costs even higher shares are common, partly reflecting the lower wage and salary levels. In Poland, for instance, supplier goods represent up to 70 percent of the total cost.

The combined BA is a very big customer. Coordination of purchasing from all suppliers has great potential if the products are standardized. The coordination aims at lowering prices, improving deliverance reliability, enhancing quality, and facilitating R&D work. In the ideal case all of these

Figure 2.1. Reduction of the number of suppliers, Guarulhos plant, Brazil.

positive outcomes would follow from the strengthening of supply management. Traditionally one single power transformer plant used to have 200 to
1,000 suppliers. The most dramatic change in supplier relationships within
the BA in recent years has been the constant downward trend in number of
suppliers. The most advanced plants now are down to a hundred or fewer
suppliers. Figure 2.1, which shows the sharp reduction, over the years 1990
to 1998, in the number of national and international suppliers at the Guarulhos power transformer plant in Brazil, illustrates this pattern in a most explicit fashion. Similar trends, although not quite as striking ones, could be
shown for almost any other plant within the BA. Some plants are close to
the single source philosophy, but most prefer at least two suppliers per product or service. The remaining suppliers are supplying more complete products than they used to do, which means that they often use suppliers in their
turn. Supplier interface at ABB has been simplified. ABB has a special Supply Management Information System (SMIS), which simplifies supplier evaluation. How important is a particular supplier moneywise? How large is
their share of total deliveries? Is it delivered on time or not? What would happen if it did not supply the item? What are the alternatives? See Table 2.6 for
a typology of supplier products.

An important outcome of supply analysis is categorizing the suppliers.
Gold Members are strategic and of highest importance. The relationships
with Gold Members are intended to be long term, reliable, participative, and
sharing otherwise secret information. The power transformer plant and its
Gold Members might manage development programs together. Future complications in supply management might be caused by ABB's ownership of

Table 2.6. Supplier Products Typology

Profit Impact	Supply Risk	
	High	Low
High	1. Strategic products	3. Leverage products
Low	2. Bottleneck products	4. Noncritical

a number of relevant suppliers, a handful of them belonging to the BA, such as Figeholm in Sweden, Micafil in Switzerland, and Alamo in the United States. The ownership is a legacy of long-ago abandoned policies of vertical integration, contrary to the present philosophy of outsourcing.

The Six Sigma Program

Leaner supply is a strong motive for higher quality standards. With only a few suppliers remaining, they have to be very reliable. All employees have to know for sure that they are reliable. One way of achieving this is to implement total quality management (TQM). Of the many brands of TQM, the power transformers BA has chosen Six Sigma. The inspiration came from Motorola, the same company that inspired ABB's time-based management investment. Six Sigma is a highly successful system of quality management codified by Mikel Harry, who worked for ABB and has since founded a Six Sigma Academy.[7]

Sigma stands for standard deviation. When a process runs on the six sigma level, it means that there are 3.4 defects per million opportunities, in other words, close to zero (an example would be two misspellings altogether in a book of this size). Many manufacturing processes run on the three sigma level, which produces 66,807 defects per million opportunities and consequently a lot of corrections or poor product quality, or both.

Deming's methodology of "measure, analyze, improve and control" is part of Six Sigma as well (Deming 1986). Statistical quality control by the operators themselves is a built-in characteristic. "The right to measure" is decentralized. "Quality is free" in the sense that efforts to reduce the number of defects are paid for in lesser costs of poor quality every time a defect is avoided. The cost of poor quality is estimated to lie in the magnitude of 30 percent of turnover, so there is a lot of potential benefit to finance the costs.[8]

With the Six Sigma approach there is a visible developmental ladder, the

[7] The Six Sigma Academy has become a market success, one of the customers being GE, in this field following in the footsteps of ABB, but GE has made their Six Sigma investment a much bigger one, comprising the whole corporation, not just one division or business area.

[8] Six Sigma implementers like Motorola and Texas Instruments have become winners of the American Baldrige Award.

different sigma levels. Six Sigma is used as a stretch goal. Many think it is impossible to obtain, but according to the Six Sigma paradigm that goal is eventually attained. Implementation of Six Sigma puts a lot of emphasis on development. There are at least three levels of quality improvement competence. The "black belts" get more advanced schooling in measurement procedures and statistical analysis than the "yellow belts" and have to pass tough exams before getting the black belt title. They are at some plants jokingly called "006s—with the right to measure." Worth highlighting is the strong belief in a "one best way" with the Six Sigma approach.

Benchmarking is the process of continually searching for the best methods, practices, and processes and either adopting or adapting their good features and implementing them to become the "best of the best."

To implement Six Sigma the BA has a special Quality Council Team with members from quality improvement–dedicated plants such as Ludvika, Bad Honnef, Pomezia, and Drammen. The team is headed by Kjell Magnusson, the vice president in charge of Six Sigma and earlier responsible for the design of "Seven-Ups." The BA has the goal of achieving the Six Sigma level by 2000.[9]

The Model Factory Program

All the programs discussed thus far tend to converge on Model Factory, in an earlier version called Common Process. One of the hypotheses about the cause of all the problems with the Common Products project is the differences in process. By operating with different processes, plants are not able to handle a common product properly. The BA management has come to the conclusion that Common Product and Common Process should be run in tandem.

The Common Process program got started in late 1994. It bears many traits of the fad called business process reengineering (BPR). Process identification and process reengineering are paramount, functional integration and continued downsizing the prioritized means. When fully implemented the Model Factory will have even leaner management than today. The few remaining management positions are renamed "process owners." The two processes given most attention are marketing and production. The interfaces between the two are far from trivial, for example, electrical design is part of marketing and mechanical design is integrated in production. Minimizing the number of steps in each process is an important objective of the program. Another one deals with improving controllability. The Model Factory relies very much on "management by facts" and continuous benchmarking. A strict adherence to the Model Factory approach would make the different

[9] *What is Six Sigma?* Windsor, Conn.: ABB Institute. 1993.

plants very similar, almost like replicas, a literal interpretation of the one best way philosophy. The Model Factory program has recently been implemented in Vaasa, Finland. The program in Ludvika, Sweden, has not reached the same level of perfection. These two plants are still very different. Of all the plants in the BA, Vaasa is closest to the model. There it has almost come true.

BA headquarters is very positive about the Model Factory program and regard it as a major competitive advantage. This evaluation has made them rather secretive concerning details of the program—and there are many details. The program characteristically goes into spelling out details, not leaving much leeway for chance or local diversity. The model factory analysis of what is core and periphery, what should be made inside a plant or bought from the outside, is classified as proprietary information. What is not classified is that an important part of the program is outsourcing components to "kit centers" in order to improve economies of scale. The exact interface between plant and kit center, on the other hand, is considered a smart secret.

The Customer Focus Program

ABB adopted time-based management (TBM) in 1990 inspired by the Motorola implementation of that organizational philosophy.[10] Boston Consulting Group[11] played a key role in ABB's early implementation. Investigations of customer expectations and demands supported the emphasis on throughput times. Swift and on-time delivery was judged to determine at least 50 percent of customer satisfaction, the quality of the product being taken for granted.

The power transformers BA was one of the forerunners in implementing TBM. That approach was soon broadened into the Customer Focus program. An indication of the early success of that program within the BA is the fact that Sune Karlsson (the BA president at that time) was promoted President of the Customer Focus Program for all of ABB.

Total throughput time from order to delivery, or TTPT, is a very relevant criterion for organizational effectiveness. TTPT is what matters to the customer. Manufacturing throughput time (TPT) measures only one of the internal processes, the one through manufacturing or "from release of documents to production till the product is ready to ship." If TPT is a swift process, but TTPT from order to delivery is not, the customer gets no advan-

[10] The ABB U.S. president at that time, Gerhard Schulmeyer, was also a member of Motorola's board of directors and had seen the effects of TBM firsthand. Schulmeyer convinced the ABB board of directors of the merits of TBM.

[11] Boston Consulting Group (BCG) coined the acronym TBM and BCG consultants wrote the book on the subject. George Stalk and Thomas Hout Jr. 1990. *Competing against time.* New York: The Free Press.

tage. If, on the other hand, a company is faster in TTPT than its competition, it is most likely to survive, especially in a shrinking market. For those with slow and late deliveries there are no customers left.

TTPT and TPT belong to the legacy of the Customer Focus program. The calculation of these indices is clearly defined in order to preserve their powerfulness. The clock starts ticking for TTPT when work starts on the electrical design and stops when the product is ready to ship. The wait time for the customer to approve the documents is not included. There are five classes of power transformers, and for each there is a target in working days. A power transformer of MVA class 4, the most complicated one, has a target of 160 days. Class 1 should be ready in 60 days. In the indices 1.00 means that TTPT for all transformers delivered from a specific plant sum up to 1.00, meaning that they are delivered according to the norm. The Finnish plant in Vaasa is remarkable in being down to 0.55 of the norm.

Management by Facts and the Prospects for Becoming a Learning Organization

The essence of the management approach at BA headquarters is "management by objectives." Because headquarters is such a lean operation, it has to rely on the smooth functioning of its benchmarking and controller systems; otherwise headquarters would lose tight control. The content of the benchmarking is attached to the different program initiatives within the BA. The framework of benchmarking within the power transformers BA is called "Seven-Ups."

The combination of the two is very important: the benchmarking is tied to the programs and vice versa. Reliable performance measurements, swift feedback, no lag in taking corrective action, and getting closer to perfection—this is the envisioned learning loop with its intellectual roots in Deming's management approach of "measure, analyze, improve, and control." Today enlarged benchmarking systems are often referred to as "Balanced Scorecards."[12] Because this BA with its "Seven-Ups" program has been practicing a kind of Balanced Scorecard for nearly a decade, there are some interesting lessons to be learned.

Managers at headquarters do not lack data, but how do they perform their analyses? How do they explain the differences in performance from one plant to the next and what kind of action follows? BA Management can combine data from the controller system of ABB, "Abacus," with its elaborate benchmarking system, Seven-Ups. The combination is intended to facilitate

[12] Robert Kaplan and David Norton. 1996. *The balanced scorecard*. Boston: Harvard Business School Press. There are also several articles in the *Harvard Business Review*, the Jan.–Feb. 1992 article, in particular: "The balanced scorecard—Measures that drive performance."

lean management and foster a learning organization. The BA's development and use of Seven-Ups is treated as a pilot project within the whole ABB Group. Seven-Ups is seen as "management by facts": What gets measured gets done. Do the local plants learn from each other and try to improve when their performance figures are not the best? Or do the benchmarking statistics bring about trumped-up excuses for performances below the norm?

Abacus was developed swiftly during the first quarter of ABB's existence (winter, 1988). The system gives management comparable economic measurements regardless of country and currency. One of the favorite yardsticks of the Abacus system is return on capital employed (ROCE). According to ROCE analysis the Finnish plant in Vaasa is outstanding in the business area. The more traditional standard, result margin, shows the Swiss plant as very strong. On the other hand, looking at revenues, the two American plants used to bring in as much as the seven smallest plants in the BA combined.

The shortcomings of economic indicators make themselves felt when one attempts international comparisons. The Abacus system is not making up for these particular drawbacks. Some plants, for instance, do not have to try as hard as others to reach the same profitability level. They are not facing tough competition. Is it fair to evaluate them with profitability as the only standard? The concept of price quality illustrates this. It refers to companies and plants living in a corporate environment that gives them good prices and financing for long-term development. Those were the good old days for many plants who had close relationships with their colleagues from the public power utilities who literally sat on the other side of the table when negotiating tender, for instance. Those days are gone for many plants. Today privatized utilities have lowered their technical ambitions and become far more price conscious than before. Privatization and deregulation are gaining ground and more plants will most likely be faced with the new challenges. Will they manage, and are they well prepared for that encounter? One way of getting closer to an answer is to start working with benchmarking, which measures performance in a more basic way than the bookkeeper.

The BA management sees organizing the feedback and evaluation process as a task of prime importance. Revenues and profitability are obvious yardsticks for measuring corporate performance, but physical measurements are of great importance too. Some measurements have a history from the old ASEA, for example, failure rates and throughput times. They have now become standards for the whole BA. Test failure rate, manufacturing throughput time (TPT), total throughput time (TTPT), and sigma rating form a hard core of very telling quality and efficiency statistics (Table 2.7).

Seven-Ups statistics are produced at most plants, but the reporting is not without problems. One concern is delayed reports that consequently leave some empty cells in the comparative statistics while the figures are still "warm." For the patient observer most statistics will be produced, but by

Table 2.7. Seven-Ups, a Forerunner to the Balanced Scorecard

1. Quality criteria: Defects per month Test failure rate Cost of poor quality On-time delivery 2. Efficiency: TPT TTPT Inventory and revenues Abacus productivity	3. Production: Shop orders on the shop floor 4. Supply Management: Supplier quality Supplier on-time delivery Number of suppliers Material cost index 5. Training: Statistics 6. Sigma rating: (Six Sigma) 7. Customer satisfaction: Receivables

then some figures are dated. The well-informed already know that the situation has changed, and new figures are required for current analysis.

Core statistics such as TPT, TTPT, and the sigma rating are delivered with great regularity. The detailed presentation of TTPT results is classified; in general the numbers are going down, and improvements are taking place. Over the years there has been a marked overall improvement in the TTPT figures. Measurements are not that complete for 1990–92 but the averages start around 3. The average TTPT figure for 1993 is 1.36; for 1994, 1.26; for 1995, 1.18; and for the first half of 1996, 1.11. The improvements were most impressive in the beginning. The law of diminishing returns seems to apply. The average from 1994–95 lowered only by 0.08 and from 1995–96, by 0.07. The whole cluster of plants is also becoming more similar, the spread narrowing from 186 points in 1993 to 117 in 1996.

It is notable that a few plants seem to fail to improve in TTPT, for example, Ludvika and Varennes, in spite of their ASEA legacy. They not only fail to improve but have very low rankings as well. Bad Honnef, the former ASEA plant in Germany, is also slow in improving but average in ranking. Some plants have their ups and downs, for instance, Dundee and Moorebank. Others have lost somewhat in both pace and ranking, like Guarulhos in Brazil and Pretoria in South Africa. Guarulhos was once an early star of this game but is now below average. Most plants, however, improve steadily each year. Vaasa in Finland is exceptional, a plant that has been the star of TTPT for four consecutive years. Among the top five in the ranking are the plants in Geneva, Legnano (Italy), Bilbao (Spain), and Guelph (Canada). The American plants were average or above average during these years and so were, surprisingly, the plants in Turkey, South Africa, and Poland.

From a headquarters perspective the overall learning curve is satisfactory. The BA is becoming more predictable and reliable in TTPT. Catch-up to the norm looks very promising. Most plants are now close or have surpassed the norm. Vaasa, the star doing much better than the norm, used innovative approaches not initially promoted by headquarters, but inspiring headquarters to step up its Common Process program to a Model Factory initiative. Thus a local plant brought new insights to global headquarters, a valuable spin-off from ABB's multidomestic structure. Why plants like Ludvika and Varennes, with seemingly excellent qualifications, fail to improve is a major remaining problem.

With the learning organization as the ideal at headquarters it has been a sobering experience to listen to all the trumped-up excuses in the face of less than satisfactory results. A favorite has been the questioning of measurement procedures; another one, blaming circumstantial evidence. The intended learning and corrective actions have many times been slow in evolving. It is hard to put up with negative feedback, harder than many proponents of the Balanced Scorecard strategy realize.

Benchmarking with the help of Seven-Ups, as illustrated by the TTPT figures, has by and large been a strong force toward less variation. It only seems to be true though for plants doing less than the norm. For performers beyond the norm there is room for innovation and new variation. Managers have to be cautious not to fall in the regression fallacy trap. New variations will be created, history will not end.

The Matrix in Principle and in Practice

The matrix organization of ABB is somewhat anachronistic. That model had its heyday in the 1970s.[13] Now few consider it an option. This quote from *The Boundaryless Organization* (Ashkenas et al. 1995) reflects mainstream opinion in the organization literature (relying a lot on previous work by, among others, Russell Ackhoff 1994):

> The matrix is ingenious in theory but confusing in practice. . . . In matrix organizations, employees have two bosses. . . . This property of the design produces what might be called "organizational schizophrenia." When an employee's bosses do not agree or have different value systems, the employee does not know how to behave. This can be very stressful. The decision regarding to whom to pay attention is usually made politically rather than in the best interests of the organization.
>
> In short, the concept of the matrix is flawed for a number of reasons. . . . It blurs accountability for results, allowing an employee to choose between conflicting priorities and to blame the priority not chosen for problems and delays. . . . In addition, the matrix organization often becomes cumbersome and costly. When all points of the organizational compass feel compelled to con-

[13] For a mostly positive appraisal, see, for instance, Harvey Kolodny. 1985. *Matrix organization, design, implementation and management.* Ann Arbor, Mich.: University Microfilms International.

tribute to decisions, decision making is slow, and travel, meeting, and communication costs high. (Ashkenas et al. 1995: 125)

Many in the BA would agree with this verdict of the matrix. Programs like Common Product and Six Sigma have been very time-consuming and frustrating. The matrix structure is often blamed. The positive effects are not as easily recognizable. Regardless of the attention and concern shown different traditions in the Common Product program, many still thought of it as a tiresome way of implementing ASEA technology. Being local worldwide might be interpreted as a matrix policy encouraging local initiatives and innovations, but it does not seem to capture the essence of the practice of program management within this BA. The role assigned to local variation and cultural diversity is limited, tolerated for a while but not in the long run, if it means below average performance. It is more a matter of how to do things than of what to do.

The BA management is also frustrated by the logic of the matrix. On many important issues they have to reach consensus decisions with the national management teams. Consequently they have to be good at persuading, if they want plant managers to comply with BA initiatives. Also the matrix is not stable: the power shifted in the BA's favor in August 1993, when top management emphasized the prominence of the BA dimension of the matrix and sent the message throughout ABB that the importance of the BAs will increase even further in the future.

For the advocates of the matrix within ABB and they include Barnevik and his senior adviser, Arne Bennborn, who has written influential texts on the merits of the matrix, the contradictions and paradoxes are not caused by the matrix but by reality. Even in other organizational designs the same problems occur but in an informal way. It is a major merit of the matrix that it makes these tensions manifest and formal, so that they can be dealt with more easily (Table 2.8).

BA headquarters has two potent means of correcting unsatisfactory plant performance, namely, export allocation and management promotion, notwithstanding the matrix. Export allocation carries a lot of weight. If no export rights are given, it might mean the end of a plant. A good reason for allocating export orders according to the BA management would be superior plant performance in general, especially swiftness and on-time delivery record. When a plant is performing below the norm and expectations, the allocation is normally withheld. The local plant has to get its house in order before it gets orders. Exports are not used as a way out of local crises.

Management promotion is a riskier way of influencing plant performance. There is a considerable turnover of plant managers, especially in important and consequently "hot" positions. Ludvika has, for example, seen seven plant managers during fifteen years without dramatic improvement in performance. A new plant manager every second year is a practice now being

Table 2.8. Comparison: Business Area Headquarters and Local Management Responsibilities

Major Responsibilities of the Business Area President	Major Responsibilities of the Local Manager
Market allocation	All business on the "domestic" market and on allocated export markets
Pricing policy	Utilization of local financing possibilities
R&D activities	R&D delegated to the country
Information systems	Benchmarking
Transfer of technology	Up-to-date use of technology
Program management	Reacting on or participating in common programs within the BA
Transfer of experience and know-how	Fostering a learning organization
Worldwide results	Local results. Catch-up if below the norm; perfection when above the norm
Development and promotion of managers worldwide	

criticized for shortsightedness within the BA. The very successful plant manager of Vaasa was in that position for eight years but is now in charge of the Hanoi venture.

What Is Left of Cultural Diversity?

Given the cosmopolitan character of this business area one might expect a melting pot of different ideas from all over the world. ABB's policy of being local worldwide might raise similar expectations. At headquarters, however, these are not the expectations. The BA management is interpreting the policy of being local worldwide as valid for customer relations but not necessarily applicable inside the plant.

Although many managers are Swedes, the BA does not look Swedish as far as management is concerned. There are no missionaries of a special Swedish or Scandinavian cultural approach. That is in line with the policy chosen by the chairman of ABB, Percy Barnevik, who has made internal impact by saying things like "Please don't connect me with the Swedish Model. I was born in Sweden, don't hold that against me, please." [14]

English is the inter lingua in ABB and the overall impression of the management ideas of this BA is certainly that most of them are American. However, just as the Japanese once matched and sometimes outperformed their American teachers in quality, ABB might rival American corporations in lean implementation of basically the same ideas and models.

The American organizational fads of the 1990s have made a great impact

[14] Quote from Barnevik's Australian visit in May 1995.

on the power transformers BA. TBM from Boston Consulting Group has been a vital part of the Customer Focus program. Six Sigma, from the Academy of the same name, has grown in importance. Japanese ideas in process management, supply management in particular, have left their mark on the slimming initiatives but indirectly by way of Boston and MIT. Lean is the catchword as in lean management, lean production, and lean supply. Lately these ideas have been presented under the heading of business process reengineering (BPR), for example, the literature dealing with the model factory. Since fads come and go, these elements make for change.

A lot of local diversity exists. Language and currency, manners and customs, wages and salaries, industrial relations and agreements—all are local. Cost is local. Wage differentials within the BA, for the same kind of job, have at least a spread of 1–20, to take just one example. The spread in performance is still important but seldom more than 1–2, sometimes only infinitesimal. Performance tends not to be local but world class, not the least owing to the many BA programs. This new combination of world class performance and local cost results in very advantageous quotas between income and cost in low-cost countries. Exports from high-cost countries are as a consequence in jeopardy. Divergence in preconditions is often combined with convergence in performance, but these might be temporary constellations. After catch-up, divergence tends to increase once more. The race for improved performance seems to be never ending.

In a sense ABB headquarters has come full circle. It started to ponder on how to encourage catch-up in distant countries such as Brazil, South Africa, China, and Vietnam. Catch-up proved a huge success, by far exceeding headquarter's expectations. Now at headquarters the question is why is it so difficult to get improvements in countries like Sweden and Germany. The problems are not exotic any longer but they may be still essentially cultural. How does management kindle an interest in learning new ways in those who think they know everything about the business? What is a motivator for change when a plant thinks it has it made from start to finish? The one best way is still an elusive objective. The national case studies, presented in the following chapters, further demonstrate the magnitude of local and cultural diversity.

3 Products, Processes, and Organizational Change in the Production of Power Transformers

Lars Bengtsson and Christoph Köhler

In this chapter we give a basic understanding of the product and the production processes. After an introduction to the product and the basics of production, the process steps in sales, design, planning and purchase, manufacturing, and testing and delivery are explained. In this context we give some hints on differences in the organization of process steps in our seven case study plants. In most of these plants, process oriented organizations are gradually replacing functional structures. However, there are still an amazing variety of combinations of functional differentiation, decentralization, and segmentation along product lines.

Basics of Product and Production

In order to differentiate the sizes of power transformers, the Power Transformers business area (BA) has defined five classes:[1] class 1, 2.0–31.5 MVA; class 2, 31.5–100 MVA; class 3, 100–315 MVA; class 4, greater than 315 MVA; and class 5, reactors. This classification is used to define the scope of production of plants and plant segments. The main product of the 24 power transformer plants of the BA is three-phase transformers for alternating current (AC). Power transformers for direct current (DC) are less common. The latter is a niche product mainly produced in the Swedish Ludvika plant and is not elaborated on further. The main parts of the DC transformers are,

---

[1] Power transformers are mainly rated in MVA. The power is a product of current and voltage according to the formula: Power (MVA) = Voltage (V) \x Current (A). A second characteristic of a power transformer is the voltage span in which it operates. To give an example, a class 2 transformer of 40 MVA may be designed for 11 kV on the primary side and 140 kV on the secondary side. Other important characteristics of a power transformer are the kind of electrical connections that are used to connect the three phases and the power losses in wires, core, and tank (0–100 kW).

however, based on the same electrical principles as the AC transformers. The active part of a power transformer consists of coils and a magnetic core (see Fig. 3.1). In a transformer there are in principle three windings per phase and coil, summing up to a total of nine windings for a three-phase AC transformer. The winding connected to the power source is called the primary winding, while the secondary winding is connected to the user side. Each winding makes many thousand turns. The third kind of winding is used for regulating irregular load on the user side.

In a core-type transformer, which is the dominant type, the three kinds of windings are wound on paper cylinders, and placed on each other in three layers. After some additional assembly and electrical connections, the final coil is placed around one of the three legs of the magnetic core. The core consists of up to several thousand thin plates (0.3 mm) placed on each other in layers to form a circular cross-sectional area. The core plates are fixed with a special clamping structure. After coil assembly the core is closed by plates fit in on the top of the core legs. To finish the so-called active part, cleats and leads are assembled to make the necessary internal and external connections on the transformer. To complete the power transformer there are several additional components needed. Most important is placing the active part into a tank filled with oil for enhanced electrical performance and cooling. The external equipment is then mounted and connected; these include control equipment, cooling equipment, tap-changers, bushings, and platforms.

The sale, design, and production of power transformers are shaped by the fact that, although there are standard aspects, each transformer is essentially custom designed to meet the requirement of the individual customers. Compared with mass production, the specifying of a transformer is a long procedure, typically a process taking several weeks or even months, and the customers are relatively few and competent. In the mature market most orders concern only single units; however, when customers buy two units, it is considered a bonus (for the transformer producer). The character of unit production is also affected by the fact that the power transformers are used in many different applications and situations, demanding different levels of power, voltage and current, as well as various numbers and types of connections. Furthermore, the always prevalent optimization between prime cost and life-cost owing to energy losses, calls for a more or less unique solution owing to various price levels on electricity around the world.

In addition, the nature of the product itself generates a high degree of complexity and uncertainty that affects production processes. With increasing levels of voltage and current the actual size of the product and its components increases: a transformer can range from room size to the size of a large house. Not the least affected is the size of the plant halls, the transport systems, and the machines. Larger transformers also mean that the risks in taking shortcuts and of large profit losses increase. This requires special design efforts for larger transformers. Furthermore, although expertise in the design and production of power transformers has developed considerably over the

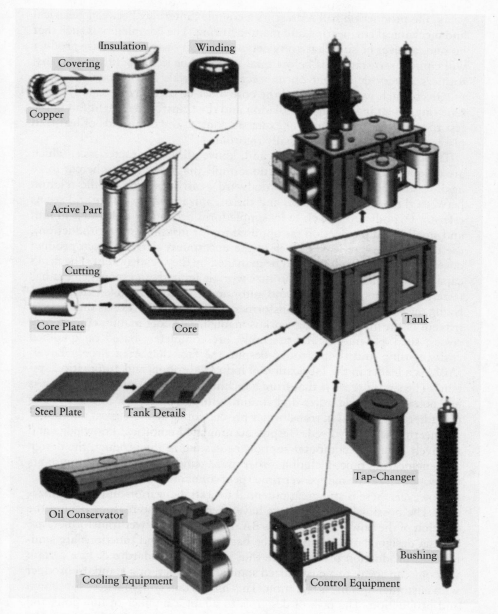

Covering
Insulation
Winding
Copper
Active Part
Cutting
Core Plate
Core
Steel Plate
Tank Details
Tank
Oil Conservator
Tap-Changer
Cooling Equipment
Control Equipment
Bushing

Figure 3.1. The different parts of a power transformer.

years, the production still represents a complex interplay between electrical and mechanical engineering and manufacturing. The complexity is such that no one can ever be sure that every detail is correct or that the costly product will conform to standards before final testing. The manufacturing of transformers is very dependent on impeccable materials and meticulous work practices. Each winding around the core must be carried out exactly right. One tiny defect in spacing or isolation and the transformer might fail in the test room. The requirements of exact stacking of the thousands of leaf-thin plates forming the core are equally rigorous.

The complexity of the product and, above all, its characteristics, which are uniquely suited to unit production, imply that there is an inherent force against standardization. Thus, Woodward's early research on the relation between the production system and the organizational structure still seems relevant (Woodward 1965). In its simple form her theory holds that in unit and small batch production (as opposed to, for instance, mass production), the technical system leaves much of the uncertainty deriving from product development and production to be managed by the social system. The firm's capacity to standardize and routinize work is limited, and management has to rely on workers' tacit skills and autonomy to a considerable extent. Analyzing the work structure in transformer production also reveals that 70–80 percent of the manufacturing work is manual. The core manufacturing processes, such as winding and assembly, are completely based on qualified craftsmanship and simple tools, despite the fact that Asea Brown Boveri (ABB) is a leader in the fabrication of industrial robots and automation systems. The simple truth is that from a technical and economic viewpoint it is not possible to standardize and routinize these operations, at least at this point in time. Typical in transformer production is also the great amount of engineering work involved. Despite accumulated empirical knowledge and relatively extensive computer support to customize the product, the design and engineering time, including order management and planning, amounts to about half of the manpower time spent in manufacturing.

However, there is still great potential for rationalization and standardization. The possible synergy effects have been one of the reasons behind the creation of the power transformers BA. Even though power transformers are custom designed and produced, the basic structure and functions are similar. The production processes are thus relatively standardized. In a certain way one can speak of a customized standard product, or a standard product with customer-specific adaptation. This has certain consequences for design and production. The task of design is to adapt a number of functions and electrical and mechanical interdependencies to customer requirements. The BA has recently managed to develop a powerful design software tool that may reduce design efforts by more than 60 percent and is intended to lead to significant reduction in total throughput time. The Common Product program (see Chapter 2) is trying to fully capitalize on this potential by defining the design of components to create synergy in components supply. Within manufacturing a certain standardization has also been achieved. The production of components, such as core cutting and spinning of copper wire, is highly automated and computerized machinery is more frequent.

The Process Chain

An average ABB plant employs between 200 and 300 people. About 5–10 orders are processed at one time on the shop floor; in a normal working week, one or two transformers are tested and leave the factory. The core process in the business of power transformers is the order process, embracing the chain from the placement of a customer order to product delivery on site. Besides this process the marketing–sales process, the process of developing new product concepts and supply management, includes close cooperation with specified suppliers. This section focuses on the value-added order process, concentrating on the production of class 2 transformers (31.5–100 MVA). This core process can be divided into the following, partly parallel, activities or subprocesses: tender; order management; design; planning and purchase; manufacturing; test and delivery. Figure 3.2 shows a simplified version of the process chain and its time structure.

The Tender Process

The quotation or tender process is normally a marketing activity taking place before the core of the value-added chain. Only about 10–15 percent of all tenders actually lead to an order. In those cases, however, the actual work on specifications and possible solutions could also be regarded as a part of the value-added process. The tender process starts with the request for a tender from a potential customer, who often uses a consultant. The request is usually made to a regional ABB sales office which, after clarifying the specifications and initial negotiations, passes it on to the transformer plant. Important and well-known customers often have direct contact with the plant and the marketing department responsible for producing the tender. The tender comprises in principal technical specifications, preliminary design, price, and delivery date. To convert the customer specifications the responsible *sales engineer* is supported mainly by electrical and mechanical designers. These designers are either organized within the marketing department or within the design department. The designers may also rotate between designing tenders and orders (e.g., Bad Honnef plant in Germany). Production planners are also consulted for capacity checking to estimate a date of delivery.

The sales engineer remains in contact with the customer during this pro-

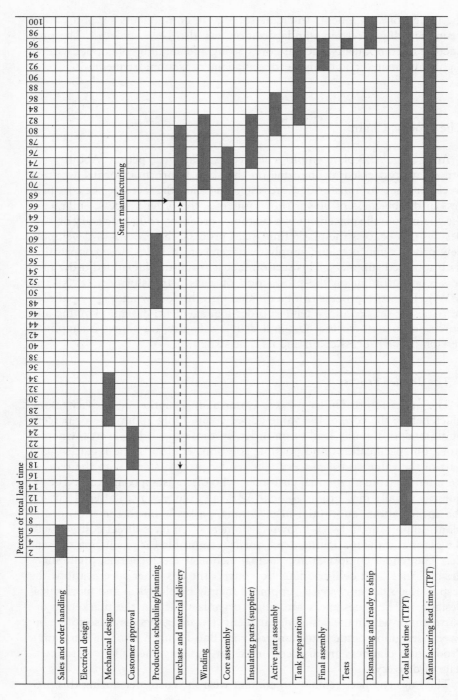

Figure 3.2. Lead times for a reference power transformer at Bad Honnef, Germany.

cess. After clarifying possible counterinquiries, and when necessary commercial and technical issues have been sorted out, the sales engineer draws up the tender. The tender is sent back to the customer via the regional sales office (in cases of a foreign customer also to the international BA). There can be several cycles in this process. The time it takes to draw up a tender varies substantially owing to the complexity of the tender. In most cases it takes between three to ten weeks.

Order Management

At best the tendering process ends up with a final order and contract agreements. This is the real start of the internal order process. The overall order process is managed by an *order handling function*. This is often a separate function within the marketing department. In some cases it is identical with the sales engineer or even an electrical designer (e.g., the Finnish Vaasa plant). In practice this generally means that one order is assigned to one project manager for order fulfillment. The project manager's responsibility covers all customer contacts needed from the time of order receipt until the transformer is assembled on site. The project manager is most active during the initial phase, when the project is defined and when the customer approves the preliminary design, and at the concluding phase, during the final on-site delivery and fulfillment of the contract.

The most decisive event, in terms of process management, is a start-up meeting, often called the *zero conference*, which is held shortly after the order has been taken. This is a cross-functional contract review in which all relevant departments participate. In most cases the sales engineer, project manager, and representatives from the electrical and mechanical design, production planning, purchasing, manufacturing, and quality departments participate in this initial meeting. In some plants (e.g., Ludvika, Sweden and Guelph, Canada) this group forms an order-specific and cross-functional *order–contract team*.

Electrical and Mechanical Design

When definite order data are stated, the engineering/technical department usually becomes responsible for order management. The design process is mainly directed by the specifications and the time schedule established. The design process actually began during the tendering phase, but definite start-up begins with *electrical design*. First, electrical calculations are done to optimize the dimensions of core and windings, mainly by using specific computer programs (e.g., Electrical Design Systems [EDS]). The results are used to forecast procurement of copper and core sheet metal. Second, calculation includes the dimensions of the cooling system and a check on how electrical impulses (e.g., lightning) will affect the transformer. Third, the design for the

electrical control equipment is rendered, including electrical layouts and design of the control panels. The designer then produces the necessary documents for mechanical design, control equipment, production, testing, purchasing, and so on. The designer also takes part in the transformer's coil
windings review in the workshop. The electrical design process can roughly
be divided into 20 percent for order and windings review; 30 percent for
calculations; and 50 percent for documentation and purchasing specifications. The work organization of electrical design varies. In most plants one
or two electrical designers do all the design work on an order. The calculations, however, are always checked by another designer (sometimes called
the grandfather principle).

Parallel with the electrical design process, *mechanical design* can start. The
first step is to create a complete (main) layout of the transformer. The second step is detailed design, in which all of the external components are designed, such as tanks and cooling equipment. The design work is partly computer supported (MDS), but the systems mainly give standard solutions and
a lot of additional manual work is often desired for each customer-specific
order. A complete layout drawing, with all measurements and components
specified, is sent to the customer together with the electrical design, and customer approved before proceeding to the order process. The third step is the
design of the cleats and leads and then the creation of a number of manufacturing documents, such as drawings, material specifications, and instructions, for every job in the workshop. The mechanical design process can
roughly be divided into 10 percent for reviews; 30 percent for layout; and
60 percent for documentation including purchasing specifications.

Normally one designer is responsible for each project; he produces the
main layout and in larger projects cooperates with 1–3 other designers. The
grandfather principle is always used. In some plants there are also draftsmen
and a specialization among designers responsible for different parts of the
transformer (e.g., the Cordoba plant in Spain). In the Bad Honnef plant a
distinct division of labor is perceivable, although it is characterized as "process oriented teamwork." The mechanical design process there is divided
among concept designers, detail designers, and draftsmen on the team. The
detailed design is furthermore split up into several subgroups who are responsible for core, windings, cleats and leads, assembly, etc. This specialization is intended to cut lead time.

Production Planning and Purchasing

After the customer has approved the design documents and the designers
have completed the mechanical design and drafting, the design process ends
and responsibility for the order moves to production. However, partly parallel with the design process, production process planning and work prepa-

ration as well as purchasing are carried out. The engineers responsible for *production and process planning* work in close cooperation with the designers during the entire design process. In the Vaasa plant the mechanical designers do design, planning, and purchasing work. Based on the material specifications sent from design, the production planning function makes a detailed manufacturing description that specifies the materials needed, if and where the components will be manufactured or purchased, and the drawings needed. Production planning also means defining the sequence and time schedule of production operations and making detailed calculations of manufacturing hours and costs. An important document produced is the Gantt plan. This defines deadlines for all manufacturing subprocesses (e.g., winding, core, and active part) and is often drawn out of standard time schedules adjusted to the current transformer order. The activities governing this plan (the critical time-lines) are winding and the start of active part assembly. The planning process ends when all technical and administrative documents for start of production are finished. The time buffer to manufacturing start-up depends on delivery dates and production capacities but lies normally between three to eight calendar days. *Purchase* of material and components is sometimes handled by a specific function within the production department, but more and more often the designers and the logistic engineers manage the purchasing.

The Manufacturing Process

A manufacturing order can be released when all drawings and manufacturing documents are available in the workshop, and when necessary capacity, material, and components (kits) have been checked and cleared. The manufacturing process (see Fig. 3.3) starts in principle with three parallel subprocesses: winding, assembly of cleats and leads, and core assembly. These are usually organized in three or more separate workshop sections. Their parallelism is governed by a common delivery time, which is the start of active part assembly. The detailed scheduling is done by production managers or work groups within each section. The coordination and production control is often facilitated by a weekly meeting in which the planners, production managers, and logistics managers participate.

Prior to winding, which is the real start of manufacturing, insulated material and spun copper have been produced and delivered to the winding section. Insulation material and copper wire can thus be regarded as supplied material, and can either be produced within special sections in the transformer plant or purchased from other companies. *The winding process* involves two steps: winding and winding assembly. They are usually carried out in two separate sections. In the first step insulated copper is wound around a paper core cylinder to build up a coil. Special insulated pressboard

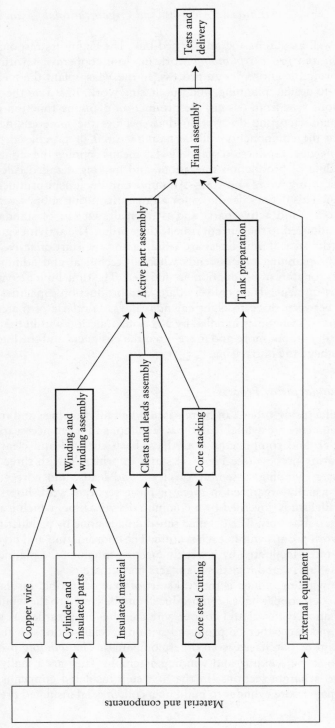

Figure 3-3. The manufacturing process of power transformers.

strips are at the same time placed within the coil to create channels for cooling. Every coil consists of three different windings placed in layers on each other (primary, secondary, and regulating winding). The work is basically manual but facilitated by special winding machines, which are rotating machines that control the tension in the winding. Horizontal machines are used for small transformers, and vertical machines for larger transformers. Normally the winder mechanic works alone with one winding. Winding is regarded as the most demanding job in the workshop. To become a qualified winder mechanic could take 5–6 years.

The second winding step is coil finishing, or *winding assembly*, which involves making electrical cross-connections by spot welding, and assembling several additional parts on the coil, such as lock cylinders, external canals, and ribbons. Furthermore, this step includes drying, pressing, and adjusting the winding to the right dimension. Several workers can work on the same coil at the same time. The winding process takes two weeks or more. Parallel with the winding process cleats and leads are preassembled. This work means mounting of wires on a wooden frame and is often organized in a separate section in the workshop. Since the work takes less time, compared with winding and core assembly, the assembly of cleats and leads can start a bit later.

The third parallel process is *core assembly*. Prior to assembly, however, the core steel has to be cut. This means producing thin plates of core steel. In some plants this is supplied material. Other plants, such as Ludvika, which is a core cutting center, have cutting machines of their own. One reason for the concentration of production resources is that the investment in advanced computerized cutting machines is substantial. Core assembly involves manual stacking of hundreds, up to several thousand, core plates with high precision. To become a good core mechanic takes about two years. The work is physically heavy, even though ergonomic aids are used, such as cranes, hydraulic lifts, and adjustable platforms. A core weighs from 500 kg up to 200 tons. In most cases two mechanics work together. It takes about two days to build a small core and up to fifteen weeks for the largest model.

Active part assembly unites the former three parallel processes and is thus the convergence point in transformer production, in which coils are mounted on the core, and cleats and leads and the upper part of the core (upper yoke) are assembled. Together with electrical connections and some additional parts, components, and insulation this process finishes the active part of the transformer. Usually two or more mechanics work together at the same transformer. A process parallel with active part assembly is *tank assembly*. This includes the mounting of external parts and components, such as the cooling system, plate forms, and control cabinet on the tank. The welded tanks and covers, expansion tanks, cooling equipment, core girders, control cabinet, and other mechanical details on the tanks are produced in advance by separate production units, either within or outside the plant.

The concluding processes—*drying, locking, tanking, and final assembly*—are often carried out within the same workshop section. In the first step the active part is dried, pressed, and retightened to the correct size. Drying is conducted in large ovens in which the entire active part stands for half a day or more, depending on size and oven type. In the second step the dried active part is installed in the tank, sealed with the tank cover, and then vacuumed and filled with oil. The final assembly also includes the last connections of electrical wires in order to prepare for the final testing of the transformer.

The Test and Delivery Process

During the test and delivery process the marketing department takes over the responsibility for the order. The transformer is moved to a special test room or test area. The tests conducted aim at ensuring that the transformer's performance meets the specifications, that it can withstand lightning bolts, and that there are no other faults. The customer is often present to accept the results of these tests, which can last for several days. These tests are nerve wracking to everybody owing to the risks of failures (and can in worst cases be a spectacular light show). If a fault is discovered, substantial and time-consuming rework may be required, and new tests have to be made. The test room results are thus crucial for the possibility of keeping delivery dates. Once testing is completed the final process step in manufacturing is dismantling and packing. Here the transformer is partly disassembled for shipping and the disassembled parts packed. Before shipping to site the necessary documentation, such as test reports, instruction manuals, wiring diagrams, and nameplate, has to be completed. After delivering the unit to site, the assembly at site concludes the order process.

Process Lead Times and Costs

When the power transformers BA was formed there were extreme differences in lead times among the transformer plants. Some plants needed more than a year and a half to deliver a large transformer; others managed in five months. The BA's key objective in line with time-based management was to reduce throughput time. With few orders on the shop floor and one finished product per week the obstacle was not planning complexity. Barriers were to be found in the customization of transformers with the consequent efforts in design and manufacturing and supply management, the step-by-step sequences of operations, and the recycling of work from production to design, etc. Generally the functionally oriented processes and organizations caused much idle and non-value-added time.

The two most important measures of lead time used within the BA are total throughput time from order to delivery, or TTPT[2], and TPT, which equals the manufacturing time. In order to foster lead time reduction the power transformers BA shortly after its constitution defined norms to aim at for the various sizes of transformers (in working days), taking the most advanced plants as the benchmark. While the most advanced plants were pushed to continue their efforts and surpass the norms, the catch-up plants had to fight to get closer to the benchmark—for some plants this meant cutting down lead time to one-third of its actual value. In general the means of reducing lead time in transformer production have been more parallel processes, in combination with compressed subprocesses. Electrical and mechanical design, which used to be subsequent processes, have become more and more concurrent. Purchasing occurs increasingly at the same time as design. The corresponding simultaneousness is also found in manufacturing. Core assembly, assembly of cleats and leads, and winding are all parallel processes preceding the start of active part assembly. Within a period of several years most plants caught up and got close to the leaders. However, as shown in Chapter 2, the actual lead time in the mid-1990s still varied among the different transformer plants. Within the framework of the Common Process project new targets have been set in the mid-1990s, amounting to another reduction in lead time by half. The new norms were clearly a real challenge that called for substantial improvements in all subprocesses. An example of how lead time is distributed among the different subprocesses may be shown from the Bad Honnef plant: sales and order management amount to about one-tenth of TTPT; design and planning, purchase and delivery, and manufacturing each make up roughly 25–30 percent of TTPT; and test and delivery about 5 percent. The potential for further lead time reduction becomes clear when analyzing the ratio between value-added activities and the number of working days. In the cases of the Ludvika and Bad Honnef plants, the value-added order work in 1994 amounted to 60–70 percent of the total number of working days. The corresponding ratio for the BA vision with Common Process was 92 percent. A first challenge for lead time reduction is thus to reduce the great amount of non-value-added time, that is, time when no work is done on the order. This potential appears mainly in the offices. Manufacturing lead time is only about half of the time spent on sales and engineering. To achieve improvements in the latter processes is thus one of the most demanding tasks even in the advanced plants of Bad Honnef and Ludvika.

---

[2] According to the BA's definition: "TTPT shall be calculated from start of electrical design to product ready for shipment." Furthermore: "Planned waiting time shall be excluded if no materials or components have been ordered before start of detailed design." The latter means that TTPT shall include the lead time for customer approval if material has been purchased in advance, which is becoming more and more common. TPT is defined as: "The time from release of documents for first operation into production to product ready for shipment."

Similar to lead time, the costs for producing power transformers vary in relation to the product type, degree of customization, and how effectively the production processes are organized. In general, however, according to the power transformers BA, the product costs are roughly divided as follows: 50 percent, material costs; 30 percent, personnel costs (10 percent, direct labor; 13–14 percent, administrative work; 6–7 percent product development); and 20 percent, other expenses (e.g., capital costs, transport).

From Functional to Process Oriented Organization

The process chain described can be seen as basic to the production of power transformers. However, the organization of the tasks and functions within this process chain has changed over time and still varies to a high degree among the plants of the BA. During the 1990s there has been more unified development of the organizational structures, concentrated mainly in three areas: (1) integrated work organization, (2) process orientation, and (3) outsourcing.

Integrated Work Organization

Traditionally the value-added order process has been more or less a sequential chain of activities, starting with order clarification and ending at delivery on site. The non-value-added time, when no work is done on the order, has dominated the total delivery time. In order to cut lead time (and to get other benefits related to this) there has been a trend among the transformer plants toward more integrated and cooperative work organization. This trend constitutes of several changes:

- The implementation of more *parallel processes*. In the manufacturing area this striving has been prevalent for a long time, not the least in order to minimize capital tied up. Current interest is focused on the establishing of concurrent engineering. In the most advanced plants electrical and mechanical design as well as purchasing have today become almost parallel processes, a restructuring based on detailed process analysis.
- The formation of *cross-functional order teams*. The idea is to speed up order preparation and to temper the problems of coordination owing to the specialization among the engineers and the classical borders between engineering and manufacturing. Such teams are today established in many plants; however, they take various forms. The teams, for example, may be order specific (Ludvika) or customer oriented (Vaasa and Cordoba). In the Bad Honnef and Varennes (Canada) plants there are as yet no teams.

- Several plants have experimented with some kind of *group work* in production. The features of these groups, however, represent a spectrum, starting with groups mainly defined by a common wage system and a common working area. At the other end of the spectrum are true semiautonomous groups or teams, in which the group members are jointly responsible for a set of manual processes and for planning of administrative tasks. The latter groups are controlled as one single planning point and the work distribution is decided within the group. The most advanced teams participate in the development of product and processes, called continuous improvement groups (*kaizen* groups).

- A related tendency is *work integration* and the *increasing flexibility* among all personnel. The reduction of lead time and buffers along the production chain has led to a greater need for multiskilled personnel that can fill the gap whenever there is one. Efforts have been concentrated at making the workers more flexible. An example is winders who learn core assembly. The same phenomenon appears with increasing pace in the offices as well. In the Bad Honnef plant, electrical and mechanical designers recently became integrated into the same group. In the Ludvika plant there has been a merger of production planning and purchasing into one logistic function. In the Vaasa plant the designers do both planning and purchasing work. Furthermore, in some plants first-line foremen have been replaced by a reduced number of production managers who coach the manufacturing groups on the shop floor.

Process Orientation

A related area of change concerns the principles of production management and the organizational structure of the entire company. One of the most revolutionary and topical changes emerging in recent years is the abandoning of functional organizational principles in favor of process orientation.[3] This change should not be confused with the *segmentation according to product lines* that exists in some plants (i.e., the so-called divisions in the Ludvika plant and focused factories in the Guelph plant). The core idea of the latter is to divide large factories into several smaller ones, each of them being focused on one product type, fully operational and independent. It is supposedly easier to control a small than a large factory. In practice this

[3] Process orientation is prescribed in both time-based management (TBM) and total quality management (TQM). The theory behind process management is, however, in some ways also a natural continuation of TBM, since the former prescribes in greater detail the organizational means to obtain a more customer oriented organization. See Eugene H. Melan. 1992. *Process management—Methods for improving products and services*. New York: McGraw-Hill; consult also M. Hammer and J. Champy. 1993. *Reengineering the corporation*. London: Nicholas Brealey.

means that there are two or more parallel sales departments, engineering departments, and workshops within the same plant. However, some functions are kept centralized, certainly the senior management level and the supportive functions of personnel, technology, finance, and supply management. More of the capital-intensive manufacturing processes, for example, wire spinning, core cutting, oven drying, and testing, are also kept undivided.

Product segmentation means smaller and more focused organization but not necessarily organizational dedifferentiation and decentralization. The idea of process management goes beyond this. *Consequent process orientation* implies the organization of business and production processes along the process chain, whereby preceding units function as suppliers to the following ones. Each process is managed by a specific process owner. In this model all planning and support functions become reintegrated into the organizational units along the process chain. The performance measurements are also process oriented. The ideal type functions like a relay race. Most of our case study plants have started to experiment with these concepts. A starting point has been the BA Common Process program. Some plants, such as Bad Honnef, have begun with the tender–sales process by integrating sales and design processes. Others, for example, the Guarulhos and Cordoba plants, began with a consequent reorganization of their manufacturing processes by decentralizing design, and process and production planning into production departments.

The most advanced plant at the time of our study was the Vaasa plant, promoted (at conferences and by documents and videos) as the best practice of process orientation within the entire BA. The most important characteristics of the Vaasa concept are:

- Process organization. In the Vaasa plant functional organization has been replaced by three main processes: management, marketing, and production. The marketing process includes not only marketing, sales, packing and delivery, and invoicing but also electrical design, main planning, project management, and testing. The production process includes the following activities: project management, mechanical design, material call-offs and reception, as well as manufacturing and quality control. A corresponding process organization was installed in one division at the Ludvika plant during 1996.
- Flat hierarchy. Each process is managed by a process owner, and below these there are only coaches and teams. No functional jobs are defined. The teams are responsible for the weekly scheduling and coordination with other groups.
- Horizontal job integration, especially in the offices. The sales engineer or the electrical designer are responsible for order management. The mechanical engineer also does planning and purchasing in advance. The guiding principle is "First one in process does the home

call" (of material). The production groups thus make the home calls of material themselves. Wages in the workshop foster multiskilled employees.

- Clear and lean production flow with low stock. The important concept is the processing of only one order at a time in each manufacturing area. Storage in the manufacturing process is owned by the suppliers. The suppliers are paid to deliver just-in-time. The supply department is thus relatively empty.
- Clear flow of production is part of a visual factory concept. Large boards for planning and performance results are placed on the walls in relevant areas. The same color is used for all documents, machines, and equipment for the same order. All engineers are placed in one landscape office next to the workshop, where large windows make visual contact easier.

Outsourcing

The third area of change is outsourcing. The widely discussed trend in outsourcing has a specific meaning in the BA. The so-called Model Factory and "kit centers" (see Chapter 2) represent a kind of virtual global factory concept. The concept mainly aims at specialization, that is, concentration on the core processes, which include design, assembly and testing, while a greater part of the components (e.g., tanks and cores) are supplied from specialized factories. The rate of outsourcing varies among the plants. The Ludvika plant is a complete plant in the sense that most components and process steps are still kept within the company, although distributed among different divisions. The Vaasa plant, on the contrary, is a highly reduced factory with a high degree of outsourcing and mainly assembly operations done in-house.

The Case Studies

The following case studies represent an interesting exercise in empirical analyses of newly emerging organizational structures rather than business recipes. The seven plants studied over time have been thrown into the cold water of the world market and the power transformers BA to learn to swim or die. The research network had the unique opportunity of studying the development of structure and strategy in these plants over a period of five years. The case studies reveal highly different points of departure and also highly different paths of development. After the five years, the previous degree of variation was reduced significantly but without having approached a new uniform Model Factory.

4 ABB in Scotland
Managing Tensions between Transnational Strategy, Market Decline, and Customer Focus

Graeme Martin and Philip B. Beaumont

Introduction

The Asea Brown Boveri (ABB) plant in Dundee, Scotland, was prominent in adopting a number of strategic initiatives associated with the Customer Focus program during the period 1992–1996. The incentive for such changes was a perceived need by management to bring about a transformational improvement in performance and in plant culture. By their own admission, the plant's management agreed that the Dundee operation was a relatively poor performer throughout the period 1992–1995, although there are quantitative and qualitative signs that some of the sought-for improvements occurred in the following years. This upturn in performance coincides with a change in pace and approach introduced by a revitalized plant management team during 1995–96. However, the ability to bring about such change was constrained by (1) a very difficult external context of economic recession and a decline in demand for its products following the privatization of its major customer, the United Kingdom (U.K.) electricity supply industry and (2) an unfavorable internal context, which has been historically characterized by an adversarial industrial relations culture and inflexible working practices.

The basic purpose of this chapter is to analyze this incentive versus ability paradox through an examination of the linkages between the "global" Customer Focus program, its "local" implementation during this period of unfavorable external and internal contexts for change, and performance of the plant over time. That is, we examine how the plant has performed during the period of ABB ownership and then investigate if its relative position in the "league table" of performance measurements and its changing fortunes over time have shaped both the extent and nature of its approach to the business area's (BA) programs and strategies. In making this the central organizing theme of the chapter we were guided by two key considerations: the incentive hypothesis and the ability hypothesis.

The Incentive Hypothesis

The first hypothesis is that relatively poor-performing plants will, in a multinational company (MNC) context, have the strongest incentive to follow and introduce business area, group, or corporatewide initiatives. This particular hypothesis is grounded in two bodies of research:

1. Existing studies of strategic change initiatives in multidivisional, multiplant companies indicating that the extent of change is highly variable between divisions and plants, with change being positively correlated with business and economic pressures stemming from problems of poor performance and dissatisfaction with the status quo (Pettigrew 1985, 455); and
2. Studies of decision making in MNCs that, at least in the industrial relations area, suggest that poorer plants in terms of organizational performance are subject to more centralized, corporate level decision making (Hamill 1984).

In short, this prior research suggested to us that the closer the ABB plant at Dundee approximated a relatively poor-performing plant, the greater the pressure or incentive it would face to follow and introduce the BA initiative. However, we recognized the possibility (not to say likelihood) that our work may not yield a simple, clear-cut relationship in this regard, not least because all the plants in the BA are assessed according to a mixture of performance measures. Moreover, as existing studies of organizational effectiveness have shown (Scott 1977), the various measures utilized are not always strongly and positively correlated. In other words, one may not obtain a clear-cut pattern across plants whereby an individual plant is always a relatively good (or poor) performer on all measures.

The Ability Hypothesis

Much of the recent research on strategic change clearly indicates that pressures stemming from poor performance are a necessary but not sufficient condition for effectively carrying through the change process. That is, there are other relevant external and internal influences such as market pressures, ownership changes, how senior management chooses to interpret or constitute its environment and, consequently, lead change initiatives, and whether the processes of managing change are internally coherent and fit comfortably with the evolving culture of the unit concerned (Pettigrew and Whipp 1991; Dawson 1994; Leavy and Wilson 1994; Bate 1996). Thus, and this is the essence of the ability hypothesis, it is often the case that those organizations which are most in need of change are, paradoxically, those that find it most difficult to generate internal, second order change.

There are three points worth making in connection with this paradox which have important implications for the management of change in the plant. The first is that coping with and managing such paradoxes are a fact of life for organizations such as ABB (Taylor 1991). The idea is that the creative tension that results from organizational paradoxes represents an essential ingredient in organizational learning and in achieving transformative or paradigmatic change (Pascale 1990; Handy 1994; Stacey 1996). Second, the achievement of excellence through the Customer Focus program in ABB is critically dependent on achieving the "cultural turn." That is, the creation of organizational excellence is inextricably bound up with the constitution of a new identity for workers at all levels which encourages "them to believe that they have control over their own destinies; that, no matter what position they hold, . . . their contribution is vital, not only to the success of the *company but also to the enterprise of their own lives*" (Du Gay 1996:60, his italics). However, as many commentators have pointed out, there are significant limitations in this project, the most important of which concern the often enormous gaps between the aspirations of senior managers, and their faith in the technologies of culture change, and the actual "consumption" of such programs by employees at lower levels of the organizational hierarchy (Anthony 1994; Legge 1995; Martin, Beaumont, and Staines 1996). Third, and following from the previous point, it is evident that in circumstances where the required scale of change is great and the time scale short in order to reposition a business unit, rather directive and even coercive styles of management, change strategies, and interventions may be required as distinct from the "softer" styles of management which had prevailed (Bate 1996; Ashburner, Ferlie, and FitzGerald, 1996; Stace 1996).

The general approach taken in this examination of change is a longitudinal, contextualist method advocated by Pettigrew (1990), in which the content, context, and processes of managing change, together with their interconnections, are examined over a period of time. From this perspective, it is the dynamics of change that are emphasized rather than temporary, static measures such as organization charts or fixed, point-in-time performance data or attitude surveys. Such an emphasis on process has some important implications for understanding and managing complexity and, as some writers have argued, planning for change, paradoxically, is likely to forestall radical or second order change (Mintzberg 1994; Bate 1996, 32–33). It is also argued that strategies and approaches to change themselves have to evolve over time in order to attune to emerging realities and circumstances.

The data for this paper were drawn from a number of sources. First, since 1992–93, one of the authors (G. M.) has had intermittent contact with the organization studied in his role as a university-based training consultant. During that period, both impressionistic evidence and attitudinal data resulting from a Dundee plant survey were collected and are referred to in the report submitted to ABB.[1] Second, material from masters-level research projects on the plant, which were supervised by one of the authors, is also drawn on to provide more systematic evidence. However, the third and main sources of data were gathered in July and August 1995, during which time semi-structured interviews were conducted with all members of the senior management team and senior union officials in the Dundee plant. These interviews were followed up between January and March 1996 with a further series of interviews with senior managers in the plant, the country-based group personnel manager, internal consultants working with plant management, and the senior corporate manager responsible for the BA Customer Focus program. This qualitative evidence was supported by unlimited access to company records and performance records.

The Context of Change

Plant History and Changes in Ownership

The Dundee plant was first established in 1937; ABB acquired it in 1988. During that long period the plant underwent a number of takeovers and mergers that have left their mark on its present situation. The plant belonged to the company that began life as Rissik Long and Co. Ltd., but in 1937 was renamed Bonar Long and Co. Bonar Long initially prospered as a result of wartime demands and its close customer relationship with the North of Scotland Hydro Electric Board; turnover increased ten-fold in the years 1937–47. It was necessary to establish new premises in 1944 on a peripheral site on the outskirts of Dundee that it shared with a number of engineering multinationals, most notably Timex and NCR (Martin and Riddell 1995).

The company was sold to Low and Bonar in 1951 and continued to expand. The range and size of products increased to the extent that the plant had the capacity to produce transformers for power stations weighing more than 200 tons. In addition the company began to produce distribution fuse-gear for the electricity supply industry, so that, by the end of the 1950s, more than 500 staff were employed in the Dundee plant and by 1961, this figure had risen to 750. Growth continued until the early 1970s when the company's U.K. markets began to diminish as the main phase of electrification in the United Kingdom came to an end. At that point the organization turned to its traditional export markets for growth which, by then, were mainly located in the former Commonwealth countries. Overseas agencies were developed and subsidiaries were acquired in Sri Lanka and Malaysia. By the

[1] Martin, G. 1995. A report on employee attitudes in ABB (Dundee) for the Investors in People program. Unpublished manuscript, University of Abertay Dundee.

The authors wish to acknowledge the work of Dr. Margaret Campbell, Andrew Edward, and Donald Mills for allowing us limited use of some of their work in producing the report.

mid-1980s the company had exported to 138 different countries and the Dundee plant had become the largest single transformer factory in the United Kingdom. However, in 1981, a new managing director was appointed who brought fresh thinking and, as a result, the Low and Bonar group decided to retrench into its core business activities in textiles, packaging, and electronics. At the same time, National Industri (NI), a Norwegian based company, whose home market was also becoming tight, was looking to expand into the fast-growing Far Eastern markets and, in a £2.2 million deal, acquired Bonar Long in 1985. A further change in ownership rapidly followed when, three years later, NI was bought out by another Norwegian multinational, Electrische Buren (EB), who renamed the plant EB Nitran.

When, in 1988, the plant became part of the EB corporation of Norway few changes in design and operations were made. However, EB brought to Dundee much tighter financial discipline and encouraged changes in working practices. Fortunately for the Dundee plant they were still prepared to invest in new plant and equipment.

The final change in ownership again came rapidly when the merger of ASEA and Brown Boveri saw the newly formed ABB embark on its aggressive strategy of growth through acquisitions. In 1988 ABB bought a 63 percent interest in the Norwegian operation. By 1992 ABB owned EB outright and, in 1994, ABB Nitran became part of ABB Power Transmission and Distribution Ltd. UK, headquartered in Telford, England.

The Effects of ABB's Transnational Strategy on the Dundee Plant

ABB's impact was seen by the local management team as "strategic" rather than the type of "financial" control exercised by the past Norwegian owners (Goold and Campbell 1987). During the short period of Norwegian ownership, the Dundee plant prospered as part of the EB international expansion program. Since EB's prime interests were in market growth and achieving financial results, the Dundee plant was rarely subject to more than arm's-length strategic or operational control. This position continued to hold for the first few years under ABB ownership since, although ABB had acquired a majority shareholding in EB in 1988, legal restrictions connected with a listing on the Norwegian stock market prevented Dundee from experiencing the full impact of ABB's matrix management structure. In effect, Dundee remained part of ABB Norway until 1992 and, as a consequence, the main impact of the ABB takeover on management style and operational controls emanated from the BA management as the latter sought to pull together the different strands of the new acquisitions.

Two areas in which the BA was particularly influential were process control and market allocation. Since the BA was very much to the fore in promoting technological and process change through the introduction of the Customer Focus program and the Seven-Ups benchmarking measures, the

Dundee plant was the object of early and direct pressure to implement these forms of performance measures. However, the local management team felt that the BA had not attempted to impose a definition of Customer Focus except through the kind of programs and operational measures introduced. Consequently, they came to interpret it as "anything you do within the company to improve effectiveness and product performance which, in turn, adds to the value of customers." The overall impression gained from the interviews was that the managers were enthusiastic and early adopters of the Customer Focus program introduced by the BA. However, there are two qualifications to this enthusiasm. The first concerns the tensions produced by rationalization and market pressures and the time and resources needed to fully implement some of the ideas such as the Six Sigma program. The second lies in the comparability of the Seven-Ups measures among the different countries. With respect to the latter, managers, without looking to excuse their performance problems, pointed to examples of where they were placed at a disadvantage in how they were measured on targets such as throughput time because of factors such as different design specifications in different countries and in the balance between bought parts and those made in-house.

To avoid national subsidiaries competing with each other for work in Third World countries and also to maintain consistency with ABB's transnational strategy, the BA management had made it very clear to the Dundee local management that plants should serve their national markets. As a result, the Dundee plant was prevented from coping with slack domestic demand by exporting to traditional "colonial" markets which had previously been part of its overall strategy and investment plans (see also Berggren 1996, 330). The consequences of this restriction were outlined by one senior manager:

> Back in the early 1980's nearly 70 percent of the output of the factory was export because the home market was very poor at that time. Now there is no possibility of going back to that situation because ABB has something like 40–50 transformer factories around the world. . . . In order to avoid ABB companies competing against each other, the BA operates a market allocation scheme where we get our domestic markets and a small share of overseas markets. But these export markets are reducing all of the time as ABB sets up or acquires new factories in places like Thailand and Eastern Europe. Not only do these acquisitions take away from our potential export markets but in turn these also have to be allocated export markets of their own. . . . So more and more we are dependent on the U.K. market and we've got to learn to survive on the basis of that market. (Interview, August 23, 1995)

Internally, ABB in Dundee has undergone a number of revisions in structure since the ABB takeover. The first of these occurred in 1989 when the company was reorganized by the BA management into three product divisions. The underlying logic behind this reorganization was the need for better financial control and measurement of different product lines which, even by that early period of ABB management, were becoming influential. However, at that point problems were anticipated that were instrumental in bringing about a further reorganization in February 1994. These included the harmful effects of competition among divisions for common resources, the increased overhead associated with duplicating resources for the divisions, and the difficulty in allocating joint costs to divisions.

Thus in line with a change in the U.K. country management structure and ABB's BA internal audit recommendation, the company established a product group structure that effectively has moved from the previous divisionalization toward a product management and matrix structure. There were five reasons given for this development:

1. To achieve a more clear profit responsibility in each product group;
2. To introduce Project Management Control through the two transformers groups;
3. To achieve better coordination between the engineering and manufacturing departments;
4. To make more effective use of declining personnel and resources; and
5. To bring about a closer alignment between the reduced size of the business and the underlying cost structure.

The new project management teams, incorporating staff with contract management, engineering, planning, procurement and manufacturing skills, were made responsible for managing contracts from receipt of orders through to final dispatch. They also had responsibility for achieving margins, delivery performance, and other internal and external measures.

Market Pressures and the Impact on Demand

By the late 1980s the Dundee plant had developed a strong position in the domestic market with approximately 80 percent of its revenue accounted for by sales to the various companies comprising the United Kingdom nationalized electricity supply industry, with whom they developed a particularly close sales and engineering relationship. However, with the introduction of the 1990 Electricity Supply Act, the industry underwent one of the most complex and largest of all privatization in the United Kingdom. The structure of the industry now comprised fifteen privatized regional companies and one nationalized corporation, Nuclear Electric. This political decision was particularly controversial because of the method of regulation introduced and the fact that it would serve as a model for deregulation of electricity supply in the rest of the European Union (Weyman-Jones 1993). These changes first had an impact on the demand and price of distribution transformers and, more recently, on power transformers. Many suggest that these market conditions may be repeated in many other European Union countries in which ABB power transformers operate.

The new companies attempted to balance capital market pressures for return on investments and the regulator's demands for real price reductions in two ways. The first of these concerns the dividend policy of the companies. Resulting from the success of the initial flotations, the companies became cash rich and responded by paying out high dividends to shareholders and allowing major increases in senior executive salaries. The second response was to achieve real price reductions on the back of major cost-cutting exercises. These included the massive labor shedding program of the generating companies and the regional electricity companies (RECs). More to the point, cost reductions have also been achieved through a more sophisticated purchasing approach in which the privatized companies have moved away from automatic replacement of capital equipment such as transformers to a policy of refurbishment by building in more "intelligence" and electronic controls to existing systems. Furthermore, the RECs are demanding increases in the life span of transformers, in the case of distribution transformers from the previous span of 40 years to 70 years. From the perspective of the Dundee managers, who are in constant contact with their customers, these changes have resulted in an overall decline in demand for transformers of all sizes and a consequent pressure on prices and margins as the existing competitors fight to retain their market share.

In the longer term there are two market problems facing ABB at Dundee. The first is the future investment policies of the electricity companies which, it is felt, has been made all the more uncertain by the atmosphere of takeovers and mergers as the RECs invest in other industries as a means of spreading their risk. The second is the maturity of the electricity supply industry itself. Between 1975 and 1993 consumer demand for energy from all sources grew by only 4 percent in the United Kingdom and most of the world's mature economies.

The Process of Change

The central theme of this chapter is the tension between the BA's global rationalization program and the local problems of implementing such changes in specific national contexts, such as that currently being experienced in the U.K. domestic market for power transformers. As noted earlier, the Dundee management team was an enthusiastic and early adopter of the BA's Customer Focus program. However, as time elapsed and as the external context for change became more difficult, managers increasingly felt that they were caught up in the paradox between the need for change and their ability to implement such change. Thus, on the one hand, they were keenly aware of the potential benefits of the company and BA initiatives and of the need to embrace these ideas with a corresponding investment in resources; on the other hand, developing market pressures and the transnational strategy had made such investment increasingly more unlikely. These tensions have been felt in the three related areas of changes in production and quality management, work organization, and industrial relations.

Production Management

The corporatewide T-50 campaign, a Swedish initiative which evolved into time-based management, was seen as the early priority in Dundee. However, since 1992, the Dundee plant began to emphasize the quality dimensions of Customer Focus. The senior management team agreed that quality was its first priority, a necessary though not sufficient condition for future success in an increasingly competitive market. Quality was seen not only as a way of securing customer loyalty through concepts like "fitness for purpose" but also as the main method of bringing their cost structures into alignment with new market conditions by avoiding previously experienced test failures and the accompanying rectification work.

Top level commitment by ABB executives to the Six Sigma program became evident and local management sought to follow their orientation. The pursuit of Six Sigma status at plant level required the appointment and training of coaches or Black Belts. The Black Belts were then to undergo a graded series of training sessions, based on the analogy of the martial arts where trainees would be awarded different colored belts comparable with the standards they had achieved (e.g., a White Belt for an understanding of the concepts, a Yellow Belt for basic and advanced statistics, and a Black Belt for experimental and process design competence).

Dundee was one of ten power transformer manufacturers who agreed to take part in a pilot scheme for Six Sigma and, by 1992, seven Black Belts had been trained. Senior management in the Dundee plant uniformly expressed commitment to the Six Sigma initiative, and many concrete measures were experimented with and implemented.

Unfortunately this commitment to quality improvement was to be severely tested with the decline in orders and the consequent pressures on costs in 1994–95. Paradoxically, market problems meant there was little cash for these types of costsaving investments and this innovation in production management had to be postponed. Typical of the senior management position on Six Sigma was the following view:

> The program that impressed me most of all the BA initiatives was Six Sigma. To carry it out properly it takes a full time team of people. Unfortunately, we just never had the resources to create a full time team. You get to a situation where you believe in the project and are driven by the BA managers to put in resources . . . we trained a lot of people . . . we really went for it in a big way. However, it demanded full time effort from these people. We didn't have the

slack. With the cutbacks these people have either gone [been made redundant] or had to be returned to their normal jobs, to look at the short term rather than the longer term. (Interview, August 18, 1995)

By 1994 it had become evident that the Six Sigma program at the Dundee plant was running into problems, as there was little or no reporting by the Black Belts to the BA. Original estimates by the BA were that these Black Belts would spend 40% of their time working on Six Sigma projects; by November of 1994, three of the employees were spending on average four hours a week on the project, while three others were spending no time at all. Eventually, the initiative was put on hold until the company could get over its difficulties.

This concern with quality did not exclude efforts in other directions such as supply management, time-based management (TBM) and, more recently, in the development of the Common Product program. The latter is seen by some as a means of ironing out the difficulties in engineering through standardization of transformer design and process technology.

Major steps were taken to implement the TBM program, initially focusing on the manufacturing process and, more recently, on the engineering-manufacturing interface. A number of changes were introduced to bring improvements in manufacturing throughput time (TPT) and total throughput time (TTPT). These included more disciplined planning and control techniques such as target setting, teamworking, communications and, more recently, project management and organizational changes. In the early stages, after the targets had been set by the BA for the different categories of transformers, simple improvements in planning for a reduction of the number of orders on the shop floor at any one time brought significant reductions in TPT.

In addition to better shop floor allocation of jobs, the manufacturing process began to be controlled by a system of target setting, in which every job had well-publicized start and finish times that were constantly made known to all employees through graphs and charts given center stage in every department. These were constantly updated by supervisors and engineers to ensure that everyone knew where the project stood in relation to the program.

Work Organization

By and large, work on the shop floor is essentially craft-based with workers enjoying considerable degrees of autonomy in how they perform their jobs, often freely interchanging with others in their work areas, where they have the capability to do so. In the literature on work organization, much has been made about the move toward functional flexibility and cross-training as a means of "leaning" out the production process. In Dundee, there have certainly been developments in the move toward greater teamworking, involving flexibility arrangements and changes in the role of supervision over the past three years. Such changes were introduced to secure the advantages accruing from not only the traditional craft-based, unit production nature of transformer manufacture but also from the production efficiencies associated with a more batch-based method of production. Thus flexibility was sought (and given), but not the type of flexibility that characterizes some of the literature (see Atkinson 1985).

Flexibility between jobs and stages in the manufacturing process was limited by the need to make full use of the "tacit knowledge" that each trade brought to the production process. Prior to 1988 strict demarcation among trades was enforced by the unions so that, for example, mechanical fitters, who belonged to the Amalgamated Engineering Union (AEU) could not do any work that came under the auspices of electrical fitters, who belonged to a different union, the Electrical, Electronic, Telecommunication and Plumbing Union (EEPTU). A flexibility arrangement was then reached with the unions whereby, in theory, any worker could do any form of job that was deemed to be in his sphere of competence. The advantages that flowed from the division of labor among different stages in the process of manufacturing a transformer, for example, between core building and assembling, were thought to outweigh the benefits of having large numbers of staff rotating between the stages of manufacture. According to one senior member of the management team, who previously had responsibility for operations: "Other than having one or two people who are multi-skilled, I don't see the requirement for it because you want men who do that part of the job really well. It increases throughput."

A further argument against wider job rotation concerned the relationship between quality and the tacit or craft-based, intuitive knowledge that was required in most stages of transformer manufacture:

> It only needs a mistake on the working part of a transformer, just a very small mistake because of the wrong interpretation of a drawing and you're in trouble. It's unlike normal mechanical engineering where everything can be measured and you know its going to fit or not fit, because in most of the work on this shop floor [the designer's drawing] is open to interpretation. You've got to consider how, for example, current is transferred because of stress points; if the corner is pronounced or not rounded, the insulation might break down. A lot of interpretation of what the designer wanted is required. (Divisional Manager, August 23, 1995)

This balance between continuity and change to meet the demands of "leaning out" production has also been evident in the development of the role of supervision over the years. In the mid-1980s the plant had approximately thirty supervisors or foremen; in 1994–95 the company devised a structure that consisted of only two superintendents or "mini-managers" and a new grade of team leaders. All team leaders have been trained in leadership and coaching skills as well as in the more technical aspects of planning and control and their jobs have developed to reflect these new competencies.

However, team leadership has not extended into these individuals being regarded as members of management. Their job is to plan and organize a team at a particular stage of the production process and to solve problems with the relevant superintendent, manager, or engineering personnel. Thus, for example, a team leader in assembly may be given a target of assembling a large transformer in two weeks. Since the sequence of work is well-known to most members of the team, there is a great deal of self-organizing and the team leader is left to focus on planning and control.

Labor Relations

The nature of industrial relations is often thought to be a major influence on the ability of MNCs to operate effectively in the United Kingdom, particularly in those areas of the country and in those industries that have a long history of collective bargaining (Ferner 1994). In Dundee, the engineering industry was generally characterized by adversarial collective bargaining with a pattern of long periods of industrial harmony punctuated by short periods of, often bitter, conflict (Martin and Dowling 1995).

At the site under study, the industrial relations history from the postwar period onward was marked by the following features:

—A relatively high proportion of long-serving employees who enforced strict demarcation lines among trades and between skilled and semi-skilled grades;
—A multiunion site (originally with four craft and general unions, before recent amalgamations), with high union density and characterized by a traditional conflictual collective bargaining relationship. Purcell and Ahlstrand (1994) refer to this pattern of industrial relations as "bargained constitutionalism"; and
—The long-standing use of work-study methods and incentive-based payment systems supplemented by extensive use of overtime paid at premium rates.

Throughout the period of the Low and Bonar ownership, industrial relations was typified by long-service managers as adversarial and "arm's length." Although they were seen locally as a family company, autocratic management initiatives and strong trade union officials ensured that collective relations were "anything but benevolent." The strike record of the Dundee plant testifies to these comments. A senior divisional manager described the atmosphere of the 1980s in the following terms:

I would say that the unions were hard, not politically militant but hard. They were used to tough negotiations, very ritualistic. We used to go through an annual strike, we used to budget for a strike each year because we knew that the shop floor wouldn't feel that they had got value for money unless they had been out on strike for a week or so. (Interview, July 18, 1995)

During the period between 1987 and 1994, the pattern and style of industrial relations began to change to a more "sophisticated consultative" approach (Purcell and Ahlstrand 1994) as the senior management team saw a need for a greater degree of commitment from the workforce. The company's strategy moved toward ability to pay rather than meeting annual expectations for cost of living claims, and the tactics used are also an attempt to introduce a problem solving, integrative bargaining approach (Walton and McKersie 1965). This was supported by a series of structured meetings with all employees to further communicate management's position. Indeed, since 1991, there have been virtually no days lost through strikes.

After this period of relatively harmonious industrial relations in the plant and the move toward a more integrative approach to bargaining, declining demand for transformers has been met with a more autocratic approach to dealing with long-standing problems of nonproductive time and overtime work. This coincided with the onset of a further questioning of the continued viability of the Dundee plant and, significantly, an internal reorganization of its management team. Early in 1995, ABB Dundee began to experience the full effects of the downturn in the market. This brought them under close scrutiny from the BA and, according to the new general manager, placed them in the "relegation zone." The Dundee management team responded with a program to further reduce the costs of production.

What underlies this return to a more adversarial and strident bargaining approach on the part of management was the need to gain control over overtime work, an issue that has long been a "festering sore" in the operation of the Dundee plant. It became clear that two interrelated factors in the plant's recent history were regarded as particularly influential in determining the ability of the Dundee plant to implement the Customer Focus program and in shaping the financial and operating performance over the period 1991–1995. These concerned major technical and production problems that the company had experienced during 1991 and the "knock-on" effects these had on excessive and persistent overtime work.

In 1991 the Dundee plant secured a major contract to build six transformers which, up to that point, were the largest and most complicated that the company had undertaken. The BA management team sent over some Swedish staff from Ludvika to advise them on engineering and production problems. Despite this, nearly all of the transformers failed during testing in the factory before being supplied to the customers. Retesting, reengineering, and major rebuilding work went on for nearly twelve months without the real cause of the problems being identified. The net result of these problems was that the company suffered its largest operating deficit during any one year of trading as customers began to exercise penalty clauses in the contracts.

In this context, the problem of overtime became more endemic than ever. It was often necessary to rectify faulty transformers through excessive use of overtime at high premium rates to avoid the client exercising further penalty clauses. An "overtime culture" emerged, which gradually became one of the most significant features of the wage-effort bargain and a major problem in management's attempts to realign the cost structure of the plant. By 1994, overtime payments in the Dundee plant accounted for 30% of the typical wage packets. Even during a period of decline in demand, "off-contract time"—time paid for but not chargeable against a contract—was running at 30 percent. This was accounted for by rectification work and other non-productive activity among the manual and white collar workers. At the same time overtime, in the order of 15 percent of total hours worked, was still being paid for at premium rates. In the past this would have been seen as largely unavoidable, owing to customer demands and to programming difficulties with a smaller workforce and the consequent heightening of labor scheduling peaks.

More recently, the plant management seized on the opportunity as a pretext to confront the overtime issue both as a way of reducing costs and as a way of attacking the "overtime culture." From May 1995, a moratorium was put on all overtime, which along with increasing productivity target levels by 15 percent, was designed to achieve the same cost reductions that would have been gained from the demand for a pay reduction. In return, the company dropped its wage reduction demands.

Such action, not unnaturally, was unpopular with workers and middle management (the latter group who had been used to managing schedules with overtime) but was supported by the full-time officers of the unions involved, who were made aware of the poor financial position and who also had the recent events of factory closures at Dundee as a backdrop to their deliberations. At the time of completing fieldwork, this moratorium was still in existence and, moreover, seems to be paying off since all departments are meeting production targets without using overtime. Moreover, when work has been due to be subcontracted out as a method of achieving deadlines, the manual unions have responded by offering to do this work in normal time as a means of keeping work in the plant.

A Change of Pace and Approach to Managing the Plant

The discussion of production management, work organization, and labor relations at the Dundee plant has traced the changes that have occurred during the period 1990–1995. However, following a reorganization of the management team during 1995, there has been noticeable changes in the pace of new initiatives and in management style at Dundee. Some of these changes have already been alluded to, most notably, the reorganization of the management team itself, the changes made to supervision and the attempts to reorganize work processes, and the adoption of a more directive or even coercive style toward industrial relations. A number of other developments and initiatives have also been introduced in 1995 and 1996, which show early signs of bringing about an upturn in the plant's fortunes.

Three of these recent initiatives are illustrative of a new management approach. First, senior managers have spent a great deal of time and energy in pressing a sense of urgency and crisis by setting out the costs of failure in headline fashion. The main vehicle for this has been through newly established briefing group meetings throughout the plant and the feedback of performance data to the shop floor during the newly-instituted weekly meetings on operational issues and monthly meetings on financial data.

Second, a number of measures were undertaken to control costs more tightly. These have largely focused on a reduction of direct labor costs by 25 percent during the same period. Accompanying changes have also included a reduction in energy costs by 25 percent during 1995, a reduction in controllable expenses involving rent, property and travel expenses by 23 percent, and a significant savings in material costs.

Third, one of the early initiatives of the new plant management team was to address the problems created by excessive "departmentalization" between the materials management, engineering, and manufacturing departments. For instance, the divisional manager explained the problems of fragmentation in the process of tendering for jobs: "We did a study that showed that from inquiry to tender—not even winning the tender—twenty four different gates had to be passed through. Everybody was working in their own box, everyone contributes but nobody owns the process. The ultimate aim is to get rid of these boxes" (Interview, January 16, 1996). This was tackled through a series of structured daily meetings and through attempts to flatten the organizational structure and develop a project team approach. Partly to symbolize this and partly to break down existing physical barriers, the architecture of the office was redesigned. With the assistance of internal ABB consultants, this process of examining organizational structures has emerged into a fully fledged business process reengineering (BPR) project aimed at securing improvements in the process of winning profitable orders—a program locally known as the Order Winning Cycle.

Performance of the Dundee Plant

Against this changing backdrop, how then has the plant performed since becoming part of the ABB power transformers BA and how have the tensions described earlier manifested themselves in actual results? In gauging these we look, first, at the financial results and, second, at some of the key operational performance indicators on the Seven-Ups measures. In doing so we find that the plant's overall record between the period 1991–1995 lays in the lower third quartile of the BA "league table." Indeed, this also corresponds to the assessment made by local management. However, there is evidence that the plant has now "turned the corner."

Financial Performance

The Dundee plant underwent an impressive transformation during and after the Norwegian and ABB takeovers. Thus turnover increased more than four-fold from 1985–1992, from £9,523,000 to £39,308,000. But by 1994, this figure was down to £30,463,000, a drop of 23% in two years. Revenues, net profits, and cash flow in the transformer division have declined from 1992–1995, in line with the plant's overall record.

Net revenues and losses in 1995, mainly associated with a greater pressure on margins as a consequence of increased market competition, caused the Dundee plant to take drastic action in the form of a £2 million cost-cutting program, which prompted the change in industrial relations and the posture regarding overtime referred to in the previous section. This downward trend in revenues and profits was also reflected in the employment reductions experienced among all sections of the workforce, which showed an overall reduction of one-third from 1992 levels.

Benchmarking Measures

The largely operational Seven-Ups measures provide both an internal and external yardstick against which companies can judge themselves. To illustrate how the company has managed its internal operational affairs we have chosen a number of key indices (from each of the three key programs, TBM, Quality Management, and Supply Management) that seem to reflect the overall aims of the Customer Focus program and which show how the company performed during the period 1990–1995. These are manufacturing throughput time, TTPT, on-time delivery rate, failure rates, number of suppliers, and supplier quality.

Time-Based Management

In relation to manufacturing throughput times (TPT), the overall picture varied over the period 1990–1995. Actual times for the smaller category transformers improved until 1992 but since then the plant's performance in these categories has declined, in recent years to levels at which the targets set for the whole BA have not been achieved. The picture with larger transformers is slightly different. Here Dundee's performance peaked in 1990 and until 1995 the trend in TTP steadily increased nearly to BA standards.

Results are different as regards TTPT, with cycles of production in all categories of transformers always being longer than BA targets. However, in line with manufacturing throughput times, performance in all categories has improved since the early 1990s. Managers account for this improvement of TTPT in Dundee by better integration between materials planning, engineering, and manufacturing.

As regards the ratio of added value to employee expenses, the Dundee plant generally performed quite well according to BA targets, showing returns of between 120–150 percent above the norm. Only in 1992, a year of major technical difficulties, did the company fall below the set standards.

Total Quality Management

On this second major aspect of the Customer Focus program, two important measures are failure rates, both in-house and in-the-field, and on-time delivery to customers. On both measures the Dundee plant has shown a marked improvement over previous years. The 1995 figures on failure rates in particular were a source of satisfaction to the management team, particularly given the problems experienced in 1992 when six major transformers continuously failed in the test room. Since 1994, no failures have occurred either in testing or in the field, a progress that was accounted for by reduced working times and increased training.

Between 1992 and 1994, managers acknowledged major problems in delivery rates to customers. However, in 1995, only one unit was delivered late to a customer, giving a near perfect on-time delivery performance. This satisfactory position was partly explained by a reduction in another of the Seven-Ups measures, "orders on the shop floor": the lower the number at any one time, the more easy it was to manage projects through the engineering and manufacturing process.

Supply Management

A final area of performance measures relates to supplier management and to the effects of operating Just-in-time programs. Since the percentage of materials, in line with most manufacturing concerns, accounts for more than half of the total value of the final product, supplier management is seen by some managers as a key to attaining targets on profit margins, delivery performance, and reducing quality problems. Here, ABB Dundee's performance was patchy. On the one hand, the number of suppliers was reduced by more than one-third since 1991. This had also led to arrangements with a smaller number of suppliers of consumables, whereby the supplier undertakes to replenish stocks on a regular basis and raises an invoice only once per year. On the other hand, these impressive improvements had to be balanced by less favorable performance in supplier quality, in which there was a recent increased trend in rejected deliveries (although this may testify to better internal goods inspection procedures), and in supplier on-time delivery, which showed a slightly negative trend over the period 1993–1995.

In summary, the Dundee plant's performance has been somewhat unsatisfactory during the period 1992–1995, largely reflecting declining markets, the efficiency problems associated with a major contract, and internal labor management. However, since 1995 the plant has convincingly begun a significant turnaround which already shows on most performance figures.

Conclusions

As the title of this chapter implies, ABB's attempts to "think globally and act locally" is likely to be accompanied by tensions and contradictions throughout the company structure. Such problems, as a matter of course, will be most acutely felt by individual plants which, in the global matrix structure, are the least able to "enact" their own environments (Tsoukas 1994). Inevitably, these tensions and contradictions will be most obvious in domestic markets, which are simultaneously open to recessionary pressures and the consequences of deregulation, that is, increased competition and uncertainty. Thus, to return to the central organizing theme of this chapter, those plants that paradoxically, have the greatest incentive to change and are most in need of reinvestment in both technological and human resources are often the least able to generate the financial and emotional energy to do so as a consequence of years of accumulated losses and pressures on both prices and costs. Such problems, as Bate (1996:35) argues, are likely to be exacerbated by "a growing cultural sickness" arising from increased feelings of pessimism, frustration, and loss of control. Thus the capacity to generate internal cultural change on which organizational transformations are so often dependent is rendered all the more unlikely. This scenario is one that is all too familiar in a British manufacturing context (see Pettigrew and Whipp 1991; Willmott, 1993).

The history of the Dundee plant has illustrated these tensions and contradictions most obviously in (1) the introduction and demise of the Six Sigma program, (2) the development of quality and design problems and the "overtime culture," and (3) the return to a more conflictual style of industrial relations as a consequence of low demand and poor performance. Thus, long-term changes such as the Six Sigma program, most obviously needed when quality and design problems were likely to impair performance, were largely abandoned because of short-term pressures, brought about by the vicious circle of poor performance, market pressures, and general feelings of lack of control. This was despite the recognition by senior management that such a program had significant potential benefits. Similarly, generating longer-term cost pressures by fending off short-term production problems through the persistent use of overtime and other decay-prone payment systems was a feature all too common in the past in UK manufacturing plants, especially those in which decentralized bargaining was the norm (Edwards 1987). Finally, the return to a more adversarial and coercive approach to industrial relations in an attempt to drive through short-term cost-cutting measures was an action that illustrates the tensions between market decline, short-term rationalization and, arguably, the longer term need for a more consultative approach to industrial relations to underpin necessary improvements in quality management and in work organization.

Since that period, however, there is evidence that the new plant management team have determined a need to bring about a more radical, "frame breaking" change (Stace 1996). Thus the noticeable change in pace and approach of the new management team using the BPR project to question existing paradigms shows signs of double loop learning and the practice of what Stacey (1996) calls "extraordinary management." More recent data on the Dundee plant's performance, and the initiatives that have been pursued, show that such action is beginning to have a significant effect.

Although it is too early to make a judgment, it appears that the Dundee plant may have turned the corner and is thus in the process of becoming a "late developer" within the family of ABB power transformer plants. If this is the case, important lessons can be learned about the processes of managing change documented in this chapter, particularly for those plants faced with the combined effects of mature and/or deregulated markets and a recessionary economic environment.

5 ABB in Spain
The Leap from Early Taylorism
to Post Taylorism

Christoph Köhler

The Cordoban plant, named ABB Trafosur, is located on the outskirts of the city of Cordoba in southern Spain (Andalusia), along the Madrid-Cordoba-Seville railway.[1] Together with a copper and electrical components manufacturer (today owned by the Finnish multinational Outokumpu), it forms part of an industrial complex with several large industrial buildings, where in its peak in the early 1970s up to 6000 people worked. A large villa from the 1920s in the center, surrounded by eucalyptus and palm trees, once was the stately home of the former owners of the company and is now abandoned. The outstanding symbol of the Trafosur plant is the test room building, a 30-meter high modern steel-concrete factory building, which looks like a huge white box with the red ABB logo added. The plant is surrounded by flat farmland of the very wide Guadalquivir river valley. Farther down the river this farmland becomes the richest agricultural area of Spain. The valley is embedded in endless hills with a view of olive trees to the horizon. The temperature in winter often reaches 25 degrees Celsius during the daytime and can climb as high as 50 degrees Celsius in July and August.

Cordoba once was the capital of the Al Andalus, the Moorish Empire in southern Spain. In the tenth century it grew into one of the largest cities of the world with about 1 million inhabitants. After the end of the *reconquista* in the late fifteenth century the city, step by step, deteriorated to a small town. Today Cordoba is a city of 300,000 inhabitants. In the twentieth century accumulated suffering and hate resulted in a strong anarchist movement

[1] The plant was visited seven times in the years 1991–1998. We applied classical case study methodology (interviews, analysis of documents, etc.). The research questions and conclusions draw strongly on a parallel research project on the machine building industry in Spain and other countries (see Fernández Steinko 1994; Köhler and Woodard 1997). Armando Fernández Steinko gave support in the fieldwork and in discussing first drafts; James Woodard helped with research and editing in the long process of writing and rewriting the case study.

which—during the Spanish Civil War (1936–1939)—expropriated and redistributed land. Some churches were also burned to punish the Catholic Church as the long-time ideological supporter of the ruling class.

This period came quickly to an end in Andalusia, after the movement was suppressed by Franco's troops who in 1936 started their conquest of Spain in nearby Seville with support of German and Italian troops and airplanes and quickly moved up the Guadalquivir River to Cordoba.

Today Cordoba remains dependent to a large degree on farming, the food industry, and public administration. However, tourism and some—mostly small—industries support the city. Unemployment is the highest in Spain affecting about one-third of the active population.

For centuries Cordoba and its province were characterized by a very polarized class structure with poor *eventuales* (farm laborers), craftsmen and shopowners on the one hand, and the *Señoritos* (landowners), bourgeois, and political leaders on the other. A very small middle class lived in the city. The old class structure is evident looking at the endless hills surrounding Cordoba. Every 5–10 kilometers there are old *cortijos* of the landowners with strong walls around them, often having a church within. Not too far away is a white village for the farm laborers, normally having a *cuartel* (barracks) for the *Guardia Civil* (country police with military organization) at the entrance to the village. After Franco's death in 1975 and the consequent democratization, old anarchist and communist traditions reemerged, until 1995 Cordoba was the only major Spanish city to be ruled by the communist party. The two so-called multinationals in Cordoba had a bad image as unreliable partners with no regional commitment. The relationship between them and the city administration was rather complicated.

The power transformer plant (formerly owned by U.S. based Westinghouse) was taken over by ABB in 1990 and named ABB Trafosur. With the long and worldwide recession in the early 1990s, tough competition from the traditional Western electrotechnical giants and new low-cost competitors from the Eastern European countries and Southeast Asia, the BA unintentionally had built up overcapacities, particularly in Europe. The ABB power transformer plants found themselves in a tough internal race for survival. ABB Trafosur in Cordoba entered this race with serious handicaps. Westinghouse had more or less abandoned the plant and there had been almost no investment in manufacturing and information technology for more than a decade. The decline and subsequent layoffs of workers created problems with industrial discipline and there were strong and conflict oriented unions in the plant. The company faced a nonindustrial economic, social, political, and cultural environment. All of these handicaps were reflected in productivity and profitability figures, which were far below the average of the industry in general and the ABB BA in particular. The plant clearly had only a few years to catch up or die. The task ahead for managers, workers, and unions was to make the improbable possible, to modernize the plant in a few years, a process that had taken more than 30 years in northern European countries. The outcome was in no way certain. When the demands and plans of the BA and ABB Spain were put on the table, many managers raised serious doubts that a modernization program of these dimensions could be carried out in such a short period of time with so many handicaps and in the difficult economic, cultural, and political climate of Andalusia.

The following section describes the history of the ABB Trafosur plant up to 1996. Two questions are at the forefront. The first is related to the development of the organizational structure: What had been the path of modernization of business and production processes? Did it follow the "Taylorist"[2] trajectory of northern European countries or alternative paths? The second question is related to structures of power and authority: What were the forces of change and resistance to change and which side succeeded? The answers to these questions for ABB Trafosur are of importance to the discussion of industrial latecomers in the capitalist world market, be it in formerly shielded and protected markets such as Spain or South America (see Dombois and Pries 1993) or the former socialist economies. They are also of importance in the ongoing discussion on organizational learning and change. The former East German communist leader Walter Ulbricht in the 1960s created a well-known slogan about how to beat capitalism economically: "Surpassing without catching up!" He obviously failed. Can the slogan be converted into a concept useful for latecomers within the capitalist world market?

History and Context of the Plant

Production of electrical components in Cordoba has had a long tradition, because the region had rich copper deposits and copper mining was established. A copper mill and factory that made cables and electrical components was founded at the beginning of this century. The power transformer company (Cenemesa) was launched in 1930 with national capital and a minority participation of Westinghouse. Cenemesa manufactured electrical motors and power transformers under license. The company grew and became an important part of the Spanish industrial system. It had a good reputation for the production of transformers and employed as many as 800 people in the 1970s. In the recession of the 1970s Westinghouse took over 91 percent of the company's capital. After a short economic recovery in the mid-1970s, a period of continuous decline started. The high forecasts of electrical energy consumption proved to be exaggerated and the plant ran into economic trouble. There was little investment and a continuous threat of plant shutdown. The company kept going only by virtue of direct and indirect subsidies from the state.

In 1987 an Italian "restructuring" specialist bought 80 percent of the

---

[2] The term *Taylorist* will be used with an unspecified meaning to describe processes and structures of functional and task differentiation in industrial companies.

Spanish electrotechnical capital goods industry (previously owned with majority by General Electric [GE], Westinghouse, Brown Boveri and others). Cenemesa formed part of this package. In 1988–1990 ABB bought a large part of the new holding and thus became the owner of more than 70 percent of the Spanish electrotechnical capital goods industry with more than 7000 employees. The deal was politically highly controversial since it involved both the national government and the unions. Both parties would have liked to have split the consortium and sold the parts to several electrotechnical multinationals. However, after long negotiations ABB successfully concluded their purchase while the state gave, in return for assurances on investment and minimum employment levels, direct and indirect support.

The technological and organizational structure of the old Cenemesa power transformer plant was in many ways typical of a large part of the Spanish and Andalusian industry and was based on Spain's model of economic development.[3] For Spain the slowed industrialization, together with much destruction of industrial capacity by the losses of capital goods and human capital during the Civil War in the 1930s, formed the background for the protectionist policies of the Franco regime. The result was a strong separation of the national from international markets and although protectionism was softened in the 1950s and 1960s, it was not abolished before Spain's full integration into the European Union in 1993. The strong direct and indirect tariff barriers generated limited and oligopolistic markets with relatively little pressure to innovate and rationalize products and production. Thus, a large part of the Spanish industry was not competitive in international markets and had to confine itself to the shielded interior Spanish market. The consequences were small research and development capacities, technologically weak and partly outdated products, small batch runs, large product variety with more scope than scale, and high production costs.

Spanish economic growth in the 1950s and 1960s was strong enough to apply Taylorist principles of functional specialization and to build up strong bureaucratic structures in medium- and large-sized companies. However, because of Spain's shielded economy, the pressure to rationalize the technical organization and technologies of the organizationally separated planning, service, and control functions was not as strong as in, for example, northern European plants. The organizational and technical support of specialized functions remained on a lower level. The consequences were an often limited and deficient planning and servicing. The resulting problems had to be handled and solved on the shop floor in order to keep production running. Therefore workers and supervisors in Spanish plants were to a high degree involved in the scheduling of jobs, in augmenting and correcting design and process specifications, in repairs of machining systems, etc.

---

[3] See Miguélez and Prieto 1991; Köhler and Woodard 1997 for a discussion of Spanish and international literature on Spain's modernization path.

The outcome was a functionally highly differentiated and bureaucratic formal organization that resembled the well-researched French structures of the 1970s (see Köhler and Woodard 1997). At the same time, the informal organization demonstrated a marked degree of functional integration. Production departments often had quasi craftlike structures with integrated planning, control, and service functions. Production workers in many Spanish factories have been more involved in planning, service, and control functions than their counterparts in comparable German or Japanese factories, known so far for their relatively high degree of shop floor involvement. The differentiation of formal and informal organization was less strong in those sectors of the Spanish economy that were exporting and exposed to the world market (as in the machine tool industry), but it was particularly pronounced in sectors that had low competition and strong ties to the public administration of the company (as owner or customer; for example, in the electrotechnical and power transformer industries).

This Spanish "syndrome" was supported by the socioeconomic, political, and cultural environment of industry. Of particular importance were the absence of a comprehensive system of vocational training and engineering schools before the educational boom in the 1980s, the strong dualization of the labor market, and "low trust" labor relations (see Köhler and Woodard 1997). In the case of Andalusia cultural traditions and highly ambiguous work orientations play an important role. Centuries of exploitation and oppression left strong marks in everyday life, in processes of socialization of children, and last but not least in attitudes to work and labor relations. Despite many regional and generational differences, some features seem to be common. First, because of the tradition of exploitation and oppression there is a tradition of low identification with dependent work. Second, because of decades of industrial decline there exists a general mistrust of employers, which was reinforced in the industrial decline of the early 1990s. Workers in many plants in Andalusia have been coerced into concessions and extra effort by threats of dismissal and shutdown, which later have been carried out anyway. Consequently workers and unions tend to disbelieve threats and promises, and they do not perceive their own action as relevant to the future of companies. Work orientations of this type can create major obstacles to rationalization and modernization programs within companies.

The Point of Departure

When ABB took over the Cordoban power transformer plant in 1990 it was in a desperate situation, being constantly on the verge of bankruptcy and depending to a great degree on direct and indirect state subsidies. ABB and the new management inherited many of the problems of the old Cenemesa plant. It had not seen significant investments in manufacturing and information technology for many years. The technical organization of the marketing, design, production and process planning, production flow, and control functions had not been modernized and was in many aspects outdated. For example, in production planning the old capacity loading concepts still dominated, throughput times were extremely long, and a large percentage of deliveries was late.

The plant operated with a classical functional organization with departments for marketing, design, product engineering, production (including process and production planning), quality, administration and finances, purchasing, personnel, and so on. The hierarchical ladder was higher than in other countries: production showed five levels of hierarchy: group leader (*lider de grupo*), foremen (*maestro*, responsible for one section and shift), head of section (*jefe de area*), production manager, and general manager. In the formal organization workers were confined to their individual jobs and not involved in planning and control functions (low degree of vertical and horizontal polyvalence).

The dramatic program of change in Trafosur had to be completely carried out by the "old" workforce. In 1976 the old Cenemesa transformer plant reached a peak, with 800 employees. There was a sharp reduction to 600 employees in 1981, followed by a slow step-by-step reduction to 520 employees in the following years until 1988. More reductions were carried out in 1989 (to 420 workers) and 1994 (to 314 workers). When ABB took over, the major bloodshed was finished. There had been almost no recruitment of new workers over the preceding 20 years. Most of the workforce entered the plant in the early 1970s. The main measure taken to achieve personnel reduction was early retirement. Because of the reduction of the older staff and little recruitment of younger personnel, the largest percentage of the workforce was in their forties and had long seniority in the plant. In the early 1990s the average age was 46 years and the average seniority, 25 years.

Because most of the workforce had entered the plant before the dramatic expansion of the Spanish educational system in the 1980s, the level of formal vocational training was relatively low. Only about two-fifths of the workforce had gone through the company's apprenticeship school or—after it was closed in the early 1970s—the state vocational training schools. Most of the employees in the technical offices did not have engineering degrees and had been promoted from the shop floor. Spanish vocational training was very limited in terms of duration and quality. The level of theoretical skills was—compared with northern European countries—relatively low. Nevertheless, the level of empirical knowledge and practical skills was quite high. First, owing to high unemployment and the high status of work in the plant, the company could be very selective about recruitment. Second, the informal craft-type organization involved workers to a high degree in all planning, servicing, production, and control functions and thus created an ideal "learning by doing" environment.

When ABB took over the plant the employee-based works council[4] and the three active unions (Comisiones Obreras [CCOO], Unión General de las Trabajadores [UGT], Confederación Nacional de Trabajadores [CNT]) were extremely powerful. Militant unionism had a long tradition in the plant and the city. Cenemesa had prospered and grown from the 1930s into the 1970s; even under unfavorable political conditions during the Franco regime the workers had some bargaining power. In the 1950s and the 1960s union structures (then illegal) reemerged, penetrated into the legal shop committees, and exerted strong influence on all aspects of the employment relationship. In Cordoba the CNT and the CCOO, the anarchist and the communist unions, were of particular importance.

ABB Trafosur in Cordoba with its inherited dramatic problems in outdated technologies, bureaucratic organization, and powerful unions was borne into an increasingly competitive environment. The Spanish home market was relatively secure but small and not large enough to support the two ABB transformer factories. Since the mid-1970s, when growth rates in energy consumption were down, the small number of newly built power plants and distribution networks left mainly the slow replacement business to the manufacturers of power transformers. Up to 1996 this market was politically protected and secure, but after that date EU regulation required open and Europewide posting and bidding of projects. Competition on the home market increased.

The future of Trafosur depends to a certain degree on a good share of the international market. ABB Trafosur in Cordoba had to fight for a part of the international market against tough competition and vested interests within the BA (see Chapter 2). After several years of hard negotiations, in 1994 it gained the right to bid in cooperation with other ABB companies in North Africa, one Eastern European country, and China. In Eastern Europe and China competition had also increased drastically. Low-cost Eastern European and Southeast Asian companies appeared on the world market and were bidding for projects at price levels that were impossible to beat by either the European based ABB plants or other Western European competitors (e.g., Siemens).[5]

On the basis of the foregoing description of Trafosur and its markets the two major questions raised in the chapter introduction can be specified. First, the "early Taylorist" informal organization of production and work with its quasi craft-type functional integration on the shop floor has strong similarities to "post-Taylorist" features. Did the plant manage to bypass northern European plants by taking a shortcut or did it follow the "Tay-

---

[4] The works council is elected by all workers of the plant. Represented were the two major Spanish unions, the communist CCOO and the socialist UGT. The CNT, a militant union with its roots in the anarchist movement of the 1930s, holds a minority vote.

[5] In a 1995 bid in Egypt, Trafosur competed against more than 20 manufacturers. Some of the Eastern European companies offered prices below the material cost of an ABB transformer.

lorist" trajectory that these plants had chosen some 40 years ago. Second, the highly staffed and bureaucratic office organization with vested interests built into it as well as the strongly ambiguous orientation of workers and unions represent massive barriers to change. What were the forces and mechanisms of change? The story of Trafosur and the answers to these questions unfold in three stages.

Stage One—Implementing Basics

Productivity and profitability of the Spanish ABB companies were very low after the takeover. They had operated in a strongly protected national market with quasi-monopolistic structures. There was very little investment since the energy crisis in the mid-1970s and the slow economic growth up to 1986. In many plants productivity was only 20 percent of the BA's world average. This situation forced ABB Spain to act quickly.

Profit Centers and Bookkeeping

One of the first steps taken by the new owners was to introduce the basic principles of ABB business organization and management to all newly acquired plants in Spain. The introduction of the profit center and matrix organization as well as the ABB controlling and reporting system (Abacus) amounted to a revolution in the traditional ways of business and management in Spain. The constitution of small and relatively independent business units with monthly reporting (Abacus) and profit responsibility created a high degree of autonomy and responsibility for management and at the same time an absolute transparency of their operations in terms of economic indicators—for themselves as well as for the BA and the regional ABB organization. Before the change of regime the financial performance of individual operations was buried and blurred in annual accounts of large corporations. Bookkeeping, as some managers said, was not part of upper level management's responsibilities. The installation and implementation of the Abacus controlling and reporting system was not easy and the approximately 200 general managers for all ABB plants in Spain had to be convinced of its importance in everyday business. The new business structure and reporting system put a tremendous amount of pressure on top management.

The new matrix organization added to the pressure. Managers were used to making decisions on their own. With the new system all managing directors of individual businesses had, according to the matrix organization, two bosses (BA and ABB-Spain), both with veto powers and—to a certain degree—different interests. This created much conflict, especially in the first years of the restructuring process when many ABB companies lived on the verge of bankruptcy. Many managing directors were used to giving and taking instructions but were not accustomed to the burden of the continuous and time-consuming conflict-consensus processes.

The situation of the Cordoban power transformer plant was even worse than that of most of the Spanish ABB plants. It had to be saved from bankruptcy. The plant was defined as an independent profit center and coupled with another transformer plant in Bilbao. They together formed the ABB Trafo (Spain) company, with headquarters in Madrid. Trafosur (Cordoba) was assigned the larger range of power transformers (classes 2–4); Trafonor (Bilbao) the smaller range (classes 1 and 2). Both plants overlapped in the medium-range product. As in the other ABB companies, the internal restructuring of Trafosur started with the financial functions and the installation of the Abacus controlling and reporting system.

A New Set of Players

After the constitution of ABB Spain a special structure was set up to initiate the reorganization of the two power transformer plants. A senior manager who had grown up in the Swedish ASEA biotop, a mixture of tough business and work ethics with the most advanced culture of participation and humanization of work, was assigned to the task. This manager had also worked in Brazil and other countries with completely different business and cultural traditions. Knowing ASEA and ABB from different positions, he also acted as an interface to the BA. He was aware that the key people for the planned high-risk process of restructuring were the managing directors of the two power transformer plants in Spain. The top management of the old Cenemesa had in the years of crisis lost its power and in a certain way almost disappeared. It had to be demonstrated that there were managers again.

This key manager selected and worked closely with the general managers of Trafonor in Bilbao and Trafosur in Cordoba (Luis Carrera). Sr. Carrera comes from a village in Santander, in the northern Spanish province of Cantabria, where he grew up on a farm. He began his career when aged 14, became a skilled worker, worked his way through technical college, and moved up the ladder in the Santander-Westinghouse plant for electric motors. He became known as an efficient and determined manager. After the ABB takeover he was asked to direct the ABB modernization program for the Cordoba plant. The unions consider him as hard headed with no sympathy for the Andalusians.

The development of a strategic plan for the two power transformer plants was the occasion to build up the cooperation between the ABB transformer Spanish headquarters in Madrid and the Power Transformers business area (BA). In this process the managing director of Trafosur built up his network of professional and personal work relations within the ABB organization. In the early stages there was much discussion about the strategic plan and the targets to be set for the coming months and years. Many of the Spanish managers were very skeptical about the possibility of a speedy and drastic change. Their main arguments were concerned with the low level of formal education and skills of the workforce, the distance of the Andalusian culture from abstract modern industrial discipline, and the powerful position of the unions.

Workers and unions of the Cordoban power transformer plant were in a very difficult position. On the one hand, they welcomed the strong modernization efforts of ABB. On the other hand, they were confronted with job losses and a loss of power in the plant. In an environment like Cordoba, where each stable job is of high importance to the community, workers cannot wholeheartedly support rationalization measures. The deeply rooted mistrust of employers in the Andalusian culture reinforced these attitudes.[6] These interests, cultural traditions, and past experiences were reflected in a very ambiguous orientation toward ABB's modernization program in Cordoba. Trafosur's workers and their unions had two souls in their chest. Under similar economic circumstances the same holds true for workers in other countries and plants as well; however, in Andalusia workers' mistrust of management is stronger than their identification with the modernization program.

Stage Two—Technology Transfer

By late 1990 the Abacus controlling system of Trafosur had already started to show profits. The 1989 reduction in personnel and other measures of cost-cutting proved to be successful. In the light of the forthcoming problems this was just a temporary relief for the managing director, Luis Carrera. Stagnating world markets, new competitors, ABB internal overcapacities, and last but not least the pressure from ABB corporate management, made clear that Trafosur had just escaped death and must then embark on a race for survival. A run-down factory with a 30-year-old organizational structure and technology had to be raised to the level of the most modern plants of the period. It was made equally clear that there was little time to catch up. The strategy in the second stage (late 1990–late 1992) was focused on "technology transfer" in a wide sense (hardware, software, and technical organization). The existing organizational structures and hierarchies were maintained. Technology transfer applied to all functions from marketing to design to process and production planning; and from supply management to pro-

---

[6] This mistrust of employers was further aggravated when multinationals like Suzuki in the years 1990, 1992, and 1994 forced massive layoffs in Linares just 50 km from Cordoba, which triggered plant occupations, sit-down strikes, and a solidarity movement in Andalusia and Spain. Suzuki had negotiated and signed investment plans and guarantees for minimum employment levels in three consecutive years and broke its promises each time after having received comprehensive public subsidies.

duction and quality. The goal was to reach northern European standards and performance levels in the shortest period of time.

Implementing New Product and Process Technologies

Dozens of projects envisaged in the strategic plan were initiated. The most far-reaching decision was related to the choice of power transformers to be manufactured in northern and southern Spain. With Westinghouse and Schneider technology the Cordoba plant traditionally produced core-type as well as shell-type transformers.[7] After the takeover Trafosur decided to continue both product lines. Some Spanish customers preferred the more expensive shell-type technology even though it showed only small advantages in performance. Nevertheless, decisions about the design of these two product lines had to be made urgently. Rationalization efforts and investments in terms of computer assistance for design and production planning as well as for manufacturing technology along the process chain were deeply affected by the choice of design.

At this time the BA-wide Common Product program was still in its early days and engineers representing the different corporate traditions merged in ABB, discussed advantages and disadvantages of the different designs. Expecting that ASEA technology would strongly influence the new Common Product, ABB Trafo chose the design that had been developed and manufactured in Ludvika, Sweden. This decision was essential for the modernization program carried out in the years 1990–1995. It affected more or less all functions and processes of the plant and required in 1990 that two staff positions be created to support the technology transfer. Major decisions were taken by a steering committee with members drawn from the BA, ABB in Ludvika, Trafosur, and Trafonor, and the ABB Trafo Spain headquarters in Madrid. This group met monthly during the next two and a half years. For each project in the plant a group was formed, the leader of each group reporting directly to the chairperson of the steering group in Madrid.

One of the early major projects was the implementation of the Ludvika system for electrical and mechanical design. The technical documentation of Trafosur had to be brought into a compatible format for its use with the new design software package. Closely related was the implementation of the Ludvika quality standards for design, manufacturing and control, affecting all steps of the process chain. The huge Ludvika quality manuals were digested and implemented by the then centralized quality department. Also the Ludvika concept was applied in production planning and control. In the old Cenemesa plant the classical planning philosophy predominated: priority

---

[7] In shell-type transformers the core is assembled around the completed coils, requiring more production hours compared with the core type (see Chapter 3).

was given to maximum capacity utilization. To achieve this, as many shop floor orders as possible were released. The plant used the standard IBM Copics system. The newly implemented Ludvika concept gave highest priority to shortening throughput times and reducing inventories. Bottlenecks in the process chain were eliminated and the capacities of final assembly were enlarged to create pull and speedup effects through the entire process chain. Capacity load was reduced, fewer orders were released, and the number of orders on the shop floor decreased drastically (from 15 to 7). Manufacturing processes were modernized by streamlining materials flow, the reorganization of logistical operations (warehouse, internal and external supplies), and last but not least by investment in manufacturing technology. Some of the important developments in this respect are the new drying cabinet, which reduced the drying time of windings from 15 to 2 days and the vertical turntable, which allows higher quality windings to be made in a shorter time.

As shown previously, ABB Trafosur could in its modernization program count on the wealth of empirical skills of the workforce in the manufacturing of power transformers. However, the strong drive for technology transfer in products and processes in a short period of time showed the limitations of practical knowledge and empirical skills. Most of the workforce had not received any classroom tuition for many years and the plant did not have younger experts who were computer-literate. Most of the personnel in the technical offices, promoted from the shop floor, were without engineering degrees. Consequently, the major bottlenecks were in implementing the modern and powerful Ludvika information technology in administration, design, process engineering, production planning, etc. Nine new employees with university degrees in industrial engineering, computer science, and economics were recruited and placed into strategic positions of the technology transfer. Trafosur at the same time began a continuous training program that initially was dedicated to educating for key positions in the technology transfer and—later—to lower levels of hierarchy and skills. This program included special training in Ludvika and stays of Swedish colleagues in Cordoba (average 6 months). Off-site classroom training in Cordoba and Madrid was given high importance.

Hundreds of large and small projects of technology transfer (in manufacturing and information technologies and in technical organization) were carried out, during which time the traditional formal organizational structure, with its high degree of functional differentiation and centralization, task specialization on the shop floor, and its various hierarchical levels were not altered. However, the strong technology transfer destroyed a large part of the craft-type, highly flexible informal organization on the shop floor. New systems in design, process and production planning, quality, and the reorganization of the logistical chain helped to make planning, service, and control functions more efficient and reduced the involvement of production workers and superiors. The rationalization of the differentiated functions allowed for a stronger separation of conception and execution. The organization lost its strong duality of formal and informal structures and approached the mature Taylorist model. There is no doubt that the organization of production and work followed the Taylorist trajectory rather than being a shortcut into the post-Taylorist world of decentralization.

Rebuilding Hierarchy—A Top-Down Approach

The organizational structure of the old Cenemesa plant, with its strong union influence and weak management, can best be described as a loosely structured network with a high degree of openness and flexibility and various centers of power. After the takeover Sr. Carrera and his top managers gave priority to reestablishment of management prerogatives, hierarchy, and control. In light of the highly ambiguous orientations of unions and workers this was seen as a precondition to implement the dramatic, speedy, and in many ways painful program of modernization, foreseen in the strategic plan of 1990. Stage two clearly was dominated by a top-down approach in trying to reestablish hierarchy, using basically two social mechanisms: personal involvement and industrial conflict.

Personal involvement was established around the comprehensive program of technology transfer, mainly the new transformer design, throughput times, and quality. Around these basic issues large numbers of projects were defined and project groups established. These groups in the beginning always involved the responsible line management and experts from all affected departments and units and at least one member of the top management structure (director, project leaders, or heads of department). The predominant culture of "muddling through" proved to be a great problem. Everyday business and social relations among colleagues was many times seen as more important than changing routines and imposing discipline. Common decisions were forgotten and deadlines overridden. The intense involvement and control of top management was crucial to coordinate projects and to push for change contrary to forces of resistance from within the organization. The extremely time-consuming (and in the long run dysfunctional) personal involvement of the general manager and his top managers was necessary to establish industrial discipline.

The second mechanism to reestablish hierarchy was industrial conflict. The shop committee and the unions had, during the crisis years of Cenemesa, taken on a dominant role in the plant. They not only had a strong position in issues such as job control but also in basic business decisions, as for example in the definition and acceptance of contracts with customers. In a certain way there existed a structure of codetermination for all aspects of the power transformer business. From the very beginning of the takeover the top management of ABB Trafosur tried to reestablish management prerogatives and to remove the employee-based works council and the unions from economic and technical decisions. At the same time the intention was to reduce the power of the unions in classical industrial relations issues (job assignment and promotion, performance, health and safety, training, wages, etc.). This was not easy to implement because the works council and the unions had strong support from the workers and the city government. Also employees could in many issues refer to the first contract of 1990 that had been negotiated for all Spanish plants by ABB Spain headquarters, the unions, and the state after the takeover. To facilitate the deal, ABB management had in many respects agreed to prolong existing plant agreements and gave its word on future minimum employment levels.

In 1992 this agreement expired and a new contract had to be negotiated between ABB Trafosur and the works council. In these negotiations several issues became critical. The old Cenemesa plant produced power transformers as well as switch gear. In the ABB structure the two lines of production were organizationally separated, located in different buildings on the Cordoban factory grounds and assigned to different BAs. ABB wanted separate bargaining units; the works council and the unions wanted to continue as one bargaining unit. As a second major issue ABB asked for the freedom to assign workers flexibly to different jobs within and between departments, called polyvalence in Spain. The works council agreed in principle but wanted more money for polyvalence. Management was not willing to give extra pay, referring to the difficult economic situation during the recession.

The dispute could have been solved at the negotiating table with minor concessions from both sides. However, the hidden agenda was about power, and management was not willing to compromise. The strike began in May 1992 and lasted for several weeks. The circumstances had been unfavorable for the unions from the beginning and they lost on most of the issues. Spain had entered a deep and long-lasting recession. ABB Trafo had only a small order book and management was willing to demonstrate its power. Since Spanish unions have very small funds for the support of their members during strikes and since the state does not pay unemployment benefits during a strike, the strike had to be called off. The unions lost the struggle as well as some credibility with the workforce. All in all, it took about three years to rebuild a functioning hierarchy and industrial discipline in Trafosur. The top-down approach and the strategy of direct control required a tremendous involvement of Luis Carrera and the half a dozen heads of departments. Going into a long strike was not without risk, but it turned out well for management.

Stage Three—Organizational Change

The third act began, by small steps, in late 1992. Whereas the second stage in ABB Trafosur's run for survival was dominated by technology transfer and a top-down approach in policies and politics, in this stage post-Taylorist ideas of reorganization were taken up. Technology transfer continued but was embedded in organizational change (decentralization, changes in hierarchy, process oriented organization, etc.). The top-down approach was loosened and selectively complemented with bottom-up politics. The top managers had earlier followed ABB's international Customer Focus program with its emphasis on organizational change via BA meetings and other measures. The systematic diffusion of these ideas, however, started later. The official Customer Focus campaign in ABB Spain kicked off in late 1993 with the setup of a nationwide organizational structure and a magazine.

Decentralization and Flexibilization

The technology drive continued strongly from 1993 to 1995. Trafosur had used the years 1990–1992 to catch up technologically with the more advanced northern European plants. From 1993 onward it actively participated in the modernization programs of the BA and implemented many of the projects being offered by the BA. Trafosur had achieved the International Standards Organization (ISO) 9001 quality certificate in 1993. In late 1994 it started its participation in the BA-wide Six Sigma quality improvement program. In 1994–95 the first modules of the Common Product and Common Process projects were implemented. New and integrated software packages for design, process engineering and production planning (Triton), and quality control had been developed by the technology centers of the BA, Ludvika, and Bad Honnef.

The distinction of this third stage in ABB Trafosur's modernization trajectory is that technology transfer is now embedded in organizational change. A slow but firm post-Taylorist trend of functional dedifferentiation and task dedifferentiation can be observed. Affected are both the organization of production and work. The reorganization first started within the framework of the traditional functional organization. Two projects serve as good general examples: first, the flexibilization of labor deployment, and second, the decentralization of quality control. One of the problems encountered after the consequent reduction of the number of job orders on the shop floor and reduction in capacity load was temporary imbalances within and between different production sections along the process chain. The regulation (plant agreement and state regulation) on work assignment and transfers of personnel made it very difficult to assign workers to different workplaces within and between sections and departments. An agreement with the employee-based works council about polyvalence of workers and flexibility in work assignment was reached after the three-week strike in 1992. The regulation on access to permanent jobs was kept; temporary transfers were deregulated, however, and made subject to unilateral management decision.

Quality control had formerly been the responsibility of a centralized quality control department with 24 employees. They had to digest and implement the Ludvika quality manuals and procedures in 1990–91 as part of the technology transfer changeover. Hundreds of inspection points were defined where work in progress had to be checked and certified by the quality department. Workers at this time had no formal quality responsibility. As part of the plantwide drive for the ISO 9001 quality certificate in 1994, the organization of the quality function was changed. Workers and foremen now took over the quality checks at the inspection points.

In 1995 a far-reaching break with the traditional organizational structure was realized by the implementation of process oriented reorganization. All departments along the process chain were defined in terms of a supplier-client relationship. The marketing and design departments were suppliers to the three production sections for components (winding core type, winding shell type, core assembly). They were also defined as suppliers to the assembly section, which in turn supplies the finished and tested product to the marketing department delivering the finished product to the actual customer. The production sections—which formed the center of the reorganization—received all the responsibilities and resources of independent business units. Planning, service, and control functions that were previously organized in separate departments and units were partially reintegrated in the production function. As a general rule the departments affected by the decentralization of process engineering, production planning, and logistical and quality control functions had to permanently delegate one person to each of the four production sections. These workers then were required to report to the head of their respective production section as well as to the head of their old department. The process engineering section was dissolved completely.

The reorganization was not easy to implement. Some of the specialized sections resisted change because this meant a loss of personnel and power. Production planning lost four schedulers, who before could be used as reserve capacity in cases of emergency. They are now fully integrated in the production sections and their assignment to general tasks requires the permission of the head of the production section. The production sections have more responsibilities, more tasks, and more pressure placed on them. They tend to become "egotistic" and hoard resources. The works council in general was not opposed to the project. However, some members represented vested interests in the mostly affected sections and opposed some decisions. Despite all these problems top management of ABB Trafosur views the new organization as a breakthrough for the continuous improvement of processes and one of the major achievements in Cordoba.

The first and second stage of modernization had pushed ABB Trafosur's organization through the Taylorist trajectory. The informal, functionally integrated, craftlike structure on the shop floor was eliminated, and the differentiated bureaucratic structure made efficient. During the third stage of modernization functional reintegration on the shop floor could be observed.

From a bird's point of view ABB Trafosur started with a highly integrated organization of production processes, which was functionally differentiated
organizationally, and then functionally reintegrated, thus returning to the
previous structure. The difference in the new integration lies in the organization's technological backbone. In stage two and three all functions from
design to planning and control have been rationalized and supported with
new concepts of technical organization and state-of-the-art information
technology.

Participation and Bottom-Up Initiatives

In stage two ABB Trafosurs's top management had reestablished management prerogatives, hierarchy, and control. This was achieved by industrial
conflict and by managerial involvement and control in projects of change.
After having regained power, the focus in the management of change shifted
to policies designed to build up trust and to stimulate bottom-up initiatives.
The mistrust in the workforce remained strong and was supported by another reduction of the workforce to 314 employees in 1994, mainly achieved
by early retirement schemes. However, this was balanced by the obvious intention of ABB to modernize and save the plant. The determination of Luis
Carrera and his top managers was observed and personally experienced by
the employees in the hundreds of smaller and larger projects that were carried out within the plant in the first years after the takeover. At the same time
the significant investment in information and manufacturing technology and
in training demonstrated ABB's commitment to the production site.

These practical demonstrations of commitment were coupled with a continuous policy of information on all levels of the hierarchy. The main message was: "We are in a bad position in the internal and external race for survival in the industry. We have a good chance to survive if we rationalize and
modernize and reduce capacities. If 100 of us leave with early retirement
schemes we can save the plant; if not we all have to leave under conditions
far worse than those that can be granted now." In the Andalusian context,
workers' orientations will remain ambivalent. However, it seems as if the
project to build up a minimum level of trust has been successful in the majority of the workforce. In 1994 continuous improvement groups were started,
designed to stimulate involvement and worker initiatives. After the implementation of the new organization, work groups were involved in so-called
internal audits, in which each section along the process chain evaluated the
foregoing supplying section for quality, timing, and other factors. The tension between mistrust and support remained strong in the workforce. It
seems, however, that management has been able to strengthen loyalty to the
modernization program and to weaken mistrust and resistance to change.

The annual negotiations at plant level took place in the framework of
reestablished management control and were less conflict prone than the pre-

vious years. Among the issues under discussion in 1994 and 1995 were performance related wage incentives (linked to throughput times and quality) for individual sections along the new internal supplier-customer chain and working time flexibility (linked to orders and capacity loading). In line with principles of militant unionism the new incentive concept was vehemently opposed by the works council because of its "desolidarization" effects. After long discussions management gave in and incentives were related to the plant performance in general and the workforce as a whole and not to individual sections.[8]

In 1995 the structure of management and control at ABB Trafosur could best be described as a mixture of hierarchy and network. During the past six years the structure has developed from a network-type organization with distributed power centers and strong unions to a hard hierarchy in 1992 and halfway back to the network structure in 1995. The latter now was based on a clear distinction of management and union responsibilities, industrial discipline and high levels of performance.

The Andalusian Modernization Path: Shortcut or Speedup?

The five-year modernization and rationalization drive at ABB Trafosur brought impressive results, which were well documented by Seven-Ups, the ABB internal benchmarking and reporting system. The most dramatic improvements could be observed in the period 1990–1993 when basic changes were implemented. The years 1993–1995 showed slower but steady improvements. Lead and throughput times were, in line with ABB philosophy, given high priority. In 1990, the first years after the takeover, only 40 percent of deliveries were on time. On-time deliveries increased by more than 20 percent each year and in 1994 100 percent of all transformer deliveries met their deadlines. Throughput times were, by 1990, up to three times longer than the BA standard. In three years ABB Trafosur more than halved its throughput times and got close to the BA standard. Improvements continued in the years 1994 and 1995. The development of the total throughput time (design and production cycle) went in parallel, their graphs showing similar shapes.

Quality records also show dramatic improvements. Each year about four dozen power transformers go through final platform testing. Failure in the test room many times implies the disassembly of a large part of a transformer. ABB Trafosur was able to reduce these wasteful events dramatically, having no test failures for the first time in 1993. The number of quality de-

[8] Interestingly enough, the overall effects on plant performance turned out to be quite beneficial. The sections did not just focus on their own activities but on timing and quality of their internal suppliers as well, which reinforced horizontal controls along the process chain.

fects detected at the inspection points was halved from 1990–1993. Productivity improvements were less strong and in part invisible owing to low-
capacity utilization. The number of MVAs per year and employee at Trafosur increased from approximately 5 in 1990 to 8 in 1992 and 10 in 1994.
Real productivity increases, however, were not so strong because outsourcing increased during this period (e.g., of tanks). The ABB internal Seven-Ups
measurement (value-added/personnel expenses) is highly dependent on sales
and capacity utilization. According to this indicator productivity has increased slightly from 1990–1995 and again brings ABB Trafosur into the
middle field of the 24 BA plants. For the years 1996–2000 high productivity increases owing to the implementation of the Common Product and
Common Process initiatives are expected.

After six years of hard work, worries, and nightmares general manager
Luis Carrera, management, workers, and unions have achieved world standards in the manufacturing of power transformers. The success story was
celebrated with an "open house" in which all employees and their families
and friends were invited. However, the happy mood was not unalloyed because some dark clouds were seen on the horizon. The phasing out of the
labor-intensive shell-type transformer as well as the step-by-step implementation of the Common Product and Common Process technologies would
foster strong productivity increases and could generate more personnel redundancies in the future. ABB Trafosur's Spanish and international markets
were under increasing competitive pressure. ABB overcapacities in Europe
and Spain remain in existence. Spain has two manufacturing sites, yet one
unit alone could supply its markets. The BA strategy of centralization of component production in so-called kit centers could be seen as a first step to re-
centralize the manufacturing of power transformers in a few centers in Europe. The Trafosur plant will have to increase its efforts if it is to survive. The
founding years of ABB Spain are just the beginning of a long struggle for survival that will reach into the twenty-first century.

These upcoming problems do not negate the achievements of ABB Trafosur in the years 1990–1996. ABB Trafosur had very little time to catch up
and managed to reach standard performance levels in the international BA
ranking in 6 years—a process that took 30 or more years in northern European plants. The rationalization and modernization drive continues and the
plant is trying hard to reach the top. Was this achieved by a shortcut, by
avoiding some lengthy and troublesome roads? Did ABB Trafosur "surpass
without catching up"? Or was it an acceleration along the same trajectory
that northern European plants, for example, had passed through? For the
technology trajectory the question is easy to answer: The accumulated experience of the 27 plants from nine different corporations and from the most
powerful producer of power transformers at this time, ABB, allowed a strong
program of technology transfer for product, organization, and manufacturing technology. Much unproductive sidetracking was avoided and state-of-

the-art production was achieved in a very short period of time. Technology transfer was a shortcut.

In looking at ABB Trafosur's organizational change during the years of observation we do not find shortcuts but rather an acceleration along the "Taylorist" trajectory. The traditional organization of the Cordoban plant was in its formal structure very bureaucratic. In its informal structure it showed modern post-Taylorist features: high integration of functions in the production system, a great informal proximity and permeability between all levels of the organization, small income differences in the workforce (i.e., between white and blue collar workers), and strong involvement of the works council and unions in managerial decisions. In the past three years the strong program of technology transfer coupled with a top-down management approach destroyed a large part of the informal structure and pushed the organization through the Taylorist trajectory on the basis of which management started to experiment with "post-Taylorist" structures.

The question is whether a shortcut from "early Taylorist" functional integration to "post-Taylorist" process orientation would have been possible. The organization of the quality function might serve as a good example. In pre-ABB times workers were informally involved in quality assurance. After the takeover the quality department was trained and made responsible in the use of the ABB Ludvika system with detailed descriptions of inspection points and procedures. In stage three of the modernization process, with the ISO certification and the new process oriented organization, quality tasks were given back to the shop floor. To a certain extent in ABB Trafosur the Ludvika quality system was implemented twice within three years, first in the centralized quality department and then on the shop floor. A shortcut would have meant to give formal quality tasks immediately to workers and foremen and provide them with adequate training thus saving one step of implementation.

There are good arguments in favor of as well as against a shortcut policy, which have been widely discussed for East German industry after reunification. For Cordoba at least two considerations speak against a shortcut. First, if catch-up time is short as it was in ABB Trafosur, many measures have to be implemented at the same time. This requires distributed centers of competence and leadership within the organization. An overload of change agents would have increased the risk of failure. Second, ABB Trafosur's strong modernization drive developed in the context of the Andalusian syndrome of low-trust labor relations and ambivalent work orientations. The decentralization of planning and control responsibilities required a minimum of trust and commitment to the "common cause," which took time to build up. In a different social and economic context, such as East Germany, a shortcut strategy might be more realistic.

The case study raises a second question on the forces and mechanisms behind ABB Trafosur's dramatically speedy—and sociologically speaking improbable—modernization drive. The discussion of Japanese transplants, as well as modern theories of organization, clearly demonstrates the difficulties in the turnaround of brown-field plants with existing organizational structures, human capital resources, labor relations, and cultural traditions. After some negative experiments the Japanese tried to avoid this set of circumstances wherever they could. ABB Trafosur succeeded in turning around a brown-field plant in the particularly difficult economic, political, and cultural climate of Andalusia. How was this achieved?

Undoubtedly a major force for change has been the chronic overcapacity and the ABB internal race for survival as well as the merciless pressure of the BA on its plants. However, external pressure constitutes a necessary but not sufficient condition of change (see Köhler and Schmierl 1992). Workforce and management of the old Cenemesa plant were, before the ABB takeover, ready to commit "collective suicide" despite the constant threat of bankruptcy. Two sets of factors seem to have been of particular importance in the case of ABB Trafosur. First, the new general manager succeeded in forming the six department heads into a cohesively acting group. This collective agent of change was embedded in a strong network of support from the Spanish holding as well as the BA structure. Second, it seems as if five years of strong involvement of top management coupled with significant investments in hardware, software, and people have been able to establish personal authority of the top managers in the workforce, thus creating the minimum of trust and loyalty necessary to modernize the company. In the words of a worker whom we met at the entrance to the plant: "The Swedes are extremely hard-headed, but maybe it's good for us."

In the light of Max Weber's theory of personal and functional authority this sounds very much like a paradox: the elimination of personal dependencies and authority and the establishment of modern organizational structures, with impersonal routines and abstract industrial discipline, seems to require personal and to a certain extent, charismatic authority. In the conflict prone and to some extent precapitalist cultural settings present in Andalusia personal authority seems to be crucial in building up a minimum of trust, initiative, and general support required to run a modern business in times of globalization.[9]

The question of "surpassing without catching up," on alternative paths of development for industrial latecomers relative to the forces and mechanisms of change are of general importance, but the answers available at this point are empirically and theoretically insufficient. More research on catch-up plants and their modernization paths is necessary. The findings will be of importance for industrial latecomers to the capitalist world market and for

---

[9] This seems to be true also for modern bureaucratic organizations that enter a phase of deep crisis and restructuring like those in East Germany after reunification. East German scholars observe a "reentry" of personal authority as a precondition to reestablish impersonal organizational routines.

the transformation of Eastern European, formerly socialist economies. It is hoped that they will shed new light on the ongoing post-Taylorist restructuring in highly developed capitalist economies, which can only be adequately understood in light of the factors differentiating it from previous stages of development.

6 ABB in Australia
Local Autonomy versus Globalization

Mark Bray and Russell D. Lansbury

Within the international activities of Asea Brown Boveri (ABB), the Australian operations are small. Within the Power Transformers business area (BA), the Australian operation is also one of the smallest. However, the Australian transformer plant is of considerable importance within the Asia–Pacific region because of the technical support it has provided to the new plants being established in countries such as China and Thailand and because it is the only regular source of profit among the mostly cash-absorbing subsidiaries.

The Australian transformer plant, which is the subject of this chapter, is located at Moorebank in the outer suburbs of Sydney. It was previously owned by Westinghouse and was acquired by ABB in 1991. In 1995 it employed around 180 persons, although a high voltage switchgear plant, which occupies the same location, employed an additional 65 employees. Like the Guelph plant in Canada (see Chapter 7 this volume), the Moorebank plant was operated in a run-down state by Westinghouse during the 1980s and has spent the 1990s trying to catch up with the performance standards set by ABB. Confronted by a stagnant, if not declining, local market, the Australian operation has also faced critical questions concerning its future viability.

The account of efforts at the Moorebank plant to overcome their difficult situation demonstrates the tensions that can arise between ABB's global strategies for change and local management philosophies and local institutional constraints. Local management, especially the plant's general manager from 1994–1996, was not convinced that the "ABB approach" was effective and it consequently sought greater autonomy to pursue its own model of business operation. In particular, the general manager questioned the appropriateness of the "Seven-Ups program" as a measure of performance and refused to introduce initiatives such as Six Sigma, preferring to assess the plant's success by reference to its profitability. Under his regime, the plant saw many improvements. An improving product market resulted in increased volumes and higher revenues. Employment levels were reduced, a more cooperative approach replaced labor-management conflict characterized by a major industrial dispute in 1993, while management has improved the planning and coordination of the production process. All of these factors contributed to a return to profit after a decade of poor financial performance, but the turnaround was arduous and the long-term success of the venture remains uncertain. There was also a residue of "political" uneasiness between the plant and the BA management.

The Socioeconomic Environment and Product Market in Australia

Australia has long been regarded as a "lucky country" (Horne 1964). By the beginning of the twentieth century, its abundant natural resources provided a standard of living second to none. In subsequent decades a national development strategy based on tariff protection of the domestic manufacturing industry, accurately described by Castles (1988) as "domestic defense," saw considerable industrial development, especially after World War II. At the same time, the working population was protected by a compulsory arbitration system that established and enforced minimum employment standards, while those outside its coverage enjoyed the protection of an effective (if limited) welfare state.

Australia's national economic prosperity began to wane during the 1970s, when international recession saw the emergence of stubbornly high unemployment, but it was the decline of international commodity prices in the face of further economic recession during the 1980s that created the sense of economic crisis necessary to produce fundamental institutional change. The Labor federal government in office from 1983–1996 oversaw the deregulation of many domestic industries, a new emphasis in the public sector on efficiency and managerialism, the end of protection, and an opening of the economy to international competition (Bell 1993).

The same government's close relationship with the union movement, referred to as "the Accord," saw significant change in labor laws and industrial relations (Bray 1994; Dabscheck 1995). At first, the focus was at a national level, in which a newly cooperative union movement worked with the government and the arbitration tribunals in a centralized incomes policy to restrain wage increases, reduce industrial conflict, and increase employment levels. After 1986, the Accord continued to produce union cooperation, but its focus moved increasingly toward negotiating productivity improvements at an industry and then an enterprise level. This decentralization and the declining influence of the tribunals culminated in a system of "enterprise bargaining" after 1991.

These national trends provide a context in which the development of the power transformer industry and the imperatives for change at the ABB Moorebank plant can be understood. The power generation industry in Australia, which represents the major market for power transformers, began on a very small scale in the late nineteenth century, but the industry grew rapidly after World War II as the domestic and industrial use of electrical power expanded (Prest 1963). Despite the end of the long postwar economic boom in the mid-1970s, the power industry continued to grow strongly as recently as the late 1970s and early 1980s as many new power stations were constructed in anticipation of a "resources boom." In response to this strong demand and, like the rest of Australian manufacturing, enjoying significant tariff protection from overseas competition, output in the power transformer industry grew rapidly.

This era of high demand ended in the mid-1980s, as the "resources boom" proved illusory, economic recession set in, and the oversupply of power generation became evident. Consequently, by the early 1990s, the power transformer market had contracted severely; there were few large power plants being constructed and the annual capacity for transformers appeared to have shrunk to around 3000 MVA. In this limited market, there were three main domestic manufacturers. ABB at Moorebank was the largest operation with around 60 percent of the market. Wilson Electric, located in Glen Waverley (Victoria) and the only Australian owned company, and General Electric Company–Alsthom (GEC-Alsthom), the Australian branch of the British-French multinational located in Brisbane, had similar capacities and accounted for broadly similar market shares. These three companies faced increasingly strong competitive pressures. On the one hand, governments more and more expected the power industry to perform efficiently and, in some cases, privatized previously state-owned power generation and distribution authorities. In this way, the customers of transformer manufacturers forced, through the tender process, reductions in costs. On the other hand, in line with broader public policy trends, tariff protection to the industry was reduced in the late-1980s and early 1990s (Bell 1993). From a high of around 25 percent in the late 1970s, the effective level of protection was to be reduced to 5 percent as of July 1996.

A Brief History of the Moorebank Plant

The ABB Moorebank site has a long and varied history of ownership. It was established after the Second World War by an Australian, William Tyree, who was a pioneer in the transformer industry. Tyree built the first 50-KVA unit for the Sydney Metropolitan Sewerage and Draining Board (as it was then known) in 1946, and so began a long career in the industry. From his initial training as a toolmaker, Tyree acquired a strong interest and expertise in the techniques of manufacturing transformers. Tyree also proved to be an astute businessman, who took advantage of the market growth, which flowed from industrial development and government protection. Starting with a small workshop in the outer suburbs of Sydney, Tyree built up a multi-million dollar business during the two decades following the Second World War. He later established another smaller plant in Perth, Western Australia.

In 1968, Tyree sold 68 percent of the shares in his company to the American-owned Westinghouse Corporation, which was then seeking to acquire interests around the world. The company became known as Tyree-Westinghouse, and Tyree retained the position of managing director. The combination of increased investment capital from Westinghouse with Tyree's local knowledge and expertise ensured that the company maintained its dominance of the Australian market. During the 1970s, Tyree expanded the company and branched into new fields, including some overseas markets. However, in 1980, Tyree retired from the company. In 1982, he recruited several key personnel from Tyree-Westinghouse and established a successful new venture making distribution transformers, which took significant business away from that division of Tyree-Westinghouse.

During the early 1980s, Tyree-Westinghouse continued to operate profitably in the medium to large power transformer markets. The "resources boom" held demand high and the Moorebank plant produced transformers with the equivalent of 3500 MVAs per year. In 1989 ABB acquired Westinghouse's international transformer operations, but the Australian plant lay in limbo until ABB finally took full control at the beginning of 1991. By this stage, the Moorebank plant was no longer as profitable. In the view of management who had worked for Tyree-Westinghouse during this period, Westinghouse used the Australian operations as a "cash cow" for many years and failed to invest in new plant and equipment. Production volumes at Moorebank fell by up to 50 percent during the 1980s.

The Moorebank plant has long been heavily unionized. It traditionally operated as a "closed shop," whereby all production workers were required to join one of the unions with coverage of the site once they accepted a job. There were three unions with members on site. The largest was the Australian Workers Union (AWU), which covered approximately 40 percent of the workforce, drawn mainly from production workers who learned their skills on the job. The other two unions covered the balance of the workforce. The Australian Manufacturing Workers' Union (AMWU) covered 25 percent of the workforce, drawn mainly from the mechanical trades. The recently amalgamated Communications, Electrical, Electronic, Energy, Information, Postal, Plumbing and Allied Services Union (CEPU) covered the remaining 35 percent of the workforce, who were mainly from the electrical trades. The emphasis on the skilled trades reflected the strong craft-related nature of the work in the plant. Even the so-called semiskilled workers had a high degree of proficiency and were required to perform often technically complex tasks.

The industrial climate at the Moorebank plant was affected by the presence of two industrially militant craft unions and the relatively large number of skilled tradespersons on the site, which gave the workers considerable bargaining leverage. Both the AMWU and the CEPU regarded the Moorebank plant as providing a well-organized base for pursuing wage increases, which became the benchmarks for wage gains sought at other sites in the metal and engineering industries. The company was regarded as profitable, with a strong and well-protected market (at least until the mid-1980s) and the ability to pass on wage increases to their customers through higher prices. There was also an element of competition between the AMWU and AWU, as they both had potential coverage of the same workers. The tensions produced by these forces were mostly accommodated during the years before 1993, with no site-specific industrial disputes occurring between 1986 and 1993. The close attention given by the unions to the plant meant that it became part of some Accord initiatives, like the Heavy Engineering Plan and the introduction of multiskilling under the Structural Efficiency Principle. However, as discussed further on, this pattern of accommodation broke down dramatically in 1993.

Under its new ownership in 1991, the Moorebank plant became ABB Power Transformer Division, one of six divisions of ABB Power Transformers Limited in Australia. During the early 1990s, through mergers with other ABB operations, further organizational and name changes took place. In 1996, the division to which the Moorebank plant belonged became known as ABB Transmission and Distribution. Former managers from the Tyree-Westinghouse period held key positions in the new ABB organizations in both Australia and Asia. The general manager responsible for the plant during the period of study (i.e., 1994–1996) initially came to Moorebank as sales manager in 1979, when it was owned by Tyree-Westinghouse. He left the plant in 1980, and then in 1982 established a new business with the original founder, William Tyree, in competition with Tyree-Westinghouse. He then left Tyree and started a venture on his own before accepting an offer from ABB to return to Moorebank as general manager early in 1994.

Within the transformer division, the new local management praised several aspects of the ABB approach. Its preparedness to invest in new technologies at Moorebank was considered admirable (if long overdue), while its efforts to encourage Customer Focus, time-based management, and new purchasing and supply arrangements were applauded. The opportunities for managers to visit transformer plants in other countries and absorb technical and managerial lessons were also regarded positively. However, there was also criticism of the ABB style of operation in some quarters, which was regarded as unduly hierarchical and bureaucratic, despite the espoused philosophy, which emphasized local autonomy, fewer layers of management and more direct forms of communication. The matrix form of organization was regarded by some managers as confusing and contradictory, with different management philosophies emanating from the headquarters and the BA office. ABB was also seen to discourage entrepreneurship and favor administrators ahead of leaders and managers. Rather than providing guidance and inspiration to local managers who then had the autonomy to develop these new ideas as they saw fit, some perceived the BA to issue directives and expect compliance from local managers irrespective of local conditions or the consequences for local profitability.

The Moorebank plant enjoyed some market success in the years following the takeover by increasing its domestic market share from around 50 percent, at the time of acquisition, to 61 percent in 1994. However, the limited opportunities for expansion in the domestic market led some to argue that the company's future depended on entry into Asian markets. The view was reflected by Percy Barnevik on a visit to Australia in March 1995 when he stated that "Australia's low-cost skill base" was a major competitive advantage for "managing the big projects that underpin Asian development and coupling that with low Asian on-site costs." He went on to say that he expected "considerable growth within Australia, but the big challenge here is Asia!" (Gill, 1995). Apparently in line with these sentiments, ABB Power Transmission in Australia assumed responsibility in 1993 to supply technical support when a major production facility for transformers in Hefei in China was developed and the Moorebank plant negotiated a technology transfer agreement. This agreement continued through 1996, with the Australian plant training significant numbers of Chinese employees and receiving considerable royalty payments. A number of managers and technical staff also transferred to other new plants in the Asia–Pacific region. However, ambitions of exporting Australian transformers to Southeast Asian countries, like Malaysia and Indonesia, were not realized. After winning allocation rights within ABB to export to these countries in 1993, new barriers to imports were erected in those countries to encourage local industry, while intense competition from Chinese and Korean companies and other factors made these export markets less desirable than anticipated. By 1995, the main focus of the Australian plant returned to the Australian domestic market.

Changes in Production Management and Work Organization

In line with the general manager's business philosophy, management strategy at the Moorebank plant in 1994–1996 emphasized changing management practices and planning. The aim was to better integrate the activities of various functional managers (e.g., sales, design, manufacture) and focus their attention on the impact of their areas on the company's "bottom line" (i.e., profit). However, as Australia is essentially a low-volume market, the plant continued to tender for a wide range of projects. The general manager argued, nevertheless, that he was attempting to be more selective and actively pursuing those contracts that were most likely to be profitable. Better planning in the supply of raw materials and components was also sought in order to avoid inefficiencies and ensure more intensive utilization of equipment and labor.

Although there was an increase in employment levels at Moorebank in 1985–86, owing to a short-lived boom in the construction of new power stations, there was a steady decline in the number of employees thereafter. After a small increase in 1994, further reductions in employment levels followed in 1995, mainly by attrition but also involving some voluntary redundancies. The main employee reductions from 1990–94 were among production workers, although more recently the number of office personnel and other white collar employees has been reduced.

Some new technology was introduced as a result of ABB's injection of $AUS 4 million into the plant. New Vapor phase (drying) equipment, mechanical handling equipment, a vertical winding machine, and improved drawing facilities brought the Moorebank's technological base closer to that of other ABB plants—the drying equipment in particular significantly reduced the time needed to produce each transformer. This investment was welcomed by local management, especially after years of neglect by Westinghouse, as tangible evidence that ABB was interested in ensuring the viability of the plant. Indeed, local management considered that new investment was essential if the plant was to operate from a sound technological and financial base that would enable it to become internationally competitive. Only then could they explore the more sophisticated innovations embodied in ABB's corporate agenda. Plans were laid, for example, to reduce the number of supervisory personnel and to flatten the management hierarchy between the shop floor and senior management. Previous attempts to foster small group activities among workers, however, were abandoned in favor of providing individual workers with more skills, which enabled them to work independently and to carry out a wider range of tasks. A consultant was engaged to plan an upgrade of supervisory skills, while it is intended that the workers will be more self-managing in the future. It is also envisaged that in the future workers will be given greater access to information and be involved in long-term planning, as currently practiced in some of the Nordic ABB plants, such as Vaasa in Finland.

Changes in Labor-Management Relations

As noted previously, the Moorebank plant was strongly unionized prior to its acquisition by ABB and was regarded as a "wage leader" by unions in the metal industry. Management generally acceded to wage demands, which they recouped through charging higher prices. By the early 1990s, however, economic difficulties in the industry eroded the unions' bargaining power. Furthermore, the introduction of enterprise bargaining meant that the unions were less able to use the Moorebank plant as a platform for industrywide wage campaigns. In the first round of enterprise agreements, in 1992, the unions gained a uniform 4.5 percent wage increase for all employees.

In the second round, in 1993, the unions sought a further 6 percent increase but this was opposed by management. Negotiations were long, relations soured, and a seven-day strike occurred. An agreement was eventually achieved that involved a general 3 percent wage increase with a further 3 percent linked to productivity improvements. The workers reluctantly agreed to targets set by management for improvements in labor utilization, production rework, and throughput time, in order to achieve the additional 3 percent wage increase. The agreement also specified that employees could be required to assist with "transfer of technology training" to other companies in the ABB group (which was a reference to cooperation between Moorebank and the Hefei plant in China).

The industrial stoppage in 1993 proved to be a turning point in labor-management relations at Moorebank. In the context of a weak product market and with government encouraging a link between wage increases and productivity improvements, Moorebank management took a hard line in negotiations with the unions. As part of the settlement of the dispute, the Workplace Consultative Committee was given a broader role within the plant.

The third enterprise agreement was concluded in September 1995 without any stoppages of work. It continued the emphasis on meeting productivity targets but also involved agreement by the unions to a program of voluntary retrenchments in order to ensure the future viability of the plant. The agreement was negotiated by the new general manager in the context of difficult economic conditions and a new group of union representatives who were focused on trying to limit job losses rather than seek wage increases. Hence, the bargaining power was now with management rather than the workforce as it had been in the 1980s.

Performance in Perspective

Production Management

Comparisons of performance within the Power Transformers BA of ABB are made by reference to a number of variables. As noted in previous chapters, these are known within ABB as Seven-Ups and include measures of quality, efficiency, production volume, supply management, customer relations, customer satisfaction, and an overall rating. These measures provide the BA management with a means of comparing the performance of different plants. They are also an important component of ABB's Customer Focus program and serve to direct the attention of management and the workforce to criteria against which their achievements are judged. Two of the most important performance measures, which form part of ABB's Customer Focus program, are total throughput time (TTPT) and manufacturing throughput time, which is known simply as TPT within ABB.

In terms of TPT for all transformer plants in 1993, it is apparent that Moorebank recorded one of the poorest performance levels. However, when TTPT was compared, Moorebank fared considerably better and was ranked in the middle range. This would seem to indicate that a major weakness in the Moorebank plant, at that time, related to its manufacturing process. On another international comparison, of average cost per employee in 1994, Moorebank was also in the middle range, but better than average for the BA overall.

Measures taken for the period from 1990 to early 1995 on ABB's Seven-Ups show a gradual improvement at Moorebank, albeit from a rather low starting point when ABB acquired the plant. TPT improved dramatically in the early 1990s, owing in no small part to the introduction of a new vacuum drier, and then stabilized before more significant improvements in 1995 and 1996. TTPT followed a similar trend. Another measure of efficiency, known as Abacus productivity (based on an internal accounting method), compares the ratio of value-added to employee expenses. This actually declined from 1992–1994, but showed strong improvement during the second half of 1995.

Test failure rates improved significantly from 30 percent in 1990 to around 4 percent at the end of 1994 (thus reducing the cost of reworking transformers), but rose again in 1995. The number of defects reported per month also improved from 50 in 1990 to 17 in 1994, after rising as high as 85 in 1992. This improvement in performance was sustained during 1995 but was still short of the target of zero defects.

The target of on-time deliveries improved dramatically from 30 percent in 1992 to 100 percent after July 1994. There was a steady improvement in inventory performance, as measured by the ratio of inventory to revenue, during 1995, with the target of less than 20 percent being reached in the second half of the year. The number of jobs released to the floor, which reflected the volume of orders received, declined from 15 in 1991 to less than 8 in 1994.

The amount expended on training reached a peak in 1993, which reflected the emphasis placed on quality improvement programs, in the effort to gain the Australian Quality Award that year (see next section). However, training expenditure subsequently fell steadily. A new training regime was introduced in 1996 in an effort to redress the neglect of training since the granting of the quality award. Under the new scheme, each department nominated a "trainer" who was attached to a "mentor," the latter being a supervisor or professional employee. It became the trainer's responsibility to ensure that all employees in his department (usually 6–8 persons) had the skills and knowledge of procedures to effectively perform their duties and each employee was guaranteed at least two hours of training per month.

Quality

In 1993, ABB Power Transmission Proprietary Limited (of which power transformers was a part) won the Australian Quality Award. The company was widely praised in the business press for having been transformed since ABB took over from Tyree-Westinghouse in 1989 (Gill 1995). Among the results quoted for the period 1989–93 were the following: 50 percent improvement in TPT for power transformers, 20 percent decline in warranty costs, a reduction in work cycle times from 75 to 41 hours, and an increase in on-time deliveries on the high voltage switch gear division from 5 to 95 percent.

The Australian Quality Award (AQA) commenced in 1989 and was similar to the Malcolm Baldrige National Quality Award in the United States and the European Quality Award. There are seven criteria for the AQA, which provided a framework for an organization to follow. The criteria are leadership, policy, and planning; information and analysis; the management of people; customer focus; quality of process, product, and people; and organizational performance. It was argued that the criteria are deliberately nonprescriptive and did not require any particular approach or structures. Rather, the AQA required that the approach and structures that were in place were appropriate to the goals of the organization and consistent with the "quality approach" to management. Critics of the award, however, argued that emphasis was placed on having procedures in place rather than on measuring an organization's quality outcomes (Saunders, 1995).

Winning the AQA award remained a rather controversial issue at Moorebank, with several managers voicing similar criticisms to those leveled at the AQAs generally. There was a view that the former managing director of ABB Power Transmission placed a higher priority on winning the award than on other more important issues that would have contributed more effectively to the business, and that the overall performance of the Moorebank plant was less than it could have been if greater attention had been devoted to improving productivity during the early 1990s. In this way, the AQA was seen as having created an unfortunate diversion, which undermined the credibility of managerial efforts to improve the overall performance of the plant.

It was also claimed that the emphasis on quality *processes* masked what were mostly very ordinary quality *outcomes*. For example, the results identified in the press need to be examined in the light of a rather low performance base of the plant when ABB took over from Tyree-Westinghouse. Furthermore, despite the high TQM score reported for ABB Power Transmission overall in 1993, customers continued to experience quality problems with the plant's products and were skeptical of Moorebank's winning the award (even to the extent of requesting their own independent audit of quality). Internal ABB measures taken over the period 1990–1993, including test failure rates, the number of quality problem reports, and the percentage of units requiring rework (discussed in the previous section), demonstrated that ABB Power Transmission overall was not meeting targets and the Moorebank plant was still exhibiting below average performance by international comparisons. An internal report showed that there were large gaps between the performance of the Moorebank plant and the maximum possible scores, particularly as regards the quality of process, product, and service. It also highlighted problems with quality assurance inspection and the need for higher levels of training in the quality area.

Between 1993 and 1996, the Moorebank plant's TQM aggregate score declined, but it still remained high and was close to target. Furthermore, on output measures, such as test failure rates and the number of defects per month, Moorebank generally performed well. However, there was a reluctance on the part of the general manager (1994–96) to become more involved in programs such as Six Sigma. While the goal of continuous improvement was accepted as admirable, it was argued by the general manager that a preoccupation with these types of measures could deflect attention from the central purpose of running a profitable business. This continued to be one of the sources of tension between the former general manager and the BA management.

Conclusions and Future Prospects

The Australian case has focused on the issue of local autonomy in the context of global strategies developed by ABB. During the three years from 1994–1996, Moorebank arrested the decline in its performance and showed a steady improvement in terms of profitability. This was achieved by the general manager (1994–96), who drew on aspects of ABB's global resources and ideas, while simultaneously pursuing a rather independent approach. A range of factors influenced the approach taken by management at Moorebank in those years and they will determine whether a similar strategy can be maintained in the future. These factors were both external and internal to the plant.

The external factors mostly provided the imperative for change in plant operations and constrained the range of change strategies available to the parties within the Moorebank plant. For example, significant declines in the level of tariff protection along with slow growth and efficiency reforms in the power generation industry brought stronger competitive pressures to bear on the Moorebank plant. Changes in the broader national industrial relations system brought expectations and opportunities for reform within the plant, although these were not always realized. Finally, the place of the Moorebank plant within its parent organization had ambiguous effects. The injection of capital that followed ABB's purchase of the plant from Westinghouse was welcomed by local management, but the obvious interplant comparisons made within ABB carried (if only implicitly) threats that made internal reform even more urgent. The promotion by ABB's BA management of programs such as Customer Focus and Six Sigma embodied expectations about how internal reform should proceed—expectations that the general manager was inclined to reject.

The internal factors affecting the Moorebank plant included its organizational structures; its particular industrial relations history; and the personalities and philosophies of its management, workers, and union delegates. The general manager in charge of the plant over the period played an especially important role. As noted earlier, he had spent a part of his early career at Moorebank during the Tyree-Westinghouse period but had left to pursue his own business interests. When he returned to Moorebank as general manager in 1994, he was critical of elements of the ABB approach but recognized that their investment and expertise were essential to the long-term viability of the plant. Rather than complying with what he regarded as dictates from the BA office, he concentrated on what he saw as the management changes needed to restore the plant's profitability. In taking a more independent approach, the former general manager emphasized the fact that he did not seek or expect to have a long-term career with ABB. Indeed, at the end of 1996, the general manager left ABB to pursue his own business interests. It is possible that his successor may have a different view of the importance of seeking to preserve local autonomy.

Looking to the future, it would appear that many of the factors that fostered autonomy at Moorebank are likely to be of declining significance compared with tendencies toward globalization. The new general manager may be more strongly influenced by philosophies espoused by ABB. The performance of the Moorebank plant will continue to be closely monitored by the BA management. As the Australian market for power transformers becomes more difficult, Moorebank will be increasingly under pressure to expand into Asia and other regions. Conversely, the Moorebank plant may have to compete with other ABB transformer plants for the Australian market. Hence, the emphasis in Australia may also become more global and less local in the future.

7 ABB in Canada
Local Hero versus Lean Learner

*Jacques Bélanger, Anthony Giles,
and Jean-Noël Grenier*

Asea Brown Boveri operates two power transformer plants in Canada, one in Varennes in the province of Quebec, the other in Guelph in the province of Ontario. The experiences of the two plants during the first half of the 1990s are a remarkable study in contrasts. On the one hand, ABB Guelph, one of the catch-up plants in the Power Transformers business area (BA), underwent a dramatic and painful transition: employment dropped from over 700 employees in the late 1980s to just 300 by 1994; the organizational structure was thoroughly redesigned and the managerial ranks pruned; new information systems, performance measures, and production technologies were introduced; and the management of employment relations was transformed. On the other hand, up until the mid-1990s, ABB Varennes, which along with the Ludvika and Bad Honnef plants, forms part of the "old ASEA core" of ABB power transformer plants, was a veritable oasis of tranquility.

This chapter takes up a double challenge: first, as do the other case studies in this volume, it seeks to explore global-national linkages, particularly the ways in which each of the two plants has sought to adapt global-level strategies to local conditions and traditions; and, second, it examines the differences between production sites located in a single national context, thus adding a level of complexity to the understanding of ABB's policy of "being local worldwide."

In the first section of the chapter, the national context of the Canadian plants is briefly outlined. The next two sections examine ABB Guelph and ABB Varennes respectively, including their recent history, organizational characteristics, local market and role within the BA, as well as a more detailed exploration of the way each responded to the corporate rationalization strategy pursued by ABB in three areas: the overall production system, work organization, and the pattern of institutional regulation. Following the presentation of the two case studies, the fourth section compares the two plants and seeks to explain why they followed divergent paths. In the conclusion, we discuss recent developments and examine the local and global factors that are shaping their ongoing evolution.

Our methodological strategy relies on several complementary research techniques. Open and sustained collaboration on the part of the managers and union organizations in the two plants enabled us to gain an understanding of innovation in the production system. In each of the two plants, direct observation was carried out mainly in two production workshops, winding and active part assembly. In addition to the numerous informal interviews that were conducted throughout the research process, a series of semistructured interviews were granted by managers, workers, and union representatives. From 1994–1997, some 56 semistructured interviews were conducted at Varennes and 61 at Guelph. Both plants also made available a wide variety of documentation.

Much of the research on which the core of this chapter is based was completed by the end of 1994. We were allowed to follow up with further fieldwork and made updated observations and conducted more interviews in each plant in 1996–97. It is therefore possible to account for recent changes in these Canadian plants in the concluding section.

The National Context

Although they are located in different provinces, each of which has its own distinctive characteristics (including, for example, its own labor relations legislation and trade union culture), the plants under study are typical examples of the broader Canadian system of labor relations.[1] For present purposes, three characteristics of this system need to be underscored.

First, in comparison with many other countries, the structure of collective bargaining is highly decentralized, with the vast majority of collective agreements in the private sector being negotiated at the establishment or enterprise level. Thus, in the case of the two Canadian power transformer plants, there was until recently virtually no coordinated approach to labor relations, except as regards some policies applying to nonunionized employees. Each plant had its own internal system of labor relations negotiated at the local level.

The second characteristic of the wider system is the central role of the collective agreement. Canadian collective agreements are typically long and complex documents that focus on remuneration and the regulation of the internal labor market (Giles and Starkman 1995). Seniority regulates a whole range of issues associated with job assignments and movements within and

---

[1] For general treatments of Canadian industrial relations, see Drache and Glasbeek 1992; Verma and Chaykowski 1992; and Gunderson and Ponak 1995.

even outside the factory gates. The underlying logic is that, through seniority, as workers progress in the job hierarchy they acquire rights attached to their position in the job classification system. As we shall see later, this level of regulation can constitute a source of considerable conflict.

A third characteristic of labor relations in Canada is the traditional arms-length nature of union-management relations. Outside of some specific areas, such as occupational health and safety and employment adjustment, there has historically been little interest demonstrated either by Canadian unions or employers in developing plant- or enterprise-level institutions devoted to participation or comanagement.

These three features of the labor relations system are part and parcel of the dominant North American version of the Fordist production model, a model that rested on a postwar compromise between employers and unions, underwritten by the state. This compromise constituted a tradeoff in which workers won relatively high wages and detailed regulation of the internal labor market, whereas management ensured that its right to manage production was enshrined in the collective agreement (Bélanger 1994, 61–66; Katz 1985). As in many other countries, this traditional model has come under intense pressure since the late 1970s. Thus, ABB's efforts to restructure production relations are consonant with a wider shift in North America, a shift that entails a search by employers for more flexibility and worker involvement in production.

From an international perspective, the interesting question is how ABB's global strategies intersect with the traditional North American model of work organization and labor-management relations. Moreover, as we shall see, there is a further level of complexity arising from more strictly local factors. Although ABB Varennes and ABB Guelph may be twins sharing the same corporate parents—the Power Transformer BA and ABB Canada— each is the product of its local environment and its own autonomous pattern of development.

ABB Guelph: The Lean Learner

The Guelph power transformer plant was built in the early 1950s by General Electric (GE). By the early 1980s, GE appeared to be losing interest in the plant, investing little and using it as a "cash cow" to fund its other operations. Then, beginning in 1986, a series of ownership changes occurred that were to fundamentally transform the plant. First, in 1986, Westinghouse and GE formed a joint venture that included the Guelph plant and a Westinghouse plant in Hamilton, Ontario. Shortly thereafter, Westinghouse assumed sole ownership of the plants, only to sell them to ABB in 1989. In early 1990, ABB closed the Hamilton plant and transferred the production of small power transformers to Guelph.

Along with the plant in Varennes, the Guelph plant thus became part of the Power Transformer Division of ABB Canada. Until 1994, the Guelph and Varennes plants were operated independently, each being run by its own general manager. However, in 1994 the managerial structure was reorganized and a single manager was put in charge of both plants.

Products, Markets, and Organizational Structure

By 1994, ABB Guelph was producing a wide range of products, including auto, generator, and substation transformers; high-voltage direct current (HVDC) transformers; phase shifters; static var compensators; and furnace transformers. It was also active in the installation and repair market.

ABB Guelph's formal market mandate encompassed Canada's five westernmost provinces, but in practice it was also serving the Atlantic provinces (which were part of Varennes' market) because Varennes had its hands full with local orders. Approximately 80 percent of ABB Guelph's total production was destined for public utilities (the most important being Hydro Ontario, the provincial power utility); 10 percent was small power transformers for industrial customers; and another 10 percent was exported to the United States.

Although it had sought to develop special links with its most important customer, Hydro Ontario, the Guelph plant faced a fiercely competitive market in the early 1990s. Besides two other companies manufacturing power transformers in Canada, foreign competition had been on the rise in recent years. Indeed, shortly after the purchase of the plant by ABB, the market for power transformers outside Quebec plunged into a deep recession affecting mostly medium and large power transformers. Demand for smaller power transformers, however, was increasing and was beginning to account for a growing share of production. In view of the downturn in the market, annual sales revenues and the number of transformers produced had been dropping since the early 1990s.

The organizational structure of ABB Guelph was modified several times during the early 1990s. As of late 1994, the plant was organized into three "focused factories" and eight other departments. Each of the focused factories brought together all of the employees involved in the design and manufacturing of a particular product range. Thus each of the focused factories included engineers, draftsmen, and production workers.

As of June 1994, ABB Guelph employed a total of 313 people. Of this total, 198 were hourly-paid employees and 115 were salaried employees. Three groups of employees were unionized. The hourly-paid production employees, who had been unionized since the 1950s, belonged to Local 541 of the National Automobile, Aerospace and Agricultural Implement Workers of Canada (known as the CAW). The draftsmen belonged to a branch of the

International Federation of Professional and Technical Engineers. They also first unionized in the 1950s. Unionization of the professional engineers occurred after ABB purchased the plant; they formed a separate branch of the same union as the draftsmen.

Production Management

Between 1990 and 1994, the system of production management at ABB Guelph was almost completely transformed. In this section we discuss that transformation in terms of four key steps: the introduction of time-based management (TBM); organizational redesign; initiatives undertaken in the area of total quality management (TQM); and the implementation of a new supply management system. TBM, TQM, and supply management are, of course, integral parts of the Customer Focus program; the organizational redesign was seen as a means of structuring activities in line with these other goals.

When ABB first took over the Guelph plant, a team of global managers was brought in to assess the state of the organization. They were shocked by the poor quality of the facilities, the confusion that reigned on the shop floor, and the huge production backlog. The new general manager's first decision was to shut down for a three-week period in order to clean up and upgrade equipment. Customers were notified of the likely delivery dates of their orders and a new master schedule was drawn up. The plant was repainted, work areas cleaned up, and machinery brought up to the standard of other ABB plants around the world.

In addition to the general clean-up and upgrading of equipment, the new management quickly introduced time-based management. The specific objectives were to reduce cycle times, over a two-year period, to the BA standard and to increase productivity by 40 percent. To this end, capacity measurements were made and the various workshops were rebalanced to overcome bottleneck problems. Over time, the TBM process developed into a sophisticated mapping of the entire design and production cycle. Aided by the adoption of a new computerized production planning system in 1992, a detailed series of "checkpoints" was established so as to measure and control the flow of production from design to delivery. Rationalization efforts then came to focus on shortening the production sequence, including efforts to outsource as many of the subassembly operations as possible and to restructure relations with suppliers. In short, then, ABB Guelph's technical production system was completely revamped by the pursuit of TBM goals.

Once TBM had been implemented, a more ambitious program of organizational change was launched, involving a combination of "focused factories" and "contract teams." Focused factories were meant to "break down the walls" between engineering, production, purchasing, and other functions. Their introduction entailed a considerable reorganization of the production management hierarchy. The multifunctional contract teams cutting across the focused factories and the service groups were established to coordinate the diverse activities involved in each individual customer order. These were meant to focus efforts on customer orders, facilitate overall planning, and coordinate the activities of the focused factories.

However, the results of this organizational change were mixed. On the one hand, coordination and communication within individual focused factories improved. Managers and unit leaders (though not necessarily shop floor workers) accepted the performance targets derived from the Customer Focus program. Indeed, shop floor managers frequently referred to "their" metrics (i.e., their unit's performance measures, which are displayed prominently throughout the plant). On the other hand, despite the existence of contract teams, the addition of the position of "master scheduler" to coordinate activities across focused factories, and weekly meetings of the focused factory managers, complaints about the lack of coordination were common.

The focused factory structure, although removing some of the traditional, functionally defined walls, erected others, thus leading each unit to focus on its own performance rather than on the efficiency of the organization as a whole. More generally, in some ways the organization redesign was not carried through to its logical conclusion. As one manager told us, focused factories "had the name and structure, but still did things the old ways." For example, employees still frequently referred to their location in the organization in terms of traditional relationships; indeed, as late as 1994, some of the signs in the building still reflected old titles and traditional departmental divisions. Finally, employees below the managerial and supervisory levels viewed the reorganization as a game of musical chairs played by management, a game that did not have a real impact on their work.

At around the time of the organizational restructuring, Guelph management introduced the idea of total quality management. At the design end of the operation, the continuous improvement and TQM philosophy translated into the establishment of checklists to reduce design errors. At the shop floor level, it meant the elimination of buffer stocks and the introduction of *kanban* methods to establish an internal customer logic between production stages and units of the focus factories. Moreover, work methods were altered to eliminate non-value-added work and the layout of the shop was transformed in a more functional sequence. This was done with some limited participation of the workforce, who were encouraged to submit suggestions to solve quality problems or improve tools and methods.

In general, however, TQM did not have nearly the same impact as TBM and seems to have been largely restricted to the managerial level. In fact, management encountered some difficulty in changing the approach of key actors whose logic was still marked by the "command and obey" tradition—

inherited from the GE era—in which their authority was based on status and their responsibilities clearly limited to areas under their direct control. Nevertheless, some TQM and continuous improvement efforts were undertaken at lower levels, at the initiative of the unit leaders, mostly to resolve quality problems and rationalize the production process to cut throughput time.

Supply management became the focus of rationalization efforts in 1993. Although steps had already been taken to reduce material inventory levels and to outsource the production of some components, the new strategy sought to reinforce the other rationalization efforts and further reduce costs. The supply management strategy was based on three central elements: shifting part of the costs of inventory to suppliers through a policy of paying for materials when they were used in production rather than when they arrived at the plant; a major reduction in the number of suppliers; and increased pressure on suppliers to meet high quality standards and tight delivery dates.

In sum, then, ABB Guelph's efforts to rationalize the production system accorded closely with the BA's strategy: TBM, TQM, and supply management policies were all directed principally toward reducing lead time, improving quality, and eliminating processes that did not add value to the production chain.

Work Organization

The most positive and durable impact of ABB management on the shop floor involved the upgrading of equipment and the elimination of strenuous work methods. In the winding area, for example, the installation of cylinders on the winding lathes was made easier and less strenuous by replacing horizontal lathes with vertical lathes and by the introduction of overhead cranes. In the insulation shop, machinery was reorganized and the layout of the shop transformed to reduce walking distances and to locate the machines in a more logical way. In the active parts assembly unit, new adjustable platforms were installed to eliminate the need to build scaffolding around the transformers prior to assembly, an operation that used to take up to two weeks.

While some changes increased the number of tasks, most were welcomed by the workforce. Work was seen as less physically demanding and as improving in quality by simplifying methods. If anything, the new tools reduced physical strain while the fact that production was based on customized individual units allowed workers to retain an appreciable degree of control over the pace of work and the sequence of operations. Management recognized the importance of tacit knowledge and so its efforts concentrated on gaining better control over uncertainties by monitoring the linkages between stages in the production process. The importance of practical knowledge can best be demonstrated through the issue of flexibility and job rotation.

In line with its overall rationalization strategy, management at the Guelph plant pursued a policy of increasing functional flexibility through a simplification of the job classification system and a policy of encouraging cross-training and job rotation. The reduction in job classifications was carried out partly through the outright elimination of some job classes through outsourcing, and partly through the merging of previously separate classifications. On the surface, the results were impressive: the overall number of job classifications fell from over 100 in 1989 to 72 in 1992, and then to less than 30 by 1994.

Nevertheless, the merging of classifications did not translate into uniform flexibility across the plant. Rather, flexibility was left to the discretion of the various unit leaders who engaged in a form of shop floor bargaining with the workers. In fact, the more skilled workers were able to resist job rotation by virtue of their tacit knowledge of the work process and the lack of similar skills among the less qualified workers. In the winding and insulation unit, for instance, even though coil finishers and coil winders were put under the same job classification, the division of labor between the two groups remained relatively unchanged, not least because of the unit leader's inability to assign coil finishers to training in winding. In the insulation section, however, the relative simplicity of the tasks allowed workers to rotate through all of the jobs by giving them responsibility for a complete order. But here also, skills and tacit knowledge came into play. Cylinder makers were able to resist flexibility by refusing to train others in their jobs, thereby protecting their position within the unit.

The third way in which work organization changed under ABB concerns supervision and control. One of ABB's first moves after buying the Guelph plant was to increase the ranks of shop floor supervisors, primarily to reassert control over production. Subsequently, supervisors were renamed "unit leaders," reflecting a shift in their focus away from the execution of work and toward monitoring work flow and ensuring that cycle time targets were met. This change was reinforced by the introduction of a new pay system that linked the unit leaders' pay to their "metrics."

The supervision and control of work was also altered by the technical dimensions of the rationalization drive. In particular, the *kanban* methods and the corresponding one-job rule of organizing the flow of materials and parts through the shop and between units had implications for shop floor management. Since workers only received work orders one at a time, the unit leader gained greater visual control of the progress of an order. This was complemented by the introduction of staging areas throughout the shop where all parts and material required for the next stage of the production process were put into "kits." Although workers retained considerable autonomy over the actual execution of tasks, a more rigorous system of work flow monitoring and control was conjoined with increased flexibility and a simplification and standardization of work.

Institutional Regulation

Production workers, considered by management to be the more militant group in the plant, were also those most affected by the downturn in the market and the rationalization of work. A product of the autocratic management style under GE, the union drew a clear distinction between its role and the rights and responsibilities of plant management. In this context, it is not surprising that the changes in the production system and in the organization of work shook the traditional pattern of institutional regulation.

One indication of the change was a significant shift in union strategy. Traditionally, the union used to load the grievance procedure prior to each round of negotiations and then used these grievances as bargaining chips to introduce changes in the collective agreement. However, more recently, the union abandoned this tactic, a clear reflection that it is on the defensive in a context of job insecurity. Moreover, in the past, bargaining centered on wages and the governance of the internal job progression structure, most movement being upward in the job hierarchy. After ABB took over the plant, however, most grievances concerned bumping rights[2] and other job security issues related to the integrity of the internal labor market.

As regards the reduction in the number of job classifications, the union sought to negotiate special arrangements to recognize seniority under the previous classification scheme in order to protect bumping rights. This, of course, was consistent with the shift of concern by union members from internal mobility and upward progression toward employment security, which depended, first, on accumulated seniority within a job classification and, second, on plantwide mobility through the accumulation of job-specific skills.

The management drive for more functional and numerical flexibility also posed a challenge to the value of the collective agreement as a framework for ensuring some measure of employment security. While the agreement required a minimum of 8 weeks' notice and allowed bumping rights for layoffs of more than 3 weeks, it also permitted exceptions. Faced with a significant decline in activity, management began to rely on these escape clauses to gain a freer hand in varying the size of the workforce. For example, layoffs of less than 3 weeks (which required only 1 week's notice and did not allow the exercise of bumping rights) came to be used frequently to adjust the size of the workforce. Furthermore, management did not hesitate to cancel these layoffs or to recall workers for short periods (less than 2 weeks) in response to production requirements. The use of the collective agreement in this way af-

[2] The group that was hardest hit were hourly-paid employees: the number of hourly-paid direct workers declined from nearly 500 to around 150, while the number of hourly-paid indirect employees dropped from around 100 to approximately 25. Salaried employees, by contrast, were somewhat better sheltered from decline; indeed, their numbers actually increased through to 1991 to just under 200, before declining slowly to just over 100 in late 1994.

fected morale on the shop floor, making workers feel as if they were effectively on "permanent layoff notice."

The vast majority of changes in the production system and work organization were carried out with little or no real involvement on the part of the union or its members. Part of the explanation is undoubtedly the weak bargaining position of the workforce in a context of reduced activity, as well as its traditional reluctance to become implicated in "management." It is also the case, however, that ABB Guelph management displayed little interest in working with the union, or indeed with nonmanagerial employees in general. The one experiment with "consultation," involving regular meetings of work groups, focused factories and all employees, was quickly abandoned, apparently because these meetings became occasions to criticize management policy. In short, by late 1994, any semblance of a workable social compromise between management and employees had all but disappeared, leaving a striking contrast between a modernized, efficient production system and a hostile and insecure labor force.

Performance

How, then, did all of these changes at ABB Guelph affect the plant's performance? In this section, we look briefly at a number of performance measures and assess the impact of the rationalization strategy.

In terms of cycle time, Guelph's progress since the early 1990s was astonishing. Total throughput time (TTPT), for all classes of transformers, fell from high on the BA's index in 1991 to good in 1994. This decrease applied equally to the production of small transformers and medium and large transformers. The trend in manufacturing throughput time (TPT) was also positive. In addition, the on-time delivery rate rose from low in 1990 to high in 1994. Clearly, then, TBM had a profound impact on efficiency, both in design and in manufacturing. Furthermore, the improvement in efficiency did not seem to involve a sacrifice of quality. Indeed, the rate of test failures was more than halved between 1990 and mid-1994; and the number of nonconformity reports (NCRs) per month declined over the same period.

Although efficiency and quality rose sharply, statistics on the plant's activity level paint a more somber picture. For instance, the number of shop orders plummeted from over 50 in 1990 to below 20 in 1993. Similarly, MVA shipped (a measure reflecting both the number and the size of transformers produced) dropped dramatically over the same period. The decline in activity was starkly reflected in employment trends: from a high of over 700 employees in total in 1989, employment at ABB Guelph had sunk to just 300 by late 1994. Management attributed two-thirds of employment losses to productivity gains and one-third to the decline in sales.

The contrasting trends in efficiency and activity may explain the trend in ABB Guelph's rating in terms of value-added as a percentage of personnel costs, which rose to 114 percent in 1991, but then began to slip after 1991 before declining sharply to just 50 percent in 1994. Thus, despite great strides in technical efficiency, it would appear that the decline in plant output was not matched by an equivalent decline in labor costs. Simply put, labor could not be shed beyond a certain minimum point, at least not without fundamentally altering the role of the plant.

Summary

Thus, after five tumultuous years as a new member of the ABB family, the Guelph plant had been transformed into a "lean learner." Management had wholeheartedly embraced and internalized the key elements of the Customer Focus program and vigorously, even ruthlessly, pursued a rationalization strategy aimed at squeezing cycle times down through a combination of borrowed and original innovations. The result was an exceedingly lean, more flexible operation which prided itself on its performance in the BA's "In-Group Olympics."

Yet rationalization was not the only reason for the leanness, for ABB Guelph went through this process of organizational change in the context of a sharply declining market. By 1994, it had become clear that a greater challenge was the need to adjust to a fundamentally different economic environment and, in particular, to develop new markets in Canada and abroad. In this respect, the greatest constraint was the firm's traditionally limited horizons: Guelph had always been a classic "branch plant", that is, a subsidiary of a multinational corporation with a specific mandate to service the Canadian market. As a subsidiary of ABB, Guelph faced the additional constraints inherent in the BA's market allocation policy.

A second fundamental challenge was internal in nature: in line with the traditional dominance of what might be called an "engineering paradigm"— begun under GE and reinforced by ABB— Guelph management had focused on technical rationalization above all else. Left by the wayside in this pursuit of efficiency were the employees and their unions. The challenge to the structure of institutional regulation, the reliance on layoffs to achieve numerical flexibility, and the deterioration of union-management relations had done considerable damage to the social fabric of the organization.

ABB-Varennes: Local Hero

The Varennes plant was built by ASEA in the early 1970s in the midst of a boom in the local electrical equipment industry created by the James Bay hydroelectric project. Indeed, ASEA was approached by Hydro-Québec (the provincial electric utility) about the possibility of sharing research and development facilities.

Products, Markets, and Organizational Structure

Varennes is a rural town situated close to Montreal. The plant is located near the research and development facilities of Hydro-Québec and both share these facilities. For instance, the transformers built in the Varennes plant are tested by the Institut de recherche d'Hydro–Québec (IREQ), the research arm of Hydro-Québec, and the Varennes plant is linked directly to these facilities by means of railway tracks. Furthermore, a joint ABB-Hydro-Québec research and development venture was set up in the early 1970s.

Over the years, Varennes developed three main product lines: power transformers (the original and still principal product), shunt reactors, and high voltage equipment. At the time of the field research, Varennes held the North American mandate for the production of high voltage transformers in the 800-kV range, as well as the North American mandate for shunt reactors.

In addition to its special mandates, Varennes' specified market included 5 of the 10 Canadian provinces — Quebec and the 4 smaller Atlantic provinces lying to the east of Quebec. However, its close relationship with Hydro-Québec meant that Varennes enjoyed a quasi-monopoly in the local market. Indeed, Hydro-Québec accounted for approximately 80 percent of the plant's operating revenues, while ABB Varennes met approximately 80 percent of Hydro-Québec's power transformer requirements. This close relationship was bolstered by a competitive advantage for ABB Varennes against outside suppliers: local content rules and the provincial utility's policy of buying from local suppliers gave ABB Varennes a 7 percent cost advantage on contract bids. Although the Varennes' plant's links to Hydro-Québec provided stability, it often had to conform to the demands of the public utility, which is renowned for asking for special features and above-average performance standards.

As of late 1994, there were two divisions in the Varennes plant, a smaller division for switch gear systems, and a larger division that manufactured power transformers. While production facilities and upper management were separate for the two divisions, they shared white collar staff. Within the power transformer division (the focus of our research), the organizational structure was relatively traditional, although quite flat. Under the general manager were department directors who received direct reports from only one further level of supervision.

Throughout the early 1990s, employment was quite stable at around 300 salaried and hourly workers. Within the power transformer division, the composition of the workforce reflected the relative stability allowed by the close relationship with Hydro-Québec. In 1994, the average age of the workforce was 41.5 years, but half of the production workers and around one-third of the office workers had more than 16 years' seniority with the company. Union-management relations were grounded in the traditional North American model. Both office and production workers were represented by the Fédération interprovinciale des ouvriers en électricité, a union with deep roots in the construction industry. Union-management relations were more or less arm's length with a history of alternating strikes and lockouts.

Production Management

Unlike the Guelph plant, ABB Varennes did not undergo any drastic organizational changes during the first half of the 1990s; indeed, an atmosphere of stability pervaded the organization. The plant was originally developed along the lines of the Ludvika model, but Varennes subsequently adapted and defined its own engineering system and resources, to the point that it was more independent than the Guelph plant in its relationships with the BA and with ABB Canada.

The organizational structure was traditional, placing heavy emphasis on the role of production management rather than on cross-functional coordination. Consequently, the planning department played a central role in coordinating operations. The planning of production built on a combination of information technology and social interaction. Based on a two-year master schedule, the planning department would draw up a fifteen-week production schedule which was then updated monthly. This schedule was the basis for planning and scheduling manpower and material requirements throughout the shop and was used extensively by foremen when forecasting the workload of their areas of responsibility. The overriding objective was to keep costs to a minimum by limiting work-in-progress and by maximizing the turnaround rate of inputs and the efficient allocation of labor within the plant.

While information on past performance was used in forecasting, the 15-week schedule also drew on tacit knowledge accumulated by the production coordinator and on consultation with those responsible for each sequence of production. Considering the uncertainties related to the nature of the product, the 15-week schedule allowed for some slack in the work flow. Of particular importance was the use of overtime. In fact, manpower requirements and capacity load were programmed for only 5 days, whereas in reality the plant often operated for 6 and sometimes 7 days a week. Overtime was thus the main buffer in balancing the system of production management.

Clearly, up until 1994, ABB Varennes had not bought the central elements of the rationalization drive in the BA. For example, whereas management at the Guelph plant focused on throughput times, Varennes put the priority on cost control. Foremen were given responsibility for throughput times, but their chief objective was to meet production schedule deadlines and not to perform in accordance with some abstract ideal. Even though the adherence to delivery dates was seen as fundamental in maintaining relationships with customers, many of the production managers challenged the validity of throughput time data as a method of comparing the performance of plants within the BA.

On the other hand, Varennes succeeded in developing a highly efficient supply management system. This just-in-time system, perfected over ten years of trial and error, was not the classic system presented in management textbooks. Instead, the idea was to keep high-cost/high-turnaround materials to a minimum so as to reduce capital outlays associated with high inventories while keeping low-cost/low-volume components on hand. For the latter category, considering the high degree of production integration, it was not considered worth risking production bottlenecks caused by a sudden shortage of material.[3] Although supply management was a central element in cost control, ABB Varennes did not adhere completely to the BA model as did the Guelph plant. Having built close relationships with its suppliers, Varennes was reluctant to break its established networks.

As for the continuous improvement and TQM activities, some progress was beginning to be made by 1994. As in many plants, it was soon realized that while a considerable amount of data was available, much of it was not useful. The quality control system then in place ran parallel with production activities rather than being a part of the process itself. This system was efficient in tracking errors and nonconformities but was not geared toward prevention. At each stage in the manufacturing sequence, a quality inspector tested the product for quality and performance and reported the results to a quality engineer. However, before an NCR was filled out, the foreman had to approve the inspector's findings. There often followed a form of bargaining over what constituted an error and what did not. This took place mostly because the foremen, concerned with meeting their monthly budget targets, were motivated either to ignore minor defects or to pass on the cost to other departments.

The quality control process therefore lacked the structure to generate permanent solutions to recurrent problems. The only forums for discussion of product quality were the quality meetings and reviews that occurred at the end of each production stage and once the power transformer was shipped to the customer. These meetings served generally to add checkpoints to the design or manufacturing checklist and not, as the continuous improvement model suggests, to find common solutions to common problems.

Work Organization

The organization of work in the Varennes plant followed a traditional model in which the foreman played a central role and reported directly to the production manager. Foremen saw themselves as responsible for manag-

---

[3] Data for 1993 confirm the application of this general principle of the just-in-time system. Of the 20 general categories of material used as inputs in the production process, the 5 categories having the highest value, namely core steel, copper, accessories, presspahn and insulation material, had an average turnaround rate of 45.2 compared with a total turnaround rate of only 6.7 for all materials. Copper, for instance, the second most expensive material, was delivered only a few days prior to its use for winding and had a turnaround rate of 126.9.

ing their areas of work, which were conceived as cost centers. Their responsibility was to monitor the status of work in progress and to coordinate efforts in line with the 15-week production schedule. While allowing a considerable amount of autonomy to individual workers and work teams, foremen were never very far away and kept a careful eye on resource allocation and time constraints. The foreman's role was, of course, closely tied to the financial performance of his cost center. Assisting in this form of "remote" control, founded on cumulative experience and technical insight, was the fact that the foreman had a good grasp of the real capacity of the sociotechnical system.

The involvement of workers and the way they were induced to use their ideas and know-how to improve their work routines did not depend on committees or other forms of participatory management. What we observed, particularly in winding and active parts assembly, corresponded instead to a high degree of worker autonomy, that is, a traditional form of job control based on craftsmanship and know-how accumulated over the years by trial and error. As one senior production manager insisted, management at ABB Varennes was not based on authority but relied on the competencies and cooperation of workers and shop floor managers. "Our management style is to bring together the skills needed to solve problems, it's shared leadership. That's because the people here have a lot of experience. They have 15 years' experience. We don't have any turnover; people know what they are doing. They want to do quality work."

Within individual departments, flexibility was built into the organization of work. Individual workers were not tied to one specific workstation, nor were they trained in or assigned permanently to a particular task. Shop rules regarding the assignment of work gave each operator full responsibility for a complete sequence of operations. In winding, for instance, the operator was given time and latitude to follow through, sometimes over several days, on the complete building of a coil. The operator worked in an autonomous fashion with design sheets, provided by the engineering department, from which he determined checkpoints and possible problem areas that required special care and verified the availability of material and tools.

In active parts assembly, many jobs were accomplished by small teams of workers. Here again, though, workers rotated from team to team and were not confined to narrowly defined jobs, thus permitting synergy between workers who had known each other for years. Once the foreman had assigned members to a team, the team leader helped the work group make consensual arrangements about the distribution of work. The team leader, who was clearly not part of management, also assisted in the technical coordination of work and kept an eye on the availability of parts and materials. The technical division of labor was not rigid at all and did not impede the individual and collective forms of autonomy that naturally emerged from such a production system. In practice, then, by 1994 workers at ABB Varennes had already gone beyond the forms of multitasking and voluntary job rotation that many firms are still seeking today.

Institutional Regulation

Labor relations were shaped around a tradeoff between a high degree of labor flexibility, within as well as across departments, in exchange for generous monetary rewards. Indeed, the local union was quite vigilant in maximizing workers' return from the wage-effort bargain. Hence good working arrangements were usually made in the application of the collective agreement, and employees were quite willing to cooperate, but, of course, everything was open to negotiation. Overtime, as we noted earlier, was a resource for buffering the tight production schedule, albeit an expensive one.[4] Within the employment relationship it also acted as a lubricant and served to strengthen the importance of the cash nexus and of the achievement of production goals. Indeed, the distribution and equitable sharing of overtime was a sensitive issue in the plant and the union guarded carefully its role in regulating this matter.

The other issue of importance in the working arrangement was employment security. While the historical employment relationship at the Varennes plant was clearly one of stability, the union never took it for granted and was diligent in protecting the jobs of its members. In sum, then, functional flexibility was allowed and overtime accepted in exchange for management efforts to avoid layoffs and outsourcing of work.

This pattern of union behavior, which puts the emphasis on job protection, internal mobility, and compensation does not foster union involvement in organizational change and broader issues. In fact, at ABB Varennes, the union drew its strength and legitimacy from its role as a countervailing power, and not as a partner with management.

Performance

As was the case with ABB Guelph, performance trends over the early 1990s at ABB Varennes were mixed. On the one hand, benefiting from its quasi-monopolistic position in Quebec and its cost advantage over competitors, the activity level at the Varennes plant was remarkably stable. Indeed, the order book was stable enough to permit production at full capacity for years. Consequently, total employment remained relatively stable at around 300 from 1991 to 1994.

Nevertheless, some of the key indicators of efficiency show a certain leveling off, albeit at an acceptable level. TPT more or less stabilized around the

---

[4] In 1992, almost 42,000 overtime hours were worked by production workers alone, representing over 11 percent of total regular hours worked and an average of 242.6 hours per production worker. Overtime in 1993 was reduced considerably, to about 26,000 hours or 7.43 percent of total regular hours and an average of 150.8 hours per production worker.

standard set by the BA, but more disaggregated data indicate that the bench-marking objectives for medium-sized power transformers were not being met, although this was compensated for by very good lead times in the production of shunt reactors, a specialized niche for which ABB Varennes held the North American mandate.

TTPT was less satisfactory and appeared to reflect what several key informants saw as an imperfect interface between engineering and shop floor assembly. Although TTPT declined from 1991–1994, it remained short of the standard set by the BA and ranked low compared with other plants.

Perhaps more important, at least in the view of ABB Varennes' management, was the performance as regards value-added as a percentage of personnel costs. This ratio jumped from 117 percent in 1988 to a high mark of 215 percent in 1992, and then remained relatively stable around 200 percent in 1993 and 1994. It would appear that Varennes was successful in preserving profitability during the recession of the early 1990s, a situation that obviously had much to do with its unique relationship with Hydro-Québec.

As regards the final test failure rate, the Varennes plant's record improved rather steadily from the mid-1980s. Nevertheless, in the 1990s further improvements were more difficult to achieve. To understand this trend one must look behind the general statistics on failure rates and distinguish among product ranges. Although the failure rate of shunt reactors was low, it was less satisfactory for transformers in the medium range. Over the five-year period from 1989–1993, several transformers in this range failed at the final testing stage. The chain-like effect of these kinds of failures were readily observable at the time of our fieldwork, when the plant's technical and physical capabilities were stretched to their limits. When units failed at the final testing stage, it caused serious bottleneck on the final assembly line that had repercussions on all other upstream areas.

Measures were taken to reinforce quality control at the different stages of production, and we have already mentioned the perverse effect of the structure of cost centers on quality control, that is, the use of NCRs to off-load costs. Nevertheless, as was also the case at ABB Guelph, this did not seem to prompt corrective measures, and the fact that many problems recurred appears to have created some frustration among the different segments of the workforce. The structure of defects reporting and the committees that oversaw and dealt with these defects represented only a first step in the direction of continuous improvement. They did not, by themselves, change the way in which each department functioned internally. At the end of 1994, the organization was still in dire need of a more structured approach to continuous improvement.

Summary

Thus, during the period when ABB Guelph was undergoing radical surgery, ABB Varennes continued to bask in its past success and its seemingly permanent stability. Indeed, stability was a feature not only of the management system but also of the organization of work and of union-management relations. Consequently, concepts such as TQM and continuous improvement made only slow headway within the managerial ranks.

Besides the lack of a change-inducing crisis, progress toward a more proactive approach also appears to have been inhibited by the traditional organizational structure. Although each departmental unit was doing its best to be cost-efficient and deliver quality within its sphere of activities, and while the sequencing of the production system was straightforward enough, communication and coordination essentially depended on individual initiative. This led to a lack of concern for the impact of decisions and actions taken upstream on the efficiency of the downstream operations. Although the interface between design and production was often cited as a key difficulty, in the sense that the former group did not consider the complexities and idiosyncrasies at the manufacturing stage, the problem was in fact embedded within existing organizational structures.

By 1994–1995, there were signs that change would have to accelerate. Not only was the Varennes plant's management becoming conscious of the internal and external pressures to foster a dynamic of continuous improvement, there were ominous signs that the Hydro-Québec gravy train was grinding to a halt. As shown in the conclusion, in this context the management of ABB Varennes began to realize that it could no longer rest on its laurels.

Comparing the Guelph and Varennes Plants

The Guelph and Varennes power transformer plants are alike in many ways. Approximately the same size, they manufacture the same range of products using methods and technology that are very similar. In both plants, workplace relations have been shaped by the Fordist model of production based on the local negotiation of elaborate collective agreements that regulate the internal labor market yet that leave management in control of strategic decisions and the organization of work. Moreover, the two plants have common corporate parents who have introduced standard performance measures as well as a range of rationalization policies and initiatives—under the general rubric of the Customer Focus program—to which the plants are expected to adhere. Finally, since 1994, a single manager has been responsible for both operations.

Yet despite these similarities, the foregoing case studies of the impact of the Customer Focus program on production management, work organization, and institutional regulation indicate that there are considerable differences in the way that ABB's policy of "being local worldwide" functions at the level of the individual plant. In this section, we identify and explain the key differences between the two plants when we completed the principal phase of fieldwork, late in 1994.

Lean Learner versus Local Hero

One of the striking differences between the two plants was the respective weight of the power transformer BA's strategies. At the Guelph plant, managers and workers frequently referred to the goals and philosophies of ABB in general and the BA more specifically. At the Varennes plant, although the BA's strategies were clearly important, they did not bulk nearly so large in the day-to-day life of the plant. In short, Guelph managers and workers felt much less independent than did their counterparts at Varennes.

This difference in the degree of autonomy can be demonstrated in various ways. One of the most notable differences was the relative emphasis each plant put on throughput times as opposed to other measures of performance. At Guelph, throughput time was accepted as the overriding priority, whereas throughput time was secondary to financial results in the plant at Varennes. This difference was reflected in the way production was managed and organized in the two plants. Whereas ABB Varennes retained a relatively traditional organizational structure built around cost centers, ABB Guelph adopted the focused factories structure, which put a greater emphasis on TBM methods.

Another indication of the different degrees of autonomy concerns quality control. Guelph more wholeheartedly adopted the principles of TQM and continuous improvement than did Varennes. An obvious reflection of this difference was the attempt at the Guelph plant to devolve responsibility for quality to shop floor workers and supervisors as a means of solving quality problems early in the production process and of making changes in designs to prevent recurrence. In contrast, Varennes retained a more traditional quality inspection function, which focused on identifying errors as opposed to preventing them.

There was also a clear difference in the degree to which each plant resorted to the strategy of outsourcing. In the Guelph plant, outsourcing was adopted as a key means of rationalizing unit production, both in financial and temporal terms. In the Varennes plant, on the other hand, outsourcing was minimal. In addition, management at Guelph saw the supply management strategies promoted by the BA as a positive step that would help to further reduce costs and rationalize production, whereas Varennes was more hesitant because of the potential disturbance to long-established relationships with its network of local suppliers.

In the area of work organization, the two plants employed very different strategies for attaining numerical and functional flexibility. At Guelph, variations in business volume and demand for labor were managed through "external" flexibility, that is, through a strategy of layoffs and recalls designed to adjust the level of manpower to immediate needs. In Varennes, an "internal" strategy that depended on extraordinary levels of overtime was the favored approach. It is true, of course, that the more stable market conditions enjoyed by Varennes allowed it more leeway than Guelph during the period studied; and it is also the case that Guelph did not hesitate to rely on overtime even when some workers were on layoff. Nevertheless, even during the early years of ABB's ownership of the Guelph plant, when the order book was full, employment levels fluctuated widely in response to market demand, whereas employment stability at Varennes was a long-term practice.

In the area of functional flexibility, the Canadian plants also adopted different strategies. At Guelph, there was a drive to achieve functional flexibility through sweeping reductions in job classifications which, in theory at least, would permit a more flexible allocation of labor. Virtually no changes in the job classification system were made in Varennes, yet on the whole our observation is that, through a more informal compromise with the union, they achieved a level of functional flexibility that surpassed that achieved at Guelph.

Turning to institutional regulation, there were differences in the degree to which management sought to make the union a partner. At Guelph, despite some superficial efforts to recognize the legitimacy of the union's role (e.g., the signing of an agreement on quality), the production workers' union was perceived as an obstacle to change. Indeed, it is not going too far to say that management took advantage of the downturn in the market to effectively sideline the union. In Varennes, although the traditional pattern of Fordist labor relations persisted, the status and role of the union was very different.

In sum, then, despite common ownership, similar products and technologies, and the existence of global strategies meant to influence workplace management, the two plants exhibited a range of significant differences during the early 1990s. Summarizing these in a general way, one might say that ABB Guelph pursued a change strategy rooted in a wholehearted acceptance of ABB guidelines, especially the focus on reducing TTPT and eliminating activities lying outside what was considered the plant's core business. In contrast, at Varennes, change proceeded at a slower pace. Although cycle times were important, the orientation continued to be on cost control within a traditional departmentalized structure with strong foremen in charge of cost centers. In the next pages we turn to the task of accounting for these differences.

Sources of Strategic Variation: Origins, Markets, and Organization

Management of the two plants faces in three directions: toward their markets, toward ABB, and toward their own employees. Each of these dimensions constitutes at once a set of constraints and opportunities. In principle, a successful strategy seeks to balance and integrate the three sets of con-

straints and opportunities. In practice, however, strategies typically are characterized by an emphasis on one of the dimensions. In this section, we explore how these forces were played out in each of the two plants. A central
argument here is that Guelph's experience is best understood in terms of its
orientation toward ABB, whereas Varennes' focus is chiefly on its market.
These strategic directions, we argue, were shaped by their differing historical ties to ABB, their different markets, and by the different structures of
power and authority that characterize each organization.

Relationship to Asea Brown Boveri

Each plant has a unique history within the ABB structure and, as many
have argued (Edwards, Ferner, and Sisson, 1993; Marginson and Sisson,
1994; Purcell and Ahlstrand, 1994), this legacy has had an undeniable influence on their response to the parent corporation. Our research indicates that
the green-field versus brown-field distinction has far-reaching ramifications.
While Varennes enjoyed a long-standing tradition of local autonomy and
played a central role in promoting ABB in Canada, Guelph was a new player.
Being a brown-field site meant that Guelph adhered more closely to the main
strategic priorities set by the BA, particularly the reduction of cycle times.
Varennes, shaped from the beginning within the ASEA model, had developed
the organizational resources and the necessary autonomy to select the elements of the benchmarking devices that they felt were most relevant to their
success as a business.

The Guelph plant, for instance, put the priority on lowering throughput times, a strategy that may in some circumstances conflict with other economic objectives, such as controlling labor costs. The Varennes plant, on
the other hand, had a long-standing history of independent organizational
growth and while the plant was originally modeled on the Ludvika operations, it had initiated changes and adjustments in accordance with the distinctive features of the local Quebec market. It was clearly more oriented
to cost control and maintaining profit margins, as reflected in the rating of
value-added by employee expenses. The priority was good financial results,
a key factor in preserving their latitude by contributing to the success of both
dimensions of the matrix. On several indices of the benchmarking measures,
however, Varennes did not compare favorably with Guelph and other plants
around the world.

Markets

Varennes was built at the express invitation of Hydro-Québec during the
boom in the electrical equipment industry of the 1970s. Subsequently, local
management developed close links with the power utility through joint research and development efforts. Moreover, Hydro-Québec's policy of favor-

ing local suppliers provided ABB Varennes with an important competitive advantage. Past performance also resulted in the allocation of the North American mandate for shunt reactors. The plant had been running at full capacity for several years and had withstood the impact of the continent wide decline in demand. All in all, these features of the local product market helped to create a margin of autonomy that local management preserved through careful management of customer relationships. As we noted earlier, however, this advantage was tempered by the fact that ABB Varennes was constrained by Hydro-Québec's demands for special features.

Guelph's market environment, in contrast, deteriorated rapidly in the early 1990s. Ontario Hydro, for instance, declared a moratorium on new capacity growth in the late 1980s, a situation that is not likely to change in the coming years. Compounding this threat was the presence of at least two major competitors in the Canadian market. These firms were competing in a tight market from which Guelph was unable to escape through the creation of barriers to entry as was the case for the Varennes plant. Nor did Guelph benefit from an exclusive mandate granted by ABB. It follows that overcapacity in the North American region posed a greater threat to this plant located in Ontario.

In sum, the different market situations and the stronger local ties built by the Varennes plant resulted in greater autonomy from the BA. Varennes had long been the main vehicle in promoting ABB in Canada and its sales volume benefited both the horizontal and the vertical dimensions of the organizational matrix. Guelph, for its part, was faced with finding ways to outperform the competition at a time when the market was crumbling. In such a context, it is not surprising that the presence of the BA was felt more strongly, since survival depended to a great extent on its performance relative to other plants.

Patterns of Power and Authority

At Varennes, the organizational structure was traditional, with a clear distinction between line and staff management as well as a strong first level of command reporting directly to the production manager. Beyond the advantage of simplicity, this system supported the rationalization of production while workers maintained a fair deal of autonomy and control over their immediate tasks. Contributing to this was an efficient planning system that provided enough breathing space to foremen in managing their areas of responsibility. It was then possible for them to make the best use of the know-how and considerable amount of tacit knowledge that was widely spread among a stable and experienced workforce. The upside of this was that efforts were directed toward production and that there was little confusion of roles and lines of authority. On the downside, this structure limited the possibilities of greater cross-functional coordination, since sharing information and expertise was a matter of individual initiative and of informal social networks. Hence each department was geared toward efficiency and cost control, but better coordination among functions and departments seemed to be necessary to move beyond and promote new standards of continuous improvement and TQM.

Structural changes promoting better horizontal coordination were introduced at the Guelph plant in the form of focused factories and contract teams. Implicit in the implementation of focused factories was the empowerment of first-line supervisors with greater managerial responsibilities for their units and a better integration of the sequences and activities related to a range of products. The implementation, however, focused each unit's attention on its own performance. Old coordination problems thus returned to the surface in a new form. Indeed, new barriers were erected as different units within the focused factories sought to protect their new territories. This was not the result of intent on the part of the workforce nor by the unit leaders but was generated by organizational features. In particular, the performance appraisal system focused attention on the results of the unit, the focused factory second, and the plant last. Hence the strategy to incite people to focus on the organization as a whole and its relationships to the market was to a great extent countered by the new structural boundaries.

Conclusion: Marrying the Lean Learner to the Local Hero?

Since 1994, a number of developments have occurred that, although considerably altering the trajectories of the two plants, serve to confirm the thrust of the general analysis we have laid out.

The most important change has been a move toward the integration of the Guelph and Varennes plants. As we noted previously, a single general manager was given responsibility for the two plants in 1994. There followed a series of measures designed to integrate the two operations, the most significant being a fundamental change in each plant's mandate. In place of the geographical division of the Canadian market, the production of new medium and large power transformers for all of Canada was given to the Varennes plant, whereas Guelph, besides retaining its small transformer mandate, was given the Canadian mandate for transformer repairs and several specialty transformers. Along with this reconfiguration of mandates has come an effort to further rationalize production through greater integration of the two plants. On the administrative level, a number of departments (including human resources management and sales and marketing) have been amalgamated under the authority of single managers either in Guelph or Varennes. At the level of production, the two plants are now producing components for each other. Varennes, for example, has been given the job of producing all of the tanks needed in both locations, whereas Guelph has been assigned the role of manufacturing all of the insulation material and cleats and lead kits for the two. It will come as no surprise that this process has been rather less smooth in practice than its architects imagined, but even taking into account its incomplete and hesitant nature, the change has been profound.

This move toward integration was driven by a dramatic downturn in orders from Hydro-Québec and the continuing slump in the medium and large segment of the North American power transformer market. Moreover, against the backdrop of an examination by ABB of the viability of retaining four transformer plants in North America, this rationalization of the two Canadian plants was meant to better position them to survive and to win more export markets—a move that appears to have been successful in view of ABB's decision to close the large power transformer plant located in Muncie, Indiana, in the course of 1998. This corporate decision obviously has symbolic importance as the Muncie factory, which was the core Westinghouse plant in this industry, was once the biggest transformer plant in the world. It also has concrete implications for the two plants studied in this chapter. In particular, Varennes is being given new mandates for the design and production of specific ranges of transformers for the North American region as a whole.

Interestingly, as closer production relations developed with the Varennes plant, as part of the adjustment to recent market opportunities in North America, we observed a lessening of the dependence of the Guelph plant in its relations with BA headquarters. As the Varennes-Guelph axis became more significant, the interface with the parent corporation evolved in a way that seems to give the Guelph plant more autonomy in the BA. In particular, neither of Guelph's two main product lines—small power transformers and the specialty and repair market—is central to the scope of the Common Product project. In redesigning the production process to handle repair jobs, for example, workers and managers have had to rely more on their own resources and ingenuity than on standardized designs and components. The changes also sounded the death knell of the focused factories, which have been replaced by the older and simpler division between small power transformers and specialty and repairs. Moreover, although the search for efficiencies continues, including a more pronounced effort to devolve decision making to the shop floor through the use of work teams and group leaders, a noticeable lessening of the importance of the BA performance measures as a guide to action was noticeable when we last visited the Guelph plant in October 1997.

Instead, the goal has been to increase the output of small transformers in order to maximize revenue generation with an eye to ensuring the plant's viability from a financial point of view and to support its effort to win niche export markets. Finally, however, labor-management relations continue to be characterized by a lack of interest on the part of management in creating a climate of employee relations consistent with their desire to foster a more participatory production model. Thus, Guelph's workforce, although greeting workplace innovations with cautious interest, retain their skepticism, scarred as they are by the brutal employment reductions and the top-down, technology-driven style of management that have characterized the ABB era in the factory.

Whereas Guelph has gained some autonomy through the forced marriage of the two plants, Varennes has seen some of its previously jealously guarded independence whittled down. Indeed, the loss of what was essentially a protected market has exposed it not only to the demands of new customers (forcing it to alter, for instance, some of its designs and production practices) but also to internal forces, notably the need to interact more frequently and more closely with Guelph as well as the need to adhere more closely to the strategies pursued by the BA with respect to production standardization and performance measurement. A striking example of this new era of interdependence is the complete redesign of the tank unit at Varennes, driven partly by the search for internal economies but also by the requirements set down by Guelph, its "internal customer" as well as by its desire to carve out a North American mandate for tank production. Varennes has now abandoned its isolationism and examined innovations in other ABB power transformer plants in an effort to learn new methods.

Organizationally, the Varennes plant has begun to fall in line with the general tendency in the BA toward cross-functional structures, notably through the adoption of committees bringing together engineers, supervisors, and shop floor workers. However, the long-standing workplace compromise has been rocked by layoffs and by managerial efforts to untie some of the delicate threads that held that compromise together, particularly collective agreement provisions concerning the assignment of tasks and the distribution of overtime.

To summarize, the closer integration of the two plants is essentially a strategic response to ongoing changes in the organizational and product market contexts, a process that has seen changes in the nature of the relationship between the two plants and their parent organizations. Integration, though, has not stamped out the distinctive traditions presented earlier. As in any marriage, although new relationships are being forged and compromises being made, tensions remain. The capacity to survive will ultimately depend on finding a balance between the individual freedom that each partner values and their joint goals. Within each plant, that challenge will depend not on technical capacity but rather on the need to hammer out internal social arrangements among workers, their unions, and management that will match the sophistication of the technical rationalization that is currently, in Canada at least, the meaning of being local worldwide.

8 ABB in Sweden
A New Start at the Old Mecca

Lars Bengtsson

The only Swedish power transformer plant of Asea Brown Boveri (ABB) is part of an industrial complex located in Ludvika, which, next to the plant at Västerås, is ABB Sweden's largest production site. Apart from power transformers, ABB also manufactures power systems, switch gear and various high voltage electrotechnical components at Ludvika. The six ABB companies located at the site presently employ a total of about 2500 people, 500 of whom work in the power transformer plant. Owing to the concentration of expertise at Ludvika, it is regarded as the center of power transmission within ABB. The old, red-brick factory buildings convey the impression of Swedish tradition and solidity. The industrial complex was built during the nineteenth century and has its roots in the mining industry. Ludvika is located about 120 miles west of Stockholm, in the heart of a historically important mining district, the cornerstone of Swedish industry. The area is surrounded by seemingly endless coniferous forests, broken only by numerous small lakes. The town of Ludvika, which today has about 30,000 inhabitants, has been closely connected to ASEA, and now ABB, since 1916. The near century-long dependence on one large employer can still be detected in the culture of this industrial community. The history of the Ludvika transformer plant also dates back to the beginning of the twentieth century. The production of power transformers is based on the Swedish patent for three-phase transformers granted to Jonas Wenström.

The Ludvika plant has enjoyed a very strong position in the world of power transformers. It produces a wide range of products and sells to customers all over the world. Because of its extensive technological competence, ABB Ludvika has been regarded by many as the "Mecca of transformers." During the ASEA era, the company licensed its technology to a number of other plants, thereby generating substantial revenue. These conditions helped it to develop considerable technological proficiency and developmental resources, which provided opportunities to enhance and develop new transformer designs. The expertise of its workers and engineers has been used in many transformer plants abroad to improve technology and processes and to introduce new product designs. Over the years, the Ludvika plant has also supplied the business area (BA) and other ABB companies with many senior managers. The strong presence of Swedes in senior managerial positions throughout the Power Transformer BA is striking.

This chapter examines how the Ludvika plant has been affected by its integration into ABB and by the introduction of corporate rationalization programs. Because the Ludvika plant started out as the star in the cast of power transformer plants, the organizational culture was suffused with a feeling of superiority. During the first few years after the creation of ABB, the plant managed to preserve its autonomy, but the will to improve and change was consequently weak compared with other plants. However, when several other plants caught up and passed by, and as the world market changed, Ludvika finally realized that its star had fallen. This revelation was the impetus to a new start, which is the main theme of this chapter.

The data for this chapter were collected mainly through semistructured interviews, but information was also gathered through direct observation in workshops and through company documents. Data collection was conducted in two main phases, in spring 1994 and spring 1995. In total, some forty persons were interviewed, many of them twice, covering most levels and functions within the company, from shop floor workers to the plant manager. Interviews were also conducted with union representatives of both the workers and the salaried personnel. Some additional data were also collected in 1996 and 1997.

Products, Markets, and Organizational Structure

Contradictory Position within ABB

For most of the decade, the position of Ludvika within the power transformer BA has been ambiguous. On the one hand, the Ludvika plant seems to play an important role, as in the "good old days" before the merger that created ABB. This is certainly the case when it comes to technological expertise. Some 40 percent of all research and development engineers in the BA are based in this large plant, mainly in the technology division. Ludvika's expertise is also used in several BA projects, such as the Common Product program, for which Ludvika carries out most of the developmental work. It is also a "center of excellence" for a niche product, HVDC (high voltage direct current) transformers, which makes the Ludvika plant responsible for all further development and manufacturing within the BA. Furthermore, ABB Ludvika is a center for cutting core plates and one of the four plants producing shunt reactors. With the recent closure of the Muncie plant in the United States, Ludvika is now the largest plant within the BA.

ABB Ludvika is also seen as a sort of regional anchor among the plants in the Nordic countries, Poland, and Scotland. Among other things, the members of this network, called the "Northern European Group," exchange know-how and take benchmarking measures on process performance and financial results. Since the mid-1990s, ABB Ludvika has been responsible for introducing new technology and coordinating market efforts in this region.

On the other hand, it might be argued that the Ludvika plant's role is modest, especially considering the size and reach of ABB as a whole. It is just 1 of more than 20 companies within the BA, representing about 11–12 percent of the total production volume in 1995 and a similar proportion of employment and revenue. Furthermore, as shown later, ABB Ludvika has so far not been a top-ranked company in terms of process performance comparisons with other plants.

Within the Swedish ABB group, Ludvika is 1 of 130 companies, although far from the smallest one. With respect to the strategic program of lead-time reduction launched in Sweden under the label "T-50" (which refers to a 50 percent reduction in lead time), ABB Ludvika has played a subordinate role. In fact, for a long time Ludvika was almost a black sheep, never featuring in the internal or external marketing of ABB in Sweden. However, the company has gradually improved its performance and position and, in December 1994, finally succeeded in being certified as a "T-50 company."

In the context of the Ludvika plant's rich history and considerable expertise in the power transformer industry, the merger of ASEA and Brown Boveri, which made the plant into just one of many players in the BA, had contradictory effects. On the positive side, the merger brought considerable advantages as regards resources for product and production development. It also offered the possibility of internal benchmarking and the diffusion of innovative managerial policies. However, becoming part of a large international group was also perceived by ABB Ludvika as a loss of autonomy in many ways. Strategic decisions regarding future product designs and market allocation would now be made in another country. Moreover, as discussed further on, until recently the ABB Ludvika plant's management and employees had too much confidence in their technical expertise to really appreciate how they could learn from other power transformer plants across the world, many of which were newcomers to the industry.

Products and Markets

The plant under study produces mainly core-type power transformers and to a lesser extent, reactors and traction transformers. Although the transformers are always customized (i.e., power, voltages, noise levels, external connections and equipment), the manufacturing process is not strictly a unit production system. Export orders (which represent the bulk of sales) often comprise two or more transformers of the same kind. Furthermore, the basic technology is largely standardized. Until 1994, ABB Ludvika's three-phase transformers were mainly based on three standardized ASEA designs representing different power levels. In 1994, the first Common Product transformers were produced to further develop the concept of a standardized product within the BA. During the 1990s, ABB Ludvika produced between 100 and 150 transformers each year, for a total of between 8,000 and 10,000 MVA.

ABB Ludvika's market mandate includes Sweden, Denmark, the Far East, and the Middle East. Historically, the domestic market was more important. A long-term relationship with a knowledgeable Swedish customer, the Swedish state public power utility (Vattenfall), played an important role in developing the technological proficiency of the Ludvika plant. Vattenfall is the single largest producer of water-powered electrical energy. Today investments in this area have gradually declined, and even though ABB Ludvika completely dominates the Swedish transformer market, domestic sales now represent only a very small part of its total production volume. The Ludvika plant has succeeded in offsetting the decline in the domestic market through exports. Indeed, contrary to the ideal established by the BA, this plant exports the greater part of its production, either as direct exports or as indirect exports via other Swedish ABB companies (e.g., ABB Power Systems).

These market changes have also been reflected in product development. The traditional and relatively standardized three-phase transformers have lost ground to more complex units, particularly HVDC transformers. At the beginning of 1994, the high voltage range of products represented nearly half of ABB Ludvika's orders and an even higher proportion of its profits.

Trends in the global market will also have an impact on the immediate future of the Ludvika plant. The Far East and the Middle East currently offer the best market opportunities; during recent years and for the coming five years its order books are full. However, within 10 years, these export opportunities could be sharply reduced as domestic production capacity grows in these areas. As for the Nordic countries, low-cost producers from Eastern Europe have already created a tougher competitive environment.

Organization and Workforce

In 1992, the plant was reorganized into four divisions and five departments. Compared with the prior functional organization, the most important changes entailed the reorganization of the design and manufacturing departments into two transformer divisions and one tank shop. Division A produces small and medium-sized power transformers, reactors, and traction transformers, whereas Division B is specialized in the manufacturing of larger power transformers and HVDC transformers. The Tank Shop mainly produces welded tanks, as well as other sheet metal components and parts.

The idea behind the reorganization was to create profit centers, each with its own resources and separate workshop, that would facilitate a process-oriented approach. Each division therefore has its own complete winding and assembly facilities. However, more costly processes were not divided. One division carries out all core steel cutting, while the other produces all wired copper and control equipment and is responsible for final processes. Marketing, as well as some purchasing, remains centralized. All testing of transformers before delivery is now carried out by the quality department. The Tank Shop, which is located in a separate workshop, is a pure manufacturing unit without design responsibility. Unique to ABB Ludvika is the large Technology Division whose engineers and technicians are recognized for their expertise in electrical and magnetic fields, transformer technology, and information systems. Indeed, a major proportion of their activities, and some 40 percent of their budget, is connected to BA projects.

In 1995, Ludvika employed a total of 530 persons. Among these, 57 percent were blue collar workers and 43 percent were salaried personnel. As many as 10 percent of the total workforce was made up of university trained engineers.[1] The average age of employees was then 43 years.

Nearly all of the employees at the Ludvika plant are unionized. The blue collar workers, numbering more than 300, belong to the Swedish Metal Workers' Union (Metall), while most of the approximately 170 white collar employees are members of the Swedish Union of Clerical and Technical Employees in Industry (SIF). Most of the university trained engineers, about 50 in all, are members of the Swedish Association of Graduate Engineers (CF). The organizational structure of the local union is not restricted to the transformer plant, but covers all six ABB companies located at the Ludvika site. This structure was inherited from the ASEA period, that is, prior to the splitting of these large production facilities into separate companies. However, the unions are internally divided into sublocals, each of which covers a single company. Similarly, ABB still has one site manager in Ludvika who deals with common issues concerning all of the six companies specialized in the field of power transmission.

The Innovation Process

During the period from 1990–1995, the Ludvika plant faced two main challenges. The first challenge was to be competitive in the context of a mature market. A small and increasingly competitive domestic market underscored the need to find new markets, minimize costs, and improve quality.

---

[1] Like all Swedes, all of the employees have spent 7, and nowadays 9, years in the comprehensive school. Most of the workers have 2 or 3 additional years of public vocational training as engineering workers. Most of the salaried personnel have the corresponding vocational training in administration, economics, or technology. Most of the university trained engineers are graduates of a 4-year school and hold a masters degree in engineering. A handful have doctoral degrees.

While cost efficiency and lead time were the critical issues in the case of the more standard products, product quality and reliability were crucial in order to compete successfully in the HVDC transformer market.

The second challenge related to the Ludvika plant's role and position within ABB, and within the BA more particularly. The integration into ABB meant a reduction of autonomy concerning market and production volume as well as the obligation to follow strategic guidelines as regards rationalization. The promotion within the larger corporation of methods such as time-based management (TBM), total quality management (TQM), and supply management created pressures on Ludvika to act in a certain way. The BA has also tried to establish a Common Product technology and, even more importantly, to reorganize the manufacturing processes in a more standardized fashion in the various plants.

To deal with this situation, the Ludvika plant adopted several strategies. One set of strategies, largely successful, aimed at widening the export market in the Far East and the Middle East. The establishment of joint ventures in Russia, Eastern Europe, and Vietnam was also part of this strategy. Because the BA's control over market allocation has not always supported these export efforts, local management has had to show some determination: "You don't gain anything by being just a nice guy," said the former general manager. The product strategy was to emphasize more complex transformers and, above all, to further develop the potential of the HVDC range of products. Another important element in the export strategy was closer cooperation with other ABB companies that sell entire power plants, such as Power Systems in Ludvika and Power Generation in Baden.

Another set of strategies entailed a drive to become more competitive, which, of course, supports and is a precondition of the export strategy. One focus here was to further develop the technological expertise of the company. This was manifested in particular by the creation of a large Technology Division, but also by the investment in specialized manufacturing equipment, for example, the cutting center. At the same time, the company sought to improve its internal and external processes by implementing several rationalization programs. The following sections explore these production management strategies, emphasizing how ABB Ludvika has implemented the corporate rationalization programs. The innovation process is then analyzed in terms of work organization and industrial relations.

Production Management

In the early 1990s, ABB's process oriented programs played a rather limited role at Ludvika. Production concepts such as T-50, TBM, and TQM were hardly promoted at all within the organization. On the other hand, the rationalization process that the Ludvika plant developed on its own did not really conflict with the principal ideas underlying the corporate programs.

From 1994–95, the commitment to these programs advocated by the BA management in Mannheim became more explicit.

TIME-BASED MANAGEMENT

Lead-time reduction and cost cutting have been long-standing objectives at ABB Ludvika. Over the past decades, several projects aiming at reduced lead time and work-in-progress were launched, mainly in manufacturing. The emphasis on lead-time reduction, expounded most prominently by ABB's former CEO, Percy Barnevik, was therefore not seen as a new idea. This partly explains why the initial commitment to the Swedish TBM program (the T-50 program) was low. Indeed, the task of promoting T-50 was not even made a full-time post but was instead added to the responsibilities of a division manager. As one manager at ABB Ludvika put it: "Should we reduce our lead times by 50 percent once again? That's not fair." The slow start was also reflected in the fact that major process mapping, in connection with the Six Sigma program, was not carried out until 1994, even though this represented the first step in implementing TBM.

Nevertheless, ABB Ludvika was active during this period. Based on its prior experience with lead-time reduction, the company gradually shifted the focus toward rationalization of the entire order process. An influential factor here was the comparisons made with other plants within the BA, which clearly showed that Ludvika's manufacturing lead times (i.e., TPT) were rather good, but that its performance was less satisfactory when the whole chain, from order and design to delivery, was taken into account (i.e., total throughput time [TTPT]). This new focus on the entire process, and particularly the design process, was also reflected in the goals that ABB Ludvika established. One division, for example, forecasted a reduction in design time by 85 percent, as well as a reduction of the total order cycle by nearly two-thirds. In the course of 1994, the commitment to ABB programs became more explicit when Ludvika sought to be recognized as a T-50 company. Then, in 1995, the new CEO ratified this stepwise approach, on the grounds that, although success in exporting depends on good TTPT performance, reducing TPT as much as possible is a crucial first step.

The Ludvika plant sought to reduce lead time and costs in two main ways. The first was a reorganization toward a more integrated and process oriented organization. Like many other companies in Sweden during this period, the management of the plant believed in decentralization, work integration, and teamwork in order to form small, effective, and cooperative units. Between 1990 and 1994, management in fact succeeded in reducing the number of employees by 20 percent without affecting production capacity. The second means was to standardize and computerize the order process. This entailed a considerable effort to define internal standards based on customer demands.

Total Quality Management and Six Sigma

For many years, product quality and quality control represented formal objectives. In particular, substantial efforts were made on quality assurance, as evidenced by both the refined standardized product designs and the quality system. Strict routines with clear checkpoints along the entire production chain and elaborate reporting systems for test failures were developed in order to reduce failure rates. In 1993 ABB Ludvika was also certified according to the International Standardization Organization (ISO) 9001 norm.

However, these measures proved insufficient. Recurring quality problems as well as average process performance compared with other transformer plants forced the Ludvika managers to consider new approaches to improve quality. This led management to gradually widen the perspective from product quality to process quality. One measure in this respect was the decentralization of quality management, which was premised on the assumption that the product divisions were best suited to manage quality improvements. Quality inspection would be conducted by operators, and quality inspectors would be assigned to the production departments. The central quality department became responsible for the final testing of the transformers and the Six Sigma activities.

The most consistent and successful TQM activities were undertaken by the division specializing in large transformers. The main problem in this division was poor quality, with every fifth transformer rejected in recent years. The division therefore launched a process oriented rationalization program aimed at improving the flow of production and fostering the involvement of all personnel. Its operationalization led to the creation of a considerable number of "improvement groups" (sixteen in 1995). These consisted of a type of *kaizen* group in which employees within the design and production departments formulated goals on the basis of an analysis of their particular problems and advantages. Some cross-functional groups that included suppliers were also set up, an organizational form later extended throughout the plant. These groups are concentrated in different workshop areas and analyze and try to solve specific quality problems when necessary. Several features of these improvement groups, together with the appointment of special process owners, relate to the Japanese *kaizen* concept, as described by Imai (1986).

Bolstered by the success of TQM, Ludvika decided, as of 1994, to adopt the BA's Six Sigma program. As a starting point, each division conducted a thorough process mapping in order to define its strategic processes, goals, and measurements. This analysis, in which all employees were actively involved, revealed a complexity in the processes that surprised everyone, and numerous simplifications were immediately identified. To support the implementation of the Six Sigma program, the idea was to build a structure of in-house competence. By 1995, the plant had 9 so-called Black Belts who were trained in Six Sigma methodology. These Black Belts, who were engineers, order managers and quality managers, were located throughout the company. Some 20 other so-called Yellow Belts, mainly quality inspectors and operators, were then trained in the summer of 1995. Although Ludvika soon became one of the most active plants within the BA on this front, it was still at an early stage in terms of the Six Sigma standards. Indeed, the company assessment was that, on average, process quality had yet to increase above three sigma.

ABB Ludvika has furthermore been an active player within the BA on the supply management model as a means to reduce costs and lead time. As a result of defining strategic suppliers and implementing a system for quality certification, the number of suppliers was successively lowered from 2,500 in 1990 down to 80 by the end of 1994.

COMMON PRODUCT AND COMMON PROCESS

Ever since the BA decided to move toward product standardization, the Ludvika plant has been involved, albeit with some reservations in the early stages. During the development and testing of the first design, Ludvika was one of the pilot plants. However, the design developed by the BA project group was heavily criticized by both the engineering and production departments at the plant. First, they felt that the technical solution was out-of-date—"A step back 10–15 years," said a former production manager—and they regarded their own standardized designs as much more advanced. Second, it was felt that the project was too narrowly focused on technical issues, with too little consideration given to the problem of finding effective processes.

In 1993, when the BA conceived a complementary project on Common Process, in which the Common Product standard was regarded more as a basis for process improvements, the designers at the Ludvika plant became more enthusiastic. One reason for their enthusiasm was that a part of the computer system package connected to the project was initiated at ABB Ludvika. The prescribed tests associated with the Common Product program were conducted from 1994 to 1996, some in collaboration with the Vaasa plant in Finland. Because of its role as an initiator of this key program promoted by the BA, Ludvika was appointed as a "grandfather" to seven other plants, which involved Ludvika personnel helping them to introduce the Common Product concept.

The BA launched the Common Process project in 1993, under the responsibility of a senior corporate manager. The core idea was to realize the potential of common products through more effective processes. At the macro level, this was to be achieved by coordinating and concentrating common resources within the BA, thereby making ideas such as the Model Factory, kit center and supply management more operational. At the micro level, processes would be optimized to find the best way of producing customized transformers in a more standardized fashion.

Ludvika gradually became more aware of the potential impact of these ideas. The management realized that such a restructuring of the entire BA would affect all plants, including major facilities such as Ludvika. The future role of each plant, however, still had to be determined; there remained considerable room for local initiatives. This insight was the starting point for a proactive approach at the Swedish plant. In particular, it invested considerable effort in becoming a kit center for cutting core plates for the various plants in the Northern region, and it has sought to become a kit center for tank fabrication.

Since 1994, the Ludvika plant has made process management,[2] which embraces several activities, a priority. Along with the Finnish Vaasa plant, it became a pilot plant for the Common Process concept within the BA as a whole. At the time of fieldwork, it was too early to evaluate the full impact of these innovations related to process management. Nevertheless, some concrete measures were soon made operational. One of these aims to obtain a more visual process and to increase the commitment to process improvements.[3] The production flows have thus been reconfigured. Up to fifteen information boards were also installed at critical points on the shop floor, so that all employees could follow and visualize the flow of production, be informed of the slippage occurring on a day-to-day basis and of the likelihood of impending bottlenecks in the production chain. These boards also show the monthly progress in projects and targets connected to continuous improvements. Such concrete measures are likely to contribute to making the related objectives—of keeping work-in-progress lower, reducing inventory costs and improving TPT and TTPT—more operational.

Another change of interest was the restructuring of the organization within one division into two core processes, the Customer process and the Production process, in order to better meet the varying customer demands.

Work Organization

The rationalization policies implemented at ABB Ludvika since the early 1990s also have had a significant impact on the organization of work. In engineering, the main focus was on the standardization and computerization of the design process. A good example was the Design 2000 project, which aimed at a major reduction of design times. The idea here was to build on the similarity of most orders and to recycle calculations, drawings, and specifications by defining parametric components. Ludvika also developed a pow-

[2] See Eugene H. Melan. 1992. *Process management—Methods for improving products and service.* New York: McGraw-Hill.

[3] This concept of the "visual company" is developed, for instance, by Michel Greif. 1989. *L'usine s'affiche.* Paris: Les Editions d'Organisation.

erful computer system for designing control equipment, which reduced design times by 85 percent for customized products and even more for more standardized ones.

Technological innovations were also made in many of the workshops. In both winding and assembly, where production will continue to depend on skilled craftsmanship, management has focused on acquiring more effective tools as well as on enhanced ergonomics. New equipment was added to improve work flow and production capacity.

The Ludvika plant strove to develop a more integrated and process oriented work organization that would promote flexibility and internal cooperation. The divisionalization carried out in 1992 and the flattening of the hierarchical structure within each department were also meant to contribute to these objectives. With the abolition of the supervisor level in manufacturing, only the level of section manager remained between the production manager and the production groups. Within the design department there is only one management level.

Goal oriented groups were established in both the offices and the workshops. In 1995, there were twenty-six of these groups in the plant, covering nearly two-thirds of the personnel, mainly in the workshops. However, the nature of these groups varied considerably. In the workshops, the basic idea is to form semiautonomous groups, each of which are responsible for manufacturing, quality inspection, and related administrative work within a certain area. The detailed planning and scheduling as well as the organization of work tasks are decided jointly by the workers based on actual orders and established goals regarding time and quality. In reality, the autonomy of the groups vary widely. The manual work in fact resembles a limited form of teamwork, since most tasks are carried out by two or more employees working together on the same unit (with the exception of the winding section, where the tasks are mostly individual).

In the offices, several forms of group and process organization emerged, all of which aimed at improving horizontal coordination. The formation of cross-functional order teams is one example. For large orders, the members of these order-specific (and thus temporary) teams include the project manager, the electrical designer, the mechanical designer, the designer of the control equipment, and representatives from purchasing, manufacturing, and quality. For minor projects, the order team is limited to the first four members. Cross-functional customer-focused order teams that work with specific customers, and not only specific projects, were also planned. The idea behind the creation of these teams was borrowed from the Vaasa and Guarulhos (Brazil) plants. Furthermore, a new form of permanent production team, consisting of both workers and engineers, was also considered.

During the reorganization process, production managers also sought to enhance flexibility and multiskilling, particularly in order to counter the ef-

fects of absenteeism and variations in workload. Some of the traditional demarcation lines between shop floor workers were removed by means of systematic training on several operations. Job rotation was established between
winding and winding assembly and between active part assembly and cleats
and leads. The recruitment policy was also seen as a tool to obtain greater
labor flexibility in these areas.

The reorganization was accompanied by a substantial amount of training,
both in TBM and TQM principles and in teamwork. Several career ladders
were defined for designers and engineers, allowing them to specialize further. This was meant to compensate in some ways for the fact that the traditional opportunities to pursue a managerial career had declined as a result
of decentralization.

Finally, the planning and control systems were altered. Until 1995, the
overall trend was toward decentralization and goal and process orientation.
This direction was evident in several areas. The divisionalization and the formation of profit centers (and, later, the information boards) have clearly
brought information on performance and financial results closer to all employees. The logistic engineers and production planners now had to develop
closer links with production workers. Furthermore, production groups are
for the most part guided by process oriented goals on delivery dates and
quality instead of detailed schedules and prescribed work plans. There is no
systematic work analysis carried out on the shop floor, and the work methods are mainly chosen by the skilled workers themselves.

Institutional Regulation

The formal position of the unions at ABB Ludvika is fairly strong. They
have two seats on the board of directors, and Swedish labor law also gives
them a right to information and to negotiate over working conditions, wages,
and major changes in company strategies. The unions should therefore be
seen as an influential actor.

However, the real influence of the unions is more limited. It is true that
managers at ABB Ludvika express a positive attitude toward the unions.
Union-management cooperation, however, during the past few years has focused mostly on negotiations concerning the 20 percent of employees who
have been made redundant. In this process, the company regarded union involvement as a valuable means of tempering the worst conflicts between
management and employees. Nevertheless, there were divergent views over
who should be laid off, with the unions arguing that seniority should be the
major principle of selection, whereas in many cases the company preferred
to keep those who possessed strategically important skills.

The unions have played a more subordinate role in the innovation process.
In common with the situation in many Swedish companies, the unions have

not been active—and indeed, have often not even been asked to take an active part—in the various rationalization projects. To some extent this lack of involvement was because they had their hands full with the massive layoffs. In addition, however, the unions were reluctant to endorse the corporate rationalization programs, since they feared new layoffs. In particular, they worried that the expertise built up at the Ludvika plant might be transferred to other plants within the BA, making these other plants more competitive and leading to losses in production volume in the plant studied.

Another matter of concern for the unions during the 1990s was the "Associate Agreements," which were based on the idea of equalizing the working conditions of blue collar and white collar workers by implementing equally structured agreements for all employees. The initiative for such new arrangements came from the national ABB management, which was seeking to promote a more integrated form of work organization in which traditional job structures would be relaxed and made much more flexible. The unions, both at the national level and in the Ludvika plant, were rather positive about the idea of equality, but the Swedish Metal Workers' Union (Metall) in particular has sharply criticized the wage setting system promoted by ABB Sweden, through which managers would decide unilaterally on the new wage structure. Metall objected that such a method could result in arbitrariness and jealousies that might jeopardize the whole idea of cooperation and goal-orientation.

Performance

In this section, we assess the impact that the process of rationalization has had on Ludvika's performance during the 1990s, focusing on the most important of the performance measures.

A first glance at Table 8.1 suggests that there have been significant improvements on all of the key process-related measures during the period 1990–95. However, a closer analysis of the data reveals a more complex picture.

A drop by nearly two-thirds in the failure rate shows that the various quality initiatives have had an effect. The TQM activities within the division producing large transformers are at the origin of much of this progress. However, the failure rate in 1995 was still far from the Six Sigma targets and resulted in substantial quality costs. A detailed analysis also reveals that, as production volumes and capacity utilization have increased, the Ludvika plant has had difficulty in keeping the rate of final test failures down. These limitations motivated management to go beyond TBM and put more emphasis on TQM and Six Sigma.

The emphasis on lead-time reduction led to some positive results. Most impressive were the improvements in on-time delivery; indeed, ABB Ludvika

Table 8.1. Performance Data at the Ludvika Plant

Measurements	Change in % 1990–95
Failure rate, %	−62%
On-time delivery, %	+82%
Lead time, TPT	−22%
Total lead time, TTPT	−34%
Productivity[a]	+27%
Orders received/revenue	+89%
Volume, MVA	−17%
No. of employees	−22%

[a](Revenue + orders received)/2 × number of employees

succeeded in delivering almost every transformer on time, despite the quality problems and the gradually increased capacity utilization. The reduction of lead time as such, which is the key objective of TBM, proved to be more difficult, although progress was significant over the five years. The performance on TTPT was still far from the BA norm. Until 1994, management tended to dismiss these results with a variety of explanations, stressing in particular that ABB Ludvika produced much more complex transformers. Our detailed analysis of the order process reveals that rationalization at the Ludvika plant has been focused more on the workshops than on the offices.[4] This also explains why the TPT figures, which were slightly better than the BA norm in 1995 (and even better in 1996) are much more favorable than the TTPT results, for which the Swedish plant remains far above the norm set by ABB Mannheim.

The improvements in productivity (by 27 percent) certainly appear to be significant. The variations over the years, however, show that the measure itself is complicated (e.g., a 54 percent increase during the period 1990–94). The productivity gain registered by ABB Ludvika reflects a combination of personnel reductions (of 22 percent) despite relatively constant volumes, higher capacity utilization, and more integrated and effective forms of work organization.

Some of these performance measures, and especially those related to quality and TTPT, were certainly a challenge and a matter of concern for ABB Ludvika's senior management. At the same time, however, strong financial results partly compensated for these problems. During the period from 1990–95, order booking (compare orders received/revenue in Table 8.1) and capacity utilization exceeded all budget targets. Moreover, compared with

[4] Lars Bengtsson. 1994. *Learning from Mecca? Rationalizations and work processes at ABB Transformers in Ludvika.* Stockholm: Royal Institute of Technology.

the other transformer plants within the BA, Ludvika was consistently one of the best in terms of revenues and profits. It is expected that the growing interest in process management, the efforts made in new design systems, and the involvement in the Common Product and Common Process projects will improve performance on these measures.

Constraints and Opportunities

Three themes are discussed in this analytical section: the introduction of corporate rationalization programs at ABB Ludvika; the drive to win the lead in the transformer production race as regards both technology and process innovation; and the significant changes in work that resulted from TBM and other process oriented rationalization programs.

A Cultural Revolution at the Old Mecca

The past ten years have seen a revolution at the Ludvika plant. The changes have affected not only structural conditions, such as new technology and reorganization, but the fundamental culture of the company as well. A culture of self-righteousness and a technological orientation have changed into a more modest search for continuous improvements and a process orientation. It is possible to identify three distinct phases in this cultural transformation.

The first phase dates back to the era prior to the creation of ABB, when the Ludvika plant played a leadership role. The former ASEA company had several licensees and exported its expertise and its managers all over the world, helping other transformer companies to improve their production.

The second phase, which was initiated by the formation of ABB and the Power Transformers BA, saw Ludvika face a new situation of reduced autonomy. Its initial reaction was to carry on as before, trying to develop the company rather independently of the corporate guidelines. Management's view was that the Ludvika plant's technological superiority in producing specialized and advanced transformers was still a sufficient basis of competitiveness. Internal rationalization continued to rely on new technology, such as computerized design systems, a cutting center, and more sophisticated product designs. Although the company accepted many of the principal ideas behind TBM and TQM, the way in which these were put into practice was defined locally. Even when the Ludvika plant took part in BA projects, it did so on the assumption that it was the "master builder" in the field of transformers and that it had much to teach the other companies. This attitude was reinforced by good financial results.

In this atmosphere of overconfidence, the benchmarking measures established by the BA were regarded with some indifference, if not simply rejected as misleading and unfair. The methodology used and the comparability of the performance figures were also criticized on the grounds of differences in the mix of products and customers. Ludvika claimed that it had a large number of new and difficult customers and that it produced the most complex transformers (and an increasing proportion of small transformers), all of which made lead-time reduction more complicated.

The third phase, which began around 1994, saw the focus shift from technology to processes and a growing interest by management in how other plants had arranged their processes. The starting point for this cultural change was the acceptance that the Ludvika plant had poor processes that had to be improved and that technological superiority was not enough to be successful in the increasingly competitive export market then taking shape. Concretely, the new orientation meant a stronger emphasis on process management and a more proactive involvement in BA projects on both products and processes. In short, this Swedish plant has sought to play a more central role within the BA.

Why did the commitment to the corporate programs take so long, and what factors accounted for this strategic change? Both the obstacles and the forces driving the change can be understood as a combination of economic and sociocultural factors. As for obstacles, the relatively strong financial situation—in terms of profits and orders—was clearly an important factor in the early 1990s, since it legitimated the perception of overconfidence. This also illustrates the complex relationship between center and periphery within a multinational organization. The BA management decided to define the concepts of TBM and TQM at the BA level, simply assuming that all of the plants in the BA would embrace the move and implement the concepts, regardless of local perceptions and strategies.[5]

A crucial factor behind the shift to the third phase was the presentation of the BA's visions of the Model Factory and Common Product and Common Process projects, which implied a complete restructuring of the BA. These visions made clear that all the plants in the BA would have to change because these new concepts were to be implemented at every location. The management at Ludvika realized that the plant's future position in the BA would depend very much on its involvement in developing and introducing these concepts.

Once this new situation was accepted, the BA's benchmarking measures were reassessed. The comparisons revealed many weaknesses and suggested the need for further improvements. Moreover, during 1994 and 1995, it became even more apparent that Ludvika was a fading star in the area of process performance, a fact that could not be ignored. For example, by the end

---

[5] According to network theory, an effective relationship between different actors in a network presupposes that the goals and expectations of *each* actor are compatible with those possessed by the others. See Håkan Håkansson and Ivan Snehota. 1995. *Developing relationships in business networks*. London: Routledge.

of 1995, Ludvika was only 19th out of the 23 power transformer plants in terms of TTPT. The TTPT of the leaders, the Vaasa and Geneva plants, were less than half of ABB Ludvika's. As mentioned earlier, ABB Ludvika was doing better on TPT; but even here it was only ranked 15th, far behind the best plants. The workshop had thus become less competitive, even though the organization of the design process was the biggest problem. The same depressing pattern held true for quality, particularly as regards the failure rate.

This painful acceptance of its own limits became the starting point for greater involvement in BA programs and for a real investment in process innovation. An additional factor was the appointment in 1994 of a new general manager who did not have to defend the previous structures and management processes.

Fighting for a Strong Position in the World of Power Transformers

The strategy pursued by ABB Ludvika since 1994 has centered on winning—or reclaiming—its role as a leading plant within the BA. To assess this strategy, it is first necessary to consider the BA strategies more closely. The opening chapters of this book stressed these objectives, emphasizing the search for greater conformity and further rationalization in the design and manufacturing of transformers. Despite ABB's slogan of "being local worldwide," programs such as Common Product, Common Process, and Six Sigma all point toward standardization and finding the "one best way"— although without affecting the capacity of individual plants to meet successfully the requirements of their various customers. However, each plant is in fact encouraged to restructure its business and processes in line with the new concepts. In this sense, all of the plants, including Ludvika, are pupils and not teachers.

To meet these new challenges, the management team at Ludvika assumed that a strong position within the BA could be based on two main elements: producing strong financial results; and taking an active part in the development of the new BA concepts in order to establish the Ludvika plant as a sort of center of knowledge in both technology and process improvements. What are ABB Ludvika's chances of realizing this ambition?

Good financial results depend very much on the market situation. Apart from the efforts to open the market in East Asia, the development of the HVDC transformer was regarded as the Ludvika plant's greatest potential for expanding exports. Thanks to the growing market for these transformers, Ludvika has been one of the best plants in the entire BA in terms of order booking, revenues, and profits. As a consequence, at the time of the study, ABB Ludvika's financial prospects appeared positive.

The ambition of developing the factory into a sort of center of expertise also seemed within reach. ABB Ludvika was rather successful in adapting the ideas of the Model Factory and kit center while at the same time preserving its character as a complete plant. On several counts, ABB Ludvika also maintained its position as a top-ranked company in transformer technology. More specifically, there seemed to be few obstacles to winning a leading position in the technology race in the BA. A much greater challenge for ABB Ludvika, however, has been to become a leader in process development. Here the picture is more complicated.

In principle, good financial results should make other plants interested in the way ABB Ludvika has rationalized and organized its production processes. However, there has been no lineup of visiting companies trying to discover the secrets of ABB Ludvika's processes. Several reasons might account for this lack of interest. First, the plant's strong profits are derived to a large extent from the HVDC transformers, which are based on Ludvika's technological strength. Second, the new forms of work organization are for the most part well-known, at least among those companies participating in the Swedish T-50 program. Complete teams, cross-functional teams, designers on the shop floor, and *kaizen* groups are advanced and farsighted but hardly unique. Third, the less than flattering results reported in the benchmarking measures have not, so far, made ABB Ludvika a star within the BA when it comes to process improvements. Naturally, such results foster little interest on the part of other BA plants in the organizational solutions and changes made at the Ludvika plant.

On the other hand, the renewal at ABB Ludvika that began in 1994 may alter this picture. First of all, Ludvika has played a more prominent role in the BA projects. For example, along with the Vaasa plant, it was appointed as a pilot plant for the development of a Common Process and reducing TTPT to 40 days. ABB Ludvika has also become a "grandfather" for seven other plants implementing the Common Product and Common Process concepts. It can now also be considered the most active plant in the BA's Six Sigma program. Moreover, for several years, it has acted as coordinator for materials purchasing, in line with the concept of supply management. Second, all these activities and initiatives are integrated into the internal Customer Focus program, through which the new general manager seeks to put the emphasis on process management and TQM. In short, in abandoning its role as a "lone ranger," the Ludvika plant has recently taken resolute and concrete steps to become a key strategic player within the power transformers BA.

Ludvika's ambition is clear: to regain its position as a front-runner within the BA, a teacher from whom other plants can learn. However, the road to becoming a process improvement star appears to be a long one. The outcome of the Common Product and Common Process projects will have a decisive effect on ABB Ludvika's future role and position.

A Revolution in Industrial Work?

This study of ABB Ludvika was conducted during a period that saw the emergence of a range of new production concepts. In this section, examination is made of the types of rationalization methods used to implement process management and what they mean for production and engineering work in the context of a mature industry characterized by a high concentration of engineers.

A general trend during recent years was the increasingly integrated and goal-oriented character of work organization, with considerable emphasis on social networks within the organization. This trend was manifested by decentralization, divisionalization and process organization, teamwork in both offices and workshops, and cross-functional cooperation. Concrete measures were taken to increase flexibility and encourage multiskilling of both blue- and white-collar workers. For all categories of employees, process management meant broader work content, more teamwork, and closer cooperation among different functions. Workers greeted this orientation positively since it gave them more autonomy and greater influence over work methods. The recent centralization of the main planning function, however, has contradicted these other trends in work reorganization, and it is still an open question whether the centralization is just temporary or a genuine break with the past.

A second important trend during 1994–95 was the drive for standardization and computerization, especially the new product standards and computer support systems. The designers, the group most directly affected by these changes, felt that the changes had provided them with better tools and had made their work smoother and more productive. However, many expressed frustration that the agreed product standards are less sophisticated and more difficult to use than the old ASEA concepts.

A third trend was the increasing interest in TQM. Compared with previous work arrangements, TQM added a dimension of continuous improvement and participation to work organization. Employees at all levels not only have to worry about the daily and order related work, they now also have to think about the development of the work processes. Examples include the introduction of quality and *kaizen* groups, the involvement of almost everybody in process mapping, and the various operational techniques associated with the Six Sigma initiative. Again, though, the employees interviewed expressed a positive attitude to this new dimension in work.

A fourth trend, which is linked to the others, was the effort put into skill development. Besides the training provided in connection with the formation of the goal oriented groups, managers were also made responsible for devising individual development plans in cooperation with each employee. These alternative and more specialized career development paths were favorably received by both the engineers and the workers, not least because the traditional upward career opportunities have declined as a result of the flatter organization.

In summary, it is quite clear that, in implementing the process oriented concepts of TBM and TQM, the Ludvika plant has abandoned Taylorism in favor of modern organizational principles.

In contrast with the principles of Taylorism, TBM and TQM, as interpreted in the Swedish debate, prescribe a completely new perspective on work, work organization, and human resource management.[6] Fundamental to this new approach is the creation of a customer- and process-oriented organization, replacing the functional form of organization. Other features include integration and decentralization (reflected in reduced hierarchies), more flexible jobs, and increased responsibility and decision-making authority at the shop floor level. Together, these ideas also stress continuous improvement combined with broad participation and the development of the skills of all employees. ABB Ludvika's version of TBM and TQM is closely related to these organizational ideals.

Nonetheless, this forging of a more modern organization, built on a wide set of measures associated with the idea of rationalization, does not present the entire picture. Although the drive for standardization and computerization is not prescribed by the concepts of TBM and TQM, it is fully consistent with them, especially considering the objectives of reducing lead time and costs and of enhancing quality. Underlying the whole process of innovation observed at the Ludvika plant is the importance of technological rationalization. Some of the improvements made, and particularly the targets established (e.g., reduced lead time in design), seem to rely more on standardization and new computer systems than on reorganization. Of course, the organizational and technological measures should not be seen as isolated from each other. The point, however, is that the implementation of TBM and TQM at Ludvika, which is an example of a company with a large number of engineers in a mature market situation, was not exclusively an organizational change. It was clearly a combination of both organizational and technological measures in a search for a more "rational" way of designing and manufacturing power transformers.

Regarding both the organizational and technological changes, ABB Ludvika's approach is similar to the concepts of "anthropocentric production systems" and even more, "agile manufacturing."[7] Aiming at increased flexibility, the agile company is characterized by cooperative, integrative, and autonomous work forms leveraging employee competence, creativity, and learning; by virtual networks of companies; and by the use of flexible and integrative production and information technology, especially different kinds of design and engineering tools.

Conclusions

The central focus of this chapter was the impact of the introduction of corporate rationalization programs on ABB's Swedish transformer plant in

---

[6] See Stalk and Hout 1990; Imai, Masaaki 1986. *Kaizen, The Key to Japan's Competitive Success*. New York: McGraw-Hill; and Bengtsson and Ljungström 1996.

[7] See Brödner 1985; Wobbe 1991; Nagel and Dove 1992; Kidd 1994.

Ludvika. A second theme was the social process through which these changes in the sphere of production affected the organization and nature of work. The analysis developed can be summarized in four concluding points.

1. The implementation of corporate rationalization programs, such as Customer Focus, TBM and TQM, in such a long-established plant is a complex process, one that demands cultural as well as structural changes. In the case of Ludvika, which was the center of knowledge about transformer technology prior to the creation of ABB, this process has entailed something of a revolution over the last several years. Although Ludvika quickly adopted the focus on lead-time reduction, it was more reluctant to commit to, and engage in, other aspects of the corporate rationalization program. Such a process demanded, and eventually caused, a degree of cultural change within the company. A culture of local autonomy and self-righteousness, and a strong belief in the primacy of technology, had to be replaced by a more humble attitude: an acceptance that Ludvika could learn from other plants and could become a more process oriented organization.

Until the early 1990s, a degree of organizational inertia was understandable in view of the Ludvika plant's unique technological expertise, its profitability, and its full order books. However, it later became evident that the market for power transformers was changing owing to the process of maturation, deregulation, and globalization in Western economies. However, besides these market forces, a further major impetus behind the transformation were the concepts of Model Factory, Common Product, and Common Process promoted by global managers in the BA. Some standardization in product design and production processes would now have to be considered seriously, independently of plant and national cultures. Ludvika's management had to recognize that all of the transformer plants, including Ludvika, would have to adapt and become involved in order to secure a solid position in the future. The Ludvika plant's consistently average ranking on the BA's benchmarking measures for process performance also contributed to this change in direction.

2. An important aspect of ABB Ludvika's fresh start was a stronger emphasis on process management through a more explicit involvement in various projects run by the power transformers BA. The drive to play a new and more proactive role within the BA represents a second conclusion of our study.

Since the change in orientation in 1994, the Ludvika plant has pursued a two-pronged strategy to regain its status as a Mecca within ABB transformer production. On the one hand, it has sought to consolidate good financial results through the opening of new markets and the development of a niche product, the HVDC transformers. So far, this strategy seems promising. On the other hand, it has become involved in BA-sponsored projects in order to develop a unique proficiency in both technology and process management. As regards technology, Ludvika seems to have consolidated its position, as demonstrated in particular by its large Technology Division and its designation as a kit center for core cutting. Furthermore, the plant has assumed responsibility for particular projects in major corporate programs such as Common Product, Common Process, and Six Sigma. Ludvika's major challenge, and its open ambition, is to become a star in process improvements. Whether this ambition will be realized was still an open question at the time of study.

3. Regardless of the outcome of ABB Ludvika's bid to regain stardom, a related conclusion is that it seems possible, in general, to acquire a prominent and unique position within a concern such as the power transformers BA, despite its drive for conformity in products and processes. However, such a role will probably be somewhat different than in a more diversified organization. More particularly, it will be based on the need for dynamics in the process of standardization. In order to develop standardization while at the same time promoting the even more important search for continuous improvements, the BA has to rely on the initiatives and activities undertaken by the individual plants. These individual plants, therefore, are called on and given the room to play an innovative role. However, this unique role will not be that of an all-knowing teacher from whom the other plants can learn, but will instead be akin to a forerunner, which, alone or in cooperation with a few other plants, can develop the new standard concepts to be implemented all over the BA. This strategy is obvious in the common projects run by the plants located in Ludvika and Vaasa.

4. The principles of TBM and TQM, at least as interpreted in Sweden, prescribe a reorganization of production that fosters a more process oriented and cooperative work organization, a sharing of information across departments, and the engagement of all employees in continuous improvement. These concepts clearly represent an abandonment of the Taylorist perspective. Their implementation at the transformer plant in Ludvika suggests that they might also have other effects on work.

It is certainly true that the organization of work at the Ludvika plant embodies many of the principles currently prescribed in the managerial literature, such as goal oriented groups in the workshops and offices, *kaizen* groups, and well-defined plans for skill development. In addition, most of the employees whom we met acknowledged that these changes have broadened the content of work and have allowed more self-regulation. It is also fair to point out that Ludvika's efforts in the area of standardization and computerization go further than what is suggested by TBM or TQM initiatives. Two points should be made in this respect.

First, the implementation of TBM and TQM at the Ludvika plant can be characterized as a combination of organizational and technological means. In fact, technology was expected to have a greater impact on lead-time reduction and costs than the organizational means. For example, the target of reducing the design time by 85 percent was mainly based on a new parametric design system.

Second, ABB Ludvika has played a central role in developing the standardized BA concepts on products and processes and the design and manufacturing tools related to these concepts. When these concepts are implemented in other BA plants, the work in these design departments and workshops will become more similar. The extent of convergence that this process will entail remains an open question. It seems clear, however, that the standardization of work has limits. It depends on the social dynamics observed at the point of production, that is, on the way engineers, managers, and production workers interpret the set of constraints and opportunities at their place of work and on how they relate to each other. It follows that within the increasingly standardized framework, there is still room for various forms of work design.

9 ABB in Germany
Is Excellence Enough to Survive?

Rainer Schultz-Wild

The Asea Brown Boveri Bad Honnef power transformer plant is located on the Rhine River near Bonn, the former capital of Germany. Along with a shoe factory and a pharmaceutical plant, it is one of the town's largest industrial employers. No comparable metal or electrical plant exists in Bad Honnef or the surrounding small towns. Thus, the fate of the workforce depends on the well-being of the plant. Many of the current employees' parents and grandparents also worked there. Workers tend to enter the plant as apprentices, work some time in production, go to engineering schools, and return to the plant after graduation. There is great pride in product quality. Compared with plants in other countries or industries, labor relations at Bad Honnef are characterized by high trust relations. A shared spirit of craftsmanship in production and technical departments, decades of hard work, and continuous step-by-step rationalization of products and processes have made Bad Honnef one of the star plants. In short, Bad Honnef is a picture book German plant.

The plant was owned by the ASEA group when the merger with Brown Boveri took place in 1987. At first glance, the merger appears to have been a success. Quite unlike many other plants under the umbrella of ABB, the multinational group, the recent history of the Bad Honnef plant is characterized by stability. Neither the fiercer competition in a context of worldwide overcapacities nor the restructuring of the power transformer business under the regime of the new corporation has so far translated into major drawbacks and job losses. The plant's basic structures and employment have remained relatively stable, although fluctuations in demand and sales have been experienced and efforts to rationalize and reshape production structures have had their costs.

On the other hand, closer examination reveals a much more complicated and open-ended story in terms of risks and of ABB Bad Honnef's long-term survival. The fact that the plant has a long history in an industrialized country with high labor costs and that it depends on exports raises a number of questions of particular interest. How long can traditional gains in productivity be defended against the encroachment of newcomers, particularly in view of the fact that product and process standardization and the transfer of knowledge are fostered centrally by the business area (BA)? Can the established, relatively high export ratios be maintained in the face of the new, explicit corporate policy of manufacturing as close as possible to customers in markets with development potential? How long can the basis of past success be maintained, that is, decades of industrial experience, the advantages of the specific institutional regulations, and Germany's particular qualification and infrastructure conditions? In short, given changing conditions, will yesterday's success story continue to be an advantage or will it become a burden in the future?

History and Corporate Context

The Bad Honnef plant's industrial history can be divided roughly into three main periods.

The *first phase* as an independent, family owned company began at the turn of the twentieth century, when August Lepper founded his firm in Bad Honnef on the Rhine River for the repair, conversion, and sale of electrical machinery. Evidence of these origins can still be found in the plant today. For example, it is still called *Plant L*. Transformer manufacturing started in 1932 and in 1951, the first 100-MVA mobile transformer was delivered, followed in 1953 by a 250-MVA large-scale transformer (220-kV).

The *second phase* began in 1964–65, when the firm was acquired on a majority basis by the Swedish ASEA group. This period as an affiliate of a foreign corporation was characterized by turbulence, the repercussions of which are still felt today. In the early 1970s, production capacity and the high voltage test fields were expanded and the first 400-kV transformers were produced. At the same time, in line with ASEA policy, acquisitions and mergers with other companies were taking place.[1] In the early 1980s, with 850 employees at its different locations, the Bad Honnef company adopted ASEA's delivery program. However, in 1986, ASEA formed three independent companies within a separate holding. The workforce at the Bad Honnef plant was first reduced to about 600, and then further decreased to 300, when tank construction and other activities were removed.

The beginning of the *third phase* of company development came with the 1987 merger of ASEA and forming the new ABB group. First, in 1989, the

---

[1] For example, in 1972, the former Dominit Power Engineering of Brilon, where the largest arc furnace transformer of its time had been built in 1970, was integrated. In the meantime, this plant has become a separate ABB company with around 200 employees involved in the production of distribution transformers.

Brilon plant was hived off. Then, in 1990, the former Brown Boveri power transformer plant (Plant M), a former competitor, was integrated into a joint ABB company: the German Power Transformer Company (DETFO) and most of the central functions, for example, engineering and sales, were relocated to the former ASEA Plant L. After German reunification, ABB became active in the new federal states of Eastern Germany and in 1991 a transformer factory (Plant H) was acquired in Halle on the Saale River.

From the time it ceased to be a family-owned, mid-size company, Plant L could no longer be called an independent organization. Its development became interlinked with that of its frequently changing mother corporations, sister companies, and daughter plants. At least three interdependencies as a result of becoming part of the ABB multinational should be mentioned. According to the corporation's matrix structure, and like all the other transformer producers, Plant L is first part of the international Power Transformers BA and, second, part of ABB's national/regional group, in this case, the Mannheim-based ABB Germany AG. Third, Plant L has served as the mother plant of German power transformer production. Its management has had to coordinate the business of the two or three transformer plants in changing organizational settings.

In the early 1990s, Germany was the only country in which three power transformer production plants were maintained by the Power Transformers BA. More or less from the beginning, it had to be regarded as uneconomical in the long term to maintain three manufacturing plants, particularly given regional and global overcapacities and overhead costs of the premises, test fields, and so on. This caused uncertainties and turmoil for several years until finally, in 1995, production at the Mannheim site was closed down.

The negotiations to reach a joint decision by the BA and ABB Germany, as required by the matrix, were difficult. Because of political and business reasons, the newly acquired East German Halle plant could not be shut down. ABB chose the Halle plant to supply the "new German Laender" (ex-German Democratic Republic, GDR) and to become a service and repair center. The BA opted for keeping the former ASEA Bad Honnef plant. However, there were strong forces in ABB Germany in favor of maintaining the former Brown Boveri Mannheim plant. As a part of the ensemble of former Brown Boveri, Mannheim plants represented the dominant traditions within Germany and thus conflicts with the rather powerful general works council were to be expected.

The Company: Markets, Personnel, and Labor Relations

Production Program and Sales Markets

The Bad Honnef plant mainly manufactures mid-size power transformers along with small quantities of large ones. In the mid-1990s, the plant's annual capacity consisted of about 65–80 units with a total performance of about 5000–6000 MVA. Only made-to-order transformers are produced, generally in unit production according to customer specifications, but occasionally in small batches. On average, 1.5 transformers are delivered per week. Their average rating was in decline from the mid-1980s onward, but then began to increase again in the mid-1990s. According to the BA-wide classification (in MVA), the product mix at Plant L corresponds to the average for all power transformer plants. In 1994, small class 1 transformers accounted for about only 5 percent of MVA; class 2, for approximately 30 percent; class 3, for more than 40 percent; and large class 4 transformers, for another 20 percent.

Although incoming orders and sales have fluctuated considerably, the situation since 1991–92 has remained stable at a volume of around DM 200 million per annum for the joint plants.

Developments in the *domestic market* have been crucial to maintaining sales. The domestic sales market consists of German power utilities. The large supraregional power plants or network operators, such as RWE AG, mainly order larger transformers and local or regional suppliers, such as municipal utilities, buy mid-size transformers. So far, these customers have basically pursued a multibrand policy. However, they prefer transformers produced domestically for the nodal points of their networks, which require sensitive, highly reliable equipment. In fact, this investment policy amounted to a sort of industrial strategy to safeguard the domestic transformer industry, and thus a relatively high price level was accepted.

The domestic market, however, is becoming increasingly competitive. This is due, on the one hand, to the appearance of a large number of manufacturers from the European Union (EU) and other countries such as Turkey, and to continuing imports from Austria, Belgium, and Holland. On the other hand, demand is on the decline, at least in Western Germany, owing to stagnating power consumption and completion of the regional grids. Above and beyond this, cost factors are becoming relatively more important than technical considerations for the major domestic customers. These days, purchasing decisions are increasingly being made by businessmen rather than by engineers, as was the case in the past. It is widely expected that even more jobs will be lost over the mid term, even though for the time being, the domestic market can be relied on owing to certain quality advantages and long-established market relationships.

Exports play a major role for the German transformer plants. DETFO is one of three BA companies that is allowed to export "professionally," that is, on a larger than usual scale. The target domestic quota is 70–80 percent. However, since 1988, the average export share has been 40 percent, with considerable fluctuations. Plant L has been even more export oriented (about 50 percent) because foreign customers have had practically no significance for the East German Plant H to date. Due to the stagnating domestic market, from 1989–90 onward, the company started to hire more personnel for the sales department to enable it to cover the export markets more thoroughly. The most important of these are the Middle East, some Asian countries, and the Benelux countries. The East European markets do not play a role for the German plants since they are served in part by ABB-acquired factories, for example in Poland, or by joint ventures, such as the one started in Russia in 1994.

Apart from the generally fiercer competition on domestic and foreign markets, the BA policy of "being local worldwide" threatens the status of "professional" exporters. The increasing localization of production in the respective regional markets entails considerable risks, particularly for plants that have previously been strongly export oriented. The Swedish plant's policy of specializing in niche products has no parallel at Plant L, with the exception of industry-type or arc furnace transformers, for which, however, there is only a relatively low demand.

Organization and Personnel

The central management for German transformer operations (DEFTO) as well as the manufacturing unit of Plant L are located at Bad Honnef. Both the plant and company are organized on a functional basis, that is, they are divided into departments with differing tasks and areas of responsibility. The central departments of purchasing, sales, commercial functions, technology, quality and manpower, which are responsible for all German power transformer operations, report to the managing directors. This is also the case, at the plant level, for the respective production sections and, above all, the technical departments concerned with order processing, electrical and mechanical design, and quality control. In terms of organization, manufacturing is one of three production subdepartments.[2]

Besides the core functions of coil winding, core assembly and final assembly, insulating parts and certain peripheral components in a mechanical workshop are also produced on site. The tank and casing components, core sheets, and insulated copper wire are the most important parts and materials purchased from suppliers.

In the turbulence resulting from the merger in 1987, the expansion to East Germany, and the closure of production in Mannheim in 1995, only Bad Honnef was able to maintain its employment level. In 1990 as well as in 1994, the Bad Honnef site had a workforce of around 270, and, contrary to the general trend, even expanded slightly. About four-fifths of the staff is employed at Plant L and one-fifth in central company administration or sales, which are largely located at the site. Roughly half of the workforce consists of salaried employees and the other half of blue collar workers.

---

[2] The other two are the planning department, with a staff of seven responsible for order management, and another small department taking care of plant and manufacturing equipment.

With about 120 mostly highly qualified, skilled workers and 6 salaried employees, the *manufacturing* department is the largest group in the plant's workforce. It is divided into five workshops according to the most important component parts of the process flow. Each workshop is headed by a foreman, whose work is coordinated with that of the others by a general foreman. Core, windings, and insulating parts are manufactured in the respective workshops and passed on to the so-called active part assembly. The tank, which comes from an outside supplier, is preassembled to enable installation of the active part in the final assembly workshop, at which point the unit is closed with the cover and the conservator. Drying, referred to as "processes," completes the manufacturing chain.

The Bad Honnef plant's employment system is highly dependent on skills and knowledge and characterized by a high degree of stability. The skill structure reflects the importance of deployment of vocationally trained workers (Facharbeiter) and qualified engineers (Schultz-Wild 1992).

Skilled blue collar workers are the largest employment group (37 percent of the workforce in 1994) and outnumber trained semiskilled (7 percent) and other workers (2 percent) together by 4 to 1. The second largest group in the workforce is made up of engineers (20 percent), who are mainly deployed to the engineering and planning departments but who can also be found in sales; this figure does not include technicians (4 percent) or other technical employees (6.5 percent). There is a large proportion of commercial and office staff (15 percent). Nine percent of the workforce is made up of apprentices and there are almost twice as many industrial apprentices as clerical ones. Since 1990, this staffing pattern has changed only slightly and has tended to increase the availability of technical knowledge and skills.

The establishment and maintenance of a stable core workforce can largely be attributed to the long existence of the plant in Bad Honnef, its strong position in the regional labor market, and the low regional mobility of the workers. Engineers and technicians are recruited from the greater region's technical colleges and universities and become familiar with the specific work areas on the job. Some of them even start their career as apprentices in the plant. The in-house apprenticeship system, which is part of the German dual system of initial vocational education and training, is central to maintaining a continued supply of production workers with the required skills.

Soon after it took over the plant in 1964–65, ASEA discontinued the traditional German form of apprenticeship training, which did not correspond to the Swedish system. However, this decision was later reversed, thus reestablishing a crucial prerequisite for the skills-oriented work system. In addition to several commercial apprentices, the plant trains 3 to 4 young people a year in electrical mechanical engineering for its blue collar area. The respective training lasts 3.5 years. During this time the apprentices are taught practical and technical skills, gain experience in all the various production workshops, and receive theoretical instruction at a vocational school. To date, all the trainees have been hired by the plant at the end of their apprenticeship, and are initially deployed to the various production areas on a timework basis for the period of one year. This settling-in period not only prevents premature specialization but also helps expand skills and the social basis for later flexible deployment.

This German system of skill formation together with the plant's strong position in the regional labor market has allowed for the development of a specific system of production and work that relies to a large extent on workforce stability, the existence of skills built up over a long period, and emphasis on personal communication. As has been shown in international comparisons, the German system of skill formation and labor deployment allows for a high degree of autonomy in production as well as for an exceptional degree of communication and mutual learning between engineering and manufacturing functions (Lutz 1992; Sengenberger 1992).

However, this system also involves constraints. Short-term capacity adjustments through numerical flexibility on the basis of a hire and fire policy, which is typical of other institutional settings and particularly of internal labor markets involving low-skilled marginal workforces, would endanger the central prerequisites of productive labor deployment. This emphasis on stability which, despite the turbulent conditions accompanying the restructuring of the company, has been more or less maintained since the formation of ABB, is also influenced by the system of institutional regulations.

Industrial Relations

The plant is embedded in the specific German system of dual representation of workers' interests (Meil 1992). The industrial union, in this case IG Metall, represents the interests of its members and, indirectly, those of nonmembers, in wage and other negotiations encompassing all companies of the respective branches in a given region. However, an important role is also played by representation of employee interests at the plant or enterprise level. In accordance with the regulations of the Works Constitution Act (1972), a *works council* is elected every three years by all the employees of an enterprise, whether they are union members or not.

The relationship between Plant L's management and works council[3] can be described as cooperative, as indicated by a statement made by the works council chairman to the effect that "management and labor have a very good and trusting relationship involving discretion on both sides." Despite the "fundamental difference between the interests of capital and labor," both sides join forces when it comes to safeguarding the plant's economic survival in crisis situations, on the condition, laid down by the works council, that

[3] The works council has seven members; four of them are blue collar and three, white collar; the chairman belongs to the former group, was previously occupied in large and medium-sized transformer assembly, and is the only works council member released from his regular job.

direct dismissals be avoided. When job cutbacks are necessary, use is mainly made of "natural fluctuation." On this basis, it has been possible to safeguard the plant's survival for the past 10–12 years.

From the point of view of the works council, one of the main consequences of integration into the ABB Group, that is, the plant's loss of autonomy and its ability to undertake spontaneous action, applies not only to production and development but also to representation of workers' interests. During the ASEA era, when the plant was ASEA's only power transformer plant in Germany, it was relatively autonomous. While previously management and the works council were able to negotiate directly, now the plant must submit to the attempts to enforce common regulations throughout all German ABB plants. The existence of a group works council also leads to a standardization of interest policy in the German plants, with Mannheim playing a predominant role in this respect. The Plant L works council has repeatedly tried to break out of this straight jacket, and has managed to assert better proposals of its own in certain areas, such as company superannuation or the rewards for improvement suggestions. On the other hand, there is no body to represent joint labor interests at the international level of the Power Transformers BA, which is playing an increasingly important role in the fate of individual companies (Schmierl, 1998).

Stability and Change: The German Way

When plants such as Cordoba in Spain or Guelph in Canada were integrated into ABB, they had a considerable shortfall, as compared with the Swedish Ludvika plant or the German Bad Honnef plant. Therefore, from the very beginning they were under great pressure to implement comprehensive technical and organizational changes in order to catch up with the front-runners. In contrast, Bad Honnef had a long-standing world market presence, decades of rationalization and modernization, as well as high productivity, quality, and overall competitiveness. Management was trying to maintain the plant's position relative to other BA plants by continuing its policies of incremental change. This pattern is characterized by constant and intrinsically unspectacular technical and organizational change rather than by erratic developments. There can be no doubt that the threat of shutting down one of the three plants and the negotiations between the BA, ABB Germany, and the Bad Honnef and Mannheim plants supported this policy. Far-reaching experiments and investments make no sense in times of high uncertainty.

Company and Plant Organization

The company restructuring that took place in 1995 following the decision to shut down production at Plant M gave rise to several organizational changes, which primarily reflect the new situation regarding product and process technologies.

During the transition period that followed the formation of ABB, Plants L and M at first continued to work with their traditional ASEA or Brown Boveri methods, respectively. Development and design tasks mainly remained their responsibility. When production at Plant M was shut down, efforts were intensified to standardize product and production techniques to a greater degree. To reinforce this process, the technical departments of the plants since then have had to report to a central corporate technology department, which in turn fortifies aspects of a functional form of organization as compared with an operations oriented form.[4]

At the same time, the switch to Common Product (CP) technology, which is only possible step by step, means that the company continues to work with two different technologies. While the East German Halle plant draws up new units solely along the lines of the new Common Product technology, at the Bad Honnef parent plant, large and special transformers continue to be developed, designed, and manufactured according to traditional ASEA methods. In terms of organization, this is reflected by the fact that the Bad Honnef plant's two subdepartments were formed in 1995 to perform both electrical *and* mechanical design for either the more standardized units built according to the Common Product concept or for other orders, for example, large units and industrial transformers manufactured according to traditional techniques.[5] Thus, the formerly separate functions of electrical and mechanical design, respectively, were brought together. The objective of the new technology-based form of specialization in subdepartments is to encourage the plant to come to terms with the new concepts and tools and accelerate their testing and improvement.

Technical development, which used to be performed in the plants' technology departments, has been upgraded in the process of company restructuring and has now been pooled into a single central department at the company level. This reflects an increased emphasis on the Common Product project, which is strongly oriented toward the whole network of BA plants. Finally, the central organization of *quality assurance* is also being strengthened. Quality-related strategic developments, that is, the further improvement of the quality system, is to become a central company function and quality control in the test bays of the plants is to be subordinated to the central quality department.

---

[4] Since 1995, Brown Boveri techniques have admittedly no longer been valid. Plant M's design department is nevertheless to be kept going to prevent bottleneck situations from arising in this area. The transfer of qualified technical personnel to the remaining plants L and H, for administrative and organizational reasons, has been only partially achieved. Only 20 employees, most of them young technicians and engineers from sales and design departments (and including only 1 production worker), have taken up transfer offers.

[5] In September 1995, there were about twice as many skilled technical employees (21 in all) involved in processing orders for large and special transformers built according to traditional methods as there were employees involved in Common Product orders (13 persons).

Apart from these changes, the organization has been characterized by a high degree of *stability*. Extensive adjustments in production volume, outsourcing and organizational structures, such as the reduction of in-house production, flattening the hierarchy and substantial reduction of extensive time and materials management, had already taken place during the ASEA era in the 1970s and 1980s. It is obvious that, rather than emphasizing large-scale campaigns, smaller and individually less evident technical and organizational changes have been used to achieve productivity gains.

This is clear from the fact that a comparatively marginal change in the interface between the technology and sales departments is regarded as being one of the most important and far-reaching internal organizational changes to have been accomplished in the early 1990s. The move toward a more strongly *order oriented* form of organization was considered but not carried out on a broad scale. Skepticism about these ideas was mainly based on its expected negative consequences for smooth functioning and short manufacturing throughput times (TPT). An *order team* was created only in the case of extremely tight deadlines or particularly demanding orders.

The Organization of Work—
Specialization and Cooperation

There is a high degree of division of labor, task differentiation, and more or less pronounced specialization below the level of plant organization, that is, within the individual plant departments and subdepartments. This applies to both production itself, as well as to design, technical order processing, and production planning.

The primary reason for the special type of work organization in the *design* department is the necessity of achieving short throughput times. Before the new Common Product techniques were generally available, a traditional-technique transformer required an average of 600–800 hours of mechanical design work. In a highly order oriented form of organization, this would keep a single engineer employed for about half a year. This is unfeasible in view of the overall delivery periods of no more than 6–7 months. A medium-sized transformer is now worked on in parallel or overlapping mode by an average of eight employees. It takes 6–8 days to design a medium-sized transformer and 7–9 days for a larger one. However, production throughput time is given top priority, particularly to ensure that as little capital as possible is tied up. This may result in delays in the technology departments' schedule, since certain tasks have to be given priority and others interrupted and attended to later.

However, this division-of-labor approach to the overall design process involves specialization of the engineers and technicians only to a certain extent. At any one time, each design engineer generally has one transformer at the design stage, a second one in detailed design, and a third one in production, thus involving his or her supervision. All the engineers are familiar with several types or size categories, but since large transformers involve higher requirements, these are more or less the domain of the senior and more experienced design engineers. As in electrical design, work results are checked by a colleague. At the same time, this *grandfather principle* is used to familiarize inexperienced newcomers with the work involved.

A similar relationship between task-based job differentiation and flexible manpower deployment also applies to *production scheduling/planning*, which is a subdepartment of production management. The complete bundle of tasks concerning work scheduling, production planning, time and materials management, and transport planning is dealt with by seven employees. Each of these has his or her own particular area of responsibility and, at the same time, is familiar with the work in any other area of the department.

Generally speaking, plant and work organization are characterized by a high degree of functional specialization and by pronounced job differentiation according to technical requirements. However, this production and work system has nothing in common with the Taylorist work organization in mass production industries (Jürgens, Malsch, and Dohse 1993; Berg 1994). Most of the jobs from production to design have high skill requirements. The skill structure of the workforce creates particular forms of close, interpersonal and unbureaucratic *communication and cooperation* within work groups, sections, and departments as well as between departments. It also allows for a high degree of flexibility.

This work and communication system applies not only to white collar jobs but also to manufacturing itself where workshops are specialized according to product components and production flow. While the requirements of various subprocesses and jobs differ considerably, 70–80 percent of production work is still manual. From core construction, which is relatively easy to learn, to coil winding, which often requires ten years of experience after completion of apprenticeship before all of its variations are mastered, the plant generally makes use of the knowledge and vocational skills of its workers.

Given the existing pressure to reduce costs, the flexible deployment of skilled workers is a central means to get by with as small a workforce as possible and manage fluctuations in manpower requirements within the stable core workforce, making minimum use of the external labor market. The daily labor deployment policy encourages close cooperation and changes in tasks and jobs so that training can be acquired in other work areas. The assignment of individual jobs takes employees' various levels of experience into consideration and is used for further training to avoid too intensive specialization.

This flexibility in manpower deployment is supported by a plant payment system for blue collar workers that was negotiated by the management and the works council as far back as 1978, modified in 1983, and currently applies to most of manufacturing. This *premium pay system*, which was very innovative when it was adopted, promotes in a particular way both the polyvalence of production workers and their actual deployment flexibility. The workers' wages, which have been paid on a monthly basis since 1993, are generally calculated on the basis of four components: basic wage rate, two premium factors for flexibility within and beyond the "home workshop," and time allowed/working speed. For particularly quality-sensitive areas such as the winding room, a quality bonus is applied as a fifth factor.

Indeed, many of the production workers can be deployed to several jobs, about half of them outside their customary workshops and about 10 percent in three workshops or more. The temporary transfer of one or more workers is part of the everyday process control work of the foremen or workshop managers, and works council approval is not required. Field service employees from the sales department can also be included in such considerations as required. Given the situation of tight staffing, such adaptation processes create significant savings in labor deployment since bottlenecks and surplus capacity can be dealt with on an almost completely in-house basis. It is only in the departments with the highest work requirements and in which temporary help cannot be used that certain manpower reserves have to be maintained.

Given the actual production structure, short-term *variation of in-house production* also creates flexibility reserves. While this does not include the core areas of production, such as coil winding, core construction, and assembly processes, which cannot be passed on to outside firms, order volume in marginal areas such as mechanical or insulating part production can be subcontracted at short notice, assuming that contacts with reliable suppliers exist. Due to the workers' deployment flexibility, those released from jobs in marginal areas can be used to reinforce work capacity in the core processes, in certain circumstances over several stages. This flexibility reserve would no longer be possible if production was permanently reduced to the core processes.

Apart from the tools to achieve flexibility that have already been mentioned, it is also possible to exchange manpower with other BA transformer plants. This is relatively easy to organize within Germany, and workers are occasionally loaned out for limited periods to other European plants. This type of exchange of personnel is further facilitated by the BA's standardization of products and processes. Provided that the interests of the workers involved are sufficiently taken into account, the works council generally approves of such moves, particularly since experience and ideas for improvements can be gained in this way.

Rationalization Programs and Competitive Position

Under labels such as Customer Focus, Time-Based Management, T-50 and Supply Management, the Power Transformers BA has produced a number of objectives and methods, all concerned with the reorganization and rationalization of business and production processes in its plants (see Chapter 2). These initiatives are part of ongoing BA-wide performance control via benchmarking and other reporting systems. They are intended to provide individual companies and local plants with incentives and suggestions. However, the plants put them into effect according to their specific conditions.

Marginal Impact of General Programs

These centrally determined programs and concepts have not triggered any extensive changes in Plant L's production management. Rather, it would seem that the rationalization or reorganization measures that were being carried out anyway have been incorporated under these labels, gaining additional stimulus or being pushed in a certain direction. There are several reasons, which are outlined below, for the fact that production management and work structures at Plant L have changed very little in comparison with the far-reaching consequences experienced by other plants.

1. The various alterations of company structures tied up available capacity. Moreover, uncertainties about the final outcome led to the postponement of in-plant optimization of organization until the framework conditions concerning product and process distribution between the two or three production sites were clarified.
2. Developments taking place as part of the Common Product and Common Process programs, in which Plant L is considerably involved at the BA's request, play an important role. This ties up capacity in both the technology departments and in manufacturing. Moreover, results of development, testing, and debugging that were applied to the new processes and work methods have to be awaited before widespread alteration of plant structures can be started, if necessary.
3. In the past, Plant L had developed very efficient structures, particularly with regard to manufacturing organization. For a certain time, these even served as a kind of reference model for other plants. Seen from another point of view, however, this meant that certain rationalization reserves, which could be used elsewhere to improve performance, had already been tapped.[6]

For these reasons, a relatively weak orientation toward centrally initiated programs should not be equated with not implementing rationalization mea-

---

[6] For example, the T-50 Program, which was very important in Sweden and which aims at halving process times within three years, was not adopted at Plant L, whereas other BA plants were getting more radically involved in speeding up throughput times by these means. This re-

sures, since other measures with similar objectives have indeed been implemented. Developments in the field of *quality assurance* are an important example.

Quality has always played a central role in transformer manufacturing. Considerable expenditures are incurred for the technology and manpower used in final testing. Since 1992–93, the BA has been promoting the Six Sigma method, developed by Motorola. Unlike traditional ex-post quality control systems, the Six Sigma method is similar to modern total quality management (TQM) concepts in that it strives to achieve a process integrated form of quality assurance with the objective of zero-defect production. Plant L has been pursuing such a modern quality assurance (QA) approach since the early 1980s, albeit without initially incorporating the new Six Sigma method.

Altogether, the plant's QA policy, as well as its production management in general, is characterized by a high degree of continuity. Neither the integration into the ABB Group nor the TQM initiative started by the BA represented a break and thus central and local activities seem to be largely compatible. On the other hand, Plant L was clearly not the fastest to respond specifically to the BA's Six Sigma method and other initiatives.

Position in International Performance Competition (Benchmarking)

Which results were produced by the more or less autonomous and continual process of change in Plant L and which position within the BA-wide international competition was reached?

Despite the turbulent developments described previously, both Plant L and the other two German plants have been able to improve their performance quite considerably. Between 1991, when Plant H was acquired, and 1995, overall productivity grew by 24 percent. Between 1987, when the merger took place, and 1995, Plant L's productivity increased by 29 percent, an annual increase of almost 5 percent. This growth does not yet include productivity improvements connected with Common Product technology. On the contrary, the increased efforts required by the implementation of the new techniques tend to hamper productivity. Apart from this, it has not yet been possible to reduce the input required for electrical and mechanical design to any great extent because of the considerable level of specifications required by customers.

Plant L holds one of the leading positions in the BA in terms of *manufacturing throughput time* (TPT). It was able to increase its TPT fairly continuously between 1988 and 1995 and progress was also made in reducing *to-*

---

flects the fact that in Plant L, speeding up manufacturing throughput times (TPT) was already a very important and decisive objective even in the ASEA days. Thus, halving the throughput times achieved is much more difficult at Plant L with much higher barriers than in the plants where such rationalization measures had not been implemented to the same extent in the past.

tal throughput time (TTPT). However, at an international level, results in this area are merely average.

In-house organization problems are also having an effect on productivity. Owing to the high priority given to short TPTs, which are crucial to capital costs savings, ongoing electrical and mechanical design processes have to be interrupted in some cases to provide support to production on changes to units already in progress. While this flexibility allows as few units as possible to be put through production at a time (8–10 in Plant L), in certain circumstances it also increases design and planning periods, thus resulting in longer total throughput times.

Plant L has successfully reduced its *failure rate*, that is by increasing the proportion of completely assembled transformers that pass the extensive final acceptance tests in the high voltage test fields (first pass yield). Indeed, its failure rate was reduced to almost zero from 1990 to 1994. However, setbacks have also been experienced.[7]

The number of defects detected during production also decreased, with the number of nonconformity reports (NCRs) falling between 1994 and 1995.[8]

However, these generally favorable performance data do not establish an uncontested position or one of long-term stability within the international network. This position can be undermined by both the turbulent sales markets and development dynamics within the BA network. The high speed of other plants in improving their performance endangers Plant L's position if it cannot keep the pace.

Labor costs are no less than 50 percent above the average of all BA transformer plants and therefore constitute a considerable hindrance. After Switzerland and the United States, the costs per employee in Germany are the highest throughout the BA, that is, 20 times higher than in China and, closer to home, 10 times higher than in Poland. Admittedly, this contrasts with a considerably higher than average turnover rate. But higher productivity only partly compensates for the cost differences. High costs and price levels entail a considerable risk for Plant L, above all with regard to the export market, which represents approximately half of its sales and is an area in which it is more difficult to build up and maintain stable customer relations. Thus the situation as a whole places Plant L under considerable pressure to rationalize and the traditional technology oriented, step-by-step rationalization policies might not be sufficient to guarantee the long-term survival of the plant.

[7] One such setback was caused by the production of a series of 7 units according to a Plant M design that—due in part to the use of new wire material—involved a design mistake. This was not discovered until 6 of the 7 units were already undergoing final testing. Only in the case of the last unit was it possible to eliminate the error during actual production.

[8] Once again, these figures should be interpreted with caution, particularly when making international comparisons. An increase in the number of NCRs can indeed refer to an increase in quality problems but it can just as easily reflect a desired increase in defect sensitivity on the part of the workers.

Common Product and Processes: Advantages and Risks

Among the BA's central rationalization initiatives, the Common Product/ Common Process project (CP project) is of particular importance. It is concerned with improving products and processes simultaneously, not for a single plant but to the advantage of the whole BA network (see Chapter 2). The bundling of resources is intended to allow for the use of development processes that would otherwise by far exceed the possibilities of one individual manufacturer. In these long and complex development processes, the best practice solutions are being sought, both in terms of product conception and the related design and manufacturing processes, which can then be applied to all plants. The innovations aim to set new standards for competitive transformer production, initiating a broad rationalization process.

The CP project has been very long and complicated. From the perspective of the BA's overall interest, there can be no doubt that in the long run it will cut costs and increase the competitiveness of the whole group of companies. In fact, one of the reasons for forming the worldwide group of power transformer plants was the expected synergy effects. However, from the perspective of the individual plants, their position vis-à-vis their clients and within the BA network, besides obvious advantages, the CP project also entails certain risks. There are contradictions between short-term productivity and implementation costs associated with producing long-term benefits. The technology alternatives favored by some plants with well-established customer relations are not necessarily the best solutions for others. General interests in increasing the competitiveness with companies outside ABB may conflict with individual plants' interests in safeguarding their relative position within the BA network.

At a formal level, the individual plants are able to decide for themselves to what extent they wish to use the CP technology, but at a practical level they are under considerable pressure to adopt the CP tools and concepts. Insofar as this involves an obligation to introduce particular methods and product design details, the CP project differs quite considerably from the other rationalization programs initiated by the BA, in that the latter do not specify to quite such an extent how the plants are to achieve the relatively abstract objectives involved.

Plant L was very much involved in the development work required for the CP project, particularly as far as the conception of Common Product is concerned. Thus it can be assumed that components, solutions, and methods that have proved their worth at Plant L have to some extent been integrated into the new developments. On the other hand, owing to the high interdependency of subcomponents and subprocesses, many compromises have become necessary.[9] This means that the expected advantages have come with

[9] A combination of the best individual solutions does not guarantee an overall optimal result. Although incomplete, the experience gathered to date has given rise to a discussion about

additional costs and efforts to implement the new technologies but their full economic effects will not be achieved as long as the development and implementation processes of the new technologies are going on. As mentioned previously, this phase is accompanied by additional expenditures, which tend to decrease the plant's current productivity and which are only partly compensated for by BA transfer payments. Although there is not yet enough experience to justify any final conclusions, it already seems clear that the new concepts entail certain risks for the Bad Honnef plant in the long run, particularly if they prove to be successful.

- In view of the sophistication already achieved at Plant L as regards the product and the production system, the application of CP developments does not hold much promise of substantial rationalization progress for *all* processes. On the one hand, it is expected that order-related design efforts will be reduced by half once the new information technology tools have been fully implemented. On the other hand, there is little indication that substantial improvements can be achieved in manufacturing, since this area already runs very efficiently at Plant L. Experience shows that the new developments create both productivity gains *and* losses, and thus a general improvement of the plant's position cannot be expected.
- Adoption of the new, jointly conceived solutions can help plants that are less productive and successful to catch up with the front-runners. Apparently there are signs that the less efficient plants are adopting the new methods faster, with fewer reservations and more obvious progress than the leading players, meaning that the cards will be reshuffled in the survival game.
- The standardization of products, subcomponents, materials, and processes opens up new possibilities for optimizing the allocation of design and manufacturing processes at the BA-wide level and for exploiting capacity or cost differences among plants. This will threaten the position of production sites in high-wage countries, in particular when customers become more price-conscious and long-standing market ties more tenuous.

Finally, the BA-wide standardization of products and processes is putting the well-established innovation capabilities in jeopardy. The ability to continually achieve product and process improvements could be lost. Until now, this factor has been a significant strength of Plant L's production system and

whether the development of a new coherent product and production concept "from scratch" would have been a faster route to a better overall result at similar costs. However, given the multitude of transformer technologies throughout the BA, having such an approach accepted would most likely have been very difficult, and thus could have resulted in higher adaptation costs in many plants.

one that ensured its dynamism. The highly qualified workforce, made up of skilled workers, technicians and engineers, which, among things such as a low degree of hierarchical structure and control, allows for independent work, process-related planning and quality assurance, as well as close communication between mechanical design and production, could lose its commitment and the ability to come up with continual improvements if these conflict with the specified standards. This is particularly true if these standards can only be modified via complicated and time-consuming clarification processes at the BA level. For this reason, the extent and precision of the standardization implemented, namely in the form of uniform solutions and methods applicable throughout the BA, will be decisive. A second question is whether sufficient scope will be left for independent local developments that allow for continued or increased use of the specific strengths of the established production system (Thomas, 1994).

In addition, the CP project also involves improving conditions for interplant optimization of *supply management*. There is pressure to standardize company production profiles. Economies of scale in the case of group-owned or external suppliers can be achieved more easily when many plants concentrate their standardized demand. Thus, standardization opens up new opportunities to reshape the network in a global perspective.

However, increased outsourcing and concentrating on a few core processes entail certain risks. For example, supply reliability may be compromised or the flexibility to reschedule production may be lost when certain processes are carried out externally. Finally, it should be recalled that the "marginal" manufacturing sectors fulfill an important function as labor reservoirs through the high deployment flexibility of the workers. This flexibility, which is particularly relevant for core manufacturing processes in which time is of the essence, may be endangered by outsourcing. Dealing with bottlenecks in these processes is all the more possible if a plant has the capacity to make certain components in-house or, as an alternative in the case of shortage of manpower, to have them made by an outside supplier. In Plant L this applies to the production of mechanical parts, for example. If the BA streamlines its plants to core processes and centralizes the supply of components, this reservoir of flexibility will be lost. This in turn would endanger the entire production system, which has been built on stability, commitment, and high trust.

Conclusion: Finding a New Position within the International Network

In view of the global state of overcapacity, the high level of labor costs in Germany, stiffening price competition, and the explicit ABB strategy of being local worldwide, the success that Plant L has achieved on the export markets in the past, as evidenced by its export rate of about 50 percent, could prove to be its weak point over the long term. Given the current domestic competition and demand situation, expectations of sales increases over the coming years cannot be justified even though there is some chance of expanding at the moment owing to the fact that the plant has taken over a large share of the clientele formerly served by the closed Mannheim Plant. However, if it is to maximize the use of its capacity, Plant L will continue to be extremely dependent on export orders. In this area, its ability to win export orders is restricted not only by external competition but also by the BA's globally oriented sales policy and its strict system of market allocation.

Given this situation, Plant L's ability to improve its productivity and performance in comparison with other BA plants is a factor of utmost importance in terms of survival.

In this respect, the BA-initiated CP project ushers in a new situation of dependency. As part of ABB's transnational strategy, it can be seen as a specific effort to combine *economies of scale* through worldwide standardization of product and processes with *economies of scope* by using resources and abilities that differ locally to adapt to regional market conditions. Successful standardization in the production of custom tailored transformers will open up a new round in business reengineering (Hammer and Champy 1993) and in the survival game within the network. The competitive situation within the network could become even more critical for plants in high-wage countries when all factories gain access to the same new rationalization tools. On the other hand, there are indications that the BA strategy that has prevailed thus far, that is, maintaining a conglomerate of functionally more or less identical factories to serve the respective regional markets, is going to be changed. Rather the strategy is moving in the direction of building up a production network in which complementary plants specializing in certain processes and components cooperate closely as a kind of virtual global factory. Centralizing of core cutting or of insulation kit manufacturing is a step in this direction. In either case, while the ability to react flexibly and to innovate will be crucial to survival within the network, at the same time this very ability is at risk, given the increasing pressure to standardize.

10 Global Policies and the Dynamics of Local Variation

Christian Berggren and Christoph Köhler

Previous chapters have presented a comprehensive sample of case studies of the transformation within ABB's transformer business: the fierce catch-up in Trafosur, Spain, the incremental improvement in Bad Honnef, Germany, the new start at Swedish Ludvika, Dundee's struggle to survive in a privatized market, and so on. But what is the direction of the Power Transformers business area (BA) when we put the pieces together? What are the central aspects of the interaction between international management and national plants during various phases in the BA history, and what are the long-term prospects? These questions have broad significance, since power transformers is such a relevant case for the study of globalization in heavy manufacturing industries. A strong version of the globalization thesis, discussed in the Introduction, implies that local and national variety are historic phenomena, which are progressively replaced by globally standardized practices, for example, in the way the Coca-Cola company has standardized local manufacture and marketing in the area of branded consumer products. From the start Asea Brown Boveri (ABB) followed a different route: combining a multidomestic (polycentric) with a globalist (geocentric) theme: local specialization and global coordination. This structure implies tensions and sometimes contradictions: the balance between the two principles, which is reflected in the matrix structure of the corporation, is not cast in concrete but constantly evolving. During the waves of mergers and acquisitions in the late 1980s and early 1990s, the principle of "being local worldwide" was repeatedly emphasized. Since then there has been a tendency toward international standardization in process and product. Does this trend mean that ABB's policy of being local worldwide was only relevant in a particular phase, when markets were still protected and fragmented? Will the multidomestic structure be superseded by a more homogeneous internationally consolidated structure, being local only at the customer interface, or are there still powerful factors sustaining a diversity of local strategies and a widespread local presence? If local variation prevails (albeit a different kind of local dynamics than in the early days of the BA), there are strong arguments against convergence to one model of business, production and work, at least in the classical manufacturing industries. On the other hand, if international convergence carries the day, the globalist ideal of one best model is strongly supported. In this chapter we analyze the dynamics of the power transformers BA from the perspective of the local companies. The concluding section returns to the question posed above about the long-term prospect of being local worldwide.

Sources of Local Variety

The power transformers BA was formed in the late 1980s, following the merger between ASEA and Brown Boveri in 1987, and the acquisition of Westinghouse's transformer business and several independent companies. An international management structure was rapidly established and a system of market allocation implemented. During these first years of the new corporation, the policy of multidomesticity was a necessity, since ABB didn't acquire local businesses to close them down, but planned to invest and expand. "Being local worldwide" was an important message to maintain commitment from local management and employees, customers, and suppliers. At the same time the BA headquarters used its global resources to enforce performance improvement. In a few cases, plants were shut and manufacturing consolidated on a national basis, but by and large, the thrust of the BA intervention in this first phase was to bring individual plants up to the level of modern international standards.

This chapter attempts to present a broader perspective on BA dynamics by analyzing the seven plants presented in this book in their relationship to the international management policies. Occasionally we will make use of an enlarged sample including four more plants: Vaasa in Finland, Elta in Poland, Sécheron in Switzerland, and Guarulhos in Brazil. They were all visited during the international research project but were not the objects of in-depth studies. Within the seven-plant sample there was in the early 1990s a clear dichotomy between historically advanced "core" companies and low-performing "peripheral" operations. On the face of it, the two categories were similar in some basic aspects. They all represented a classical functional organization, with strong boundaries between main departments, marketing, design, purchasing, process engineering, and production. Manufacturing was organized as unit production (in contrast to more efficient batch or mass production), heavily dependent on tacit worker knowledge, which had been acquired through years of accumulated experience.

Despite these basic similarities, the performance of the newly acquired plants was a world apart from the performance of the old core plants (nearly all of them previously part of ASEA). Within their functional organization, the core plants had carried rationalization very far and created a highly efficient technical structure: strict planning systems, elaborate work methods, well-defined interfaces, comprehensive quality manuals, and so on. As part of the old ASEA tradition, manufacturing flow and short throughput times (TPT in the BA parlance) had high priority. The functional specialization of the workforce was combined with flexible labor deployment, high levels of skills, and interpersonal communications. Thus the transformer plants avoided the rigidities of the Taylorist division of work in typical mass production operations. Industrial relations were characterized by stability and predictability, ranging from the close cooperation between management and Betriebsrat at Bad Honnef to the carefully regulated mechanisms of conflict resolution at Varennes, Canada.

The newly acquired peripheral plants, on the other hand, displayed a low level of functional rationalization and technical organization, and suffered from a lack of investments in tools and computer support. Deficient systems of planning, logistical control, and quality assurance were compensated for by repeated cycle-backs between departments and informal and undocumented problem solving at the factory floor, which resulted in uneven workload and high manpower needs. The main target of production control, as far as it existed, was to "load the plant," not to secure a smooth flow. As a result factory floors tended to be cramped by orders waiting for further progress. This planning method was captured by a manager at Guelph, Canada, in the biting sarcasm: "We were eating like an elephant but shitting like a mouse." At Spanish Trafosur, the inefficiencies of the formal hierarchy resulted in a dual structure. Workers enjoyed a high degree of unstructured autonomy in order to deal with problems that in theory had been solved by planning and engineering offices. Industrial relations were conflictual and management weak. When production volumes and profits declined in the 1980s, the Moorebank plant in Australia entered a vicious circle of conflicts, whereas in Trafosur, management more or less retreated from the plant. At Scottish Dundee, an overtime culture emerged that effectively undermined any system of production and cost control.

Core and periphery are important concepts to capture the BA in its first phases, but to understand the subsequent development it is important to dig somewhat deeper into the sources of local variation. Three major factors could be identified: competitive intensity, corporate history, and local strategies. The first of these, competitive intensity, refers both to internal, intracompany competition as well as external competitive pressure. Bad Honnef, for example, was a case of high internal competitive pressure until the previous Brown Boveri plant in Mannheim, Germany, was finally closed. In the early years of the BA, Brazil was another case. The closure of the second Brazilian plant in 1992 might have contributed to the slowdown of Guarulhos performance improvement since 1993. Vaasa in Finland experienced a very serious threat from the Ludvika plant, located in the same Nordic region. Sécheron in Switzerland is potentially exposed to competition from German Bad Honnef. International orientation as measured by ratio of exports is a proxy for external competitive pressure. This aspect has to be qualified, however. The most strongly export oriented plants have been Ludvika, Bad Honnef, and lately also Vaasa. A significant share of their exports has been addressed to more or less government controlled markets, but there has been strong competition to drive the development of technical expertise and particular competencies. The plants in our sample historically least exposed to competitive pressure were the Spanish and Australian plants with their overwhelming dependence on protected and insulated home markets. As part of ABB, however, Spain is also a case of internal competition between Trafosur in Cordoba and Trasonor in Bilbao, which certainly has helped to drive performance at Trafosur.

Corporate history is a second major factor. The traditional ASEA plants constitute the core plant category in our sample; the previous General Electric/Westinghouse plants (Guelph, Trafosur, Moorebank) the other category: the low-performing peripheral plants. Dundee and Polish Elta are close to the Westinghouse heritage. ASEA used to be strong in design for manufacture and production planning and control, but had no tradition of multidomestic operation; on the contrary, it represented a "one best way" approach with a strongly centralized control system. Brown Boveri, the other parent of the ABB Group, embodied a different culture, an emphasis on technical excellence combined with a federalist international structure. As a result of the merger of the two the philosophy of multidomestic operation ("being local worldwide") was born, with its dynamics and tensions between the national and globalist themes. In the power transformers BA the previous Brown Boveri plants generally were strong in engineering but weak financially, rather similar to ASEA before Barnevik. Several have been closed as part of the policy of national consolidation. One of the survivors, the Sécheron plant, has become a star performer in the business area, which the ASEA-dominated international management group has been very slow to acknowledge. Another stellar performer, the Vaasa operation was part of Finnish Strömberg, an early and successful acquisition of ASEA in 1986. The plants most exposed to competitive pressures tended to be most advanced in terms of technical organization and functional rationalization. The market variable being equal, ASEA plants historically outperformed the others, for example, the Brown Boveri plants. Varennes stood out as a special case, a solid representative of the ASEA tradition, but operating on a protected market, and experiencing few incentives to improve above a certain level.

The third factor refers to subjective action. The trajectory of individual plants is not decided by external factors such as competitive pressure and corporate systems in a deterministic way. Managerial action and local ingenuity, which use sociocultural traditions to their advantage, are important in the final outcome. The ascendancy of Finnish Vaasa, for example, could not be explained if this factor is left out.

In the next two sections we analyze developments at the local company level. The previous discussion points to many sources of variety in ABB's vast international network of transformer operations. The most conspicuous aspect of BA development in the first half of the 1990s, however, was the rapid catch-up in the acquired facilities which did not belong to the historic ASEA core. At the start, the technical organization and functional rationalization of the North European core plants were the distinct role models. There was a strong emphasis on manufacturing throughput and investments in basic functional efficiency: engineering, planning, logistics, order control, and quality assurance. However, as a result of the BA's emphasis on a total approach to time-based management in the business area, the focus of rationalization shifted from technical efficiency and shop floor throughput to an emphasis on reduction of total lead times, from order receipt to delivery. This also meant an organizational reorientation, from functional differentiation to integration, process optimization, and a flow-type organization.

Catch-Up at the Periphery, Stability at the Core

In this section we discuss three main elements of catch-up at the periphery plants: technology transfer; functional rationalization and managerial shake-out; remolding of industrial relations, and reassertion of management control. Next attention is focused on the traditional core units in our sample—Ludvika, Sweden, Bad Honnef, Germany, and Varennes, Canada—and their way of combining external integration into the international business structure with a highly independent internal operation.

Technology Transfer

For a long time before the ABB takeover the previous owners of the peripheral plants had ceased being committed to the transformer industry. Because of a protracted period of overcapacity and slow growth, these companies had neither invested in tools nor training. As new members of the ABB family, the plants started as worn-down brown-field sites with outdated production technology and idiosyncratic product designs, as well as an entrenched management culture, or—in the Spanish case—a sheer lack of management. A first, basic step in the catch-up process was modernization of plant hardware. From Elta in Poland, Dundee in Scotland and Guelph in Canada, ABB renovated facilities, painted plant floors and enforced cleanliness, reorganized physical layout and introduced modern tools and equipment for winding and assembly, many of them developed in Ludvika (e.g., the hydraulic assembly platforms introduced in Guelph). The ABB takeover included several harsh measures, principally layoffs. The investments were very important from a psychological point of view. They signaled the new company's firm commitment to the industry, in contrast with the previous owners.

Another crucial hardware aspect is product technology. A significant disadvantage of ABB's acquisition strategy is the resulting mixture of technologies in the same field, each transformer technology having its own design specifications, component content, installed customer base, and maintenance and spare parts requirements. To achieve economies of scale commensurate with its international sales volume, the new BA management early on launched a Common Product project. As we have seen previously, however, the merging of product technologies has been a much more time-consuming endeavor than BA management had anticipated. In some cases, such as Spain, management decided not to wait for the launch of the common product technology, but to adopt the Ludvika technology in the meantime. As a complementary strategy to enforce worldwide quality standards and reduce variation BA management strongly emphasized the use of common components and BA-wide suppliers, even in the case, such as Poland, in which local suppliers could offer significantly lower prices.

Functional Rationalization and Management Reform

The modernization of plant equipment was accompanied by efforts to rationalize the technical organization along functional lines: to improve process engineering, overhaul planning priorities, and systematize quality inspection procedures. At Dundee and Cordoba, a new planning system, which enforced a strict control and limitation of orders on the shop floor was key to improved performance and lead time. This emphasis on manufacturing throughput time (TPT) was part of a long ASEA tradition, which had been perfected by the German operation and now was introduced in the catch-up plants.

Overall, the arrival of ABB meant a stress on accountability and systems, from cash management and financial reporting to quality control. Many of the acquired plants had been operating in an insulated and protected environment. A crucial part of ABB's management transformation was to break with isolation and instill a sense of urgency and an awareness of world standards. The international BA metrics, above all the TPT and total throughput time (the time from order receipt to transformer on-site delivery, or TTPT) measures, have been an essential tool to create such an awareness, but more important in the initial phase was to send managers and management teams from the acquired plants to well-performing European units such as Sécheron, Bad Honnef, and Ludvika. Extensive training of local management and assignments of international managers to important positions have been other tools. Elta in Poland has been supported by managers from Sweden, Switzerland, and Germany; Guelph, by a Swedish general manager. Trafosur in Andalusia used managers from northern Spain and Brazil to break with the local management culture.

The basic approach to inherited local management was similar across the world; the force and scale of change varied quite considerably, however. At Guelph there was a real shakeout to get rid of the old Westinghouse culture. All managers were assessed on the basis of past performance complemented by independent test procedures. People who had been working at the plant for 25 years had to apply for their jobs anew and those who failed had to leave. The Elta plant in Poland stood out as a contrast to this radical approach. Apart from some international assignees, most of the managers from the old state socialist period were retained in key positions, and there was no comprehensive screening and selection in the manner of Guelph, Canada. Australia was also something of an exception, with a rapid management turnover at the top positions, but no real shakeout, and no support from international assignments. This probably contributed to the fact that Moorebank has been slow to fall into line with the BA mainstream, using arguments about its particularity to defend lagging performance in the Seven-Ups system.

Remolding Industrial Relations, Reassertion of Managerial Control

Whereas performance improvement in old brown-field plants has been remarkably swift, the remolding of traditional systems of industrial relations and working practices has been more complicated. The agenda of ABB can be summarized in a few key points:

—Improvement of physical environment and introduction of rational methods;
—Enhancement of flexibility and multiskilling;
—Shedding of excess labor to create a lean workforce, focused on core activities;
—Reestablishment of management control on the shop floor; and
—Replacement of conflictual relations with a consultative approach, within the framework of clear management priorities.

ABB's massive investments in equipment and facilities, the basis for the catch-up efforts, contributed to significant improvements in physical working conditions. According to the Guelph study, the new methods reduced physical strains and unnecessary work, without taking away workers' control of the pace of work and sequence of operations. Another general pattern was heavy investment in training, not only of management but also of non-managerial personnel. In Trafosur, for example, all operators were supposed to participate in general training programs, covering basic principles of electricity. At Elta, Poland, language education was a priority subject. However, the emphasis on training and skill acquirements tends to come into conflict with the lean management principles and the need to be profitable in spite of adverse market conditions. This is borne out by the Guelph case. Here it was not possible to include skilled workers such as winders in the job rotation schedule. This would have required a several-year-long training of semiskilled workers and the tight manpower planning did not allow such long-term commitments. In less skilled departments, such as the insulation shop, it was much less costly to cross-train workers, and hence to realize the flexibility goal. At Dundee, Scotland, the dramatic deterioration in market conditions following the privatization of electric utilities dealt a heavy blow to the training efforts. As described in Chapter 4, local management decided to put its efforts in the Six Sigma program "on ice," and the Black Belt operators, who had already been extensively trained, had to return to their normal jobs or were made redundant.

On the downside, an important aspect of the ABB regime has been the massive layoffs. In all of the newly acquired plants in our sample—Guelph, Trafosur, Dundee, and Moorebank—employment was cut by half during the first years in the 1990s. The intention was probably to eliminate the overmanning of the acquired plants once and for all by a swift operation early on. This would make it possible to operate with a lean but stable workforce, and invest profitably in further training. However, because of worsening market conditions, the initial massive layoffs were followed by a continuing erosion of the remaining employment at many plants. This has negatively affected training and created a widespread feeling of insecurity. In the Guelph case, for example, plant management became increasingly oriented toward numerical flexibility, combining overtime with layoffs on short notice. This resulted in a feeling among workers of being "on a permanent notice of layoff."

A crucial theme on the ABB agenda was to reassert management control. Trafosur, Spain, represents the most radical break with a previous period of union control and shop floor influence. When ABB took over, the message was clear-cut: "The plant has managers again." At Dundee, the problem as perceived by management was the long-standing "overtime culture," in which workers were economically dependent on heavy overtime assignments at premium wage rates. In this environment cost control and productivity planning were most difficult to establish. Taking advantage of the crisis situation in 1995, management demanded productivity improvement instead of overtime in a determined effort to break with previous practices. At the Elta plant the role of the foremen was significantly strengthened. As a Polish unionist pointed out:

> Under the socialist regime it was almost a punishment to be promoted to a foreman position: many more responsibilities, but only a small wage increase and no effective authority. Now, with ABB there is a more distinct difference between

workers and foremen and the company trains this cadre extensively. In a situation where there is always a risk of getting fired, the power of first-line management naturally increases.

A part of this ABB agenda has been to weaken various forms of informal worker collectivism or seniority-based job control practices that traditionally served as a basis for independent unionism and worker autonomy. ABB has striven to translate formal management into real management, restricted only by a minimum of collective agreement rules. The emphasis on management prerogatives is in line with ABB's focus on flexibility and lean staffing. However, in a production system heavily reliant on skilled work and tacit knowledge acquired through long-term on-the-job training, there are important limits to these staffing policies. The Canadian comparison indicates that daily horizontal cooperation is functioning better in the traditionally regulated Varennes plant than in Guelph, where more formal arrangements are in place to foster teamwork (fewer job classifications, organization into focused factories, etc.). The new priorities have to be supported by a culture conducive to long-term commitment and broad responsibilities.

Several of the acquired plants, as for example Trafosur, Dundee and Moorebank, had a tradition of conflictual industrial relations. The ABB takeover resulted in a general decline in the power and militancy of organized labor, but ABB management has also made determined efforts to foster more cooperative and consultative relations. This has been successful insofar as the tradition of conflict and confrontation seems to have faded away. However, in times of worsening market conditions, management seems to have reverted to more autocratic methods. This is seen, for example, in the way numerical flexibility is utilized at Guelph, or in the coercive manner Dundee chose to change the overtime culture. The prospects of even more serious cost and market pressure on the plants in the future will mean further strains on industrial relations, not only at the peripheral plants but also at some of the core plants, which hitherto have enjoyed a high level of stability.

Stability at the Core Plants

For the core plants in our sample, which all belonged to ASEA in the 1970s and 1980s, the first acts in the formation of the power transformers BA did not imply any radical change. Varennes, in particular, continued operating very much in the same commercially successful way it had before ABB was formed, protected by the support of its main customer Hydro-Québec. Bad Honnef was previously a stand-alone ASEA operation in Germany. When this was merged with Brown Boveri in Germany to form a part of ABB, the independence of Bad Honnef was significantly reduced. As highlighted in Chapter 9, Bad Honnef's loss of "individuality and spontaneity" was deplored by the works council. Ludvika is a special case. It used to pride itself on being the "Mecca of transformers," riding high on its technological strength and steady stream of license revenues. The creation of the BA transferred decision-making power concerning markets, capacity, future products, and technology projects from Dalecarlia to the BA center in continental Europe and made them subjects of complicated organizational considerations. Thus, in contrast with Varennes, Ludvika lost much of its traditional independence already in the early phases of the BA formation. However, compared with the catch-up plants at the periphery, all the core operations maintained a significant degree of autonomy in their internal operations. This was reflected in the very limited impact of the BA-wide programs in these plants. Varennes continued to focus on cost and customer relations as it had for many years, not bothering too much about its modest rating in the BA metrics concerning throughput times. At Bad Honnef there was a similar distanced attitude to the BA programs and concepts of time-based management (TBM), total quality management (TQM), and the like. Neither plant triggered any new rationalization or reorganization initiatives. Rather, the Bad Honnef plant continued to build on its ASEA tradition of rationalizing the production process, and in terms of throughput time in manufacturing the plant performed excellently. Similar to Varennes, organization and work structures at the Bad Honnef plant were remarkably stable. The plant was already a model of manufacturing efficiency, so why change? The most important organizational innovation was a minor rearrangement of the interface between sales and engineering.

In Sweden, Ludvika displayed a similar weak interest in the ABB's nationwide TBM effort, the highly publicized T-50 program. Despite the reduction in its external autonomy, Ludvika maintained a solid self-confidence, bolstered by healthy financial results and a continued strength in technology. A divisional structure was implemented in order to improve product focus and process flow but it did not challenge the basic functional structure. In short, all three core plants continued on their path of rationalization along established functional lines. In this endeavor, Bad Honnef was most successful, whereas Ludvika experienced difficulties, partly because of the managerial brain drain referred to previously.

Another important aspect of the core plants was the stability of their employment. During the years 1991–1994, Varennes maintained a workforce of 300 people. Bad Honnef went through a period of restructuring in the early 1980s, but from 1985 to 1994, employment was stable at 300 people. At Ludvika, there was a crisis in 1990–91, when Sweden plunged into a deep recession. The workforce was reduced from 660 to 500 employees, and the strategic capacity of the plant was cut by BA decision from 10,000 to 8000 MVA annually. Since 1991, however, employment has been stable, and in 1994, BA management decided to bring the strategic capacity of the plant back to the 10,000 MVA level.

This pattern of stability included labor-management relations. In Quebec, relations are characterized by traditional arm's-length distance, based on respect. In Germany, mutual trust was combined with close cooperation, and a common interest in safeguarding the future of the plant. As a part of this package, management has worked hard to avoid any layoffs in times of downturns. In Sweden, ABB pioneered an offensive by the Confederation of Employers (Svenska Arbetsgivareföreningen [SAF]) to change the overall employee relationship from a traditional separation in different bargaining units for blue-collar and white-collar workers into one single category. This was presented as a necessary adaptation to the requirements of new technologies and markets. The proposal also entailed a political dimension, since it intended to replace a previous collective identity as "wage earner" with a company-specific individual identity as "associate" (see Mahon 1994). It also contained a system for individualized wage determination with a much stronger role for local management than in the traditional collective agreements. This sparked heavy criticism among several local sections of the metalworkers' union at ABB. The power transformers plant in Ludvika kept a low profile in these discussions. Stability was the most characteristic aspect also of its system of industrial relations.

The Diversity of Local Response—From Compliance to Innovation

The dichotomy core-periphery is a helpful tool to understand the consolidation of the international BA at the plant level in the first half of the 1990s, but it is not enough to explore the variety of local response. Drawing on our expanded sample, it is possible to distinguish between four different profiles: compliance, opposition, independence, and innovation.

Compliance and Catch-Up

In our sample, two plants have distinguished themselves for a most obedient application of BA policies. These are the Cordoba, Spain, and Guelph, Canada, plants, the "BA zealots." Both of them started from a position as worn-down Westinghouse plants, and had to strive very hard to achieve international standards. Further, they did not enjoy any particular strong client relationship; in the Canadian case this contrasted very much with the situation of the Varennes plant. Moreover, both Trafosur and Guelph were plagued by overcapacity and a constant uphill battle to increase their order intake. In the absence of any independent power base, the local plant strategy was very much oriented toward the BA center. The efforts to become the most diligent absorbers of the BA programs have not been enough to sustain a stable level in the BA internal ranking. In some years Guelph reported top-ranking throughput times, but in the TPT statistics for 1995–96, for example, both plants ranked below average.

Dundee, Scotland, is a more complicated case. Plant management responded quickly to the opportunities presented by Six Sigma and had high ambitions to use the program for streamlining and improving its processes. The plant had suffered from underinvestment for a long time, and management was expecting a much more competitive market situation, so it certainly had an incentive to change. Black Belt instructors were trained and pilot projects started. These ambitions were thwarted by the vicious decline in sales and earnings when the U.K. electricity market was deregulated and utilities privatized. Dundee very much desired to adhere to the BA policies, but these required investments that the plant could no longer afford. The BA process goals thus ran into conflicts with the more immediate priorities of cutting costs to run a profitable operation.

Opposition

Financial strength and strong customer relations breed local independence, but there is no general correlation of the opposite type, that is, between financial pressure and responsiveness to BA policies. This is borne out by the Moorebank story. The Australian operation is interesting as an instance of open opposition. Australian managers have criticized the ABB structure for being too complex and hierarchical, for encouraging administrators instead of entrepreneurs, and for being unduly concerned with operational, as contrasted to with, financial efficiency.

Comparative plant visits undertaken in the research project in the mid-1990s demonstrated the difference in attitudes between Moorebank and Trafosur, the "BA zealot." At Trafosur, graphs of BA metrics were displayed everywhere on the shop floor, and the general manager constantly reminded the workforce of the need for catch-up. In Australia, virtually no BA metrics were exhibited in the factory. Management explained this absence by pointing out that pupils who always receive bad marks tend to be demoralized rather than stimulated if their ranking is constantly displayed. The critical attitude at Moorebank has not been supported by any strong commercial performance or market prospects. Rather, it seems to be rooted in a specific sociocultural and managerial tradition, hardened by the long distance to BA headquarters. However, as Chapter 6 points out, it also reflects the disappointing experience of an exercise in process focus at Moorebank: the successful campaign for the Australian Quality Award, which diverted management from pursuing critical business opportunities.

Independence and Inertia

When the power transformers BA was formed, its historic core plants maintained their established way of operating, as we have seen. They were externally integrated in the overall BA structure and its system of market allocation, but there was no real impetus for them to change their internal organization. Successively, the pressure to revamp their traditional functional structures increased. In spite of this, several of them retained a strong attitude of independence, or what the BA management would call inertia. Bad Honnef presents such an example of resistance to any radical change. One reason was that the German plant, in contrast with Ludvika, Sweden, never ceased improving its technical organization, although in recent years (1995–1996) the plant no longer belonged to the top three performers. The Bonn plant is located quite close to Mannheim where the BA was headquartered until 1996, and BA management seems to have exerted considerable pressure, asking for more rapid and radical improvement. The BA management does not enjoy any direct line authority, however, and as Chapter 9 demonstrates, there was virtually no organizational change at Bad Honnef from 1990 to 1995.

Varennes did not display any superior manufacturing capability but enjoyed extraordinary relations with its main customer and could report stable revenues and earnings. The Quebec plant was remarkably relaxed about central guidelines, tacitly treating the BA metrics as a menu, and selecting the parameters most suitable to its own best interests. This was in stark contrast with the behavior of Guelph, the obedient BA pupil in English Canada. In terms of BA metrics, such as TTPT or TPT, Guelph outperformed Varennes. The Quebec plant, however, enjoyed superior financial results, was working to full capacity, and in terms of close customer relations, it simply had no equal.

Innovation

The compliance and catch-up efforts of the Guelph and Trafosur, Spain, plants were very much in accordance with the "script" of the international management. The stability and stagnation at the traditional core plants deviated from BA expectations of constant improvement, however. International convergence was not supposed to imply regression to the mean! Another unexpected, but positive, phenomenon was the innovative response coming from noncore locations—which is a testimony to the dynamic character of the BA. Finland's Vaasa plant is the most high-profile of these cases. After the acquisition by ASEA in 1986, management at Vaasa was seriously worried by the plant's long-term perspective. As a small acquired plant, with no particular technical or economical advantages, the potential threat was obvious, underlined by the announced or actual closures of plants in Sweden and Norway. The Finnish plant had no illusions of the Common Product and Common Project initiatives that were espoused by the BA management at this time, and absorbed much of the energy at Ludvika. "Even if we had a design advantage in Vaasa, it would soon be made common within the worldwide BA" they argued. On the face of it, Vaasa supported the Common Product concept, but all real management attention was focused on creating a specific competitive advantage by developing a seamless engineering and manufacturing flow. Indirect staff was eliminated, and all traditionally separated administrative and engineering tasks were integrated into the core teams in production and sales. The result was a process-type organization going far beyond conventional notions of lean production. No component of this system was unique by itself; unique was the consistency and singular focus of the local management effort. The results were outstanding both in terms of performance levels and improvement rate. From the late 1980s to the mid-1990s, average throughput time was reduced from 130 to 32 days. Every year from 1993 to 1996 Vaasa was on the top of the TTPT index.

Toward the Year 2000—Redefinition and Repositioning?

In its early years, the power transformers BA had enjoyed a robust increase in order intake and turnover. In 1992 sales declined, and by 1993 it became clear that this development was not transitory. In 1994 total orders received by the BA stood at only 80 percent of the 1991 figure. The American market turned out to be a disaster, but Eastern Europe too was a great disappointment. ABB became riddled with overcapacity, and the BA management exerted strong pressure on local operations to downsize and lower their break-even levels. Every operation was expected to improve, old core plants as well as the acquired catch-up plants. At the BA level, the Common Product and Common Project programs with their federalist approach had run into severe difficulties, and management started to put much more emphasis on process development and process standardization. The new wave was signified by projects such as Common Process and Model Factory, which were not based on the structure of any traditional core plant. The most far-reaching of these globalist one-best-way approaches was the Six Sigma program. Taken to its ultimate conclusion, this program would result in a rigorous standardization of every measurable process. Despite these central policies driving convergence, a review of the local responses indicates new sources of diversity. In contrast with the first phases, however, the major part of this variety could not be attributed to backwardness and inertia, but to contradictory pressures and goals, to local ingenuity and opportunities, and to the dynamic character of the BA structure itself.

Local management is inspired and pressured by the BA management, but even more so by markets and bottom-line results. At the end of the day, the strength of the BA management relies on its capacity to anticipate emerging market trends, to translate them into strategic and structural policies, and to identify and leverage innovative local responses by encouraging horizontal cooperation and knowledge exchange. Previous sections have highlighted the effectiveness of the BA management in supporting the catch-up process at the periphery plants, but also its limited leverage against the independent attitude of the old core plants. One important reason for this limitation is ABB's matrix structure. The BA management does not decide on the future of a plant, but has to negotiate with the national ABB organization. In these negotiations key customers have a very strong voice. If they have a clear preference for one particular operation, irrespective of its performance in the internal BA Olympics, then that plant is chosen, and the other closed down. BA metrics is important, but no matter how hard a plant tries, other aspects may be even more important. Early on the power transformers BA adopted a program of national plant consolidation, and in the Scandinavian as well as Latin American countries this policy was implemented comparatively smoothly. In a number of cases, such as Canada, the United States (until 1998), Italy and Spain, a dual plant structure survived. The cost of closing a plant was much higher than business area managers had anticipated, and the basic structure of manufacturing plants remained surprisingly stable.

Externally, the most significant trends in the late 1990s were the structural changes in markets and competition. Traditionally, the transformer markets had always been national. Long-standing customer relations, public ownership of utilities, and national technical standards raised effective barriers to international competition. This situation was the basis for ABB's strategy of "being local worldwide." Now this situation started to change in the Western world, by the combined forces of domestic deregulation and international integration. The British market was a forerunner in the deregulation wave, but in the mid-1990s, this trend also reached countries such as Canada, Sweden and Finland and was starting to make inroads in continental Europe. Beginning in 1996, open posting and bidding was made mandatory within the European Union. In principle every public utility planning to invest in a transformer has to make its request public in Brussels, which will make it possible for all competitors to submit a quote. The implementation of this procedure will take years, but the end result will be a destabilization of traditional networks, and a decline in the overall prices. The same is happening in the Americas. On average, transformer prices fell 20 percent in the years 1992–1995. For a mature product like power transformers, such a decline is very difficult to absorb. At protected and regulated markets, ABB still enjoyed a price premium of 20–30 percent, but deregulation will erode these premiums. This development presents a formidable challenge for every transformer manufacturer. Another problem is the general stagnation in the American and Western European markets. The U.K. experience demonstrates that deregulation will increase the market for refurbishment rather than for replacement.

Within the BA, the development in the first half of the 1990s had blurred the distinction between core and periphery plants. The old functionally oriented core plants were not at the forefront any more. New role models started to emerge and previous teachers had to become pupils! A symbolic demonstration was the pilgrimage of Ludvika, Sweden, managers to Vaasa, Finland. Previously the historic core plants remained true to their established ways, in spite of declining relative performance and increasing market pressures. In 1995, the chilly winds of change started to blow. This was most apparent in Ludvika, the quintessential core plant. From an atmosphere of self-confidence and self-sufficiency in the early 1990s, management at the Swedish plant started to realize that technological strength and successful product niches were not enough. In a highly significant move, the general manager at Guelph, Canada (a previous production manager from Ludvika) was repatriated to become the general manager at Ludvika. The new head brought international managers to Ludvika for the first time in its history, and started sending study groups to the new model plants in the BA. Ludvika started to participate much more actively in international BA projects in order to develop its processes and organization. The result was a dual strategy: to continue to build on long-term technological capabilities, and to revamp its manufacturing organization, reinforce process orientation, and become a pilot plant for testing out the Common Product.

Increased market pressure is a vital factor in making a local company rethink previously successful operations. However, timing seems to be crucial. If local management waits too long, the resources necessary for long-term change will not be available. Ludvika started its reorientation in due time, when export sales were still booming. At Varennes, Canada, too there was an increasing awareness of the need for change, illustrated by the problems of "functional silos" in its established organization. By the mid-1990s, its strategy of countering BA pressure by fostering local embeddedness was reaching its limits. The prospect of drastically altered future market conditions prompted the plant to embark on a route of comprehensive change. As demonstrated by these cases, the crucial management skill is not to run a turnaround program when the company is already bleeding but to anticipate external change in order to avoid the need for a turnaround.

The Shifting Meaning of Being Local Worldwide

Improved performance and diffusion of best practices within the historically existing manufacturing system will hardly be enough to respond to the pressures of the integrated and deregulated markets. Economy of scale and specialization are again becoming priorities, and it is debatable if being multidomestic is an advantage in the Western countries anymore. One response to these pressures would be to redefine the concept *domestic* from national to regional, for example, from being Swedish to being located somewhere in the Nordic countries, or from meaning Canadian to meaning North American. This redefinition approach will certainly be tested.

Consolidation might be facilitated both by the standardization of processes encouraged by the Six Sigma program as well as the diffusion of the Common Product technology in 1997–98. Ideally, these efforts will make the plants transparent and interchangeable. However, after all these years of strenuous efforts to catch up and meet moving targets, closedown decisions will be very painful. As we have seen, it has been exceedingly difficult to consolidate plants on the national level. It will hardly be easier to close plants as part of a regional restructuring. An intermediate solution, at least, will be to build on the two-tiered manufacturing structure being implemented in 1995–96. In Europe this structure means that the capital-intensive process of cutting core steel is concentrated in three centers: Sweden, Germany, and Italy, whereas the labor-intensive manufacture of insulation materials is transferred to a low-cost site. At the same time the overall degree of vertical integration is lowered, in favor of a more comprehensive use of external high-volume component suppliers. In this structure "being local" essentially means keeping a nationally dispersed structure of final assembly and service.

The only major area of long-term market expansion is Southeast Asia. Here local presence is of strategic importance. The problem of the BA is that there are too many transformer factories in the stagnating markets of the world, and far too few in the expanding parts. The overcapacity in Europe and North America, and the long-term need for repositioning tend to unleash a Darwinian survival game between plants. Local management and local networks strive to develop innovative counterstrategies and to embed their operations in wider organizational and market structures. To increase survival chances plants will probably adopt dual strategies. First, they will "compete" on performance improvement and by learning from new role models. This will drive further convergence.

Second, they will compete on differentiation (which partly will frustrate the central interest of transparency). They will attempt to develop unique capabilities and devise strategies to build *organizational* embeddedness, which is different from the previous local embeddedness. Ludvika is an example of this differentiation strategy. Its preferred way of safeguarding exports has been to develop a specialized and highly profitable niche, high voltage direct current transformers. In 1994, such transformers accounted for 50 percent of all orders. Another method is to take on particularly demanding orders within the general products program. In that way, Ludvika could continue to differentiate itself from the rest of the group. Product differentiation is complemented by a strategy of organizational embeddedness, in which Ludvika builds strong relations with ABB customers outside the BA, for example, Power Systems, which also is operating in Ludvika. Creating this organizational link does not shelter the plant from the pressures of world market competition, but it is an important vehicle for making plant operation more robust.

Another way to compete within the BA is to build on particular cost advantages and develop simplified designs for designated markets. In Eastern Europe and Third World countries, ABB's main products tend to be over-engineered.[1] In 1995 Elta in Poland manufactured transformers of its own design using core steel from local suppliers and not from any BA-wide supplier. According to supply managers in Elta, the Polish steel producers will never be able to match the quality level of the Japanese, whose advanced materials have been so important in minimizing the weight of new transformers. For Eastern European customers purchasing price is the overriding concern, however. To continue its use of local sources, the Polish plant will need design capacities to modify the BA-wide Common Product technology. This might affect the emphasis on strict product standardization.

In some aspects, the international structure evolving in this new phase of the BA drama will display less diversity and more of globally adopted best proved practices. A basic reason is that the first source of variation discussed previously, the economic context of the Western plants, will be much more similar. Further, the second source, differences in company history and context, is increasingly losing its relevance. Other sources of diversity, sociocultural environment and local action, have not disappeared, however. In their struggle for survival, selective international learning and skillful mobilization of local resources will be a most important combination for individual plants. In the discussion of BA-wide standardization programs, Chapter 9 on ABB Bad Honnef points to increasing constraints for local action and innovation, however. Specifically, the German plant worries about risks for the local ability to realize future improvements in increasingly standardized products and processes. Chapter 8 demonstrates that ABB Ludvika is more optimistic, stressing the continued dependence of the BA on initiatives and activities by local plants to foster further development of standardization concepts. There are certainly elements of command and control within the BA, but it must also be understood as a dynamic web, making final outcomes more open-ended than an analysis of management intent would suggest. For proactive plants it will still be possible to be forerunners, to forge horizontal alliances and build local superiority, but not as permanent and stable leadership positions in the way the BA was structured at its start.

In addition to these sources of dynamic variation across Western plants, future operations in Asia will create new cases of both economic and cultural diversity. It is important to remember that Asia's increasing importance in the world economy does not necessarily equate to an integration within a free-trade regime. It seems rather naive to predict that China will become more liberal and less protectionist than Japan, for example. In an ironic twist of history, the idea of being "multidomestic" is being eroded in Europe, where many companies are centralizing and streamlining production, mar-

---

[1] In a bid in Egypt in 1995, Trafosur, Spain, competed against twenty other offers. Some Eastern European plants quoted prices below the Spanish costs for material!

keting, and distribution on continental lines (see, for example, Beckérus & Edström 1995) but at the same time showing more interest than ever in the Asian growth economies. The decision in 1996 to transfer the highly successful management team at Vaasa, Finland, to Vietnam in order to launch a new Asian transformer operation symbolizes the changing priorities. The international engineering and manufacturing structure of power transformers will be reconfigured, but it will still be a multisite operation. The necessity of improvement and learning across plants will remain, and thus also will the tension between the global and local initiatives.

I I Power Plant Production
Continuity and Innovation in a Core Business

Marhild von Behr

This chapter presents a study of changes in work organization in Asea Brown Boveri (ABB) European turbine production network, a business area (BA) within the Power Generation Segment.[1] This BA is a striking example of skill-based manufacturing, whose effect on management policies will be examined. The chapter begins with an overview of the structure of ABB Power Generation and a comparison of production in the transformers and turbine networks. Although the Power Transformers BA has opted for universal implementation of best practice in all sites, policies within the turbine production network are much less uniform. Next, I examine the significance of work organization for corporate strategy. I then focus more specifically on how change is affecting work organization within the turbine production network. In the concluding section, I discuss the dynamics of local variation in the Power Generation segment and their implications for the general debate on "convergence or divergence" in international production networks.

Contrasts between Turbine and Power Transformer Production

ABB Power Generation is responsible for the development and production of power generation systems for utilities, industries, and independent power producers. Its main products are different types of power plants (hydro, coal, diesel, gas) and their components: boilers, steam and gas turbines, as well as generators. Services, repairs, and retrofits are also an important part of the business.

[1] Prof. Dr. Hartmut Hirsch-Kreinsen collaborated with the author in this study. I would like to thank the many people with whom we talked in the offices and workshops we visited in Germany, Sweden, Switzerland, Poland, and the United States. We are particularly grateful to Dr. Helmut Klepper for his continuous support throughout this study.

The world market for power generation equipment is mature and characterized by local customers and global competitors. In addition to ABB, these mainly include General Electric, Hitachi, Siemens, Toshiba, Mitsubishi Electric, and GEC Alsthom. All are established equipment suppliers and their technologies have a great deal in common. Because the customer base is limited, there is tough competition on the basis of price, performance, and service. All players are under pressure to meet escalating standards for environmental performance and resource productivity, forcing them to continuously invest in new technology.

In 1995, ABB Power Generation employed 46,000 people and reported total revenues of $US 10.3 million. The segment is divided into ten business areas, some of the most important of which are Gas Turbine and Combined-Cycle Plants (PGT), Utility Steam Power Plants (PSU), Power Generation Industry (PGI), Fossil Combustion Systems and Services (PCS), and Environmental Systems. Power Plant Production (PPP) was established in 1992 to coordinate and control turbine production.

The distribution of ABB's turbine production plants worldwide is quite similar to that of the transformer production sites, especially in Europe. However, there is a profound difference between these two production networks. Although transformers are shipped from the factory as complete products, ABB's turbine factories usually produce only some of the parts necessary for a power generation unit. A network of complementary and partly interchangeable factories supplies products to foreign and domestic assembly plants or directly to construction sites.

The manufacturing operations within the production network of power plants can be roughly divided into three categories: Lead Centers, Centers of Expertise, and Local Support Centers. The aim is to realize the concept of "focused factory." Thus, wherever possible, not more than two factories in the network are responsible for one product and component. The lead centers in Sweden, Switzerland, and Germany are mainly responsible for production development and transfer of new technologies to other plants. Plants in the centers of expertise group are mainly located in Eastern Europe, Brazil, and the United States. Apart from one Polish plant in the lead center group, the others are responsible for low-cost production in the generator sector and the assembly of turbines. The local support centers in southern and eastern Europe (Spain, Portugal, Italy, and Romania) operate in service and retrofitting for the local market, meet statutory "local content" requirements, and facilitate export trade financing. In addition, there are plans to set up parallel manufacturing units in the Far East in the near future.

The following discussion focuses on the core components of a turbine, namely stators, rotors, and blades. As production of these components requires capital-intensive machine tools designed for unit and small-batch production, high capacity utilization is thus critical for cost-effective manufacturing. It is therefore necessary to concentrate production at a limited number of sites, and exports to other regions and countries continue to play a large part in ABB Power Generation. In contrast, transformer factories are less dependent on economies of scale, owing to the relatively simple and assembly-intensive nature of their manufacturing processes. Thus, the strategy of "being local worldwide" can be pursued by dispersing production facilities around the world according to market requirements. In the Power Generation Segment, the equivalent of this strategy is to set up local distribution and assembly branches in the major markets, which operate in close cooperation with the European engineering and production units.

Another difference between the two networks is that transformer production, except for some critical sections such as winding, requires skills that are easy to find in any industrialized country. Production of complex turbine components, however, can only be entrusted to highly skilled production workers. Moreover, developing and improving turbine production requires a sophisticated industrial infrastructure of machine builders, research institutes, and consultants. These conditions are primarily met in ABB's established sites in Sweden, Switzerland, and Germany.

The Power Plant Production BA (PPP) holds an extra position in the ABB matrix, which is something of an anomaly. Not being a profit center in the usual sense, it consists of a multinational team of a dozen managers, most of whom are from the management of various power segment BAs in Sweden, Switzerland, and Germany. The others come from major national production sites. This group bargains on central decisions concerning production and investment. There is no similar BA in any other segment. The group's main task is to allocate turbine orders to the various production facilities according to the rules of market allocation and calculations of optimal distribution in terms of delivery, costs, and capacity utilization. PPP's other main task is to coordinate investment programs in the network. Moreover, PPP management strives to control performance according to a special benchmarking system. The results of the bargaining processes are valid for the operative units belonging to the BAs within the power generation segment, such as Utility Steam Power Plants (headquartered in Mannheim), Gas Turbine Power Plants (BA management in Baden), or Power Generation Industry (based in Finspong). The PPP management team is under pressure from three levels: the international BAs within the segment, the national holding companies, and the production locations requesting orders and investment. ABB corporate strategies, for example, Customer Focus, total quality management (TQM), and time-based management (TBM), also apply to PPP decisions but only in an indirect way. These corporate programs are chiefly promoted by the operative BAs, whereas PPP's focus is on the outcome of the bargaining process.

In contrast to the power transformers BA, the turbine production network has no central policy for an extensive modernization of the plants acquired in Eastern Europe. In the core plants, there are initiatives to implement common technology, for example, high-speed processing machinery for special components. Subsequently, this new technology will most likely be made available to all plants in the network, and this will ultimately lead to convergence in machining techniques. However, in addition to these initiatives, different technological concepts continue to exist.

Within the network, local facilities are exposed to strong competitive pressure. Owing to overcapacity, there is ongoing competition among the plants, which intensifies as the economic situation deteriorates. Thus, each site has to keep abreast of developments in the other factories. A high ranking in the international benchmarking system may secure eligibility for special support by the PPP in terms of investment in new technology or allocation of profitable orders, and so on. Although it is in a competitive position similar to transformer production, the PPP management does not seem to be particularly interested in "ABB Olympics" or a "one best way" factory model. All plants are expected to improve their results in terms of costs, throughput times, and quality; however, during this study, each factory maintained its own profile in the network, its particular advantages and problems, as well as its "mitigating circumstances," which are partially based on the sociocultural environment.

In current debates on the development of industrial work, the key question is whether there is a convergence of work structures in countries with widely differing cultural and socioeconomic traditions. The internationalization strategies of ABB Power Generation provide an opportunity to test the convergence thesis empirically. As stated earlier, the power generation segment is exposed to fierce international competition. Within the network, certain largely identical products are manufactured at a number of sites in different countries. In such a situation, central management might adopt a standardizing approach, that is, identify the best practice in work structures within the sites involved and then implement the practice at all the other sites. The argument against this approach relates to cultural and socioeconomic factors, such as educational system, labor market, and industrial relations, which continue to exert a major influence on the organization of skilled production work. According to this view, to obtain optimum production results, there must be scope for organization at local sites, and international networks must allow for differing regional conditions and historically evolved structures. If this argument for diversity is valid, it is likely that our study of the turbine production network provides an example of continued national variation in work structures.

Corporate Strategy and Plants

Typically in a matrix organization, each network's local plant manager has several superiors. In this case, the matrix includes three levels: the business area management, the national company management, and the PPP management board. In economic and financial areas, autonomy is restricted and control becomes more and more rigorous as uniform reporting systems are implemented. Moreover, in the PPP network, factories are regularly monitored on the basis of a central benchmarking system, which includes a dozen performance parameters, such as orders, revenues, calculated results, productivity, and quality. Because of the special cost structure of production within ABB Power Generation, additional reports are required for machinery-related data such as capital expenditure, depreciation, and capacity utilization. Failure to meet the agreed-on performance standards initially results in discussions and critical advice, possibly also in reduced operational autonomy. In extreme cases, the continued existence of the site might be in jeopardy. The result of my research is that specific incentives for improvement are not derived from centrally espoused programs such as Customer Focus, TBM and TQM, but mainly from increasing customer demands regarding delivery times and precision, price, and quality. Another principal factor is the dramatic increase in competitive pressure, both from external competitors and other plants in the network. From this perspective, implementing central programs means "translating" actions, which are in any case necessary, into the terms of a relevant program and reporting them as program activities.

A central issue in my investigation relates to the development of work organization in the network. First, it should be asked whether there are any explicit corporate goals relating to work organization or any central initiatives aimed at diffusing organizational best practices. The answer so far seems to be no, since the top executive level, the international Power Generation Segment, does not specify any binding goals for work organization in its operational units. There are no parallels to corporate programs such as Customer Focus, TBM and TQM, or to other precisely defined central objectives, such as cutting lead time by half or cutting costs by 25 percent. Nor are there any explicit general goals at the level of national management, such as flat hierarchies, reduction of interfaces, or decentralization of responsibility. The influence of these much-discussed models of "modern" corporate work organization can be seen in the Western European plants. However, it can be attributed more to national and international seminars, publications, state sponsorship, and so on rather than to the influence of high-ranking national management bodies. A partial exception is the Swedish national holding, which recommends the implementation of Swedish style "group work" in its plants.

Furthermore, the PPP's central management committee is not seeking a "patent remedy" for work organization in all its production facilities. Nor is it looking for a systematic transfer of know-how relating to work organization development in certain sites to other plants in the network. As part of investment projects at individual sites, the latest technical developments may well be diffused to other units in the network, in compliance with PPP guidelines on technology transfer. At the same time, the need for continuous improvement of work processes is regularly emphasized. Nevertheless, there are no identifiable signs of pressure to implement standardized work structures. Thus, with regard to work organization, the scope for autonomy in the power plant production field is wide, and can be used for country-specific or even factory-specific approaches, which respect local traditions and exceptional circumstances. Changes in work organization at the plant level are not closely monitored as long as they conform to performance targets. Thus, the situation in the network's plants is not fundamentally different from that in factories that are not part of a multidomestic company. They are subject to the same requirements, which are, in this case, imposed by the market.

Why then does management not focus more on the convergence of work structures? The underlying theory, which is often seen in the literature, states that centrally controlled standardization of production and work structures is essential in highly integrated production networks. This theory is justified on the grounds that the integration of parallel and complementary processes calls for a high degree of compatibility between production and work structures in the various plants (Flecker and Schienstock 1994). Obviously, the uniformity of production results and the compatibility of the components in the network studied can be adequately guaranteed by the application of uniform design specifications and quality standards. This seems to provide the desired degree of flexibility in plant utilization without a need for standardizing production and work structures in the various factories.

Changes in the Organization of Production Work

The results presented here are based on a comparative study of three plants in Western Europe (Germany, Switzerland, and Sweden) and one in Poland. These four plants manufacture more or less the same products. This makes it possible to compare work structures directly, since intervening variables such as complexity, batch size, and quality requirements are kept as constant as possible. The products manufactured in the factories observed are turbine blades, which are machine components of medium to high geometrical complexity, ranging from a few centimeters to a meter and a half in length. Turbine blades are subject to extremely high quality requirements and are produced in small- to medium-sized batches. Most of the work is performed on Numerical Controlled (NC) machines. The manufacturing process can be classified as capital-intensive component production. Thus, the factories observed operate under conditions that are typical of the high-quality machine building industry. During the two-year survey (1993–1995), the four plants were in a transitional stage. They were just starting to adjust to new technology and reorganizations of labor practice. Rather than examining an established status quo, we were in a position to compare nationally differentiated processes of change. The close relations among the factories also made it possible to analyze the way cooperation and competition within an international production network affect reorganization of work structures within plants. The four factories are to some extent both interchangeable and complementary. In other words, they are linked by supply relationships, but they are also in competition for certain orders. The PPP network is at the beginning of a consolidation phase in which plants are repositioning themselves with regard to their strategic status in the network.

Goals and Approaches to Reorganization

In all the Western European plants observed in the network, efforts are being made to move away from the conventional, Taylorist principles of work organization. The guiding image for the new organizational forms is group work and process-oriented production design. The above interpretation of the findings, if it were not carried any further, could lead us to conclude that the growing convergence of work structures has been confirmed. However, further research on the division of labor shows that only the terminology is the same. Numerous studies (e.g., Altmann, Köhler, and Meil 1992; Moldaschl and Schultz-Wild 1994; von Behr 1995; von Behr and Hirsch-Kreinsen 1998) have already demonstrated that the term *group work* is used to denote widely differing forms of cooperation. Similarly, in the three Western European plants observed, there are considerable differences in the understanding of group work, its interpretation being based on national contexts. Consequently, each plant pursues different organizational objectives, different degrees of decentralization, and different approaches to reorganization.

A clear idea of national conceptions of group work can be derived from the goals that these Western European factories define for its implementation. These goals vary widely both in terms of the area in which group work is introduced and the nature of the groups, the degree of functional and technical division of labor, and the extent of intragroup hierarchy (Figure 11.1).

In line with the primary goals of the rationalization processes, approaches to reorganization, that is, means of implementation, also differ in the observed plants. If the focus is on the modernization of production technology (as in the Swiss and German cases), then work organization issues tend to be put on hold. They are not addressed until the workforce is considered to have the specialized skills required to operate the highly automated systems effectively. If the overhaul of work structures is pursued as a rationalization measure in itself (as is the case in Sweden), both progress in the reorganization process and requalification of the production workforce have special significance. The following is a detailed presentation of each country's goals and approaches to reorganization:

—*Switzerland*. The goals of the Swiss plant include a partial reorganization in which different organizational principles continue to exist alongside one another in individual areas of production. Work

Switzerland	Germany	Sweden
Partial reorganization in formal groups with functional division of labor and skill-based specialization Coexistence of differing organizational principles	Reorganization in production islands in terms of technology and work organization	Complete reorganization in self-regulating groups with integral operations and extensive decentralization of responsibility

Figure 11.1. Defined goals for "group work" in three western European plants.

groups are formed on the basis of technical criteria such as batch size and machine layout. The division of labor between work preparation and production is shifted in favor of production, but the emphasis is on the physical relocation of the work preparation departments—production planning, order processing, scheduling and programming—to the shop floor. This is done to ensure that work preparation is carried out "down where the chips are flying." Internal group structures are characterized by technical specialization and a hierarchical division of labor among foreman, assistant foreman, and machine operator. Work planning and task allocation, among other things, remain in the hands of the foreman and assistant foreman.

The approach to reorganization is based on investments in new production technology. Therefore, changes in work organization are assigned a lower priority. Management views group work as a possible approach that is appropriate for the new NC technology and flexible manufacturing systems, but not as the only alternative. It does not rule out the fact that the new systems can operate successfully using the traditional structures with their strict division of labor. Workers' representatives are getting involved in these issues and are generally in favor of a switch to group work in various areas of production. As a first step, a narrowly defined production area has been converted to group work, as described previously. Then, further introduction of group work is planned for the state-of-the-art manufacturing systems, which were installed in the mid-1990s. In this case, the new work structures are characterized by the tendency toward continued hierarchical division of labor, which was already identified in the plant's goals.

—*Germany*. The goals of the German plant include a step-by-step reorganization of all production areas along group work lines. The guiding principle is the "production island" as defined by the AWF (Ausschuss fuer wirtschaftliche Fertigung [Economic Manufacturing Committee]). This institution has been active in promoting production islands in Germany since the early 1980s (AWF 1984). This concept's key objectives are the complete production of a family of parts, pooling of all the requisite resources, group work with little division of labor, and self-determination within defined boundary conditions. The aim is to reintegrate scheduling functions into the production process not only by physically relocating the department, as in the Swiss plant, but also by returning the associated duties to the production groups. In the German plant, concepts such as low division of labor and flat hierarchy are central to the desired work organization. The idea is to set up *"self-regulating groups"* in which the machine operators are actually responsible for personnel assignment, machine scheduling, and holiday coordination. Qualifications of the group members should be similar enough to allow rotation among workplaces. There is one leading role, that of the group leader, which should be open to rotation among group members.

In Germany as in Switzerland, the approach to reorganization is based on the introduction of new and highly automated manufacturing technology. Group work is viewed as an inevitable consequence of technological innovation. Thus, thorough technical training of personnel takes precedence over preparation for working in group structures. The consequence of this approach is that the technical initiation process is protracted and old structures are likely to survive for a considerably long time. In both the German and Swiss plants, there is a "partially implemented" group in one production area (Computer Numerical Controlled [CNC] grinding). Although this group work is exceptional, its positive results make it an important prototype for the rest of the plant. By referring to this example, workers can see the benefits of group work as well as being aware of the problems that may arise.

—*Sweden*. In the Swedish plant, the goal is to organize the entire factory along group lines. Old structures should not continue to exist beside the new ones. Guided by the concept of integral operations, scheduling and programming, among other things, are integrated in the production groups. The aim is to decentralize responsibilities to a far greater degree than in the German plant. The production groups are to be granted budgetary autonomy, including costing and cost control and, to some extent, investment decision making. Group work is embedded in a series of other activities associated with the actual work process, for example, regular group meetings to optimize processes, the creation of problem-solving groups, and the promotion of informal group meetings. In Sweden, the change to group work is an end in itself, without any direct link with the concurrent modernization of production technology. When the transition was made in the early 1990s, it was carried out in a single step over a very short period of time without any exception. The workforce's acceptance of change is attributed to active participation of the unions and their representatives at the plant level, who were instrumental in defining the groups and allocating duties to them (in the associated group meetings). In this approach to reorganization, there is no stopping halfway. The total switch to group work is now followed by continuous development of the groups, bringing them progressively closer to the established goals, for example, budgetary autonomy.

To sum up, the Western European plants under study do not only differ in their interpretation of the new work structures' content, but also in their pursuit of different strategies for change. The divergent goals and approaches to reorganization are indicative of the continued variation in future work structures within the turbine production network.

Divergence in the Future Work Structures at the Western European Plants

The emerging work structures in the three plants can be characterized according to a typology developed in a previous research project (Moldaschl and Schmierl 1994). In theory, each type can outperform the others, depending on the costs of change and on the way socioeconomic specifics or individual factors fit in with the basic characteristics.

—A *structurally conservative division of labor* means that strict separation between production planning, work preparation, quality control, and maintenance is maintained. Production groups are assembled on the basis of formal production-related criteria and characterized by rigid internal division of labor and hierarchy.

—*Polarized division of labor* means that work preparation is integrated into shop floor activities, but skills within the groups are polarized, that is, some are at the top and others are at the bottom of the qualification scale. Since the levels are far apart, there is no opportunity for rising to the top of the hierarchy on the basis of increasing professional experience. This division of labor also means that there is restricted flexibility in worker deployment.

—Structurally, *innovative division of labor* means that work preparation, tool management, and quality inspection are integrated into the groups' duties. Groups operate on the principle of self-regulation, and there is little or no hierarchy within the group. Group responsibility is wide-ranging, extending as far as independent management of a group's budget and decision-making powers for small-scale investments.

If we attempt to relate this typology to the interim solutions and the foreseeable trends at the three plants observed, only the Swedish plant can be clearly assigned to one ideal type. In this case, the completed reorganization of production means that the path of future development in work structures will belong to the structurally innovative type. At the Swiss plant, organizational development seems to be highly ambivalent. On the one hand, the structurally conservative type is already in place in the production area that has switched to "group work." It is therefore very likely that this style of group work will be applied to other areas of reorganization. On the other hand, management plans for the new highly automated manufacturing systems tend toward a polarized division of labor. A group leader with academic technical qualifications will be in charge of machine operators in the skilled worker category. These plans imply a division of labor which, even in the long term, will make it difficult for machine operators to take over the group leader's position as they acquire more professional experience.

In the German plant, future development could follow any of these three paths. The one group in which this has already been partially implemented does not have the scope for scheduling that is inherent in the production island concept. If this interim solution were applied to other areas of production, the result could be a move toward the structurally conservative variant. At the same time, the technical implementation of the new highly automated systems will require qualifications that are higher than the skilled worker level. This will probably result in a polarized division of labor, which is already the case at a neighboring German turbine manufacturing plant. However, the production island concept still remains the stated goal. If the plant were to directly implement this goal in other areas of reorganization, further developments would lead to the structurally innovative division of labor.

To sum up, the coexistence of different work structures within the network seems to be necessary for Western European plants. The analysis of the work structures in the Eastern European plant reinforces the conclusion that, currently, it cannot be assumed that the turbine production network is moving toward standardization of work structures.

Traditional Work Structures in the Polish Plant

The term *group work* is also commonly used in the Eastern European reference plant, although the content is basically different. In the Polish factory, group work characterizes a formal series of individual workplaces with the same type of machines. This group work relates to a traditional grouping of machine operators, which has occurred naturally without any requirement for special organizational structures. There are no plans for structural innovations involving decentralization along the lines of Western European models. The Polish plant is concentrating on rationalization to catch up and rapid implementation of the most recent technical systems. These systems are integrated into the traditional hierarchical work structures; there is no attempt to imitate the work structures of the Western European core plants.

The Polish case illustrates the contrast between the rationalization strategies in Western and Eastern European plants. Western European plants are forced to combine a high level of automation with changes in work organization to compensate for the disadvantages of their location (high labor costs), and at the same time make full use of their competitive advantages (highly skilled work force and developed industrial infrastructure). In contrast, Polish managers hold the view that the production of complex items can currently only be carried out within the traditional structures based on strict hierarchy and division of labor because of their socialist history, the country's cultural conditions, the skill structure of the workforce and the strongly hierarchical mindset. In this case, it is again the combination of different qualification structures and cultural factors that imposes different approaches to work organization.

Interaction within the Production Network

There is a long tradition of international comparative studies of industrial labor practices (e.g., Lutz 1976; Maurice et al. 1982; Sorge et al. 1982; Düll and Bechtle 1991). However, under the conditions of internationally integrated production, another important step needs to be added to this tradition. Hitherto, the methodology has been based on relatively static observation of existing arrangements in individual countries, with the primary objective of emphasizing the differences in skill structures, work organization, and industrial relations. The external pressure for change, although it has certainly been at work in the past, was neglected. Thus, to assess the contemporary development of industrial work, it is necessary to consider the pressure for change resulting from global corporate strategies. To describe the dynamics of change as fully as possible, we will examine a further dimension, namely the reciprocal influence of units within the international network. There are two ways through which reciprocal influences can affect work organization within plants, that is, through direct exchange of experiences among factories, and indirect forms of learning and borrowing within the network.

—Analysis of the data shows that there is no systematic exchange of experience relative to organizational changes. Contacts among plants are primarily related to questions of technological developments, current orders, and quality. Thus, there is no direct reciprocal influence on local work structures. This is in stark contrast with conditions in the power transformers BA.

—However, it is possible to detect implicit forms of learning among plants. Being part of the production network results in a broadening of cooperation relationships, for example, joint technology development initiatives or task forces for solving common problems of quality. On these occasions as well as at management meetings, in trainee programs, and on reciprocal visits, plant and production managers gain insight into how the other factories operate. This extended knowledge base may allow a plant to emulate a solution adopted by another plant or to learn from another plant's mistakes.

—Implicit impacts on local work structures are also the result of the "battle for survival" shifting from the marketplace to the network. As already described, relations within the turbine production network are not only cooperative but also highly competitive. In this constant battle for relative superiority, the central benchmarking system has a special significance. Its comparative performance data are a source of detailed information for all local managers, that is, each unit has a specific frame of reference when making its own decisions. Formerly, information about competitors could only be obtained by observing their success on the market, and this information was, moreover, relatively anonymous and brief. Nowadays, the environmental factors that shape a plant's course of action not only include the national conditions and market requirements but also the differentiated performance data from the other units in the network. Detailed insight into the successes and failures of the parallel production units may implicitly lead to changes in local work structures.

These changes may operate along two opposing lines: based on its performance level and on the resources being activated at the individual plants, a plant may be forced to emulate another plant's successful solutions. These effects of reciprocal influences would confirm the thesis of convergence. However, a plant can also use the advantages of a particular status in the network and of unique local resources to implement its own solutions, which differ greatly from those in the other plants, thus producing or perpetuating diversity.

Dissemination Effects of Production Engineering Solutions

The state-of-the-art machinery implemented in the Swiss and German plants is creating interest among units in the other countries in using the new technology for their own rationalization processes and for keeping in touch with technological developments in the network. Thus, they are attempting to obtain the authorization of PPP management to purchase similar machines and systems. If these investments are approved, the technologies developed in Switzerland and Germany will be implemented in the other factories. It must be stressed, however, that the transfer of these technologies does *not* necessarily mean that the other units in the network will have to adopt the Swiss or German work structures. According to a well-known thesis, international production networks tend to accelerate the diffusion of best practice (Flecker and Schienstock 1994). This applies to production engineering, but cannot be confirmed in the area of work organization. Even after the implementation of identical technical systems, the work structures in the cases studied here continue to be governed primarily by national conditions. Contrary to theses that claim otherwise, the development of national work structures for the production of highly complex components is not dominated by the introduction of technology.

Ambient Pressures

Plants are continuously compelled to make changes not just by hard economic and technological facts but also by ambient pressures imposed by the network. We now demonstrate these effects on factory structure by once again referring to the German plant. Since all the German production facilities in the network have to cope with factors such as high wages and company taxes, inflexible working hours, and rigorous environmental protection targets, they are under continuous pressure to compensate for the disadvantages of their location by making the best use of the resources available in the German environment. This also applies to the German plant in our sample, in which three aspects of changes in philosophy have been identified:

—There is growing awareness of the urgent need for effective responses to new competitors from low-wage countries. Without the opportunity for direct comparison with internal production facilities in Eastern Europe, in this case the Polish factory, there would have been a delay before the new competitors and their impact could be identified by means of shifts in demand on the international market.

—There is growing acceptance of the new necessity for transferring know-how, a duty that is very important for German factories in the altered landscape of internationalized production, but which has, in the past, been viewed very skeptically. The dangers of withholding know-how become apparent when they act as an obstacle to cooperation with the less advanced factories in the network. The Swiss factory steadily pursues a policy of knowledge transfer in keeping with its own traditions and those of the neighboring surrounding industry, thereby ensuring that it can influence technological processes in other factories in the network and reinforce its position as a leading center.

Following this model, the German factory is, in the mid-1990s, passing on its own knowledge to representatives of the Eastern European plants that are catching up more extensively than before.
—The plan to modernize work organization along the lines of lean hierarchies, decentralization, and reintegration of functions on the shop floor has long been an issue of debate in the German factory. It is now being fleshed out and accelerated by a change to production islands and self-regulating group work. Structural innovations in the parallel Swedish plant are, indirectly, weakening the continued existence of old structures in the German plant. The Swedish reference plant has taken the lead in decentralizing responsibilities and embedding group work on the shop floor in other activities within the plant. Presently, the German plant is under pressure to act rather than prolong the discussion. Ambient pressures lead the German plant to catch up with the nationally defined goals. Hence, reorganization is not aimed at adopting the far-reaching Swedish model of group work, but at speeding up the achievement of the German production island model.

Conclusion

When examining the increasing international convergence of industrial structures, it is necessary to distinguish between two main levels: company and work organization. The units compared in the turbine production network are becoming more similar as regards the management of the business: accounting, financial controls and the creation of cost center structures, and so on. Current research does not, however, allow us to assume convergence at the level of work organization, which is the main focus of this study.

Our results relate to a particular form of production network: the manufacture of complex machine components in small batches involving highly skilled production workers. To a greater or lesser degree, all the Western European factories observed are moving away from the old work strategies. The common guiding image for new work structures is group work. The main goals are decentralization and flattened hierarchies, reduction of interfaces, and utilization of the whole spectrum of worker skills. At this level, we certainly find convergence of work structures in the Western European countries. On the other hand, worker skills and management mindset vary greatly among the plants in the network, depending on social conditions and the characteristics of the surrounding operational structures. The national and, to some extent, regional differences in the potential of the workforce are reflected in local work structures. Plant managements are mainly aware of the organizational know-how available in their own country. National labor markets also play a part in goal setting and decision making at individual plants. When implementing new organizational structures, the Western European plants studied here go their own way, influenced by international models but strongly colored by their national background.

Internal competition and comparisons are an important stimulus for change within the production network. Participation in the network does not directly lead to standardization of work structures but it accentuates the pursuit of nationally differing goals and approaches to reorganization. For the time being, the most probable outcome is the continuing diversity of these work structures. All of the four units observed will increase their efforts to implement their own solutions adapted to the national context, assuming that the work structures envisaged are well suited to face the competition with the other plants in the network. Thus, differences in work structure seem to be one of the fundamental aspects in this international network of skill-based complex production. Attempts to bypass national and regional peculiarities and to force local work structures into a uniform shape are bound to fail because they disturb, and may even destroy, the relatively stable equilibrium and accord that have grown up historically between social and industrial conditions and the skill structures in individual factories. This entails a whole range of division of labor from process planning to production. There may be an increasing convergence in other areas of production, for example transformer manufacturing, but this is not a general trend applicable to the capital goods industry as a whole. In the international production network of the power generation segment, work organization ranges from conservative hierarchical structures to innovative autonomous work forms, with neither showing any sign of future predominance.

12 Distributed Development in a Multinational

Christian Berggren

In the Introduction to this book we claimed that Asea Brown Boveri (ABB) represented a third-model multinational, a hybrid striving to integrate the different logics of global business and local embeddedness, combining a geocentric and a multidomestic approach. So far we have studied the meaning of "being local worldwide" in one business area (BA). The Power Transformers BA represents a classical electrotechnical technology, and has a structure uniquely well suited to broad international comparisons. However, this BA is only one of ABB's 35 business areas. What in our study is specific to the power transformers BA, what is generally representative of the predicaments of the ABB Group? It is important to compare the case of the power transformers BA with business areas operating under different technological and commercial conditions. Such a contrasting case is the Automation BA, which delivers process control systems (mainly consisting of software) to a wide array of different industries. The power transformers BA represents a mature, slowly evolving technology. Efficient local manufacturing plays a major role in its business success. By contrast, the Automation BA builds on a rapidly evolving technology and high research and development intensity. Custom engineering and continuous development are the major sources of value. Instead of an international manufacturing network the automation BA has a globally dispersed structure of engineering and project management centers. Thus of central concern is the organization and management not of production plants but of engineers.

Comparing the power transformers and automation BAs underlines the variation in management practices and possibilities within ABB. Consider the notion of best practices, which gained such currency in many industries during the 1990s. The belief in an international best practice, or a globally valid "one best way," has guided many of the programs within the power transformers BA. To identify a best practice, however, it is necessary to be able to measure and compare performance in physical as well as financial terms. That is also the objective of several of the indices of the Seven-Ups metrics within ABB Power Transformers. Within ABB Automation, however, it turned out to be extremely hard to measure the engineering and development practices in a consistent way across projects in one country, and even more difficult across countries. Accordingly, it is not possible to identify any best practices. This difficulty in measurement and comparison implies that the pattern of local variation and central initiatives, of national autonomy and international directives, will be different in several ways.

In this chapter ABB Automation is compared with ABB Power Transformers. In the first section, a brief profile of the automation BA, and the research methods I used in investigating this business area, are presented. The second section contrasts the differences between the Power Transformers BA and the Automation BA. The next section elaborates on six significant similarities between the two BAs. The specificity of ABB's principle of "being local worldwide" is brought out by a brief comparison between the way ABB Automation and its competitors are organizing their engineering activities. The remainder of the chapter focuses on the problems of rationalizing international engineering and development processes.

ABB Automation—A Brief Presentation

ABB Automation designs and delivers integrated systems for control and supervision of various industrial processes: in paper mills, chemical plants, steel mills, water treatment facilities, offshore oil exploitation, and the like. The basic idea is to automate process control and information management, not manufacturing operations, which is the realm of another business area, ABB Flexible Automation. ABB Process Automation (here called ABB Automation to simplify the discussion) started as a separate company within the Swedish ASEA group in 1986. It was based on the ASEA Master System and its flexible network of operator stations, normally located in a central control room, and process stations, connected to various subprocesses across the plant. Figure 12.1 provides a schematic overview of the Master System with its various levels. The General Master System is supported by industry-specific optimization packages: control programs for reheat furnaces in rolling mills, packages for bleachery control in pulp mills, and so on. Most of the BA's automation systems are sold in the form of project deliveries. In the case of paper machine controls, for example, ABB basically delivers a function: a specified process capability in terms of paper thickness, moisture, opacity, and so on. International projects involving extensive plant engineering and commissioning often require several years to conclude.

In the early 1990s, ABB Automation had 6000 employees worldwide. Each of the operations in Sweden, Germany, and Switzerland employed 1000

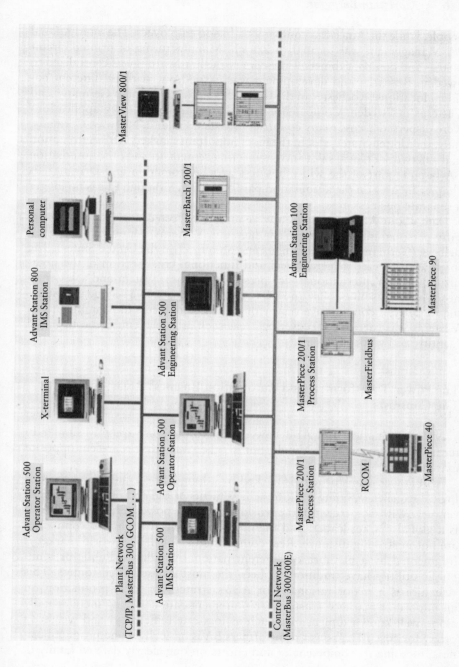

Figure 12.1. Overview of ABB Master Automation System.

people, while the American company had 1600 employees. The international BA Management was located to Zürich. Manufacturing of printed circuit boards and control cabinets—the core of the hardware—was centralized to Sweden. Research and development was carried out at three different national locations: Rochester in the United States, Mannheim in Germany, and Västerås in Sweden. Competence centers for various industry applications were dispersed across many countries: Sweden, Finland, Norway, Germany, Italy, the United States, etc. In the most important markets ABB Automation had a network of local sales and engineering centers. In 1994 the automation BA became part of the wider business area, Automation and Drives. This chapter focuses on the automation part of the BA, although this is no longer a separate business area.

Data about ABB Automation were mainly collected during 1993–1995. Fifty personal interviews were conducted in Västerås, Mannheim and Heidelberg (Germany), and Columbus and Stamford (in the United States). The interviews covered a hierarchical and functional cross-section of the organization, from international vice presidents to local system and sales engineers, as well as blue collar and white collar unionists. In a second step starting in 1995, a comparative survey of software engineers in Mannheim and Västerås was carried out, covering areas such as management, professional identity, and work problems.

The Power Transformers and Automation Business Areas: The Contrasts

ABB Automation and ABB Power Transformers are roughly similar in terms of employment worldwide, but in other ways they represent opposite extremes (Table 12.1).

ABB Power Transformers is backed by a long ASEA tradition of technological excellence, going back to achievements at the end of the nineteenth century. With 20 percent of the world market for power transformers, ABB is a global market leader, and the other major electrotechnical companies are not in striking distance. Real competition is local. The world market is fragmented by a plethora of different national standards. Public or semipublic utilities have traditionally been the most important customers. This structure is a major rationale for ABB's strategy of local production on all important markets. Customer requirements are changing incrementally along well-known dimensions, such as loss rate (efficiency) and weight (a proxy for cost). The power transformers BA is basically a one-product business, focusing its competencies and efforts on one clearly defined family of products.

In all these aspects, ABB Automation is different. In this sector, there are 5–6 companies fighting for global leadership. Launching its first commer-

Table 12.1. The Power Transformers Business Area Compared with ABB Automation

	Power Trafo	ABB Automation
History within ASEA/ABB	100 years	10 years
Research and development intensity	2–3%	10%
Product technology	Mature	Rapidly evolving
Manufacturing structure	Distributed	Centralized
Manufacturing technology	Mainly manual	Mainly automated
Global market position	World leader	No market leader can be identified
Main processes of learning	Between production plants	Between centers of engineers

cial automation platform (for control of paper production) in 1985, ABB is a relatively new contender in this group, challenging established rivals such as Siemens in Germany and Honeywell in the United States. Technology and market conditions are evolving rapidly. A transition to open systems, in which hardware and software are "unbundled," means that customers are no longer completely dependent on their first-time suppliers. Customer demands are becoming much more stringent, especially in Europe, where environmental concerns are raising the standards for industrial process control. Local manufacture is of no importance for maintaining a high market share. For key components, such as printed circuit boards, there are decisive economies of scale, and therefore ABB Automation has consolidated manufacturing to its Västerås facilities in Sweden. In contrast with ABB Power Transformers, there is no competition among different plants within the automation BA and no equivalent to the sophisticated system of transformer plant comparisons. The majority of automation systems are sold as part of complex project deliveries, involving extensive plant engineering and customer interaction. To handle this ABB has a global network of national sales and engineering operations divided into local branches on major markets, such as Germany, the United States, and Sweden.

The Automation and Power Transformers Business Areas: The Significant Similarities

In spite of all the differences, however, there are important and interesting similarities between the two business areas.

1. Both are a result of ABB's strategy of mergers and acquisitions. As a consequence, they are not only far-flung multinational operations but they are also struggling to integrate the heritage of different cor-

porate cultures, to merge different technologies, and to cope with diverse types of customer relationships.

2. In both BAs, management is dominated by Swedes, but located outside Sweden, and espousing methods and principles developed in the United States. When ASEA merged with Brown Boveri the headquarters of the new automation BA was first located in Mannheim. Three years later, when Combustion Engineering was acquired, it was transferred to Stamford, Connecticut. When the automation BA was merged with Drives to a form a combined business area, the international management center was relocated a third time, now to Zürich.

3. Both the power transformers and automation BAs embraced the concept of time-based management (TBM) as efficiency drivers in blue collar as well as white collar areas. TBM measures, such as manufacturing throughput time (TPT) and total throughput time (TTPT), rank as the most important among the international plant comparisons for the power transformers BA. The automation BA tried a TBM-inspired approach to its production operations, as well as its product development and project delivery processes. The effort was successful in manufacturing, but much less so in the other areas, for reasons that are discussed in detail later in the chapter.

4. Both business areas are grappling with the challenge of combining a multidomestic presence with cross-border learning and diffusion of common approaches and standards. This sets ABB apart from the competition, although in different ways in the two cases. In the power transformers BA, the major rivals are local, competing on cost, speed, and customer adaptation. The "automation industry" represents the opposite extreme. All of ABB's major rivals are internationally centralized. Siemens, the main European competitor, has concentrated its engineering resources to one German center, Erlangen. This makes it easier to manage large-scale projects, and to gather information from various applications in a systematic way. ABB's dispersed engineering network is exceptional in the industry. The ABB difference is borne out by an applications engineer interviewed in the mid-1990s. He used to work for the American specialist in paper machine controls, AccuRay, when it belonged to Combustion Engineering and accompanied AccuRay to ABB:

AccuRay had one big European applications center, located in Ireland. Engineers were sent out all over the continent to negotiate contracts and commission delivered equipment—a typical bachelors' job. In this way, AccuRay developed competence and effective information and learning among engineers. Communications between sales and engineering in Ireland and the development center in Columbus, Ohio was direct and simple. When a new product was launched, American engineers came over for a few weeks to teach and train the applications engineers. Such a direct and personal contact is not possible within ABB's dispersed structure. Here new products are mainly introduced by formal documentation. The ABB advantage is our close customer contacts entertained by the local engineering offices. This is of particular importance in complex deliveries, where it's hard to finalize the commissioning phase, if the customer is not assured of future support. Personal trust is crucial, since it is not possible to specify everything in the contract. . . .

Within the power transformers BA, cross-border learning mainly takes place between plants, and is supported by a powerful set of metrics. Within the Automation BA, learning and diffusion of standards and practices have to take place between engineering companies and development centers. To match the advantage of its centralized competitors, the diffusion of common processes, as a basis for international knowledge transfer, is of decisive importance.

5. Both BAs have invested heavily, but with modest success, in developing Common Product platforms. Improved economies of scale are a major rationale for corporate mergers. In reality, it takes a long time and much effort to bring about the Common Product platform prerequisite to economies of scale. When ASEA and Brown Boveri merged there were suddenly two competing automation systems, ASEA's Master System and Brown Boveri's ProControl System. Which one should survive? In the popular image, engineers are supposed to be highly rational and instrumentally oriented, but in reality issues of competing products are very difficult to resolve on the basis of technical merits. The rivalry between the Master and Pro-Control systems triggered hard arguments, and when management decided to cease development of ProControl there "was blood on the floor," according to one participant. In 1990, ABB acquired Combustion Engineering in the United States. Combustion Engineering was a loosely organized conglomerate including Taylor Instruments, which had developed a control and supervision system, MOD 300. MOD was more similar to Master in terms of architecture than Pro-Control and enjoyed a higher market share in the chemical industry. ABB Automation decided to keep both systems but to merge them successively in future product generations, and eventually market only one system worldwide.

The Common Product project within the power transformers BA started from seven different technologies. In 1996 it was in a crucial try-out stage after several years of frustratingly slow progress. In the Automation BA "only" two different platforms were to be merged. After the acquisition of Taylor Instruments in 1990, a huge joint project was set up, consisting of twenty subprojects. The intention was to launch a fully integrated system in three years. In 1996, six years after the start, the goal of a common hardware platform was almost achieved, but only 60 percent of software was fully integrated (Bresman and Birkinshaw 1996a,7). There were several reasons for the difficulties. One was the installed base of MOD and Master systems. This was an important asset for the company, since customers rarely switch to a new system supplier. However, it also was a major obstacle for the development of a unified platform, since new product releases had to be compatible with all the existing MOD and Master installations. Another reason for the difficulties in integrating the systems was the multisite development structure with a relatively weak central staff. At Rochester there was a limited interest in eliminating all the specific MOD features in favor of an international platform, since this would pose a threat to their own future.

The main obstacle to knowledge utilization by far at the early stages was lack of trust, on both sides. This was usually manifested in serious not-invented-here problems, e.g., refusal to adopt systems and ideas from the other party. Rivalry and duplication came as a result of this. (Bresman and Birkinshaw 1996b, 9).

A corporate strategy of mergers and acquisitions is a fast track to international presence, and the administrative merger of a new company may be quickly executed. However, as both the power transformers and automation BAs testify, integration at the point of technology and research and development is often painstakingly slow and difficult.

Central Initiatives and Local Variation: Toward Common Processes in Project Delivery?

Of the total price of an automation system, platform hardware is only a minor part, and the components are increasingly sourced from external suppliers. A smooth manufacturing process, which efficiently assembles customized systems in short delivery times is a precondition for ABB Automation's business. Its decisive competitive advantages, however, reside in other capabilities: constant development of new platform components and features; expertise in design of optimization packages for industry-specific processes; and effective applications engineering and project management.

Within the power transformers BA, management attention has been focused on making its global net of manufacturing plants operate in a reasonably standardized way, using similar factory layouts, production technology, and quality assurance systems; and identifying best practices and diffusing them to low performing plants. Another important activity is to standardize local designs, by introducing the same computer tools and design packages in the whole business area. The progress in both manufacturing and custom design is monitored by throughput measures. In the automation BA, standardization across plants is not relevant, but effective and compatible processes in project delivery and plant engineering certainly are. However, there are no simple metrics measuring and driving these processes.

Traditionally, project delivery and engineering within ABB Automation have been a world apart from the standards of manufacturing. Manufacturing is continuously exposed to a wide range of physical metrics for assessment of productivity, production yield, quality, lead time, inventories, and so on. The culture of the sales managers and custom engineers is one of individual autonomy and personal style.

> Project managers are "lonely wolves." It's a one-man show. Of course we discuss various experience within the department. But there is no regular interchange, no uniformity and no common approach, not even within this regional Swedish department. (Swedish project manager, 1994)

In the project delivery process, constant customer interaction is key. After a contract is signed, the project is dependent on the input of process data from the customer, and the data are often supplemented and corrected at several points later in the process. Normally the delivery date is determined by the supplier of the mechanical equipment, for example, the paper machine. Compressed engineering lead time (throughput time) in the automation BA is not seen to have any direct competitive value. Thus it was very difficult to introduce the TBM approach in the delivery process. In manufacturing, physical parameters are the most important metrics; in sales and project delivery, the dominating performance indicators concern financial outcomes and customer relations, such as gross margin and enhancement of long-term customer relations (to secure future contracts). When ABB Automation launched its TBM program in the early 1990s, a vice president for internal efficiency was appointed to encourage more effective procedures and methods within sales and project delivery. The intention was to collect regular measurements of sales efficiency, man-hours spent in preparing bids and proposals, cycle times for plant engineering activities within different projects, and so on. The response was not enthusiastic. A recurrent problem was the difficulties in measuring white collar efficiency in nonstandardized and customized projects; another difficulty was to get application engineers to devote enough time and effort to the kind of detailed structuring and reporting of their activities necessary to make projects comparable. In 1994, four years after the start of the T-50 program, the delivery projects were still entirely measured and evaluated on the basis of financial items. In that year the Swedish organization initiated an effort to develop a completely computerized project environment: specifying activities lists, designing a reference library, a system for handling and retrieving old solutions, and so forth. This effort was supported by a broader group representing six important ABB countries. The ambition was to make the activities in the project delivery process transparent and measurable. This was not necessarily appreciated among sales engineers and project managers, with their entrenched individualistic culture.

Before being implemented the project was replaced by an international effort in the business area called total optimization, or TOPS. Using a business process reengineering (BPR) model, the total value chain from proposal to plant commissioning was analyzed. Consultants compared the methods of ABB and other major players in the industry. According to this analysis, ABB's centralized competitors were more effective in employing engineering standards, in reusing old solutions, and in utilizing information technology. For ABB it ought to be the opposite: in order to work effectively its dispersed network of local centers should be using information technology more, not less, than its centralized rivals. The next step in the TOPS effort was to gather an international task force on so-called neutral territory, in this case the United Kingdom, in order to devise a pilot project for Bid and Proposal. If this up-front step in the delivery process could be made more standardized and have a more well defined interface with project management and engineering, the entire process chain would work much more effectively. The pilot project initiated several follow-on projects for subsequent phases in the delivery process. Again, however, it is important to note the absence of systematic metrics and comparisons of local engineering centers, which makes it difficult to estimate the diffusion of more efficient processes.

According to the hard-core BPR school (Hammer and Champy 1993), a true reengineering effort must be a directive, top-down exercise, in many cases outright coercive. In ABB Automation, there is much more emphasis on horizontal collaboration and local initiatives. The TOPS project developed a common framework in 1994, but the next step was not a centralized effort, but rather the opposite, to bring the common ideas to the local organization and make them part of local development initiatives. This decentralized approach was congenial with ABB's multidomestic structure, but how effective was it? In the Swedish organization, several key people argued that the new organizational technology (the common procedures and framework) was not effective per se but had to be embedded in informational technology. This argument was strongly emphasized by the previous vice president for internal efficiency: "Only if and when we have new and effective computer tools will there be a breakthrough for new and common processes."

The comment illustrates an important theme in this chapter: that engineering practices are not integrated easily, "in an engineering way." Within manufacturing, a crucial benefit flowing from new technologies is the possibility of redesigning organizations and redefining the division of labor and lines of communication. New production technologies are not tools to be used at will, but constitute integrated systems that often make specific tasks and forms of cooperation mandatory. Within engineering, computer support often just means support. In 1997, management took a new step in its efforts to create a common framework for the local engineering and delivery process. A new business unit, BU TOPS, was formed and located in Zürich, as a part of the management structure of the BA. This move signalized a more centralized strategy and an emphasis on standardized processes worldwide, such as common workflow and systems of document handling.

Software Engineering—So Far, National Strategies

With 10 percent of revenues spent on research and development and an industry in rapid technological change, the creativity and efficiency of the product development process are of great importance. The largest projects encompass the development of entirely new platforms involving new operator and process stations and communication systems. A majority of these activities consist of software development. This is a general trend within ABB, in which software development has become a dominant aspect of new product design in a range of business areas: Robotics, Network Control, Signal, Traction, Relays, Information Systems, etc. ABB has been an innovative player in the field of industrial automation, but from a management perspective there were numerous problems with the organization of its system development in the early 1990s, many of them similar to the experiences of other companies in the software engineering field. In the absence of effective process control and metrics, managers have often resorted to time pressure as their main control mechanism:

> The traditional management ideology is that people have to feel the whip. Every time a schedule has to be changed, modifications are only minimal and as a result it soon has to be changed again. The belief is that people will stop working hard if the dead-line pressure is relaxed. (Swedish middle manager, interview 1994)

The belief in the importance of constant time pressure is related to endemic problems in scheduling and controlling the development projects. When engineers in Västerås and Mannheim were asked about how resources are allocated to various projects, and what kind of learning takes place between projects, the answers were not encouraging:

> There is no database. You have it in your head. Our manager is joking about the pi factor: estimate the time, and then multiply with a factor pi. We don't de-

vote enough time to planning, but often we don't know enough about what we are supposed to do, that is, the product requirements are too unspecified.

We are lousy in follow-up on finished projects. A project goes on for an awfully long time, and when we've finished a project, everybody wants to forget it as soon as possible and start something new. The project just fades away, and there is no meeting afterward for a joint discussion.

A consequence of scheduling problems and project delays is heavy use of overtime. The launch of the Advant system in 1993 was accompanied by enormous strains: unreliable time schedules and repeated delays necessitated massive overtime work, especially during system testing. An engineer in Västerås' system test department gave the following account (Interview 1995):

It was incredible. We worked from 08.00 in the morning to 02.00 in the middle of the night for weeks and more. Part of it took place in the middle of the summer and some people had to postpone their vacations.

Histories of excessive overtime are part of the international folklore of software engineering, especially in the United States. DeMarco and Lister, for example, provide a vivid illustration of this: line managers who suspect laziness and overstaffing if a project ships on time, project managers who brag about the number of divorces and nervous breakdowns during the development work, etc. (1987, 12–13).

In the case of the Advant project there were several reasons for these difficulties, the most important being the challenge of mastering unproved technology. A basic component of the Advant system was the new real-time UNIX operating systems for the operator stations. The station was to be supplied from Hewlett Packard (HP), but HP had no experience in running UNIX in real-time applications (and neither did anyone else), and this created a mass of unforeseen difficulties. Another reason was the inherent difficulties in planning and scheduling complex software development. These problems have been debated, at least since the 1960s when International Business Machines (IBM) experienced unprecedented difficulties in developing the operating system for its famous 360 series. This experience has been analyzed by Frederick Brooks in the classic book *The Mythical Man-Month* (1975): "First, our techniques of estimating are poorly developed. More seriously they reflect an unvoiced assumption, which is quite untrue, i.e., that all will go well. Second, our estimating techniques fallaciously confuse efforts with progress . . . and when schedule slippage is recognized, the natural (and traditional) response is to add manpower." However, complex software projects require so much communication, that delays cannot be cured by the addition of more engineers. This is formulated in Brooks's law: "Adding manpower to a late software project makes it later" (Brooks 1975, 14, 20, 25). The problems confronted by Brooks are still very relevant thirty years later, as illustrated by the titles of recent books and articles in the field, such as *Software's Chronic Crisis* (Gibbs 1994), or *Death March* (Yourdon 1997). In the debate concerning the organization of software engineering, there have been two opposing approaches. One emphasizes software development as a creative art, requiring a decentralized organization where autonomous groups of skilled systems engineers integrate user demands and computer technology into innovative solutions (Borrum 1987). The other approach seeks to employ industrial principles of discipline, systematic training, statistical project planning, rigorous quality inspection, and so on. The factory approach was tested in Japan during the 1980s, but proved to be too rigid and inflexible (Berggren and Nomura 1997). In the mid-1990s, two modified approaches to change were being tested within ABB Automation, one in Sweden and one in Germany, but with no direct international coordination.

The Swedish effort was inspired by a participative version of BPR with an emphasis on process analysis, cross-functional flow, and interdisciplinary teams. When this process redesign effort, called T-50 in systems development, was initiated in the Swedish organization, the idea of cutting design lead times by half met with resistance among engineers, understandably so given the tradition of heavy time pressure in the organization: "We are doing our utmost already. Will we now have to work double shifts?" A laborious analysis and mapping of the current development process was conducted. The idea was to define the product development process rigorously in terms of input data, process characteristics, and output data. Similar to the rationalization efforts within project delivery and plant engineering, a crucial problem for the T-50 project in product design is to make its processes measurable, that is, to define relevant metrics for productivity, quality, and time precision and to monitor them in a consistent way. At ABB Sweden, the new product development model was being introduced gradually in 1995–96, including preliminary tests for the new metrics.

The German approach to change belonged to the total quality management (TQM) camp, stressing standards, documentation, and repeatable and predictable processes. This approach was inspired by the American capability maturity model (CMM), which originally was developed for the U.S. Department of Defense to evaluate and rank software vendors according to their process maturity. CMM is a very structured method for analyzing and grading development organizations. Coincidentally, Mannheim's incremental strategy seems to be rather similar to the approach of the Power transformers BA at the Bad Honnef plant.

The different tacks of the Swedish and German organizations does not mean that they will be forever different. Compared with the power transformers BA, the automation BA enjoys the advantage of having a young and dynamic technology. There is much less of entrenched national standards and traditions. A rapid diffusion of programming tools, languages, and methods from the United States, which enjoys a hegemonic position in the software field, helps to create a common professional basis. The Swedish and German organizations are pursuing different approaches to change, but they also have several elements in common, for example, the emphasis on defining and using process metrics and of involving end users throughout the development process. One important obstacle toward genuine international efforts, however, has been the deeply held assumptions about differences in national cultures. Within the Swedish organization, there is a widely held opinion that the German organization is more hierarchical and authoritarian than the Swedish culture of consensus and horizontal communications. German managers, on the other hand, lack clear lines of command and responsibilities in the Swedish organization:

> In Västerås authority and responsibility appear to be dispersed and fragmented. Everybody seems to have a management task. Line managers are not the same as product managers, and project leaders are a third group. As a result the projects are pulled in different directions. Responsibility is distributed, but as soon as someone makes a decision everybody starts discussing it. (German middle manager, interview 1994)

However, interviews of rank and file systems engineers and other software engineers in Mannheim and Västerås demonstrate a remarkable similarity in perceived problems and professional identities. In both places, engineers displayed a strong commitment to their work and a high appreciation of job features such as challenge, complexity, and demands on creative problem solving. Indeed, the similarities of these professional attitudes seem to be more important than the perceived cultural divergence.

Engineering Practices—Far from Global Convergence

This chapter has contrasted the research and engineering intensive ABB Automation with the streamlined international organization of ABB Power Transformers. Two specific efforts within the automation BA have been analyzed: the endeavors toward common standards within project delivery, and the efforts to rationalize the product development processes. A recurring theme has been the gap between managerial intent and organizational outcomes. Obviously, this business area is far from the global convergence discernible in the mature power transformers BA. ABB is strongly committed to maintain a local engineering presence "worldwide," but to stay competitive this has to be combined with processes for effective cross-border learning. ABB Automation has devoted considerable effort to internationalize top management and to set up temporary international task forces. Early on managers acknowledged the importance of extended transfers among the development centers to achieve effective integration, but they lacked the means to bring about such a cross-flow of engineers. The internationalization of engineering practices in a multidomestic company, which is a merger of different corporate as well as national cultures, seems to be a much more difficult task than is often assumed.

13 The ABB Attempt to Reinvent the Multinational Corporation

Jacques Bélanger and Torsten Björkman

The Need for Restudying the Multinational Corporation

Multinational enterprises are rightly seen as a prime manifestation of the forces of globalization. They embody internationalization by their omnipresent marketing and worldwide production processes. This book presents the results of an international study of the social organization of production within one single giant multinational. Asea Brown Boveri (ABB), on which our study focused, is a corporation widely regarded as one of the most multinational of them all. Some of the key arguments refer to its multidomestic structure, its non-national management policies, and its uncommonly internationalized design and manufacturing processes. Our research methodology sheds light on the way the forces of globalization actually operate within this corporation, top-down and bottom-up the hierarchy, geographically back and forth from center to periphery. We based our analyses on an abundance of performance data from the point of production.

By way of introduction we want to discuss the American-Japanese bias in the research literature on multinationals. Corporations founded in the United States or Japan all but monopolize the literature on multinationals. According to some studies more than 95 percent of the references in the international literature on multinationals are made to American and to a lesser extent, Japanese corporations. That bias is debatable. It is true that these two nationalities are very important among the giants; for instance on *Fortune*'s list of the 500 largest corporations in the world, they comprise almost 60 percent, but then 40 percent are not American or Japanese and may be worth looking into. If we analyze a more comprehensive population of "multinationals," for instance the 35,000 multinationals in the United Nations' data bank, then the American-Japanese share shrinks to 30 percent. Germany, the United Kingdom, France, Switzerland, the Netherlands, and Sweden together are equally important on that list. Our study of ABB, a predominantly European multinational, helps to diminish the American-Japanese bias. If European multinationals are different, it would be interesting to know how. A hint is the fact that European multinationals in general, of small country origin in particular, are among the most multinational of them all. One could add that multinationality develops out of necessity, since their domestic markets do not suffice to make them really large, but then one should keep in mind that there are numerous small countries with none or very few multinationals. Even if one knows the necessary conditions for the growth of multinationals, do all the conditions add up as being sufficient?

In our study of ABB we try to advance theoretical debates in the fields of management, industrial sociology and comparative industrial relations, a cross-disciplinary approach more difficult to implement than to express. The existent literature on multinationals is vast and rich, but still has some obvious shortcomings, one being its polarization. A characteristic is the overwhelming share of books and articles on top management. This management literature is preoccupied with top managerial opinion, while complementary data from middle or lower management are mostly lacking, not to mention the rank and file on the shop floor. The managerial perspective also has a preference for opinion to the detriment of observation and performance data.

We have compared "what they say and what they do." We have data on both management and shop floor reality. In management science this is seldom the case. In mainstream literature on multinationals managerial opinion is evidence enough. In 1994 and 1995 Ghoshal and Bartlett published two influential articles in the *Harvard Business Review* dealing with trend-setting multinationals, ABB as one of them, but their empirical findings were from headquarters only. What managers say is taken at face value.[1] Tom Peters in *Liberation Management* (1992) refers to a conversation with ABB's legendary chief executive officer at the time (in 1991), Percy Barnevik. Although interesting in itself, it is strangely interpreted by Peters. He takes it for granted that he knows what is happening at lower levels in the corporation, since he has met Barnevik in person. Peters makes very odd statements, for example, that ABB consists of only three hierarchical levels. One visit to any ABB plant or company would have been sufficient to convince him that the levels are more numerous. In political science few would dream of interpreting the statements of politicians literally. In managerial science it is a common habit to place what managers say on an equal footing with what managers do.

Now to the other end of the panorama we are trying to cover. In the literature of industrial relations and work sociology there is much to read on research from the shop floor level. That literature is strong where manage-

[1] Bartlett, Christopher A., and Sumantra Ghoshal, Changing the role of top management: Beyond strategy to purpose, *Harvard Business Review*, November-December 1994, pp. 79–88. Ghoshal, Sumantra, and Christopher A. Bartlett, Changing the role of top management: Beyond structure to process, *Harvard Business Review*, January-February 1995, 86–96.

rial literature is weak, that is, findings on everyday realities for the rank-and-file. Managerial levels, on the other hand, are often treated in a more sweeping manner. Management is said to be acting according to "new," "modern," "changing" concepts, leaving readers astray on the more precise content of what they say and do. Differing opinions and contradictory actions on the managerial level seldom enter the analysis. In other words, the industrial relations and work sociology literature would benefit from the managerial literature's well-informed account of management. To paraphrase Kipling, it is likely that "never the twain shall meet." [2]

In this book, however, we have tried to arrange such a meeting, in spite of all the prophecies of calamity. We have studied all levels of management from BA president to foreman. We have a lot of performance data from the shop floor, but we lack the full picture of opinions and experiences of all employees—there we ran out of resources. We have not succeeded in a complete merger of management and shop floor research, but we have hopefully taken important steps in that direction.

We have had the advantage of benefiting from a grand field experiment, the Power Transformers business area (BA) within ABB. By studying plants in so many countries within one corporation, plants that employ essentially the same technology to manufacture a similar range of products, we are able to focus on the importance of the local and national setting. We do not have to bother with the usual differences owing to varying products, technologies, and company sizes. Such differences do not help but hamper the analyses.

Since ABB has been saluted by an almost unanimous business press as a master of the game of becoming truly transnational, we have been keen on presenting our findings on the many difficulties and complications in fulfilling the corporate policy of "being local worldwide."

We now return to the three major issues addressed in the Introduction to the book. At the end of our research are we in a better position to answer them? We think so, and start by addressing them each of the three in turn.

Answering the Issues from the Introduction

Program Management and Internal Coordination:
Issue 1. Globalization versus the Dynamics of Local Variation

Have we been able to identify the most important mechanisms of internal coordination? None of the extreme positions can best describe the coordination pattern within the BA we have studied, neither strict formal control nor very subtle methods of communication. It is evident from the case study chapters that the BA operates with a composite coordination strategy that is formal as well as informal (see Martinez and Jarillo 1989). We have recog-

---

[2] Rudyard Kipling: "Oh, East is East, and West is West, and never the twain shall meet." Kipling's poem can be found in "The Ballad of East and West" (1889).

nized the whole range of methods from obvious to understatements, from brusque to subtle. Simply stating this is not enough, however, to capture the characteristics of how coordination is achieved within the ABB company and the power transformers BA in particular.

Our major finding in this respect is the role of programs. The BA management meetings for confirmation of achievement and sharing of common beliefs and values are of importance. They do not represent the core of coordination though; this is achieved by the internal programs. Company managers are invited to meet at BA headquarters, but the meetings have become less frequent (twice yearly) and with declining attendance. We think it is crucial to emphasize the BA's focus on its programs. The independent power transformer companies are "taxed" by BA headquarters. This taxation finances a number of "common" programs within the BA (see Chapter 2), for example, Common Product, Model Factory, lean supply, time-based management (TBM), Six Sigma, and Customer Focus. These programs were described and analyzed at length in the previous management and case study chapters.

Program Management is in many ways strict and formal. The impact of the programs is much enhanced by internal comparisons. The benchmarking system is a kind of internal ABB "Olympics," under the name of Seven-Ups, with the BA management as organizer and referee. What is called "Seven-Ups" in the power transformers BA is a forerunner of the Balanced Scorecard (Kaplan and Norton 1996). Seven-Ups data combine economic and technical information with attitude data on customer satisfaction. The different "sports" have been selected by the BA management. There are seven all together, as the name implies: quality, efficiency, production, supply management, training, sigma rating, and customer satisfaction. The metrics deal with total throughput time (TTPT), test failure rate, Six Sigma value, training statistics, and so forth.

Internal coordination is channelled through the various programs, the foremost coordination structure as well as coordination mechanism of the BA. We conclude that these programs are important enough to merit a special category on how internal coordination is achieved. We like to label it Program Management and think that it has not been given due attention in management literature.

The programs are not only ordinary change programs, of which there are always a bundle of in a larger company, but also programs in combination with benchmarking. It is this combination that we want to emphasize. The programs in tandem with benchmarking are a design for implementing semi-automatic systems. The idea is that the programs should run without much maintenance and supervision, as substitutes for management, of which there is so little present in this lean corporation. This idea might turn out to be an illusion, since metrics, as our data demonstrate, can be denied, subverted, or corrupted. The need for human intervention likely remains.

Seven-Ups is benchmarking according to the principle that "what gets measured gets done." Measurement procedures are defined and prescribed, and the scores are exact, but still they might be questioned. Is the selection of "sports" and indices representative and fair? Are the measurements taking all contingencies into consideration? Is anyone cheating, reading their measurements wrongly? These objections are tempting and, as described in the next section, sometimes used as excuses when the figures fail to be flattering.

A Cross-Border Teaching and Learning Organization: Issue 2. Organizational Learning within a Multinational Corporation

The study of the power transformers BA illustrates several important implications of the combination of global (geocentric) and multidomestic principles, defined as the "third model" multinational. There is no way corporate management can achieve strict top-down control over the manufacturing process. In such a context, global management is mostly about control of financial resources and of market allocation, the monitoring and comparison of plant performance, and the diffusion of best practices and new ideas about management processes. Hence the matrix system allows for both decentralization and close monitoring of performance.

A necessary condition for such a managerial approach, which judges on results but is also very active in promoting innovative programs such as TBM or Six Sigma, is a valid collection of data on performance and its operationalization in benchmarking measures. The accounting system, which collects on a monthly basis a large set of performance data, including manufacturing throughput time (TPT) and total throughput time, final test failure rates, and value-added per employee expenses, effectively represents such a management device. These data are studied and analyzed closely by corporate management, mostly at the BA level. In the current context in which market allocation is crucial considering that most Western plants want to export more, and on which strategic decisions on investment and divestment will follow the course, this actually contributes to a form of coercive comparison between plants.

Central initiatives such as the Six Sigma program developed far-reaching ambitions for international convergence, implying a rigorous standardization of processes and management systems. In its ultimate form, this hardcore TQM message views all kind of process variations as disturbances that are to be eliminated if the plants are to be made interchangeable. In an internationally standardized system, it would be possible to retain a dispersed structure but optimize production globally, without carrying the excess capacity which has been necessary to date. If a local plant is overloaded, excess orders would be smoothly transferred to another plant, operating in a clone-like fashion. Another benefit would be the enhanced economy of scale in hardware and software. Further, the protagonists of global standardization view this as an important vehicle for organizational learning, based on identifying and diffusing "best practice": find the one best way for every operation, make it the global standard, improve and elevate the improved routine to the new global standard, and so on.

However, there are other dimensions of learning not captured by the global standardization logic but building on local ingenuity and using customized production and local customer relations. Such initiatives may be more creatively diffused horizontally as exemplars for others to emulate than by rigorous international programs. In short, dynamic diversity may create another logic of learning than the Taylorist one of finding the "one best way." The matrix structure of ABB tends to stimulate a complex interplay of initiatives. The emphasis on strong external relations with suppliers and customers also increases the potential for diverse initiatives and different logics of learning. The theoretical economies of scale within a BA such as power transformers may never be reached. On the other hand, local initiatives and strategies may create competitive advantages, more effective in taking on local contenders than cost reduction based on global standardization.

New role models emerge; in 1993–1996 the most prominent case of successful flow organization was Finland's Vaasa plant. Convincing benchmarking measures from one plant then help global managers persuade any self-confident local management of the need for further improvement if they are to keep pace with the leaders within their own BA. Hence a process of emulation between comparable organizational units is created and supports the diffusion of better practices. The learning process also often takes the form of a cross-national mutual exchange between two local organizations that have more in common as regards technology or sometimes cultural and social acquaintance. In short, these forms of cross-organizational learning are not imposed and not even organized by corporate headquarters, but the BA plays a crucial role in showing the way toward best practices.

Our findings show a very successful catch-up learning in the periphery of the BA but slower improvements at the old core plants (see Chapter 10). Catch-up in several of the peripheral plants is sensationally swift and close to the ideal of mutual and shared learning, truly a "learning organization" as it was once coined by Arie de Geus.[3] The downside is, of course, the slow learning at the core plants. Benchmarking has obviously great potential as a learning device but does not guarantee success.

If the catch-up methodology is spreading, the way it did in ABB Power Transformers, it might have significant consequences for relative competitive advantages. Plants and countries that used to compensate for low performance by low wages and costs are now performing on a world-class level. They still have low wages and costs. Their new differential between income

---

[3] De Geus, Arie. 1997. *The living company*. Boston: Harvard Business School Press. Arie de Geus is the retired head of planning coordination at Shell, the classical European example of a cross-border corporate merger.

and cost, often a staggering quotient, gives them a heavy competitive advantage and makes them very attractive for relocation of work and jobs, and secures their potential as future exporters.

Lessons might be learned from the ABB experience, not the least by those interested in the Balanced Scorecard (Kaplan and Norton 1996). Who is teaching whom in a learning organization? The "Seven-Ups" program attempts, as mentioned, to keep track of seven performance indicators. The tracking is pretty accurate; whether it strikes a balance is more debatable. First total throughput time and later Six Sigma have worked as the most important indices, in which both profitability and personnel data are downplayed. The most important dimension of the whole endeavor is not balance but an accumulated "track record." Each and every company is able to trace its own performance and "learning curve" as well as benchmarking it with the rest of the BA.

Theoretically, this might sound like an ideal setting for effective mutual learning, something that Bartlett and Ghoshal dreamed of when they envisioned the "transnational organization." Empirically, we have a few things to add. Bartlett and Ghoshal categorized multinationals according to how they learn and develop in *Managing across Borders* (1989).[4] Bartlett and Ghoshal contributed to the popularity of the *transnational* epithet. In "multinational" multinationals (MNs) "knowledge is developed and retained in each unit"; in "global" MNs "knowledge is developed and retained at the center"; in "international" MNs "knowledge is developed at the center and transferred to overseas units." In "transnational" MNs, the most advanced category, "knowledge is developed jointly and shared worldwide." Interestingly, the authors have failed to name a category for the corporation in which knowledge is developed locally and transferred to the center. That would come close to the role of the Finnish plant at Vaasa in the power transformers BA we have studied.

Bad ratings do not only inspire learning and improvements but a lot of excuses as well. One of the most frequent ones is to question the measurement system. Creativity is triggered on explaining away the bad results, not on planning and taking action with the aim of improving them. This unlucky outcome seems to be most likely when the ranking list is revolving, that is, when plants and companies that used to look on themselves as the very best, as teachers and missionaries, have difficulties in readjusting to new roles as hopeful pupils. Denial and repression are two well-known psychological defense mechanisms that apparently function on an organizational level as well. How to handle falling former stars is a challenge that the Seven-Ups approach has difficulties in coping with, but it has worked very well for some of those in an early catch-up position.

---

[4] See Chapter 4 in particular.

Process Management and the Tearing Down of Organizational Boundaries. Issue 3. The Implementation of a New Production Regime at the Plant Level

We have studied in some detail the various programs by which the power transformers BA has tried to improve the flow of production, giving priority to a shortening of throughput times from order to delivery and reducing variations in quality. A common denominator of the many programs is a focus on process. Lean management and supply, TBM, TQM, BPR—all these faddish programs are preoccupied with process identification and process management, radical reengineering shortcuts as well as more incremental day-to-day improvements. Process management is aiming for increases in productivity and efficiency through simpler, swifter and more controllable processes.

Clearly, from the beginning of this decade, time-based management (TBM) became the real focus within ABB as a whole[5] and the search for drastic reductions in cycle times actually became a trademark of the ABB management style. The impetus for change is the need to become even more cost-efficient and driven by customers' requirements as competition intensifies. In a mature industry such as power transformer manufacturing, it is now well understood that organizational innovation is the main source of competitive advantage. The participants we met, in various countries, insisted on this reality with remarkable consistency.

A key management idea, transcending the many programs and projects implemented at the point of production, is often referred to as process management or the horizontal organization. While this notion has recently become trendy in the managerial literature (see in particular Ashkenas et al. 1995), there is in fact a long tradition of process management in this corporation; it was already practiced within ASEA in the 1960s and 1970s.[6] The idea is to move beyond the traditional hierarchical and vertically integrated organization, because the many "walls" corresponding to the main functions (marketing, design, planning, manufacturing, etc.), departments, managerial layers, and professional status impede the necessary flow of information and know-how. Various devices of social engineering are now being developed to

---

[5] In 1990–91, middle managers within the whole of ABB were more or less ordered to study the TBM methodology. They were "recommended" books such as George Stalk and Thomas Hout Jr. 1990. *Competing against time: How time-based competition is reshaping global markets.* New York: The Free Press; and Philip Thomas. 1990. *Competitiveness through total cycle time: An overview for CEOs.* The reading was thought of as mandatory. If not all of it was obeyed, they knew they should be familiar with the TBM terminology. Consultants from the Boston Consulting Group also helped them to gain a better understanding of TBM. In February 1993, Robert Taylor wrote an article entitled "Resetting the clock" in the *Financial Times*, in which he emphasized that "Asea Brown Boveri is transforming its factories by slashing lead times" (10 February 1993, 14).

[6] Curt Nicolin, who was still chairman of ASEA at the time of the merger, was an early advocate and also a theoretician of process management.

foster a transition from functional differentiation to total process optimization. Besides TBM, they consist of initiatives such as the Six Sigma program (first developed by Motorola), which represents a more rigorous approach to process variance than previous methods and offers a solid basis for TQM. The emphasis moves from functional rationalization to a flow-type organization and the compression of total lead time.

This is not to suggest that these traditional "frontiers" are now to be dismantled easily and forever. On the contrary, our research shows that various forms of cross-functional teams and horizontal coordination are currently experimented with some success, with major implications on social organization and social relations. In particular, in workplaces in which the manufacturing process was much dependent on the autonomy and tacit skills of a stable workforce, there is now some pressure for moving beyond "artisan" forms of coordination and control. This process of innovation is well under way and stepping up in most local organizations, independently of national frontiers.

Reformulating the Issues

The Dilemmas of Being Local Worldwide

A favorite theme when categorizing multinationals is trying to grade them according to multinationality. Being ranked as the most multinational of multinationals means prestige. But which is the most multinational, multinational?

> Those that can claim to be global are exceptions, companies from small countries like Switzerland or Sweden. That is also why Asea Brown Boveri (ABB) is cited in every book or article about the subject as a model global firm: it is a Swiss-Swedish engineering firm, has 85 percent of its sales outside its two homes and does organize itself to blend an extremely decentralized structure with a global strategy and some global functions such as R&D. But it is not at all typical. Nor is the typical multinational becoming more like ABB. It is becoming a regional firm.[7]

In the multinationality discourse the notion of "culture" is often superficial, as if there were a deterministic relationship to country of origin. "Swedish managers trying to look local worldwide" is an internal ABB joke seemingly valid because it is supported by statistics. In 1988, the first year of operation, top management for ABB as a whole did consist of 119 persons[8]:

---

[7] A survey of multinationals: Everybody's favourite monsters. *The Economist* (March 27, 1993).

[8] CEO plus executive committee (13); heads of corporate staff (19); business area presidents (47) plus country segment presidents (11); and regional and country managers (29).

53 of them (44 percent) were Swedes, while the Swedes made up 19 percent of all employees. In 1997, the tenth year of operation, top management consisted of 138 persons[9]: 43 of them (31 percent) were Swedes, and their contribution to all employees was down to 11 percent. By comparison the Swiss are roughly half as many, 16 percent. Swedes and Swiss, together roughly half of top management, tend to be used at the start-up of a BA or national company but are then replaced by "local" professionals when the operation matures. The Group Executive Committee has after ten years more Swiss than Swedish members.

If we go from appearance to content and try to characterize what the Swedes are promoting, they neither seem particularly Swedish nor local. Take the Process Management initiative we have just discussed. It has a clear origin and it is not Swedish. Although some models and programs started their career in Japan, they have been named and packaged in the United States. To be even more precise, almost all are from Boston. MIT and Harvard Business School and a few consultancy firms, for example, McKinsey and the Boston Consulting Group, have coined all the important models of the 1990s. The American dominance over the "fashion industry" called management is overwhelming. When it really comes to the point, ABB can make few valid claims of originality program per program. The ideas and models have been imported from the United States. The creativity of ABB in this context is shown in its combination of programs, for instance, uniting an older American idea like the matrix organization with a newer one like lean management and doing it very consistently. That is a rare, almost unique, combination in the present world of multinationals.

The fact that the American ideas in ABB are promoted mostly by Europeans (a third of them Swedes) might have some implications. One might be that of more of a long-range perspective. ABB management has been holding most of its convictions for a decade now. They keep on promoting lean management in combination with the matrix. The American fads tend to live a lot longer in the ABB environment than where they came from, in Boston. By American standards some of the core ideas of ABB are actually becoming a bit dated, TBM for instance, but as cultural elements they still have an American marking.

ABB in general, and the power transformers BA we have focused on in particular, is part of a cosmopolitan world culture of management. The American influence is strong. What ABB is doing and striving for is pretty much commonplace amongst all the competitors and multinationals. How they do it is a lot more distinguishing, however.

During the 1990s the meaning of "transnational" became trendy and

---

[9] CEO plus executive committee (11); heads of corporate staff (22); business area presidents (32) plus country segment presidents (20); and regional and country managers (48). A few BA managers are presidents of more than one BA, e.g., like Bo Göran Persson, who is in charge of both the Power and Distribution Transformers BAs.

inflated. Any company with ambition might use "transnational" as a catchword for their up-to-dateness and progressive outlook. "Multidomestic" is a more informative categorization of ABB than "transnational." [10] The problem with "multidomestic" is that domestic must be qualified. The more than forty domestic markets where ABB supposedly feels at home are domestic in varying degrees. ABB is more domestic in Sweden and Finland than in Norway and Denmark, more domestic in Switzerland than in Italy, more domestic in Canada than in the United States. ABB might feel "domestic" in Germany and the United States but it is more doubtful how many of their customers are of the same opinion. A lesser ambition was once formulated by ABB, to "become an insider, not an invader," [11] which might be more realistic than becoming "domestic" in the same sense as the local market leader.

Being local and domestic has many different meanings, depending on which country we are discussing. It is harder to become "domestic" in some countries than in others. Siemens and General Electric (GE) still have strong grips over their home countries, but in the case of GE, it is head to head with ABB only on some products, since it has abandoned vast parts of the electrotechnical spectrum. In many countries ABB is facing competition from smaller national niche players. Since the customers are professionals, we do expect the price–product performance ratio to play a major role, though. Investigations prove that price elasticity, as well as on-time delivery performance according to specifications are important to customers. In most countries nationality is becoming less vital; performance, quality, and service more expected. World markets are in short becoming more competitive, and local presence is increasingly being judged on merit.

ABB is pursuing the "triad strategy" [12] in line with so many of the other giant multinationals. Up until 1998, that meant having special regional (read: continental) executive committee members for Europe, the Americas, and Asia–Pacific/South Asia. That executive layer was then dissolved. Still the regional character of ABB is obvious. Sixty-five percent of its employees work in Europe, 20 percent in Asia and Africa, and 15 percent in the Americas (1997 figures). Even ABB, this most "transnational," "multidomestic," multinational corporation, according to the business press, is still close to what *The Economist* called a "regional" firm, as quoted earlier.

It is easy to locate ABB to Europe, but harder to pinpoint it culturally and temporally. ABB's self-characterization of being a company of "contradictions," global and local, big and small, centralized and decentralized, is an apt one. ABB is basically European but trying to implement American

[10] The phrase "multidomestic" was once coined by ASEA's sales manager, Arne Bennborn. Until his retirement in 1996, he was responsible for "large composite plants" (read big "turnkey" orders).

[11] By the very same Arne Bennborn.

[12] A strategy associated with one of its most eloquent advocates, Kenichi Ohmae, formerly at McKinsey.

ideas, not the least in the growing economies of Asia. ABB is an American-ized European-based company giving priority to a local presence in Asia. The more than forty national ABB companies have to cope with at least that many "local" cultures, often more in countries such as China, India, Canada, Spain, and Italy. That is the polycentric, multidomestic part of ABB. Because the global (geocentric or monocentric) part of ABB is not ethnic in the sense of most American, Japanese, German, French, and other big country multinationals, namely propagating their culture of origin,[13] the difficulty of characterization rests with the global side. On the global level ABB's culture is corporate, cosmopolitan, but as we keep emphasizing, Americanized. ABB's policies and programs mostly fit with the latest American fads, for example, trying TBM, Six Sigma, BPR, the Balanced Scorecard, and so forth. Fads come and go, but some fads, long ago faded, live on in ABB. The matrix was popular in the 1970s; few species have survived, ABB being one of them. The list of ABB contradictions might be enlarged with "out of date" as well as "up to date."

The matrix conceals ABB's character of an Americanized cosmopolitan multinational. Becoming truly local takes time; at best you only come half way by acquisition. With the matrix structure a dual character remain, particularly so if the BA is strengthened at the expense of the national companies, as has so far been the tendency. The matrix also produces a number of problems of its own, to which we return later in the chapter.

Beyond Convergence and Divergence

The debate on convergence or divergence has attracted a lot of interest for decades. The arguments tend to be given in parallel. Numerous arguments are presented supporting the convergence thesis, but there is also a lot of evidence in favor of understanding the situation as one characterized by divergence. Proponents of the different positions have turned into entrenched camps.

In the convergence perspective, multinational enterprises are seen as the embodiment of globalization, spearheading the breakdown of national variety. The growing importance of multinationals in forming a global economy has been one of the leading convergence themes. In this brave new world standardized multinationals are triumphant, while national variation is considered to be of lesser and lesser importance. The early successes of worldwide American multinationals, such as Ford and IBM, McDonalds and Coca-Cola, are referred to as evidence. However, when, for instance, IBM

[13] The employees in most Japanese transplants are encouraged to study Japanese culture, to get a deeper understanding of *kanban, kaizen,* and so on. See Fucini, Joseph J., and Suzy Fucini. 1990. *Working for the Japanese.* New York: Free Press. In ABB there is no such push for studying Swiss or Swedish culture.

showed record losses and downsized half its workforce in the early 1990s, they looked less triumphant.[14] Another important reference, the swift establishment of Japanese transplants in the late 1980s in the United Kingdom, the United States, Mexico, and Malaysia, has also become a bit dated. Companies such as Toyota, Nissan, and Honda were heralded as the first of the "machines that changed the world" (Womack, Jones, and Roos, 1990). The authors focused not only on the market transformation but also on the changing workplaces, the establishing of the same rigorous production regimes, the uniform ways of the corporations' lean organizations and workforce skilling. The spreading of that "machine" is obviously in a slowdown in the late 1990s.

The divergence camp used to be equally self-confident in its claims of understanding the diversity and divergence of the global situation. Wage and cost differentials are still there. The same kind of task might cost a hundred times more to get carried out in Germany than in China, for instance. The national economies differ dramatically. They might be converging regionally but not globally. Along a number of dimensions the gaps are widening, for example, in income, education, skills, and possession of technologies. The world is becoming more—not less—polarized. Even in the divergence camp, though, there are some signs of repositioning, and certain discourses are becoming more flexible.

The ABB case provides abundant material to move beyond the many simplistic notions of global convergence or national variety, and understand both the parameters driving globalizing trends and the factors sustaining national and local diversity. The field studies support a deeper understanding of this dialectic movement between corporate efforts to rationalize and optimize on a global scale and, on the other hand, efforts at the local level to do the same but according to distinct logics and by drawing on local resources and opportunities. We have sought to describe and analyze the way each of these two competing forces are at play and how their synthesis may actually foster innovation and the diffusion of learning throughout the corporation.

Our observations reveal and confirm that, even in times of "global production," the "problem of labor" still has to be confronted in every workplace. Work rules have to be established, some form of bargaining has to occur. The same holds true for the organization and process of management. The wide variety of managerial structures in each plant, the degree to which managers have adapted and introduced innovations in the organization of work, and the extent to which they involve workers in the day-to-day management of the production process depend on local factors and cannot be determined by corporate policy.

[14] The literature on what went wrong with IBM has become a genre of its own. See, e.g., Heller, Robert. 1994. *The fate of IBM*. London: Little, Brown; and Carrol, Paul. 1994. *Big blues: The unmaking of IBM*. New York: Crown.

This pattern of labor regulation is molded to some extent by national institutions. The case study chapters offer further evidence of the possibilities for joint regulation, which are built into the Swedish and German systems, as opposed to the plant studies from the United Kingdom, Australia and Canada, which show how managers and unionists alike still relate to a different tradition, which certainly had more to do with arm's length bargaining and pressure at the point of production. Moreover, local forces are at play here. The two Canadian plants follow the same general framework of collective bargaining. However, the relationships between management and union representatives are widely contrasted. In one plant, workplace innovations such as TQM are proceeding slowly, out of a concern to maintain the equilibrium between management goals and the cooperation of the workforce. In the other plant, management has confronted the internal labor market and, in the process, torn the social fabric on the shop floor.

A recent surge of interest in comparative industrial relations is stimulated by an apprehension that the forces of globalization may reduce the influence of national regulatory systems on workplace relations. While industrial relations scholars have traditionally conceived their field of study as made of distinct national systems, new research problems now arise on the agenda (see, in particular, Hyman 1999; Locke, Kochan, and Piore 1995). Several empirical studies have shown how national institutions still make a real difference in structuring relations at the point of production, in spite of forces for more convergence. John Paul MacDuffie has proposed some interesting avenues in insisting on scholars to look beyond usual explanations and not use exclusively their "country lens." He suggests in particular that "it may make sense to first examine company-level factors affecting the adoption and diffusion of new approaches to work organization and then to turn to national-level explanations to explain residual variation" (1995, 106). The research methodology applied in this comparative study of ABB helps uncover some of the complex forces at play here.

As for institutional forces, market forces do not structure local relations in any deterministic way. In protected markets, which still comprise the majority worldwide, operations can command premium prices and cultivate intimate economical and technical relationships with their main customers. In deregulated and open markets, such as the United Kingdom, Sweden, Finland, and the major part of North America, the downward pressure on price is intensive, and local networks tend to destabilize. Nevertheless, the characteristics of the local market and the degree of competitive pressure is related to the relative autonomy of local plants, by itself a source of variety. The relative autonomy of a given plant is also strongly influenced by the structuring of relationships with its local economic and political environment. The case study chapters show how much the process of management is influenced by the insertion of the productive organization in the wider political and social systems. The pressures felt by any given plant to reform its management systems are mediated by its position in the local product and labor markets. Indeed, embeddedness in the local environment sometimes generates additional resources for a local company to develop more autonomy in its relations with corporate management.

We would like to transcend the simplistic debate on convergence or divergence and view the two as complementary. Visions of convergence are often founded on trend extrapolation and consequently running the risk of a regression fallacy. Howard Perlmutter, well-known for his typology of multinationals, predicted in the early 1970s, that the top layer of multinationals would control 80 percent of the noncommunist world's productive assets in 1985. In 1990 the top 100 still did not control more than 16 percent of Western assets;[15] although this is a lot, it is very little compared with Perlmutter's doomsday forecast. Diversity springs eternal, but since it is often the result of creativity, innovation, and deviation, it is almost by definition harder to predict than convergence.

It is also relevant to be specific in assessing the forces of convergence and divergence. In which fields do they apply? Convergence might be true as regards fads (such as downsizing, time savings, optimal sizes of plants, etc.) and at the same time we might have divergence in matters relating to performance, that is, on labor productivity, profitability, learning, and growth. A learning organization, to take just one example, could be seen as converging toward a norm during a catch-up phase. If and when they do, management is likely to move the target, with the intention of improving performance even further, to continuous improvement. Convergence tends to breed divergence, in other words. When many have reached the norm, they get the message or insight to go on improving. In this phase their learning becomes more innovative, developmental, and entrepreneurial in character to gain competitive advantages both internally and externally. This process is amply demonstrated in our case chapters. When Vaasa proved itself and became a BA model, all the other companies were encouraged to learn from it, with revolving role models but still the pattern of role models. In the survival of the fittest, fitness is a moving target. Competition is producing convergence, in the sense that the low performers tend to lose terrain, go bankrupt, and disappear. At the same time it is bringing forth new, innovative ways, making for divergence. Contrary to what many expect the pursuit of "the one best way" does not automatically result in convergence. Best practices are constantly redefined.

In ABB the integration after the merger and acquisitions, when the former competitors had become parts of the same corporation, did result in a growing degree of standardization. Nevertheless, the divergence process started all over again owing to innovative plants like Vaasa that improved beyond

---

[15] A survey of multinationals: Everybody's favourite monsters. *The Economist* (March 27, 1993).

expectations and certainly owing to new acquisitions, for example, the ones in China and Vietnam.

The Trendsetter Issue: Reinventing the Multinational

In the business press and management literature the focus has not been on ABB as much as on the person, policies, and philosophies of Percy Barnevik, the chairman of ABB and its chief executive officer (CEO) during its first nine years, 1988–1996. He was the mastermind behind the merger between ASEA and Brown Boveri and of the strategy of acquisitions and growth that followed. Barnevik was also responsible for major choices of organizational design such as the matrix and lean management on all levels, particularly at headquarters.

ABB has had the advantage of very good investor relations and consequently high stock ratings from its very first year of operation. That success is not self-evident given the company's revenues and profitability; it is more a proof of the appeal of ABB's plans and policies as presented by Barnevik than a reflection of past performance. In the investigations by *Financial Times* and Price Waterhouse[16] on Europe's most respected companies, ABB has come out on top and Percy Barnevik has twice been ranked as the most respected European manager, in particular for his strategic vision. Our study confirms his strong influence.[17] It is striking to note that in the local plants visited by our team of researchers, in so many countries, Percy Barnevik is seen as the driving force behind the ABB philosophy of decentralized management and corporate accountability. Many policy slogans are well communicated.

The other side of the coin of Barnevik's excellent reputation has been the claim that ABB stands or falls with him.[18] We cite from a page profile published by *The Economist* in 1996, titled "The ABB of management":

Not long ago, pundits held that globalisation would erase national differences and homogenise consumer tastes. Mr Barnevik's view is more nuanced. He argues that purely national companies have little chance of thriving as govern-

[16] Presented so far in 1994, 1995, and 1996 and each year relying on interviews with 1,400 managers of the largest European corporations. Companies close to ABB have been British Airways and Marks & Spencer.

[17] Just to give one example, the opening of an extensive interview with Barnevik in the *Harvard Business Review* reads as follows: "Percy Barnevik, president and CEO of ABB Asea Brown Boveri, is a corporate pioneer. He is moving more aggressively than any CEO in Europe, perhaps in the world, to build the new model of competitive enterprise—an organization that combines global scale and world-class technology with deep roots in local markets" (Taylor 1991, 91). For a most laudatory assessment of Barnevik's bold leadership, see also Tom Peters (1992, Chap. 4).

[18] See Nils Elvander. 1995. Gränslös samverkan: Fackets svar på företagens internationalisering. Stockholm: SNS.

ments deregulate and as the cost of travel and information plummets. But he stresses that companies need to keep deep roots in local markets, because markets will continue to differ. His answer is a cosmopolitan conglomerate diverse enough to respond to local tastes but united enough to amount to more than the sum of its parts.

. . . But ABB's current structure—and indeed the modern management fashion which Mr Barnevik has done so much to influence—has thrust an awesome amount of responsibility to the very top of the organization. The more global it has grown, the more it has relied on a strong leader to hold it together. The bigger test of Mr Barnevik's skills may be not how well the company performs while he is still in charge, but what happens to it after his departure.[19]

That test is now under way. It is a test of Weberian dimensions, the ABB corporation going from charismatic leadership to reliance on strategies and organizational designs, systems, and programs. Barnevik was a trendsetter—will ABB prove to be a trendsetting corporation?

ABB is not an ordinary multinational. On the one hand, its small-country origin makes it special. Its start from a cross-border merger is even more uncommon. Cross-border acquisitions are frequent but cross-border mergers are not and especially not mergers between equals like the old ASEA and Brown Boveri, close to identical in size and age. The merger resulted in two truly domestic markets, Switzerland and the Nordic countries, and many claimed "domestic" markets of debatable status in which ABB is not the dominant player. The purpose of ABB's merger and acquisitions offensive of the late 1980s was, on the other hand, to become less special, more like its major competitors, GE and Siemens. In particular ABB intended to reach similar economies of scale. These features might make ABB a role model for other small-country multinationals wanting to quicken the growth process. Few seem to have been inspired—GEC-Alsthom is an exception.

The size goal was reached with the strategy of focusing on one industry, the electrotechnical one. ABB has grown to command the world's biggest market shares in the core businesses of the electrotechnical industry, that is, generation, transmission, and distribution. $US 35 billion dollars in revenues and some 220,000 employees make ABB one of the top hundred largest corporations in the world (it ranked 70 in revenues in 1996). Still GE and its conglomerate strategy, with only a sample of the electrotechnical products in combination with the strangest products and services from other lines of industries, has so far been markedly more successful in profitability. The one-industry strategy is risky and fateful if your chosen industry is suffering from overcapacity and price falls due to deregulation and privatization and no new star product, such as the cellular phone that salvaged the aging telecommunications industry. The other extreme, the conglomerate, is seldom

---

[19] "The ABB of management," *The Economist.* January 6, 1996, p. 56.

very successful either. GE is one of the very few fast-growing conglomerates; its profitability is truly exceptional.

ABB has become big but it is questionable to what extent the potential for economies of scale has been realized. That goal seems elusive, as we have demonstrated with the history of Common Product and the ABB preferred policy of one plant per domestic market. Economies of scale are a main responsibility of the BA headquarters, but in the matrix structure of ABB their authority is tempered by the national companies, responsible for economies of scope. The efforts to develop a Common Product technology have so far not resulted in a final breakthrough, even if the toughest period seems to be over. This testifies to the costs and time needed to realize the economies of scale promised at the time of the mergers, which is an often poorly understood problem. Other business areas within ABB, for example Process Automation, have experienced the same problem of merging diverse technologies. There is no doubt about the international management's determination to bring about the Common Technology platform; when that is accomplished there will probably be a reduction in variety in other respects as well. The issue of merging technologies reminds us that studies of integration must adopt a very long perspective.

ABB has possibly the leanest headquarters organization of all multinationals. Central headquarters at Oerlikon, a suburb of Zurich in Switzerland in the center of Europe employs less than 200 people. The CEO himself is seldom present at headquarters; instead he is meeting customers and visiting ABB companies. The entire ABB corporation has for several years had a workforce of more than 200,000 employees, so international headquarters only represents one-thousandth of the total workforce. If we add all the BA headquarters and national company headquarters, the total is about 600 people altogether. This very sharp reduction cut nine-tenths of the staffs of the merging companies forming ABB in 1987—around 6,000 managers, specialists, and secretaries. That is a remarkable downsizing. The transition to lean management is a major reorganization and an important feature of ABB. In this respect ABB is a trendsetter. Now downsizing of headquarters has become common practice, although seldom as drastic as in ABB. Many corporations talk about the merits of becoming leaner; ABB has realized this type of reorganization.

Downsizing of staff and headquarters can be relatively easily achieved by central decisions and policies. This was a very important measure during ABB's restructuring of acquired companies. A more demanding task is to translate lean management into low-cost production and development. Here the balance is more mixed at ABB. The power transformers BA has been driving down costs relentlessly. In other BAs it could be argued that a more resourceful, and less lean management, is needed in order to cope effectively with international coordination of capacity, planning of investments, and so on. This leads to the broader question: Is being lean necessarily a virtue? In recent years, an increasing number of researchers have questioned the "lean ideal" and the wisdom of repeated rounds of downsizing, arguing that this practice is exhausting organizations, making them heavily dependent on outside consultants and depleting resources for long-term strategic reflection and development. The excessive burdens of the small BA management in the power transformers BA seems to illustrate some of these concerns.

With its lean headquarters the ABB organization is very dependent on the functioning of the roughly 35 business areas (BAs) and more than 40 national centers and some 1,000 companies. In a crisis there is not much help or backup to be expected from headquarters. Whom should they send? The lean structure is repeated on all levels. The BAs, the equivalent of divisions, vary a lot in size but most of them consist of between 5,000 and 10,000 employees. Military divisions have around 15,000 soldiers; their corporate counterparts are generally smaller. Started by Sloan at GE, the business "division" became one of the most important organizational reforms of this century. ABB has promoted a potential alternative, that is, "companies." The more than 1,000 companies of the ABB group are often called "company-companies" to make it clear that they are small and medium-sized enterprises (SMEs). More than 200,000 employees split up into 1,000 companies would make us expect companies of around 200 employees. The variation in company size is considerable but many effectively have around 200 employees. This shoal of small companies is a vastly more radical way of structurally forcing the organization to decentralize than the divisionalization of earlier decades. Even in this respect ABB has got a following. A number of giant corporations are trying to multiply by reproducing more daughter companies, new companies of mostly company size. In short they are trying to create more local autonomy within the framework of the giant corporation.

In contrast with lean management and company-companies, the ABB matrix organization has inspired little or no following, because the reputation of the matrix has dwindled since its heydays in the 1970s. The matrix system of management attempts to strike a balance between economies of scale and scope. The corporation is searching for synergy between globally oriented and nationally directed managerial structures. Each local plant is responding to the influences of a national policy and to the requirements of a global strategy. ABB's corporate article of faith on the importance of local presence and preaching respect for local cultures represent softer sides of the matrix. ABB slogans of "Think globally, act locally," and "Being local worldwide" recognize that local responses and solutions cannot be unilaterally prescribed from headquarters. Local management should always question the way things are done. The empirical material presented in this book highlights that the matrix seems to be responsible for slow decision making as well as implementation: to quote the critics, "More friction than action."

Many of the initiatives within ABB's Program Management have a following. GE is pursuing Six Sigma with more enthusiasm and purposefulness than ABB Management. Siemens is copying the ABB time-based management approach under the name of time optimized processes (TOP) and with the help of managers recruited from ABB. The competitors keep track of each other and try to copy what seems to be working. ABB has been a sender of many new messages.

Even with ABB's major emphasis on managerial initiatives, there is sometimes a huge gap from executive policy statements to plant reality. These considerations have a general significance and could be related to many large organizations, but they take on a special meaning in the structures and policies of ABB. How does a company sustain a globalist profile within a multi-domestic structure?

ABB's Program Management provides a clue. When the international transformer business was organized, it was only natural that the technically highly competent old ASEA plants would assume the role of being teachers for the acquired operations. Who would have expected that only a few years later a small Finnish plant would be elevated to master of process efficiency within this traditional heavy industry, with its classical strongholds in Germany, Sweden, and North America? This ability to distance itself from the old core and identify "new stars" could be seen as the litmus test of a combined geocentric and multidomestic organization, sometimes called the "third model" of multinational organization. The European ABB corporation might prove a trendsetter in its ambitions of combining global resources and local flexibility, as opposed to the ethnocentric cultures of most American and Japanese multinationals.

A second clue concerns the importance of a cohesive managerial structure in a matrix organization. The power transformers BA might be an exception to matrix management because of the presence and commitment of an undisputed network of senior managers, most of them originating from the old ASEA. Other BAs are less fortunate. Without strong, sometimes informal, managerial networks, it is very difficult to run international operations effectively, especially in hard times. Consequently the performance of the matrix system cannot be judged in the abstract, but has to take these factors into consideration.

We have studied ABB in depth within the power transformers BA, the business area that is considered a role model for ABB's multidomestic strategy. We would like to end with a few words of caution. The power transformers BA is a special case, deviating from most others in ABB. No other BA is as equally decentralized and multidomestic or has as many plants and companies around the world. Most other BAs work with more dynamic technologies characterized by swifter change. Seven-Ups, the very important benchmarking system used in the power transformers BA, a key to the efficient functioning of Program Management in this sector has run into many difficulties already under the relatively stable and advantageous contingencies of this BA.

In conclusion we want to summarize that our study demonstrates that "being local worldwide" has been a valid strategy for ABB and the Power Transformers BA, but that its implementation has been vastly more demanding and time-consuming than expected. By focusing on a specific business area, and combining detailed plant studies from a variety of countries, our study highlights the actual workings of the geocentric and multidomestic principles—and the enormous effort, skill, and energy needed to maintain this orientation. The strategy has been only a partial success under relatively advantageous circumstances.

In the debates of the 1990s concerning modern management, globalization, and cross-border operations, ABB and Percy Barnevik have been enormously influential as a point of reference. ABB has stimulated or triggered reorganization and internationalization in many previously ethnocentric firms, from Alsthom to Siemens. However, Barnevik also argued that while it is relatively easy to copy products, it is very difficult to emulate a complex international organization. In that sense he might be more prescient than many of the management gurus and business journalists preaching "the ABB gospel." As several of ABB's competitors have experienced, internationalization and the building of multidomestic structures do not come easy, nor do cross-border mergers. Our study can be read as another warning to the copycats. In quite an epical way, the ABB story demonstrates how much work and effort are needed to build and manage a coordinated multidomestic structure. After ten years of hard work with program management, harvest time remains elusive. The challenge of global management is still there to be met.

References

ABB Ltd. Zürich, Annual Report 1988–97.

ABB Power Transformers Management GmbH. 1996. *Common Process documentation: A description of the Common Process obtained as a result of the implementation project in Vaasa and Ludvika.* Compiled by Pierre Comptdaer. Mannheim: ABB Power Transformers BA.

ABB Transmit Oy. 1995. *Power transformers: Construction.* Vaasa: ABB Transmit Oy.

Ackoff, Russell. 1994. *The democratic corporation.* New York: Oxford University Press.

Ahlskog, Marina. 1992. *Koncernfackligt samarbete inom ABB Strömberg.* Helsinki: Työministeriö.

Altmann, Norbert, M. Deiss, V. Döhl, and D. Sauer. 1986. Ein "Neuer Rationalisierungstyp"—neue Anforderungen an die Industriesoziologie. *Soziale Welt,* p. 2/3.

Altmann, Norbert, Christoph Köhler, and Pamela Meil, eds. 1992. *Technology and work in German industry.* London: Routledge.

Anthony, P. D. 1994. *Managing culture.* Milton Keynes: Open University Press.

Ashburner, L., E. Ferlie, and L. FitzGerald. 1996. Organizational transformation and top-down change: The case of the NHS. *British Journal of Management* 7, no. 1: 1–16.

Ashkenas, Ron, Dave Ulrich, Todd Jick, and Steve Kerr. 1995. *The boundaryless organization: breaking the chains of organizational structure.* New York: Jossey-Bass.

Atkinson, John. 1985. Flexibility, uncertainty and manpower management. *Institute of Manpower Studies,* Report No. 89. Falmer: University of Sussex.

Ausschuss fuer Wirtschaftliche Fertigung (AWF). 1984. *Flexible Fertigungsorganisation am Beispiel von Fertigungsinseln.* Eschborn: AWF.

Bartlett, Christopher, A. 1986. Building and managing the transnational: The new organizational challenge. In *Competition in global industries,* edited by Michael E. Porter. Boston: Harvard Business School Press: 367–401.

Bartlett, Christopher, A., and Sumantra Ghoshal. 1989. *Managing across borders: The transnational solution.* Boston: Harvard Business School Press.

——. 1990. Managing innovation in the transnational corporation. In *Managing the global firm,* edited by Christopher Bartlett, Yves L. Doz, and Gunmar Hedlund. London: Routledge.

——. 1994. Changing the role of top management: Beyond strategy to purpose. *Harvard Business Review,* November–December, 79–88.

Bate, S. P. 1996. Towards a strategic framework for changing corporate culture. *Strategic Change* 5, no 1: 27–42.

Beckérus, Åke, and Anders Edström. 1995. *Den europeiska rockaden: Svenska företag väljer ny strategi*. Stockholm: Svenska Dagbladet Executive.

Behr, Marhild von. 1995. Gruppenarbeit im amerikanischen Maschinenbau—Die tayloristische Variante eines post-tayloristischen Modells. *WSI-Mitteilungen* 4, 48: 277–283.

Behr, Marhild von, and Hartmut Hirsch-Kreinsen, eds. 1998. *Globale Produktion und Industriearbeit—Arbeitsorganisation und Kooperation in Produktionsnetzwerken*. Frankfurt/New York: Campus Verlag.

Bélanger, Jacques. 1994. Job Control under different labor relations regimes: A comparison of Canada and Great Britain. In *Workplace industrial relations and the global challenge*, edited by Jacques Bélanger, P. K. Edwards, and Larry Haiven. Ithaca, N.Y.: ILR Press: 43–69.

Bell, S. 1993. *Australian manufacturing and the state: The politics of industry policy in the post-war era*. Melbourne: Cambridge University Press.

Bengtsson, Lars. 1994. *Learning from Mecca? Rationalizations and work processes at ABB Transformers in Ludvika*. Stockholm: Royal Institute of Technology.

Bengtsson, Lars, and Martin Ljungström. 1996. *Total quality management and work organization: The relationship between TQM and work organization in Swedish industrial companies*. Gävle: University-College Gävle-Sandviken.

Benson, Harris. 1996. *University Physics*. New York: John Wiley & Sons.

Berg, Nina. 1993. *Medbestemmelse i et overnasjonalt konsern: En studie av ABB ASEA Brown Boveri*. Bergen: Universitetet i Bergen.

Berg, Peter. 1994. Strategic adjustments in training: A comparative analysis of the German and U.S. car industries. Edited by Lisa Lynch. *Training and the private sector*. Chicago: University of Chicago Press.

Berggren, Christian. 1994. Building a truly global organisation? The case of ABB and the hard task of integrating a multi-domestic enterprise. Proceedings of an International Conference on Corporate Change, Sydney.

——. 1996a. ABB: Local presence and cross-border learning within a multinational. In *Blackwell cases in human resource and change management*, edited by John Storey. Oxford: Blackwell: 320–343.

——. 1996b. Building a truly global organization? ABB and the problem of integrating a multi-domestic enterprise. *Scandinavian Journal of Management* 12, no. 2: 123–138.

Berggren, Christian, and Nomura, Masami. 1997. *The resilience of corporate Japan*. London: Paul Chapman.

Björk, Stellan. 1991. Arne Bennborn, den dolde tänkaren på ABB. *Ledarskap* no. 7:

Björkman, Torsten. 1991. *The ABB project. The whole is more than the sum of its parts*. Stockholm: Royal Institute of Technology.

——. 1994. ABB: Les nouveaux possibles. In *La fin du modèle suédois*, edited by Jean-Pierre Durand. Paris: Syros, 135–158.

Björkman, Torsten, and Karin Lundqvist. 1981. *Från MAX till PIA* [A study of new Rationalization strategies in the Swedish engineering industry, within ASEA in particular]. Lund: Arkiv.

Borrum, F. 1987. Beyond Taylorism. The IT-specialists and the deskilling hypothesis. Working paper, Copenhagen School of Economics.

Bray, Mark. 1994. Unions, the Accord and economic restructuring. In *Developments in Australian politics*, edited by J. Brett, J. Gillespie, and M. Goot. Melbourne: Macmillan.

Bresman, H., and J. Birkinshaw. 1996a. *ABB & Combustion Engineering*. Stockholm: IIB, Stockholm School of Economics.

——. 1996b. *Knowledge management in international acquisitions*. Stockholm: IIB, Stockholm School of Economics.

Brödner, Peter. 1985. *Fabrik 2000. Alternative Entwicklungspfade in die Zukunft der Fabrik*. Berlin: Sigma Bohn.

Brooks, Frederick. 1975. *The mythical man-month*. London: Addison & Wesley.

Carrol, Paul. 1994. *Big Blues: The Unmaking of IBM*. New York: Crown.

Castles, F. 1988. *Australian public policy and economic vulnerability*. Sydney: Allen & Unwin.

Catrina, Werner. 1991. *BBC. Glanz—Krise—Fusion. 1891–1991: Von Brown Boveri zu ABB*. Zürich: Orell Füssli.

Cohen, Roger. 1992. The very model of efficiency. *The New York Times*, 2 March.

Dabscheck, Braham. 1995. *The struggle for Australian industrial relations*. Melbourne: Oxford University Press.

Dawson, P. 1994. *Organizational change: A processual perspective*. London: Paul Chapman.

De Geus, Arie. 1997. *The living company*. Boston: Harvard Business School Press.

DeMarco, T., and T. Lister. 1987. *Peopleware*. New York: Dorset House.

Deming, W. Edwards. 1986. *Out of the Crisis*. Cambridge: MIT Press.

Dombois, Rainer, and Ludger Pries. 1993. *Modernización empresarial: Tendencias en America Latina y Europa*. Caracas: FESCOL.

Dore, Ronald. 1973. *British factory—Japanese factory: The origins of national diversity in industrial relations*. London: Allen & Unwin.

Drache, Daniel, and Harry Glasbeek. 1992. *The changing workplace: Reshaping Canada's industrial relations system*. Toronto: Lorimer.

Du Gay, Paul. 1996. *Consumption and identity at Work*. London: Sage.

Düll, Klaus, and Günter Bechtle, unter Mitarbeit von Manfred Moldaschl. 1991. *Massenarbeiter und Personalpolitik in Deutschland und Frankreich—Montagerationalisierung in der Elektroindustrie*. Vol. I, Frankfurt/New York: Campus Verlag.

Edwards, P. K. 1987. *Managing the factory*. Oxford: Blackwell.

Edwards, P. K., Anthony Ferner, and Keith Sisson. 1993. People and the process of management in the multinational company: A review and some illustrations. *Warwick Papers in Industrial Relations*, no. 43.

Elvander, Nils. 1995. *Gränslös samverkan. Fackets svar på företagens internationalisering*. Stockholm: SNS.

Evans, Paul, and Peter Lorange. 1989. The two logics behind human resource management. In *Human resource management in international firms*, edited by Paul Evans, Yves L. Doz, and André Laurent. London: Macmillan: 144–162.

Ewing, Per, and Lundahl Lennart. 1996. *The Balanced Scorecards at ABB Sweden. The EVITA project*. Stockholm: EFI, Stockholm School of Economics.

Fernández Steinko, Armando. 1994. La competividad en el sector de maquinaria mecanica: Una comparación Alemania-España. *Economía Industrial* Mayo/Junio.

Ferner, Anthony. 1994. Multinational companies and human resource management: An overview of research issues. *Human Resource Management Journal* 4, no. 2: 79–102.

Flecker, Jörg, and Gerd Schienstock. 1994. Globalisierung, Konzernstrukturen und Konvergenz der Arbeitsorganisation. In *Umbrüche gesellschaftlicher Arbeit, Soziale Welt*, edited by N. Beckenbach, and W. van Treeck. Sonderband 9. Göttingen, 625–642.

Frenkel, Stephen. 1994. Patterns of workplace relations in the global corporation: Toward convergence? In *Workplace industrial relations and the global challenge*, Edited by Jacques Bélanger et al. Ithaca: ILR Press, 240–74.

Fucini, Joseph J., and Suzy Fucini. 1990. *Working for the Japanese*. New York: Free Press.

Gallie, Duncan. 1978. *In search of the new working class: Automation and social integration within the capitalist enterprise*. Cambridge: Cambridge University Press.

Ghoshal, Sumantra, and Christopher A. Bartlett. 1995. Changing the role of Top Management: Beyond Structure to Process, *Harvard Business Review*, January-February, 86–96.

——. 1997. *The individualized corporation: A fundamentally new approach to management*. New York: HarperBusiness.

Gibbs, W. W. 1994. Software's chronic crisis. *Scientific American*, September: 86–95.

Giles, Anthony, and Akivah Starkman. 1995. The collective agreement. In *Union-management relations in Canada*, edited by Morley Gunderson and Allen Ponak. 3d ed. Don Mills, Ontario: Addison-Wesley: 339–371.

Gill, M. 1995. "Labour gives the edge, says ABB chief." *Australian Financial Review*, 30 March, 29.

Glasmeier. A. and K. Fuellhart. 1996. What do we know about firm learning? Paper presented at Innovation and International Business, 22nd Annual Conference of European International Business Academy, Stockholm.

Glete, Jan. 1983. *ASEA under hundra år, 1883–1983*. Västerås: ASEA AB.

Goold, M., and A. Campbell. 1987. *Strategies and styles: The role of the center in managing diversified companies*. Oxford: Basil Blackwell.

Greif, Michel. 1989. *L'usine s'affiche*. Paris: Les Editions d'Organisation.

Gunderson, Morley, and Allen Ponak, eds. 1995. *Union-management relations in Canada*. 3d ed. Don Mills, Ontario: Addison-Wesley.

Håkansson, Håkan, and Ivan Snehota. 1995. *Developing relationships in business networks*. London: Routledge.

Hamill, G. 1984. Labour relations and decision-making in multi-national companies. *Employee relations* 15, no. 2: 30–34.

Hammer, Michael, and James Champy. 1993. *Reengineering the corporation*. London: Nicholas Brealey Publishing.

Handy, Charles B. 1994. *The empty raincoat*. London: Hutchinson.

Hedlund, G. 1986. The hypermodern MNC: A heterarchy? *Human Resource Management* 25, no. 1: 9–35.

Hedlund, G. 1994. A model of knowledge management and the N-form corporation. *Strategic Management Journal* 15: 73–90.

Heller, Robert. 1994. *The fate of IBM*. London: Little, Brown.

Hirsch-Kreinsen, Hartmut. 1994. Die Internationalisierung der Produktion: Wandel von Rationalisierungsstrategien und Konsequenzen für Industriearbeit. *Zeitschrift für Soziologie* 6, no. 23: 434–446.

Hirsch-Kreinsen, Hartmut. 1995. Einflussgrössen, Verlaufsformen und Arbeitsfolgen internationaler Rationalisierungsstrategien—Erste Befunde eines laufenden Projektes. In *Verbund Sozialwissenschaftliche Technikforschung, Mitteilungen* 14: 6–26.

Hirst, Paul, and Grahame Thompson. 1996. *Globalization in question*. Cambridge: Polity Press.

Hoffmann, Klaus, and Frank A. Linden. 1994. Kommando Zurück. *Manager Magazin*. 11: 34–45.

Hofheinz, Paul. 1994. ABB's big bet in Eastern Europe. *Fortune*, 2 May, 24–30.

Hofstede, Gert H. 1980. *Culture's consequences, international differences in work-related values*. Beverly Hills: Sage Publications.

Homburg, Heidrun. 1991. *Rationalisierung und Industriearbeit. Arbeitsmarkt, Management, Arbeiterschaft im Siemens-Konzern Berlin 1900–1939*. Berlin: Haude and Spener.

Horne, Donald. 1964. *The lucky country*. Harmondsworth: Penguin.

Huber, Achim, and Kotthoff Hermann. 1994. *Das Modell der Reorganisation im ABB-Konzern*. Saarbrücken: Institut für Sozialforschung und Sozialwirtschaft.

Hyman, Richard. 1999. National industrial relations systems and transnational challenges: An essay in review. *European Journal of Industrial Relations* 5, no. 1: 89–110.

Hyman, Richard, and Anthony Ferner, eds. 1994. *New frontiers in European industrial relations*. Oxford: Blackwell.

Imai, Masaaki. 1986. *Kaizen: The key to Japan's competitive success*. New York: McGraw-Hill.

Inserra, André, and Patrik Olsson. 1995. *A study of inter-firm linkages in Brazil and Sweden*. Gothenburg: Chalmers' International Master's Programme.

Jürgens, Ulrich, Thomas Malsch, and Knuth Dohse. 1993. *Breaking away from Taylorism: Changing forms of work in the automobile industry.* Cambridge: Cambridge University Press.

Kanter, Rosabeth Moss. 1989. *When giants learn to dance.* New York: Simon and Schuster.

Kaplan, Robert, and David Norton. 1996. *The balanced scorecard: Translating strategy into action.* Boston: Harvard Business School Press.

Kapstein, J. 1990. Preaching the Euro-gospel: ASEA Brown Boveri redefines multinationalism. *Business Week*, 23 July, 34–38.

Katz, Harry C. 1985. *Shifting gears: Changing labor relations in the U.S. automobile industry.* Cambridge: MIT Press.

Keller, Maryann. 1993. *Collision. GM, Toyota, Volkswagen and the race to own the 21st century.* New York: Currency.

Kidd, Paul. 1994. Agile Manufacturing: Key issues. In: Paul Kidd and Waldemar Karwowski, eds. *Advances in Agile Manufacturing.* IOS Press: 29–32.

Köhler, Christoph. 1995. Arbeits- und Produktionssysteme im internationalen Vergleich—Deutschland, Spanien, Frankreich und Japan. *Industrielle Beziehungen* 3, no. 2: 223–250.

Köhler, Christoph, and Klaus Schmierl. 1992. Technological innovation—Organizational conservatism? In: Norbert Altmann, Christoph Köhler, and Pamela Meil, eds. *Technology and work in german industry.* London: Routledge.

Köhler, Christoph, and James Woodard. 1997. Systems of work and socio-economic structures: A comparison of Germany, Spain, France and Japan. *European Journal of Industrial Relations* Vol 3: 59–82.

Kolodny, Harvey. 1985. *Matrix organization, design, implementation and management.* Ann Arbor, Mich.: University Microfilms International.

Lansbury, Russell D., and John R. Niland. 1994. Trends in industrial relations and human resource policies and practices: Australian experiences. *International Journal of Human Resource Management* 5, no. 3: 581–608.

Leavy, B. and D. Wilson. 1994. *Strategy and leadership.* London: Routledge.

Legge, Karen. 1995. *Human resource management.* London: MacMillan.

Leppänen, Rolf. 1994. *ABB action recipe.* Helsinki: Hakapaino.

Levitt, Theodore. 1991. The globalization of markets. In Cynthia A. Montgomery and Michael E. Porter, eds. *Strategy: seeking and securing competitive advantage.* Boston: Harvard Business School Publishing Division, 187–204.

Littlechild, Stephen. Office of electricity regulation: The new regulatory framework for electricity. In *Regulators and the market*, edited by Cento Veljanovski. London: Institute of Economic Affairs, 107–118.

Locke, Richard. 1992. The demise of the National Union in Italy: Lessons for comparative industrial relations theory. *Industrial and Labor Relations Review* 45, no. 2: 229–249.

Locke, Richard. 1995. The transformation of industrial relations? A cross-national review. In *The comparative political economy of industrial relations*, edited by Kirsten S. Wever and Lowell Turner. Madison, Wisc.: IRRA. Industrial Relations Research Association Series: 9–31.

Locke, Richard, Thomas Kochan, and Michael Piore, eds. 1995. *Employment relations in a changing world economy.* Cambridge, Mass.: The MIT Press.

Lund, Robert, Albert Bishop, and Anne Newman, eds. 1993. *Designed to work: Production systems and people.* New Jersey: Prentice-Hall.

Lutz, Burkart. 1976. Bildungssystem und Beschäftigungsstruktur in Deutschland und Frankreich—Zum Einfluss des Bildungssystems auf die Gestaltung betrieblicher Arbeitskräftestrukturen. In *Betrieb—Arbeitsmarkt—Qualifikation.* Frankfurt/München, ISF: 83–151.

Lutz, Burkart. 1992. Education and job hierarchies: Contrasting evidence from France and Germany. In *Technology and work in German industry*, edited by Norbert Altmann, Christoph Köhler, and Pamela Meil. London: Routledge, 257–273.

MacDuffie, John Paul. 1995. International trends in work organization in the auto industry: National-level vs. company-level perspectives. In *The comparative political economy of industrial relations*, edited by Kirsten S. Wever and Lowell Turner. Madison, Wisc.: Industrial Relations Research Association Series: 71–113.

Mahon, Rianne. 1994. Wage-earners and/or coworkers? Contested identities. *Economic and Industrial Democracy* 15: 355–383.

Malnight, Thomas. 1993. Globalization of an ethnocentric firm: An evolutionary perspective. *Strategic Management Journal* 16, no. 2: 119–41.

Marginson, Paul, and Keith Sisson. 1994. The structure of transnational capital in Europe: The emerging Euro-company and its implications for industrial relations. In *New frontiers in European industrial relations*, edited by Richard Hyman and Anthony Ferner. Oxford: Blackwell, 15–51.

Martin, Graeme, Phil B. Beaumont, and Harry J. Staines. 1996. Corporate culture change in a Scottish local authority: Paradoxes and tensions. In *Experiencing human resource management*, edited by Chris Mabey, Tim Clark, and Denise Skinner. London: Sage, 73–92.

Martin, Graeme, and Martin Dowling. 1995. Strategic change, HRM and Timex. *Journal of Strategic Change* 4, no. 2: 77–94.

Martin, Graeme, and Tom Riddell. 1995. The wee firm that decked IBM: "Manufacturing" strategic change and leadership in the "cash." *Journal of Strategic Change* 5, no. 1: 3–26.

Martinez, Jon I., and J. Carlos Jarillo. 1989. The evolution of research on coordination mechanisms in multinational corporations. *Journal of International Business Studies* 20, no. 3: 489–514.

Maurice, Marc, François Sellier, and Jean-Jacques Silvestre. 1982. *Politique d'éducation et organisation industrielle en France et en Allemagne—essai d'analyse sociétale*. Paris: Presses universitaires de France.

Maynard, H. B., G. T. Stegemerton, and J. L. Schwab. 1948. *Methods—Time measurement*. New York: McGraw-Hill.

Meil, Pamela. 1992. Stranger in Paradise—An American's perspective on german industrial sociology. In *Technology and work in German industry*, edited by N. Altmann et al. London: Routledge, 12–25.

Melan, Eugene H. 1992. *Process management—Methods for improving products and service*. New York: McGraw-Hill.

Miguélez, Faustino, and Carlos Prieto. 1991. *Las relaciones laborales en España*. Madrid: Siglo XXI.

Mintzberg, Henry. 1994. *The rise and fall of strategic planning*. New York: Free Press.

Moldaschl, Manfred, and Klaus Schmierl. 1994. Fertigungsinseln und Gruppenarbeit— Durchsetzung neuer Arbeitsformen bei rechnerintegrierter Produktion. In *Arbeitsorientierte Rationalisierung*, edited by Manfred Moldaschl and Rainer Schultz-Wild. Frankfurt/New York: 51–103.

Moldaschl, Manfred, and Rainer Schultz-Wild, eds. 1994. *Arbeitsorientierte Rationalisierung: Fertigungsinseln und Gruppenarbeit im Maschinenbau*. Frankfurt/New York.

Morgan, Gareth. 1993. *Imaginization*. London: Sage.

Nagel, Roger N., and Rick Dove. 1992. *Twenty-first-century manufacturing enterprise strategy*. Bethlehem, Pa.: Lehigh University.

New world order. 1995. *Asia Week*, 8 September.

Noble, David. 1977. *America by design*. Oxford: Oxford University Press.

Ohmae, Kenichi. 1990. *The borderless world*. London: Collins.

——. 1995. Putting global logic first. *Harvard Business Review*, January/February, 119–25.

Pascale, Richard. 1990. *Managing on the edge: How successful companies use conflict to stay ahead*. London: Viking.

Perlmutter, H., and D. A. Heenan. 1979. *Multinational organization development: A social architectural perspective*. Reading, Mass.: Addison-Wesley.

Peters, Tom. 1992. *Liberation management: Necessary disorganization for the nanosecond nineties*.New York: Macmillan.

Pettigrew, Andrew M. 1985. *The awakening giant: Continuity and change in imperial chemical industries*. Oxford: Blackwell.

——. 1990. Longitudinal field research on change: Theory and practice. In *Longitudinal field research methods: Studying processes of organizational change*, edited by George Huber and Andrew H. Van de Ven. Thousand Oaks, Calif: Sage, 91–125.

Pettigrew, Andrew M., and Richard Whipp. 1991. *Managing change for competitive success*. Oxford: Blackwell.

Porter, Michael. 1990. *The competitive advantage of nations*. London: Macmillan.

Prahalad, C. K., and Yves L. Doz. 1991. Managing DMNCs: A search for a new paradigm. *Strategic Management Journal* 12: special issue 145–64.

Prest, Wilfred. 1963. The electricity supply industry. In *The economics of Australian industry*, edited by Alex Hunter. Melbourne: Melbourne University Press, 112–140.

Purcell, John, and Bruce Ahlstrand. 1994. *Human resource management in the multidivisional company*. Oxford: Oxford University Press.

Rapoport, C. 1992. How Percy Barnevik makes ABB work. It's Europe's best cross-border merger since Royal Dutch and Shell. *Fortune*, 29 June, 24–27.

Reason, John. 1994. Special report on power transformers: Performance improves in many small steps. *Electrical World*, June, 48–60.

Saunders, P. 1995. Understanding the Australian Quality Awards, *QBIZ: Journal of the Faculty of Business*. Brisbane: Queensland University of Technology.

Schienstock, Gerd. 1994. Globale Konzerne: Netzwerkstrukturen, Organisationsstrategien und Arbeitsbeziehungen. In *Arbeit* (Zeitschrift für Arbeitsforschung, Arbeitsgestaltung und Arbeitspolitik), Vol. 3, no. 3: 254–69.

Schmierl, Klaus. 1998. Amorphie im "Normierten Verhandlungssystem"—Wandel industrieller Beziehungen im internationalen Unternehmensverbund. In *Globale Produktion und Industriearbeit*, edited by Marhild v. Behr and Hartmut Hirsch-Kreinsen Frankfurt/New York: Campus Verlag: 161–207.

Schultz-Wild, Rainer. 1992. Bringing skills back to the process. In *Technology and work in German industry*, edited by Norbert Altmann, Christoph Köhler, and Pamela Meil. London: 185–197.

Scott, W. Richard. 1977. Effectiveness in Organizational Effectiveness Studies. In *New Perspectives on organizational effectiveness*, edited by Paul S. Goodman and Johannes M. Pennings. San Francisco: Josey Bass: 63–95.

Sengenberger, Werner. 1992. Vocational training, job structures and the labour market— An international perspective. In *Technology and work in German industry*, edited by N. Altmann et al. London: 245–256.

Slater, Robert. 1992. *The New GE. How Jack Welch Revived an American Institution*. New York: Irwin.

Sorge, A., G. Hartmann, M. Warner, and I. Nicholas. 1982. *Mikroelektronik und Arbeit in der Industrie—Erfahrungen beim Einsatz von CNC-Maschinen in Grossbritannien und der Bundesrepublik Deutschland*. Frankfurt/New York.

Stace, Doug. 1996. Transitions and transformations: Four case studies in business focused change. In *Blackwell cases in human resource and change management*, edited by John Storey. Oxford, Blackwell: 43–62.

Stacey, R. 1996. *Strategic management and organizational dynamics*. 2d ed. London: Pitman.

Stalk, George, and Thomas Hout Jr. 1990. *Competing against time: How time-based competition is reshaping global markets*. New York: The Free Press.

Taylor, William. 1991. The logic of global business: Interview with ABB's Percy Barnevik. *Harvard Business Review*, March–April, 90–105.

Thomas, Robert J. 1994. *What machines can't do. Politics and technology in the industrial enterprise*. Berkeley: University of California Press.

Thurow, Lester C. 1996. *The future of capitalism: How today's economic forces shape tomorrow's world*. New York: William Morrow.

Tichy, Noel, and Stratford Sherman. 1993. *Control your destiny or someone else will. How Jack Welch is making General Electric the world's most competitive company*. New York: Doubleday.

Tsoukas, Harimodos, ed. 1994. *New thinking in organizational behaviour*. London: Butterworth Heinemann.

United Nations (UN) Conference on Trade and Development, Division on Transnational Corporations and Investment. 1995. *World investment report*. New York and Geneva: UN.

Verma, Anil, and Richard P. Chaykowski, eds. 1992. *Industrial relations in Canadian Industry*. Toronto: Dryden.

Vernon, Raymond. 1994. Research on transnational corporations: Shedding old paradigms. *Transnational Corporations* 3, no. 1: 137–158.

Walton, Richard, and Robert B. McKersie. 1965. *A behavioural theory of labor negotiations*. New York: McGraw Hill.

Wever, Kirsten S. 1995. Markets, strategies and institutions in comparative perspective. In *The comparative political economy of industrial relations*, edited by Kirsten S. Wever and Lowell Turner. Madison, Wisc.: Industrial Relations Research Association Series: 181–192.

Weyman-Jones, Thomas G. 1993. Regulating the privatized electricity utilities in the UK. In *The political economy of privatization*, edited by Tom Clarke and Christos Pitelis. London: Routledge, 93–107.

Willmott, H. 1993. Strength is ignorance: Slavery is freedom; managing culture in modern organizations. *Journal of Management Studies*, 30, no. 4, 515–52.

Wobbe, Werner. 1991. *Anthropocentric production systems: A strategic issue for europe*. APS Research Paper Series, vol 1. Brussels: CEE-FAST.

Womack, James P., Daniel T. Jones, and David Roos. 1990. *The machine that changed the world*. New York: Rawson Associates.

Woodward, Joan. 1965. *Industrial organization: Theory and practice*. London: Oxford University Press.

Yourdon, E. 1997. *Death march*. N.J.: Prentice-Hall.

Notes on Contributors

PHIL BEAUMONT is Professor of Employee Relations at the University of Glasgow Business School. He has published extensively in the field of industrial relations and human resource management in the United Kingdom and the United States. He is also the author of several books including, most recently, *Human Resource Management: Key Concepts and Skills* (1993) and *The Future of Employment Relations* (1995).

JACQUES BÉLANGER is a Professor in the Département des relations industrielles at Université Laval, Quebec. The results of workplace studies he completed in companies such as Bombardier and Alcan have appeared in various industrial relations and sociological journals. He is also co-editor (with P. K. Edwards and L. Haiven) of *Workplace Industrial Relations and the Global Challenge* (1994).

MARHILD VON BEHR works as Senior Researcher at the Institut für Sozialwissenschaftliche Forschung (ISF) in Munich, Germany, a registered nonprofit organization engaged in both theoretical and empirical research in the field of industrial sociology. She has an electrotechnical background formation and studied sociology, economics and social psychology. Her research interests are in the area of technical and organizational change in industry, work design, and development of skill structures including new aspects of globalization.

LARS BENGTSSON earned his doctoral dissertation in 1993 and was employed at the Royal Institute of Technology in Stockholm from 1983 to 1995. Since 1991 he has been Senior Lecturer in industrial management at the University College in Gävle. His research field concerns changes in work organization, technology, and management in industrial companies.

CHRISTIAN BERGGREN is Professor in Industrial Management at Linköping University in Sweden, and is strongly involved in its executive training program, where ABB plays an important role. He has done extensive research in the automotive industry with major works published in English, German, and Japanese. He is also conducting long-term studies of Japanese industries in cooperation with scholars in Japan.

TORSTEN BJÖRKMAN is Professor of Sociology with special emphasis on organization and leadership at the National Defence College in Stockholm and is Adjunct Professor of Human Work Sciences at Luleå Technical University. He first studied ABB (ASEA at that time) in the 1970s, so this book is a revisit. His publications mostly deal with organizational development or the changing universe of professions and vocations; a few of his writings deal with history.

MARK BRAY is Professor in the School of Management at the University of Newcastle, Australia, where he chairs the Industrial Relations and Human Resource Management Group. His research interests include workplace and industry level studies in road and air transport as well as comparative studies of public policy issues.

ANTHONY GILES is an Associate Professor in the Département des relations industrielles at Université Laval, Quebec. His recent publications focus on the impact of globalization on work, employment, and labor relations, particularly within multinational corporations.

JEAN-NOËL GRENIER is a Ph.D. student in the Département des relations industrielles at Université Laval, Quebec. After completing a degree in economics, he received an M.A. in industrial relations from Laval. His research interests are globalization, multinational corporations, and the regulation of labor.

CHRISTOPH KÖHLER is Professor of Sociology at Friedrich-Schiller-Universität in Jena, Germany. He has worked for many years at the Institute für Sozialwissenschaftliche Forschung (ISF) in Munich, Germany, where he conducted studies on internal labor markets, personnel policies, and job rights in West Germany and the United States as well as on technological and organizational change in industry. His current research interests are globalization and the dynamics of convergence and divergence in regional structures of production and work.

RUSSELL D. LANSBURY is Professor and Head of the Department of Industrial Relations at the University of Sydney, Australia. His recent publications include *After Lean Production* with T. A. Kochan and J. P. MacDuffie, and *International and Comparative Employment Relations* with G. J. Bamber.

GRAEME MARTIN is the Director of Dundee Business School, University of Abertay Dundee. He has published widely in the area of human resource management (HRM) and strategic change. Currently, he is researching into culture change and HRM in multinational firms with Phil Beaumont.

RAINER SCHULTZ-WILD is board member and works as a Senior Researcher at the Institut für Sozialwissenschaftliche Forschung (ISF) in Munich, Germany. He studied sociology, economics, and political science. His research interests are in the area of the structures of the labor market, technical and organizational change in industry, globalization of production, work design, and development of skill structures in companies including aspects of international comparison.

Index